THE AUTOBIOGRAPHY OF
MARK TWAIN

THE
AUTOBIOGRAPHY OF
MARK
TWAIN

As arranged and edited,
with an Introduction and Notes, by
CHARLES NEIDER

PERENNIAL LIBRARY

Harper & Row, Publishers

New York, Evanston, San Francisco, London

THIS BOOK IS DEDICATED

WITH PLEASURE

TO MARK TWAIN'S DAUGHTER

Clara Clemens Samossoud

75—1

Maria Fernanda Van Zyle

◇◇◇◇◇◇◇◇◇◇◇◇◇◇

CONTENTS

INTRODUCTION

by Charles Neider

In my opinion Mark Twain's autobiography is a classic of American letters, to be ranked with the autobiographies of Benjamin Franklin and Henry Adams. I think that it will be regarded as such over the years. The final work of one of our country's most beloved authors, it is the product of one of those nineteenth-century giants whom we of this century are slow in replacing. It has the marks of greatness in it—style, scope, imagination, laughter, tragedy.

It is the product of a highly original yet representative mind and it brings back the tone and flavor of an America which was young and optimistic, a homespun, provincial America but an America with greatness in its heart. Thoreau's America may have contained many lives of quiet desperation. Mark Twain's decidedly did not. The midwestern and western frontiers were not the America of Concord and Boston. The difference between these places accounted, in the autobiographical context, for the difference between Mark Twain and Henry Adams, and in the literary one between Mark Twain and Henry James.

It must be said at once that now for the first time the material of the present volume is being presented as autobiography, and in the sequence which one would reasonably expect from autobiography. And for the first time the whole manuscript is being used as the source, not parts or selections of it. Also, the present volume contains from 30,000 to 40,000 words which have never before seen print. Mark Twain left a manuscript of unwieldy proportions, which included whole small books, such as *Is Shakespeare Dead?* He had thrown them into the grab bag which he thought of as his autobiography. Leaving such books out, we have a more reasonable manuscript. Bernard DeVoto has reckoned that Albert Bigelow Paine used about half of the latter manuscript in his edition of the Autobiography (1924) and that he himself used about half the remainder in *his* edition (1940).

To put it briefly, Paine either did not envision the possibility of a true autobiography or did not care to undertake to make one. The same can be said of DeVoto. Both said in their introductions that what they were presenting was not really autobiography but a kind of table-talk. To both men I owe thanks because they gave me the opportunity to do the exciting job which remained to be done.

When Mark Twain died in 1910 he was widely regarded as the most prominent and characteristic American writer of his generation. He had a large and devoted public, and this public had some reason to expect from him, as a posthumous publication, an autobiography which was the equal if not the superior of any yet written in the United States. It had been known for some time that he was writing such a book, and a number of chapters had appeared in twenty-five installments of the *North American Review* of 1906 and 1907. But his public was disappointed, for Mark Twain had some curious notions about writing an autobiography, notions which kept changing over the years except in one respect: they became ever more curious.

He began with composing sections by hand and ended with a series of autobiographical dictations. As early as the 70's he was writing fragments. Around 1873 he wrote a brief autobiographical sketch for his friend Charles Dudley Warner; in 1877 he recalled the early days in Florida, Missouri; in 1885, on the death of General Grant, he dictated a series of recollections of his meetings with the General; in 1890 he set down the Paige typesetting machine episode, that fiasco of his middle years, and his memories of his mother; in 1897-1898, while in Vienna, he wrote the brilliant chapters on the early days spent on his uncle's farm; in 1899 he composed an autobiographical sketch for the use of his nephew, Samuel Moffett, on the basis of which Moffett wrote a biographical essay for the Uniform Edition of Mark Twain's works, issued in the same year; in 1904 he wrote the notes on the Villa Quarto and the memory of John Hay while living on the outskirts of Florence; and in 1906 he undertook the sustained series of dictations which added so greatly to the Autobiography's bulk.

The task alternately irked and pleased him. In 1877, at the age of forty-two, he had resolved to begin his autobiography at once, in a formal way. "I did begin it," he wrote in 1904, "but the resolve melted away and disappeared in a week and I threw my beginning away. Since then, about every three or four years I have made other beginnings and thrown them away. Once I tried the experiment of a diary, intending to inflate that into an autobiography when its accumulation should furnish enough material, but that experiment lasted only a week; it took me half of every night to set down the history of the day, and at the week's end I did not like the result.

"Within the last eight or ten years I have made several attempts to do the autobiography in one way or another with a pen, but the result was not satisfactory; it was too literary. . . .

"With a pen in the hand the narrative stream is a canal; it moves slowly, smoothly, decorously, sleepily, it has no blemish except that it is all blemish. It is too literary, too prim, too nice; the gait and style and movement are not suited to narrative. That canal stream is always reflecting; it is its nature, it can't help it. Its slick shiny surface is interested in everything it passes along the banks—cows, foliage, flowers, everything. And so it wastes a lot of time in reflections."

Later he experimented with newspaper clippings. "I shall scatter through this Autobiography newspaper clippings without end. When I do not copy them into the text it means that I do not make them a part of the Autobiography—at least not of the earlier editions. I put them in on the theory that if they are not interesting in the earlier editions, a time will come when it may be well enough to insert them for the reason that age is quite likely to make them interesting although in their youth they may lack that quality."

He was not afraid to wander. "In this autobiography it is my purpose to wander whenever I please and come back when I get ready." Once he thought he had found the "right" way. "Finally in Florence, in 1904, I hit upon the right way to do an Autobiography: Start it at no particular time of your life; wander at your free will all over your life; talk only about the thing which interests you for the moment; drop it the moment its interest threatens to pale, and turn your talk upon the new and more interesting thing that has intruded itself into your mind meantime. . . .

"And so, I have found the right plan. It makes my labor amusement—mere amusement, play, pastime, and wholly effortless."

But early in 1906 he was having difficulties. "The difficulties of it grow upon me all the time. For instance, the idea of blocking out a consecutive series of events which have happened to me, or which I imagine have happened to me—I can see that that is impossible for me. The only thing possible for me is to talk about the thing that something suggests at the moment—something in the middle of my life, perhaps, or something that happened only a few months ago. It is my purpose to extend these notes to 600,000 words, and possibly more. But that is going to take a long time—a long time."

At other times he was quite proud of what he was composing.

"I intend that this autobiography shall become a model for all future autobiographies when it is published, after my death, and I also intend that it shall be read and admired a good many centuries because of its form and method—a form and method whereby the past and the present are constantly brought face to face, resulting in contrasts which newly fire up the interest all along like contact of flint with steel. Moreover, this autobiography of mine does not select from my life its showy episodes, but deals merely in the common experiences which go to make up the life of the average human being, and the narrative must interest the average human being because these episodes are of a sort which he is familiar with in his own life and in which he sees his own life reflected and set down in print. The usual, conventional autobiographer seems to particularly hunt out those occasions in his career when he came into contact with celebrated persons, whereas his contacts with the uncelebrated were just as interesting to him and would be to his reader, and were vastly more numerous than his collisions with the famous.

"Howells[1] was here yesterday afternoon and I told him the whole scheme of this autobiography and its apparently systemless system—only apparently systemless, for it is not that. It is a deliberate system and the law of the system is that I shall talk about the matter which for the moment interests me, and cast it aside and talk about something else the

[1] William Dean Howells.

moment its interest for me is exhausted. It is a system which follows no charted course and is not going to follow any such course. It is a system which is a complete and purposed jumble—a course which begins nowhere, follows no specified route, and can never reach an end while I am alive, for the reason that if I should talk to the stenographer two hours a day for a hundred years I should still never be able to set down a tenth part of the things which have interested me in my lifetime. I told Howells that this autobiography of mine would live a couple of thousand years without any effort and would then take a fresh start and live the rest of the time.

"He said he believed it would and asked me if I meant to make a library of it.

"I said that that was my design but that if I should live long enough the set of volumes could not be contained merely in a city, it would require a state, and that there would not be any multibillionaire alive, perhaps, at any time during its existence who would be able to buy a full set, except on the installment plan.

"Howells applauded, and was full of praises and indorsement, which was wise in him and judicious. If he had manifested a different spirit I would have thrown him out of the window. I like criticism, but it must be my way."

And in a similar vein:

"This Autobiography of mine differs from other autobiographies—differs from *all* other autobiographies, except Benvenuto's, perhaps. The conventional biography of all the ages is an open window. The autobiographer sits there and examines and discusses the people that go by—not all of them, but the notorious ones, the famous ones; those that wear fine uniforms, and crowns when it is not raining; and very great poets and great statesmen—illustrious people with whom he has had the high privilege of coming in contact. He likes to toss a wave of recognition to these with his hand as they go by and he likes to notice that the others are seeing him do this, and admiring. He likes to let on that in discussing these occasional people that wear the good clothes he is only interested in interesting his reader and is in a measure unconscious of himself.

"But this Autobiography of mine is not that kind of autobiography. This Autobiography of mine is a mirror and I am looking at myself in it all the time. Incidentally I notice the people that pass along at my back—I get glimpses of them in the mirror—and whenever they say or do anything that can help advertise me and flatter me and raise me in my own estimation I set these things down in my Autobiography. I rejoice when a king or a duke comes my way and makes himself useful to this Autobiography, but they are rare customers, with wide intervals between. I can use them with good effect as lighthouses and monuments along my way, but for real business I depend upon the common herd."

And in March of 1907, while on vacation in Bermuda, he recorded still another objective of the Autobiography. "I do not need to stay here any longer, for I have completed the only work that was remaining for me to do in this life and that I could not possibly afford to leave uncompleted—my Autobiography. Although that is not finished, and will not be finished until I die, the object which I had in view in compiling it is accomplished: that object was to distribute it through my existing books and give each of them a new copyright of twenty-eight years, and thus defeat the copyright statute's cold intention to rob them and starve my daughters. I have dictated four or five hundred thousand words of autobiography already and if I should die tomorrow this mass of literature would be quite sufficient for the object which I had in view in manufacturing it."

In his Autobiography Mark Twain let out most of the stops in whatever disciplines he had managed to maintain during his writing career. Bernard DeVoto believed that Twain's failure to write a coherent autobiography was due to a certain dread. "When he invoked Hannibal [that is, his early years] he found there not only the idyll of boyhood but anxiety, violence, supernatural horror, and an uncrystallized but enveloping dread. Much of his fiction, most of his masterpiece [*Huck Finn*], flows from that phantasy-bound anxiety.

"I think that the impulse to write his autobiography was in part an impulse to examine and understand that dread. And I think that the impulse was arrested short of genuine self-revelation because the dread was so central in him that he could approach it only symbolically, by way of fiction."

But one does not need to rely on such a theory in order to account for Mark Twain's difficulties with his Autobiography. His mind, rich in memory and nostalgia, kept seeking anecdotic forms of recollection, forms which did not easily suit the chronological organization of the classic autobiography. And it was a case of the storyteller irked by "facts," the dross which inhibited fancy. If the facts were sometimes the losers, that worried Mark Twain not at all. "I don't believe these details are right but I don't care a rap. They will do just as well as the facts," he once wrote in his Autobiography. In this respect he had good company, even the meticulous Henry Adams. Speaking of a journey to Washington with his father as a twelve-year-old in 1850, Adams wrote in his own autobiography, "The journey was meant as education, and as education it served the purpose of fixing in memory the stage of a boy's thought in 1850. . . . This was the journey he remembered. The actual journey may have been quite different, but the actual journey has no interest for education. The memory was all that mattered. . . ."

Mark Twain's life was a long and rich one; it seemed to him an inexhaustible mine of recollection. The associations streamed out from it in a million directions and it was his quixotic hope to capture most of them with the irony and humor and storytelling gift which were his own way of regarding the human drama. He was staggered by the size of the task and justly so. The real question is whether he actually failed, as has been generally believed. It is true that he did not use a comprehensive, a strategic approach, that he kept winning tactical battles at the cost of winning a war. But many works of art are approached in such a way, works which reach a great culmination. Perhaps if he had lived a few years longer he would have found a sufficient perspective to organize the Autobiography and edit out of it all the irrelevant materials which his odd methods of composition had allowed to sneak in. The fact is that the greatness is *there*. You can edit the trivia out but you cannot edit the greatness in. One of the ironies of art is that it is possible to win a war and lose the battles, and that it is more tragic to lose the battles than the war. Formal neatness and comprehensive sweep: and dead or dying details. The details in Mark Twain's Autobiography are intensely alive, those which are part of the true birth.

Mark Twain was trying to amuse himself: that was his chief aim during the dictations. (It was during the dictations, near the end of his life, that he let most of the trivia in. And the trivia is always set apart; there is no case of a brilliant section which contains it. Everything is distinctly of a piece: the good is good, the bad is clearly bad.) He had produced his share of work in the world; he had outlived most of the people he cared for; the world was in a bad way and he was not averse to leaving it. And so he reminisced, and by so doing he amused himself—reminisced on his own terms, not on the world's, not according to some theory of autobiographical composition.

It was in 1906 that Albert Bigelow Paine began to have an influence on the Autobiography. Meeting Twain at a dinner in New York, he asked if he might visit him soon. At their next meeting he proposed to write the official biography of him and Mark Twain agreed. As a result, Twain undertook a series of autobiographical dictations, to be used partly by Paine as the basis of the biography and to be published in and for themselves at an appropriate time. The word "appropriate" in this connection turned out to have a surprisingly flexible meaning. At first it was Mark Twain's intention to publish no part of his autobiography until a century after his death; then, shortly afterward, he set about publishing numerous chapters of it in the *North American Review*. In some parts of the typescript he indicated marginally that they were to wait for fifty years after his death; in others seventy-five; and in several places five hundred years after the year of composition. Some of these injunctions have been adhered to by his heirs and executors; others, for good reasons, have not.

The dictations were begun in Twain's New York home at 21 Fifth Avenue, were continued for a while near Dublin, New Hampshire, then in New York again and eventually in Redding, Connecticut, in Stormfield, Twain's last home. They went on fairly continuously for two years, then intermittently for another two, and were ended by Twain's death in the spring of 1910. The dictations, although rarely the equal of certain of the reminiscences Mark Twain composed earlier, by hand, are nevertheless invaluable for a complete account of his life, and in many instances they are excellent.

Paine had the unhappy choice of publishing the Autobiography as he found it or of regarding it as raw material and bringing it to a more or less finished state. I say unhappy because he faced a very special dilemma. What he found was a manuscript of unwieldy size, consisting of a series of extended notes—a bundle of things relevant and inspired mixed with items irrelevant and dull; all in so disorganized a condition as to be bewildering, although the sections and fragments in themselves were thematically, stylistically and factually complete. If Paine had published the manuscript as he found it he would have been charged with lack of an understanding of his whole responsibility; if he had edited the manuscript he would probably have been criticized even more strongly. He decided to leave the responsibility with Mark Twain, except for the omissions he made whenever the spirit moved him, usually in the interest of "propriety" as he understood it, often failing to warn the reader that something had been left out.

Paine had another choice to make. Mark Twain had requested him to publish the Autobiography not in chronological order but in the sequence in which it was written and dictated. What an extraordinary idea! As though the stream of composition time were in some mysterious way more revealing than that of autobiographical time! To gauge Paine's problem adequately one must keep in mind the fact that Mark Twain had approached his autobiography from all directions simultaneously. Paine offered no details of the manner or wording of Mark Twain's request, nor did he suggest whether it was written or given orally, or whether made at the beginning of their relationship or near the end. And so we are unable to judge how much earnestness there was behind it. He merely noted: "The various divisions and chapters of this work, in accordance with the author's wish, are arranged in the order in which they were written, regardless of the chronology of events." Ought Paine to have taken Mark Twain's wish regarding sequence so literally? It was a delicate problem, but by no means either the first or the last of its kind to be presented to a literary executor. At any rate Paine adhered to Mark Twain's wishes, and as a result it is impossible to call to memory another autobiography by a major writer which made its debut so inauspiciously and in so confusing a manner.

The shortcomings of the two volumes were plain. The Autobiography of 1924 was incomplete, raw, badly arranged. It was a grab bag, a repository for anything and everything;

its chief flaw was that it correctly reflected Twain's notions and methods. Beginning with fragments composed by hand as early as 1870, it ranged over sublime and ridiculous chapters down to dictations of April, 1906. Much of it was embarrassing: fragmentary notations on news stories of the day, exchanges of letters, opinions of the moment. Parts, such as the reminiscences of the uncle's farm, were among the best things Mark Twain had ever written, and cried out to be saved. But it was difficult to save such an inauspicious edition, and the good things in it began to be forgotten with the bad. In time there were literate readers, and admirers of Mark Twain, who barely realized that he had tried his hand at an autobiography. Paine's hope of issuing more volumes in the autobiographical series was doomed, and his desire to fulfill Mark Twain's request by ending the work with the latter's account of the death of his daughter Jean was frustrated.

Reviewing the two volumes, Carl Van Doren wrote in the *Saturday Review of Literature,* "Are there still further candors to be expected? Or was Mark Twain really so cautious that the occasional objurgations of this book seemed to him untempered violence? These questions ought to be answered one way or the other, and not slurred over as they have here been by Mr. Paine." He spoke of the work as being "casual and repetitious and disorderly" but added that it was "far from being a damp fizzle." He asked insistently, "Is there more of it somewhere?" Richard Aldington attacked Twain as not being very funny or much of a writer, and spoke of "the tedium of these desultory disconnected pages" in a review in the *Spectator*. Mark Twain's friend, Brander Matthews, liked the book as the expression of a great and wise man, yet wrote, "There is here no consecutive record of a career, but only tumultuous recollections, poured forth as the spirit moved him. . . . It begins anywhere; it doesn't end at all; it has no skeleton and no adroit adjustment of members; it ranges through the Cosmos and arrives at Chaos; it is compounded of unrelated fragments; it is haphazard and helter-skelter; it is casual and fortuitous. . . ."

The best review was written by Mark Van Doren for *The Nation*. Van Doren warned that the book would be disappointing to anyone who "expected a consecutive or otherwise ordered account" of Mark Twain's life. "How much order anyone had a right to expect from the mind of this man is a question; but the fact remains that the book as it now appears is a jumble of things some of which are consequential and some of which are not. . . . Unpublished articles and other scraps on hand were shoveled in to make the manuscript 'complete.' The sections were arranged in the order of their composition, not in the order of the events related. . . . But the Autobiography, shapeless and disappointing as it is, must still be called a great book. Perhaps by very reason of its imperfections it reveals, in the plainest and most naked way, the quality of Mark Twain's literary sinew." After comparing Twain with Fielding, Shakespeare and Rabelais, Van Doren wrote, "He shares with those men their vast riches in the mine that is so indispensable to a writer of the first rank, the mine of eloquence. This is shown here not only in numerous paragraphs and pages which mount to the top pitch of expression, not only in eulogies and diatribes which sweep the reader from his bearings, but more convincingly yet in the evidence everywhere that Mark Twain's interest in the arts of language was unbounded."

Sixteen years after the appearance of Paine's edition, Bernard DeVoto issued *Mark Twain in Eruption*, which brought to the public a large new portion of the autobiographical typescript. DeVoto did not like Paine's edition, which he called shapeless and annoying. He did not emulate Paine's technique of "sampling" the contents of the Autobiography but instead depended on "omitting trivialities and joining together things that belonged together." He did not hesitate to select, rearrange and edit. The organization of his volume was thematic. But the book he issued was supplementary to and conditioned by the edition of his predecessor; consequently it was as incomplete as Paine's two volumes.

Speaking of the order which he gave his volume, DeVoto said, "It is a loose order but it is the tightest one that can be given the Autobiography; and occasionally I have chosen to let the original order stand, at some cost in incoherence." But DeVoto was in error. His thematic order was an imposed one and could not accurately be called the tightest which can be given the Autobiography, the essence of whose internal order is time. The tightest order of any work is the order functional to it, inherent in it, the order which is in harmony with its subject.

DeVoto worked only with the unpublished parts of the typescript and as he did so he had occasion to make omissions. "I have left out what seems to me irrelevant or uninteresting," he wrote; yet later in his introduction he admitted that he left out certain passages because they contained matter which was "fantastic and injurious." He added that he had omitted other passages "because the exaggeration gets so far into phantasy that it becomes a trivial rage." I have been able to examine the passages in question and have reached the conclusion—not an unexpected one—that the wise course is to let Mark Twain have his say in these matters of high emotion.

In some of the omissions DeVoto was no doubt influenced by opinions which he could not ignore, such as those of the Estate and of the surviving daughter; but in others, such as the suppression of the concluding observations relating to the Bret Harte matter, he exercised a kind of judgment which can be questioned. The remarks which I have included on temperament are all publishable and important, without involving the sensibilities of living persons, now or in 1940; they were among the remarks DeVoto omitted. "I have left out nothing that seemed to me important, and I assume responsibility for the omissions as well as for what is printed," DeVoto wrote. In fact, he did leave out matter which he considered important; and the full responsibility for omissions was not his if in his role of editor he was deferring to the wishes of others.

But aside from such peculiarities as I have mentioned, DeVoto's was a good volume, and the judgment and ability of its editor were clearly superior to those of Paine. It had clarity and organization. It resurrected forgotten chapters from the pages of the *North American Review*. It revealed new facets of Mark Twain which until 1940 had been observable only by scholars. It deserved the good press it received. The tone of its reception may perhaps be exemplified by Clifton Fadiman's review in *The New Yorker*. "It seems Mark Twain, scared to death of what Mrs. Grundy would say, left a whole pile of manuscripts to be issued at intervals after his death. Some of these odds and ends were published in Albert Bigelow Paine's edition of the Autobiography, about as disappointing a book as ever came from the pen of a first-rate writer. Out of a part of the remainder, that sagacious Resurrection Man, Bernard DeVoto, has carpentered a book which may add little to Mark

Twain's literary stature but a good deal to our understanding of his split temperament. . . . All in all, a valuable book, readable for itself and indispensable for the new light it throws on the author. Mr. DeVoto's industry, taste and knowledge of his subject have combined to produce a volume in which Mark Twain's voice speaks unmistakably, though from the grave."

By now the reader will have surmised what my own plan has been. Working with the autobiographical manuscript as a whole, both unpublished and published parts, I weeded out a variety of material. I did this for several reasons: in order to make a wieldy volume which would meet certain requirements of the general reader (for whom this book is designed); in order to unburden the excellent parts of the dated, dull, trivial and journalese sections of the work; and in order to concentrate less on opinion and secondhand recollection and more on the more truly autobiographical, the more purely literary and the more characteristically humorous material. My volume is to a high degree anecdotic, but I believe this to be a virtue rather than a defect, in that it correctly represents the creative slant of Mark Twain's mind.

From the published parts I have omitted such matter as the lengthy notes on the Grant memoirs, the beauties of the German language, the Morris incident, much of Susy's biography, various comments on the news or correspondence of the day, elongated remarks on Theodore Roosevelt, Andrew Carnegie, the plutocracy and so on. From the unpublished parts I have omitted material on the San Francisco earthquake, which I believe to be under par (besides, Mark Twain did not experience the quake personally), on a mining friend's literary effort, on spontaneous oratory, on the supremacy of the house fly (both of these pieces being rather strained, in my opinion), on simplified spelling, on palmistry, and other matters. I do not believe that it would do justice to Mark Twain's literary reputation to publish these sections.

Unlike DeVoto, I do not assume responsibility for all of the omissions. Had the authority been mine I would have included in this edition the dictations of five days—June 19, June 20, June 22, June 23 and June 25 of 1906. But I would not have put them into the body of the Autobiography, for they are more essayistic than autobiographical; I would have made an appendix of them. Mark Twain's surviving daughter, Mrs.

Jacques Samossoud, who has the authority and the responsibility, has decided that it would serve no good purpose to publish the chapters at this time. It was also DeVoto's desire to publish them but he did not do so because Mrs. Samossoud (then Mrs. Gabrilowitsch) requested him not to. Three of the chapters have penciled on their title pages, "Edited, for publication in *Mark Twain in Eruption*, but omitted at the request of Mme. Gabrilowitsch." It was these especially which I had in mind when I said earlier that DeVoto omitted matter which he considered important, and that he did not, as he claimed, have full responsibility for the omissions.

In a letter to William Dean Howells, Mark Twain wrote: "Tomorrow I mean to dictate a chapter which will get my heirs and assigns burned alive if they venture to print it this side of A.D. 2006—which I judge they won't. There'll be lots of such chapters if I live 3 or 4 years longer. The edition of A.D. 2006 will make a stir when it comes out. I shall be hovering around taking notice, along with other dead pals. You are invited." He was referring, apparently, to the first of the five chapters mentioned above. On the title pages of two of the chapters is a penned note in his hand: "Not to be exposed to any eye until the edition of A.D. 2406. S. L. C." In his biography of Mark Twain, published in 1912, Paine offered sample tidbits of the chapters (Vol. III, pages 1354-57). If read superficially the chapters seem savagely irreverent, but they are the work of a profoundly religious man. They are attacks on orthodoxy, cant and sham in religion, and are an indication of the boldness and strength of Mark Twain's mind. He discusses, among other things, the character of God, the defects of bibles, the immaculate conception, the evil influence of the Bible, his belief that the present God and religion will not endure, and his belief that Christ did not prove that he was God.

I have considered it an essential part of my task as an editor of the Autobiography to hold judgment in abeyance and to bring into the light of publication as much of what Mark Twain wrote as possible, without doing injury to his literary reputation. For this reason I have tried to fill various omissions. I have found forgotten important material in the pages of the *North American Review*—pages on bowling, bad pool tables, "Quaker," Redpath, Dean Sage. (I also found there material which I did not think worth reprinting.) It was necessary to hunt in the *North American Review* because the manuscript and typescript of the Autobiography as they now exist at the university library at Berkeley are incomplete, whole chapters and sections of material which were published in the magazine and in Paine's edition being no longer among the papers. I have put into its correct place in the Autobiography the final chapter, the death of Jean, now published as part of the Autobiography for the first time. I have included material from the unpublished typescript which struck me as being too important to leave out (in this too I have disagreed with DeVoto). Examples are the experiments in phrenology and the village phrenologist (Chapter 13), the recollections concerning Louisa Wright (Chapter 16), the remarks on the significance of repetition in humor (Chapter 28), the further ruminations on Webster (in Chapter 49), the remarks on the effrontery of amateur literary efforts (Chapter 58), the comments on man which are the concluding section of the remarks on Bret Harte (Chapter 63), the illness of Mark Twain's wife (Chapters 67-70), the receiving of honorary degrees (Chapter 73), the final comments on Mrs. Aldrich (in Chapter 76), and the remarks on baldness and cleanliness in man (Chapter 78). I have also included the pages on the death of Mrs. Clemens (Chapter 71), written immediately after the event. These are filed separately from the autobiographical typescript among the Mark Twain papers in Berkeley, but I believe them to have been intended as part of the Autobiography. Mark Twain described the deaths of Susy and of Jean and included the detailed notes on his wife's illness in his Autobiography, and it is likely that he desired to include the death of his wife also. Finally, I have picked up many corrections of the text by Mark Twain which my predecessors overlooked, and have put whole paragraphs and pages back in their rightful places, which were either suppressed or forgotten. These are too numerous to list here, but important examples are the anecdote about Dr. McDowell in Chapter 3, the unflattering comments on the actor Raymond in Chapter 5, the anecdote in dialect about the venerable lady in Chapter 6, the anecdote about Orion in the bathtub in Chapter 43 and also the one about Billy Nye in the same chapter.

Having prepared such a manuscript as I have just described, I then arranged it in a chronological sequence. Strict chronology was undesirable; it would have too often interrupted the flow of Mark Twain's thoughts and style, for he liked to range here and there in time, according to his narrating habits. But then strict chronology is to be found only in biographical statistics, not in autobiographies. The advantages of the chronological arrangement are self-evident.

The original typescript contains many summarizing titles, which Paine carefully published. I have agreed with DeVoto that they are boring and unnecessary. The division into chapters is mine. In the earlier editions the dates of composition were printed prominently. I have regarded these as of minor importance and have indicated such dates only when the context required them and then only in footnotes. Finally, I edited the manuscript for consistency and, following DeVoto's practice, modernized the use of commas by deleting hundreds of them. It is probably a pity to take liberties with Mark Twain's commas, but the practice in this instance is not without some justification. There is no definitive text; there is only a typescript in most cases, often in more than one draft. We do not know whether, in his dictations, Twain specified punctuation. The probability is that he did not. The punctuation is not stable. It is true one can argue that the punctuation has some authority, inasmuch as he corrected at least some of the pages; but even here it has many inconsistencies. Furthermore, sections of the original manuscript and typescript are missing, as I have already said, and we must depend on Paine's published version and on the pages of the *North American Review* to know what they contained, and these are not authoritative sources as far as punctuation goes. An interesting sidelight on this problem occurs in the margin of a typescript page. "*Private:* Discard the stupid Harper rule for once: don't put a comma after 'old'—I can't *have* it! S L C" The notation is in Twain's hand. He was referring to a phrase—"beyond that old safe frontier."

In a very few instances I have inserted a connective sentence such as "But to go back a bit" or have brought in a sentence or two from the autobiographical sketch which Mark Twain wrote for his nephew Sam Moffett, or I have deleted a sentence which was repetitive under the new arrangement; otherwise the language is Mark Twain's. I have worked in the belief that the main facts and outlines of his life are sufficiently known to the reader to preclude the insertion of biographical data either in the form of connective paragraphs or of footnotes.

In a tradition established by Paine, I should like to inform the reader that not everything that Mark Twain says in this book is gospel fact. He may have thought it was the fact, or he may have invented or forgotten. Contemporary documents such as diaries and letters lead one to be wary of accepting as gospel all that Mark Twain says here, although on the whole, and in the profoundest sense, in the poetic and psychological sense, it is true. In particular, his attacks on persons ought to be read with caution as well as with delight.

New York
September 3, 1958

ACKNOWLEDGMENTS

It gives me pleasure to thank the several persons who have generously helped in the making of this book: my wife Joan Merrick, Mrs. Clara Clemens Samossoud, Thomas G. Chamberlain of the Mark Twain Estate, Elizabeth Lawrence, Cass Canfield, Jr. and Frank S. MacGregor of Harper & Brothers, Henry Nash Smith and Frederick Anderson of the University of California in Berkeley, Walter Blair of the University of Chicago, and Herbert Cahoon of the Pierpont Morgan Library of New York.

                                                                C. N.

A NOTE

on the Present Arrangement

Readers who do not have the Paine and DeVoto volumes handy and who would like to see at a glance how my arrangement differs from those of my predecessors may be interested in the following list of the contents of the earlier autobiographical books.

Paine, Volume I. A bit on the Tennessee land; the early years in Florida, Missouri; the Chicago G.A.R. Festival; General Grant and the Chinese; a call with William Dean Howells on Grant; concerning Grant's *Memoirs;* Gerhardt and the Grant bust; the Reverend Dr. N. visits General Grant; the machine episode; the Clemenses; Colonel Sellers; the Tennessee land; uncle's farm; boyhood days; Twain's mother; playing "bear"; village tragedies; Jim Wolf and the cats; Macfarlane; old lecture days in Boston; Ralph Keeler; beauties of the German language; a Viennese procession; comment on tautology and grammar; private history of an MS. that came to grief; Villa Quarto; Villa Viviani; a memory of John Hay; notes on *Innocents Abroad;* Stevenson, Aldrich, et al.; Henry H. Rogers; about the Big Bonanza in Nevada; on making certain speeches; the Morris incident; birthday speeches and other matters; the dream of Henry's death; a burglar-alarm incident; the Morris incident; notions about news; on writing an autobiography; John Malone; General Sickles; the Morris incident; John Malone; dueling.

Paine, Volume II. A meeting in Carnegie Hall; Twichell and an unpleasant political incident; the character of man; voting for Cleveland; Twichell's unpopular vote; recollections of Twain's wife; death of Susy Clemens; recollections of Susy; Dr. John Brown; recollections of Susy; playing *The Prince and the Pauper;* Susy's biography of her father; comments on the trade of critic; Susy's biography and its associations; strong language; Susy's biography; memories of Henry and boyhood; the Hannibal days; Susy's biography; courting Olivia Langdon; Susy's biography; notice of the death of Mary Wilkes; memories of Anson Burlingame; memories of Twain's father-in-law; Susy's biography; Charley Langdon; how Twain became a businessman; Susy's biography; memories of General Grant; Susy's biography; authors' readings; visiting President Cleveland at the White House; various matters; letter to ex-President Cleveland; on Cleveland; Susy's biography; model for Huck Finn; Hannibal days; comments on the killing of 600 Moros; sundry matters; Hannibal days; mental telegraphy; Twichell; the Players' Club; Susy's biography; curious letter superscriptions; memories of Harriet Beecher Stowe; comments on newspaper clippings; the scheme of his autobiography; Higbie's letter; memories of Higbie; a scheme for finding employment for the unemployed; Orion Clemens; sundry matters; Orion Clemens; interview with Tchaykoffsky the revolutionist; first meeting with Helen Keller; Orion Clemens; old days in Nevada; the Morris case; Ellen Terry's farewell banquet; Orion Clemens; letter from a French girl; *Huck Finn;* various matters; Frank Fuller.

DeVoto. The monarchy; the panic of 1907; Theodore Roosevelt; the hunting of the cow; the President as advertiser, naturalist and nature-faker; the true character of Mr. Roosevelt; the American gentleman; Domitian; Andrew Carnegie; the drift toward centralized power; purchasing civic virtue; Senator Clark of Montana; the teaching of Jay Gould; the teaching applied; Mr. Rockefeller's Bible class; the little tale; illustration of a fine art; A B C lesson; a corn pone prayer; the minstrel show; the mesmerist; Jim Wolf and the wasps; "The Jumping Frog"; the American Publishing Company; James R. Osgood; setting up as a publisher; General Grant's publisher; failure of a publisher; when a book gets tired; humorists; "1601"; *A Connecticut Yankee;* platform readings; the Snodgrass letters; *What Is Man?;* "Extract from Captain Stormfield's Visit to Heaven"; "The Fortifications of Paris"; the report of Twain's death; Bret Harte; the memorial meeting to Thomas Bailey Aldrich; Murat Halstead and Bayard Taylor; Kipling; Elinor Glyn; the last visit to England; Marie Corelli; Winston Churchill; Sidney Lee; the Holy Grail; miscellany.

PREFACE

In this Autobiography I shall keep in mind the fact that I am speaking from the grave. I am literally speaking from the grave, because I shall be dead when the book issues from the press.

I speak from the grave rather than with my living tongue for a good reason: I can speak thence freely. When a man is writing a book dealing with the privacies of his life—a book which is to be read while he is still alive—he shrinks from speaking his whole frank mind; all his attempts to do it fail; he recognizes that he is trying to do a thing which is wholly impossible to a human being. The frankest and freest and privatest product of the human mind and heart is a love letter; the writer gets his limitless freedom of statement and expression from his sense that no stranger is going to see what he is writing. Sometimes there is a breach-of-promise case by and by; and when he sees his letter in print it makes him cruelly uncomfortable and he perceives that he never would have unbosomed himself to that large and honest degree if he had known that he was writing for the public. He cannot find anything in the letter that was not true, honest and respect-worthy; but no matter, he would have been very much more reserved if he had known he was writing for print.

It has seemed to me that I could be as frank and free and unembarrassed as a love letter if I knew that what I was writing would be exposed to no eye until I was dead, and unaware and indifferent.

MARK TWAIN

CHAPTER 1

I was born the 30th of November, 1835, in the almost invisible village of Florida, Monroe County, Missouri. My parents removed to Missouri in the early 'thirties; I do not remember just when, for I was not born then and cared nothing for such things. It was a long journey in those days and must have been a rough and tiresome one. The village contained a hundred people and I increased the population by one per cent. It is more than many of the best men in history could have done for a town. It may not be modest in me to refer to this but it is true. There is no record of a person doing as much—not even Shakespeare. But I did it for Florida and it shows that I could have done it for any place—even London, I suppose.

Recently some one in Missouri has sent me a picture of the house I was born in. Heretofore I have always stated that it was a palace but I shall be more guarded now.

The village had two streets, each a couple of hundred yards long; the rest of the avenues mere lanes, with railfences and cornfields on either side. Both the streets and the lanes were paved with the same material—tough black mud in wet times, deep dust in dry.

Most of the houses were of logs—all of them, indeed, except three or four; these latter were frame ones. There were none of brick and none of stone. There was a log church, with a puncheon floor and slab benches. A puncheon floor is made of logs whose upper surfaces have been chipped flat with the adz. The cracks between the logs were not filled; there was no carpet; consequently, if you dropped anything smaller than a peach it was likely to go through. The church was perched upon short sections of logs, which elevated it two or three feet from the ground. Hogs slept under there, and whenever the dogs got after them during services the minister had to wait till the disturbance was over. In winter there was always a refreshing breeze up through the puncheon floor; in summer there were fleas enough for all.

A slab bench is made of the outside cut of a saw-log, with the bark side down; it is supported on four sticks driven into auger holes at the ends; it has no back and no cushions. The church was twilighted with yellow tallow candles in tin sconces hung against the walls. Week days, the church was a schoolhouse.

There were two stores in the village. My uncle, John A. Quarles, was proprietor of one of them. It was a very small establishment, with a few rolls of "bit" calicoes on half a dozen shelves; a few barrels of salt mackerel, coffee and New Orleans sugar behind the counter; stacks of brooms, shovels, axes, hoes, rakes and such things here and there; a lot of cheap hats, bonnets and tinware strung on strings and suspended from the walls; and at the other end of the room was another counter with bags of shot on it, a cheese or two and a keg of powder; in front of it a row of nail kegs and a few pigs of lead, and behind it a barrel or two of New Orleans molasses and native corn whisky on tap. If a boy bought five or ten cents' worth of anything he was entitled to half a handful of sugar from the barrel; if a woman bought a few yards of calico she was entitled to a spool of thread in addition to the usual gratis "trimmin's"; if a man bought a trifle he was at liberty to draw and swallow as big a drink of whisky as he wanted.

Everything was cheap: apples, peaches, sweet potatoes, Irish potatoes and corn, ten cents a bushel; chickens, ten cents apiece; butter, six cents a pound; eggs, three cents a dozen; coffee and sugar, five cents a pound; whisky, ten cents a gallon. I do not know how prices are out there in interior Missouri now but I know what they are here in Hartford, Connecticut.[1] To wit: apples, three dollars a bushel; peaches, five dollars; Irish potatoes (choice Bermudas), five dollars; chickens, a dollar to a dollar and a half apiece, according to weight; butter, forty-five to sixty cents a pound; eggs, fifty to sixty cents a dozen; coffee, forty-five cents a pound; native whisky, four or five dollars a gallon, I believe, but I can only be certain concerning the sort which I use myself, which is Scotch and costs ten dollars a gallon when you take two gallons—more when you take less.

Thirty to forty years ago, out yonder in Missouri, the ordi-

---

[1] Written in 1877.

nary cigar cost thirty cents a hundred, but most people did not try to afford them, since smoking a pipe cost nothing in that tobacco-growing country. Connecticut is also given up to tobacco raising, today, yet we pay ten dollars a hundred for Connecticut cigars and fifteen to twenty-five dollars a hundred for the imported article.

At first my father owned slaves but by and by he sold them and hired others by the year from the farmers. For a girl of fifteen he paid twelve dollars a year and gave her two linsey-woolsey frocks and a pair of "stogy" shoes—cost, a modification of nothing; for a Negro woman of twenty-five, as general house servant, he paid twenty-five dollars a year and gave her shoes and the aforementioned linsey-woolsey frocks; for a strong Negro woman of forty, as cook, washer, etc., he paid forty dollars a year and the customary two suits of clothes; and for an able-bodied man he paid from seventy-five to a hundred dollars a year and gave him two suits of jeans and two pairs of "stogy" shoes—an outfit that cost about three dollars.

I used to remember my brother Henry walking into a fire outdoors when he was a week old. It was remarkable in me to remember a thing like that and it was still more remarkable that I should cling to the delusion for thirty years that I *did* remember it—for of course it never happened; he would not have been able to walk at that age. If I had stopped to reflect I should not have burdened my memory with that impossible rubbish so long. It is believed by many people that an impression deposited in a child's memory within the first two years of its life cannot remain there five years but that is an error. The incident of Benvenuto Cellini and the salamander must be accepted as authentic and trustworthy; and then that remarkable and indisputable instance in the experience of Helen Keller. For many years I believed that I remembered helping my grandfather drink his whisky toddy when I was six weeks old but I do not tell about that any more now; I am grown old and my memory is not as active as it used to be. When I was younger I could remember anything, whether it had happened or not; but my faculties are decaying now and soon I shall be so I cannot remember any but the things that never happened. It is sad to go to pieces like this but we all have to do it.

CHAPTER 2

My uncle, John A. Quarles, was also a farmer, and his place was in the country four miles from Florida. He had eight children and fifteen or twenty Negroes and was also fortunate in other ways, particularly in his character. I have not come across a better man than he was. I was his guest for two or three months every year, from the fourth year after we removed to Hannibal till I was eleven or twelve years old. I have never consciously used him or his wife in a book but his farm has come very handy to me in literature once or twice. In *Huck Finn* and in *Tom Sawyer, Detective* I moved it down to Arkansas. It was all of six hundred miles but it was no trouble; it was not a very large farm—five hundred acres, perhaps —but I could have done it if it had been twice as large. And as for the morality of it, I cared nothing for that; I would move a state if the exigencies of literature required it.

It was a heavenly place for a boy, that farm of my uncle John's. The house was a double log one, with a spacious floor (roofed in) connecting it with the kitchen. In the summer the table was set in the middle of that shady and breezy floor, and the sumptuous meals—well, it makes me cry to think of them. Fried chicken, roast pig; wild and tame turkeys, ducks and geese; venison just killed; squirrels, rabbits, pheasants, partridges, prairie-chickens; biscuits, hot batter cakes, hot buckwheat cakes, hot "wheat bread," hot rolls, hot corn pone; fresh corn boiled on the ear, succotash, butter beans, string beans, tomatoes, peas, Irish potatoes, sweet potatoes; buttermilk, sweet milk, "clabber"; watermelons, muskmelons, cantaloupes —all fresh from the garden; apple pie, peach pie, pumpkin pie, apple dumplings, peach cobbler—I can't remember the rest. The way that the things were cooked was perhaps the main splendor—particularly a certain few of the dishes. For instance, the corn bread, the hot biscuits and wheat bread and the fried chicken. These things have never been properly cooked in the North—in fact, no one there is able to learn the art, so far as

4

my experience goes. The North thinks it knows how to make corn bread but this is gross superstition. Perhaps no bread in the world is quite so good as Southern corn bread and perhaps no bread in the world is quite so bad as the Northern imitation of it. The North seldom tries to fry chicken and this is well; the art cannot be learned north of the line of Mason and Dixon, nor anywhere in Europe. This is not hearsay; it is experience that is speaking. In Europe it is imagined that the custom of serving various kinds of bread blazing hot is "American," but that is too broad a spread; it is custom in the South but is much less than that in the North. In the North and in Europe hot bread is considered unhealthy. This is probably another fussy superstition, like the European superstition that ice water is unhealthy. Europe does not need ice water and does not drink it; and yet, notwithstanding this, its word for it is better than ours, because it describes it, whereas ours doesn't. Europe calls it "iced" water. Our word describes water made from melted ice—a drink which has a characterless taste and which we have but little acquaintance with.

It seems a pity that the world should throw away so many good things merely because they are unwholesome. I doubt if God has given us any refreshment which, taken in moderation, is unwholesome, except microbes. Yet there are people who strictly deprive themselves of each and every eatable, drinkable and smokable which has in any way acquired a shady reputation. They pay this price for health. And health is all they get for it. How strange it is! It is like paying out your whole fortune for a cow that has gone dry.

The farmhouse stood in the middle of a very large yard and the yard was fenced on three sides with rails and on the rear side with high palings; against these stood the smokehouse; beyond the palings was the orchard; beyond the orchard were the Negro quarters and the tobacco fields. The front yard was entered over a stile made of sawed-off logs of graduated heights; I do not remember any gate. In a corner of the front yard were a dozen lofty hickory trees and a dozen black walnuts, and in the nutting season riches were to be gathered there.

Down a piece, abreast the house, stood a little log cabin against the rail fence; and there the woody hill fell sharply away, past the barns, the corncrib, the stables and the tobacco-curing house, to a limpid brook which sang along over its gravelly bed and curved and frisked in and out and here and there and yonder in the deep shade of overhanging foliage and vines—a divine place for wading, and it had swimming pools, too, which were forbidden to us and therefore much frequented by us. For we were little Christian children and had early been taught the value of forbidden fruit.

In the little log cabin lived a bedridden white-headed slave woman whom we visited daily and looked upon with awe, for we believed she was upward of a thousand years old and had talked with Moses. The younger Negroes credited these statistics and had furnished them to us in good faith. We accommodated all the details which came to us about her; and so we believed that she had lost her health in the long desert trip coming out of Egypt and had never been able to get it back again. She had a round bald place on the crown of her head and we used to creep around and gaze at it in reverent silence and reflect that it was caused by fright through seeing Pharaoh drowned. We called her "Aunt" Hannah, Southern fashion. She was superstitious, like the other Negroes; also, like them, she was deeply religious. Like them, she had great faith in prayer and employed it in all ordinary exigencies, but not in cases where a dead certainty of result was urgent. Whenever witches were around she tied up the remnant of her wool in little tufts, with white thread, and this promptly made the witches impotent.

All the Negroes were friends of ours, and with those of our own age we were in effect comrades. I say in effect, using the phrase as a modification. We were comrades and yet not comrades; color and condition interposed a subtle line which both parties were conscious of and which rendered complete fusion impossible. We had a faithful and affectionate good friend, ally and adviser in "Uncle Dan'l," a middle-aged slave whose head was the best one in the Negro quarter, whose sympathies were wide and warm and whose heart was honest and simple and knew no guile. He has served me well these many, many years. I have not seen him for more than half a century and yet spiritually I have had his welcome company a good part of that time and have staged him in books under his own name and as "Jim," and carted him all around—to Hannibal, down the Mississippi on a raft and even across the Desert of Sahara in a balloon—and he has endured it all with the patience and friendliness and loyalty which were his birthright. It was on the farm that I got my strong liking for his race and my appreciation of certain of its fine qualities. This feeling and this estimate have stood the test of sixty years and more and have suffered no impairment. The black face is as welcome to me now as it was then.

In my schoolboy days I had no aversion to slavery. I was not aware that there was anything wrong about it. No one arraigned it in my hearing; the local papers said nothing against it; the local pulpit taught us that God approved it, that it was a holy thing and that the doubter need only look in the Bible if he wished to settle his mind—and then the texts were read aloud to us to make the matter sure; if the slaves themselves had an aversion to slavery they were wise and said nothing. In Hannibal we seldom saw a slave misused; on the farm never.

There was, however, one small incident of my boyhood days which touched this matter, and it must have meant a good deal to me or it would not have stayed in my memory, clear and sharp, vivid and shadowless, all these slow-drifting years. We had a little slave boy whom we had hired from someone, there in Hannibal. He was from the eastern shore of Maryland and had been brought away from his family and his friends halfway across the American continent and sold. He was a cheery spirit, innocent and gentle, and the noisiest creature that ever was, perhaps. All day long he was singing, whistling, yelling, whooping, laughing—it was maddening, devastating, unendurable. At last, one day, I lost all my temper and went raging to my mother and said Sandy had been singing for an hour without a single break and I couldn't stand it and *wouldn't* she please shut him up. The tears came into her eyes and her lip trembled and she said something like this:

"Poor thing, when he sings it shows that he is not remembering and that comforts me; but when he is still I am afraid he is thinking and I cannot bear it. He will never see his mother again; if he can sing I must not hinder it, but be thankful for it. If you were older you would understand me; then that friendless child's noise would make you glad."

It was a simple speech and made up of small words but it went home, and Sandy's noise was not a trouble to me any more. She never used large words but she had a natural gift for making small ones do effective work. She lived to reach the neighborhood of ninety years and was capable with her tongue to the last—especially when a meanness or an injustice roused her spirit. She has come handy to me several times in my books, where she figures as Tom Sawyer's Aunt Polly. I fitted her out with a dialect and tried to think up other improve-

ments for her but did not find any. I used Sandy once, also; it
was in *Tom Sawyer*. I tried to get him to whitewash the
fence but it did not work. I do not remember what name I
called him by in the book.

CHAPTER 3

I can see the farm yet, with perfect clearness. I can see all
its belongings, all its details; the family room of the house,
with a "trundle" bed in one corner and a spinning wheel in
another—a wheel whose rising and falling wail, heard from a
distance, was the mournfulest of all sounds to me and made
me homesick and low spirited and filled my atmosphere with
the wandering spirits of the dead; the vast fireplace, piled
high on winter nights with flaming hickory logs from whose
ends a sugary sap bubbled out but did not go to waste, for we
scraped it off and ate it; the lazy cat spread out on the rough
hearthstones; the drowsy dogs braced against the jambs and
blinking; my aunt in one chimney corner, knitting; my uncle
in the other, smoking his corncob pipe; the slick and carpetless
oak floor faintly mirroring the dancing flame tongues and
freckled with black indentations where fire coals had popped
out and died a leisurely death; half a dozen children romping
in the background twilight; "split"-bottomed chairs here and
there, some with rockers; a cradle—out of service but waiting
with confidence; in the early cold mornings a snuggle of children in shirts and chemises, occupying the hearthstone and
procrastinating—they could not bear to leave that comfortable
place and go out on the wind-swept floor space between the
house and kitchen where the general tin basin stood, and
wash.

Along outside of the front fence ran the country road, dusty
in the summertime and a good place for snakes—they liked to
lie in it and sun themselves; when they were rattlesnakes or
puff adders we killed them; when they were black snakes or
racers or belonged to the fabled "hoop" breed we fled without
shame; when they were "house snakes" or "garters" we carried them home and put them in Aunt Patsy's work basket for
a surprise; for she was prejudiced against snakes, and always

when she took the basket in her lap and they began to climb out of it, it disordered her mind. She never could seem to get used to them; her opportunities went for nothing. And she was always cold toward bats, too, and could not bear them; and yet I think a bat is as friendly a bird as there is. My mother was Aunt Patsy's sister and had the same wild superstitions. A bat is beautifully soft and silky; I do not know any creature that is pleasanter to the touch or is more grateful for caressings, if offered in the right spirit. I know all about these coleoptera[1] because our great cave, three miles below Hannibal, was multitudinously stocked with them and often I brought them home to amuse my mother with. It was easy to manage if it was a school day because then I had ostensibly been to school and hadn't any bats. She was not a suspicious person but full of trust and confidence; and when I said, "There's something in my coat pocket for you," she would put her hand in. But she always took it out again, herself; I didn't have to tell her. It was remarkable the way she couldn't learn to like private bats. The more experience she had the more she could not change her views.

I think she was never in the cave in her life; but everybody else went there. Many excursion parties came from considerable distances up and down the river to visit the cave. It was miles in extent and was a tangled wilderness of narrow and lofty clefts and passages. It was an easy place to get lost in; anybody could do it—including the bats. I got lost in it myself, along with a lady, and our last candle burned down to almost nothing before we glimpsed the search party's lights winding about in the distance.

"Injun Joe," the half-breed, got lost in there once and would have starved to death if the bats had run short. But there was no chance of that; there were myriads of them. He told me all his story. In the book called *Tom Sawyer* I starved him entirely to death in the cave but that was in the interest of art; it never happened. "General" Gaines, who was our first town drunkard before Jimmy Finn got the place, was lost in there for the space of a week and finally pushed his handkerchief out of a hole in a hilltop near Saverton, several miles down the river from the cave's mouth, and somebody saw it and dug him out. There is nothing the matter with his statistics except

---

[1] Mark Twain meant chiroptera.

the handkerchief. I knew him for years and he hadn't any. But it could have been his nose. That would attract attention.

The cave was an uncanny place, for it contained a corpse—the corpse of a young girl of fourteen. It was in a glass cylinder inclosed in a copper one which was suspended from a rail which bridged a narrow passage. The body was preserved in alcohol and it was said that loafers and rowdies used to drag it up by the hair and look at the dead face. The girl was the daughter of a St. Louis surgeon of extraordinary ability and wide celebrity. He was an eccentric man and did many strange things. He put the poor thing in that forlorn place himself.

Dr. McDowell—the great Dr. McDowell of St. Louis—was a physician as well as a surgeon; and sometimes in cases where medicines failed to save he developed other resources. He fell out once with a family whose physician he was and after that they ceased to employ him. But a time came when he was once more called. The lady of the house was very ill and had been given up by her doctors. He came into the room and stopped and stood still and looked around upon the scene; he had his great slouch hat on and a quarter of an acre of gingerbread under his arm and while he looked meditatively about he broke hunks from his cake, munched them, and let the crumbs dribble down his breast to the floor. The lady lay pale and still, with her eyes closed; about the bed, in the solemn hush, were grouped the family softly sobbing, some standing, some kneeling. Presently the doctor began to take up the medicine bottles and sniff at them contemptuously and throw them out of the window. When they were all gone he ranged up to the bed, laid his slab of gingerbread on the dying woman's breast and said roughly:

"What are the idiots sniveling about? There's nothing the matter with this humbug. Put out your tongue!"

The sobbings stopped and the angry mourners changed their attitudes and began to upbraid the doctor for his cruel behavior in this chamber of death; but he interrupted them with an explosion of profane abuse and said:

"A pack of snuffling fat-wits! Do you think you can teach me my business? I tell you there is nothing the matter with the woman—nothing the matter but laziness. What she wants is a beefsteak and a washtub. With her damned society training, she—"

Then the dying woman rose up in bed and the light of battle was in her eye. She poured out upon the doctor her whole insulted mind—just a volcanic irruption, accompanied by thunder and lightning, whirlwinds and earthquakes, pumice stone and ashes. It brought the reaction which he was after and she got well. This was the lamented Dr. McDowell, whose name was so great and so honored in the Mississippi Valley a decade before the Civil War.

Beyond the road where the snakes sunned themselves was a dense young thicket and through it a dim-lighted path led a quarter of a mile; then out of the dimness one emerged abruptly upon a level great prairie which was covered with wild strawberry plants, vividly starred with prairie pinks and walled in on all sides by forests. The strawberries were fragrant and fine, and in the season we were generally there in the crisp freshness of the early morning, while the dew beads still sparkled upon the grass and the woods were ringing with the first songs of the birds.

Down the forest slopes to the left were the swings. They were made of bark stripped from hickory saplings. When they became dry they were dangerous. They usually broke when a child was forty feet in the air and this was why so many bones had to be mended every year. I had no ill luck myself but none of my cousins escaped. There were eight of them and at one time and another they broke fourteen arms among them. But it cost next to nothing, for the doctor worked by the year —twenty-five dollars for the whole family. I remember two of the Florida doctors, Chowning and Meredith. They not only tended an entire family for twenty-five dollars a year but furnished the medicines themselves. Good measure, too. Only the largest persons could hold a whole dose. Castor oil was the principal beverage. The dose was half a dipperful, with half a dipperful of New Orleans molasses added to help it down and make it taste good, which it never did. The next standby was calomel; the next rhubarb; and the next jalap. Then they bled the patient and put mustard plasters on him. It was a dreadful system and yet the death rate was not heavy. The calomel was nearly sure to salivate the patient and cost him some of his teeth. There were no dentists. When teeth became touched with decay or were otherwise ailing, the doctor knew of but one thing to do—he fetched his tongs and dragged them out. If the jaw remained, it was not his fault.

Doctors were not called in cases of ordinary illness; the family grandmother attended to those. Every old woman was a doctor and gathered her own medicines in the woods and knew how to compound doses that would stir the vitals of a cast-iron dog. And then there was the "Indian doctor"; a grave savage, remnant of his tribe, deeply read in the mysteries of nature and the secret properties of herbs; and most backwoodsmen had high faith in his powers and could tell of wonderful cures achieved by him. In Mauritius, away off yonder in the solitudes of the Indian Ocean, there is a person who answers to our Indian doctor of the old times. He is a Negro and has had no teaching as a doctor, yet there is one disease which he is master of and can cure and the doctors can't. They send for him when they have a case. It is a child's disease of a strange and deadly sort and the Negro cures it with a herb medicine which he makes himself from a prescription which has come down to him from his father and grandfather. He will not let anyone see it. He keeps the secret of its components to himself and it is feared that he will die without divulging it; then there will be consternation in Mauritius. I was told these things by the people there in 1896.

We had the "faith doctor," too, in those early days—a woman. Her specialty was toothache. She was a farmer's old wife and lived five miles from Hannibal. She would lay her hand on the patient's jaw and say, "Believe!" and the cure was prompt. Mrs. Utterback. I remember her very well. Twice I rode out there behind my mother, horseback, and saw the cure performed. My mother was the patient.

Doctor Meredith removed to Hannibal by and by and was our family physician there and saved my life several times. Still, he was a good man and meant well. Let it go.

I was always told that I was a sickly and precarious and tiresome and uncertain child and lived mainly on allopathic medicines during the first seven years of my life. I asked my mother about this, in her old age—she was in her eighty-eighth year—and said:

"I suppose that during all that time you were uneasy about me?"

"Yes, the whole time."

"Afraid I wouldn't live?"

After a reflective pause—ostensibly to think out the facts—"No—afraid you would."

It sounds like plagiarism but it probably wasn't.

◇◇◇◇◇◇◇◇◇◇◇◇◇◇◇◇◇◇

CHAPTER 4

The country schoolhouse was three miles from my uncle's farm. It stood in a clearing in the woods and would hold about twenty-five boys and girls. We attended the school with more or less regularity once or twice a week, in summer, walking to it in the cool of the morning by the forest paths and back in the gloaming at the end of the day. All the pupils brought their dinners in baskets—corn dodger, buttermilk and other good things—and sat in the shade of the trees at noon and ate them. It is the part of my education which I look back upon with the most satisfaction. My first visit to the school was when I was seven. A strapping girl of fifteen, in the customary sunbonnet and calico dress, asked me if I "used tobacco"— meaning did I chew it. I said no. It roused her scorn. She reported me to all the crowd and said:

"Here is a boy seven years old who can't chaw tobacco."

By the looks and comments which this produced I realized that I was a degraded object; I was cruelly ashamed of myself. I determined to reform. But I only made myself sick; I was not able to learn to chew tobacco. I learned to smoke fairly well but that did not conciliate anybody and I remained a poor thing and characterless. I longed to be respected but I never was able to rise. Children have but little charity for one another's defects.

As I have said, I spent some part of every year at the farm until I was twelve or thirteen years old. The life which I led there with my cousins was full of charm, and so is the memory of it yet. I can call back the solemn twilight and mystery of the deep woods, the earthy smells, the faint odors of the wild flowers, the sheen of rain-washed foliage, the rattling clatter of drops when the wind shook the trees, the far-off hammering of woodpeckers and the muffled drumming of wood pheasants in the remoteness of the forest, the snapshot glimpses of disturbed wild creatures scurrying through the grass—I can call it all back and make it as real as it ever was, and as blessed. I can call back the prairie, and its loneliness and peace, and a vast hawk hanging motionless in the sky, with his wings spread wide and the blue of the vault showing through the fringe of their end feathers. I can see the woods in their autumn dress, the oaks purple, the hickories washed with gold, the maples and the sumachs luminous with crimson fires, and I can hear the rustle made by the fallen leaves as we plowed through them. I can see the blue clusters of wild grapes hanging among the foliage of the saplings, and I remember the taste of them and the smell. I know how the wild blackberries looked, and how they tasted, and the same with the paw-paws, the hazelnuts, and the persimmons; and I can feel the thumping rain, upon my head, of hickory nuts and walnuts when we were out in the frosty dawn to scramble for them with the pigs, and the gusts of wind loosed them and sent them down. I know the stain of blackberries, and how pretty it is, and I know the stain of walnut hulls, and how little it minds soap and water, also what grudged experience it had of either of them. I know the taste of maple sap, and when to gather it, and how to arrange the troughs and the delivery tubes, and how to boil down the juice, and how to hook the sugar after it is made, also how much better hooked sugar tastes than any that is honestly come by, let bigots say what they will. I know how a prize watermelon looks when it is sunning its fat rotundity among pumpkin vines and "simblins"; I know how to tell when it is ripe without "plugging" it; I know how inviting it looks when it is cooling itself in a tub of water under the bed, waiting; I know how it looks when it lies on the table in the sheltered great floor space between house and kitchen, and the children gathered for the sacrifice and their mouths watering; I know the crackling sound it makes when the carving knife enters its end, and I can see the split fly along in front of the blade as the knife cleaves its way to the other end; I can see its halves fall apart and display the rich red meat and the black seeds, and the heart standing up, a luxury fit for the elect; I know how a boy looks behind a yard-long slice of that melon, and I know how he feels; for I have been there. I know the taste of the watermelon which has been honestly come by, and I know the taste of the watermelon which has been acquired by art. Both taste good, but the experienced know which tastes best. I know the look of green apples and peaches and pears on the trees, and I know how entertaining they are when they are inside of a person. I know how ripe ones look when they are piled in pyramids under the trees, and how pretty they are and how vivid their colors. I know how a frozen apple looks, in a barrel down cellar in the wintertime, and how hard it is to bite, and how the frost makes the teeth ache, and yet how good it is, notwithstanding. I know the disposition of elderly people to select the speckled apples for the children, and I once knew ways to beat the game. I know the look of an apple that is roasting and sizzling on a hearth on a winter's evening, and I know the comfort that comes of eating it hot, along with some sugar and a drench of cream. I know the delicate art and mystery of so cracking hickory nuts and walnuts on a flatiron with a hammer that the kernels will be delivered whole, and I know how the nuts, taken in conjunction with winter apples, cider, and doughnuts, make old people's old tales and old jokes sound fresh and crisp and enchanting, and juggle an evening away before you know what went with the time. I know the look of Uncle Dan'l's kitchen as it was on the privileged nights, when I was a child, and I can see the white and black children grouped on the hearth, with the firelight playing on their faces and the shadows flickering upon the walls, clear back toward the cavernous gloom of the rear, and I can hear Uncle Dan'l telling the immortal tales which Uncle Remus Harris was to gather into his books and charm the world with, by and by; and I can feel again the creepy joy which quivered through me when the time for the ghost story of the "Golden Arm" was reached—and the sense of regret, too, which came over me, for it was always the last story of the evening and there was nothing between it and the unwelcome bed.

I can remember the bare wooden stairway in my uncle's house, and the turn to the left above the landing, and the rafters and the slanting roof over my bed, and the squares of moonlight on the floor, and the white cold world of snow outside, seen through the curtainless window. I can remember the howling of the wind and the quaking of the house on stormy nights, and how snug and cozy one felt, under the blankets, listening; and how the powdery snow used to sift in, around the sashes, and lie in little ridges on the floor and make the place look chilly in the morning and curb the wild desire to get up—in case there was any. I can remember how very dark that room was, in the dark of the moon, and how packed it was with ghostly stillness when one woke up by accident away in the night, and forgotten sins came flocking out of the secret chambers of the memory and wanted a hearing; and how ill chosen the time seemed for this kind of business; and how dismal was the hoo-hooing of the owl and the wailing of the wolf, sent mourning by on the night wind.

I remember the raging of the rain on that roof, summer nights, and how pleasant it was to lie and listen to it, and enjoy the white splendor of the lightning and the majestic booming and crashing of the thunder. It was a very satisfactory room, and there was a lightning rod which was reachable from the window, an adorable and skittish thing to climb up and down, summer nights, when there were duties on hand of a sort to make privacy desirable.

I remember the 'coon and 'possum hunts, nights, with the Negroes, and the long marches through the black gloom of the woods, and the excitement which fired everybody when the distant bay of an experienced dog announced that the game was treed; then the wild scramblings and stumblings through briers and bushes and over roots to get to the spot; then the lighting of a fire and the felling of the tree, the joyful frenzy of the dogs and the Negroes, and the weird picture it all made in the red glare—I remember it all well, and the delight that everyone got out of it, except the 'coon.

I remember the pigeon seasons, when the birds would come in millions and cover the trees and by their weight break down the branches. They were clubbed to death with sticks; guns were not necessary and were not used. I remember the squirrel hunts, and prairie-chicken hunts, and wild-turkey hunts, and all that; and how we turned out, mornings, while it was still dark, to go on these expeditions, and how chilly and dismal it was, and how often I regretted that I was well enough to go. A toot on a tin horn brought twice as many dogs as were needed, and in their happiness they raced and scampered about, and knocked small people down, and made no end of unnecessary noise. At the word, they vanished away toward the woods, and we drifted silently after them in the melancholy gloom. But presently the gray dawn stole over the world, the birds piped up, then the sun rose and poured light and comfort all around, everything was fresh and dewy and fragrant, and life was a boon again. After three hours of tramping we arrived back wholesomely tired, overladen with game, very hungry, and just in time for breakfast.

CHAPTER 5

My father was John Marshall Clemens of Virginia; my mother Jane Lampton of Kentucky. Back of the Virginian Clemenses is a dim procession of ancestors stretching back to Noah's time. According to tradition, some of them were pirates and slavers in Elizabeth's time. But this is no discredit to them, for so were Drake and Hawkins and the others. It was a respectable trade then and monarchs were partners in it. In my time I have had desires to be a pirate myself. The reader, if he will look deep down in his secret heart, will find—but never mind what he will find there. I am not writing his autobiography but mine. Later, according to tradition, one of the procession was ambassador to Spain in the time of James I, or of Charles I, and married there and sent down a strain of Spanish blood to warm us up. Also, according to tradition, this one or another—Geoffrey Clement, by name—helped to sentence Charles to death.

I have not examined into these traditions myself, partly because I was indolent and partly because I was so busy polishing up this end of the line and trying to make it showy; but the other Clemenses claim that they have made the examination and that it stood the test. Therefore I have always taken for granted that I did help Charles out of his troubles, by ancestral proxy. My instincts have persuaded me, too. Whenever we have a strong and persistent and ineradicable instinct we may be sure that it is not original with us but inherited—inherited from away back and hardened and perfected by the petrifying influence of time. Now I have been always and unchangingly bitter against Charles, and I am quite certain that this feeling trickled down to me through the veins of my forebears from the heart of that judge; for it is not my disposition to be bitter against people on my own personal account. I am not bitter against Jeffreys. I ought to be but I am not. It indicates that my ancestors of James II's time were indifferent to him; I do not know why; I never could make it out; but that is what it indicates. And I have always felt friendly toward Satan. Of course that is ancestral; it must be in the blood, for I could not have originated it.

And so, by the testimony of instinct, backed by the assertions of Clemenses, who said they had examined the records, I have always been obliged to believe that Geoffrey Clement, the martyr maker, was an ancestor of mine and to regard him with favor and, in fact, pride. This has not had a good effect upon me, for it has made me vain, and that is a fault. It has made me set myself above people who were less fortunate in their ancestry than I and has moved me to take them down a peg upon occasion and say things to them which hurt them before company.

A case of the kind happened in Berlin several years ago. William Walter Phelps was our minister at the Emperor's court then, and one evening he had me to dinner to meet Count S——, a Cabinet Minister. This nobleman was of long and illustrious descent. Of course I wanted to let out the fact that I had some ancestors too; but I did not want to pull them out of their graves by the ears and I never could seem to get the chance to work them in in a way that would look sufficiently casual. I suppose Phelps was in the same difficulty. In fact, he looked distraught now and then—just as a person looks who wants to uncover an ancestor purely by accident and cannot think of a way that will seem accidental enough. But at last, after dinner, he made a try. He took us about his drawing room, showing us the pictures, and finally stopped before a rude and ancient engraving. It was a picture of the court that tried Charles I. There was a pyramid of judges in Puritan slouch hats, and below them three bareheaded secretaries seated at a table. Mr. Phelps put his finger upon one of the three and said, with exulting indifference:

"An ancestor of mine."

I put my finger on a judge and retorted with scathing languidness:

"Ancestor of mine. But it is a small matter. I have others."

It was not noble in me to do it. I have always regretted it since. But it landed him. I wonder how he felt! However, it made no difference in our friendship; which shows that he was fine and high, notwithstanding the humbleness of his origin. And it was also creditable in me, too, that I could overlook it. I made no change in my bearing toward him but always treated him as an equal.

Among the Virginian Clemenses were Jere and Sherrard. Jere Clemens had a wide reputation as a good pistol-shot and once it enabled him to get on the friendly side of some drummers when they wouldn't have paid any attention to mere smooth words and arguments. He was out stumping the state at the time. The drummers were grouped in front of the stand and had been hired by the opposition to drum while he made his speech. When he was ready to begin he got out his revolver and laid it before him and said, in his soft, silky way: "I do not wish to hurt anybody and shall try not to but I have got just a bullet apiece for those six drums and if you should want to play on them don't stand behind them."

Sherrard Clemens was a Republican Congressman from West Virginia in the war days, and then went out to St. Louis, where the James Clemens branch lived and still lives, and there he became a warm rebel. This was after the war. At the time that he was a Republican I was a rebel; but by the time he had become a rebel I was become (temporarily) a Republican. The Clemenses have always done the best they could to keep the political balances level, no matter how much it might inconvenience them. I did not know what had become of Sherrard Clemens; but once I introduced Senator Hawley to a Republican mass meeting in New England and then I got a bitter letter from Sherrard from St. Louis. He said that the Republicans of the North—no, the "mudsills of the North"—had swept away the old aristocracy of the South with fire and sword and it ill became me, an aristocrat by blood, to train with that kind of swine. Did I forget that I was a Lambton?

That was a reference to my mother's side of the house. My mother was a Lambton—Lambton with a p, for some of the American Lamptons could not spell very well in early times and so the name suffered at their hands. She married my father in Lexington in 1823, when she was twenty years old and he twenty-four. Neither of them had an overplus of property. She brought him two or three Negroes but nothing else, I think. They removed to the remote and secluded village of Jamestown, in the mountain solitudes of east Tennessee. There their first crop of children was born, but as I was of a later vintage I do not remember anything about it. I was postponed—postponed to Missouri. Missouri was an unknown new state and needed attractions.

I think that my eldest brother, Orion, my sisters Pamela and Margaret, and my brother Benjamin were born in Jamestown.

There may have been others but as to that I am not sure. It
was a great lift for that little village to have my parents come
there. It was hoped that they would stay, so that it would become a city. It was supposed that they would stay. And so
there was a boom; but by and by they went away and prices
went down and it was many years before Jamestown got another start. I have written about Jamestown in *The Gilded
Age*, a book of mine, but it was from hearsay, not from personal knowledge.

My father left a fine estate behind him in the region roundabout Jamestown—75,000 acres.[1] When he died in 1847 he
had owned it about twenty years. The taxes were almost nothing (five dollars a year for the whole) and he had always paid
them regularly and kept his title perfect. He had always said
that the land would not become valuable in his time but that
it would be a commodious provision for his children some day.
It contained coal, copper, iron and timber, and he said that in
the course of time railways would pierce to that region and
then the property would be property in fact as well as in
name. It also produced a wild grape of a promising sort. He
had sent some samples to Nicholas Longworth of Cincinnati
to get his judgment upon them and Mr. Longworth had said
that they would make as good wine as his Catawbas. The land
contained all these riches; and also oil, but my father did not
know that, and of course in those early days he would have
cared nothing about it if he had known it. The oil was not discovered until about 1895. I wish I owned a couple of acres of
land now, in which case I would not be writing autobiographies for a living.[2] My father's dying charge was, "Cling to
the land and wait; let nothing beguile it away from you." My
mother's favorite cousin, James Lampton, who figures in *The
Gilded Age* as Colonel Sellers, always said of that land—and
said it with blazing enthusiasm too—"There's millions in it—
millions!" It is true that he always said that about everything
—and was always mistaken too, but this time he was right;
which shows that a man who goes around with a prophecy-
gun ought never to get discouraged. If he will keep up his
heart and fire at everything he sees he is bound to hit something by and by.

Many persons regarded Colonel Sellers as a fiction, an invention, an extravagant impossibility, and did me the honor

[1] Correction (1906)—it was above 100,000, it appears. (M.T.)
[2] Written 1897-1898.

to call him a "creation"; but they were mistaken. I merely put him on paper as he was; he was not a person who could be exaggerated. The incidents which looked most extravagant, both in the book and on the stage, were not inventions of mine, but were facts of his life; and I was present when they were developed. John T. Raymond's audiences used to come near to dying with laughter over the turnip-eating scene; but, extravagant as the scene was, it was faithful to the facts in all its absurd details. The thing happened in Lampton's own house and I was present. In fact, I was myself the guest who ate the turnips. In the hands of a great actor that piteous scene would have dimmed any manly spectator's eyes with tears and racked his ribs apart with laughter at the same time. But Raymond was great in humorous portrayal only. In that he was superb, he was wonderful—in a word, great; in all things else he was a pygmy of pygmies. The real Colonel Sellers, as I knew him in James Lampton, was a pathetic and beautiful spirit, a manly man, a straight and honorable man, a man with a big, foolish, unselfish heart in his bosom, a man born to be loved; and he was loved by all his friends, and by his family worshiped. It is the right word. To them he was but little less than a god. The real Colonel Sellers was never on the stage. Only half of him was there. Raymond could not play the other half of him; it was above his level. That half was made up of qualities of which Raymond was wholly destitute. For Raymond was not a manly man, he was not an honorable man nor an honest man, he was empty and selfish and vulgar and ignorant and silly, and there was a vacancy in him where his heart should have been. There was only one man who could have played the whole of Colonel Sellers, and that was Frank Mayo.[3]

It is a world of surprises. They fall, too, where one is least expecting them. When I introduced Sellers into the book, Charles Dudley Warner, who was writing the story with me, proposed a change of Sellers's Christian name. Ten years before, in a remote corner of the West, he had come across a man named Eschol Sellers, and he thought that Eschol was just the right and fitting name for our Sellers, since it was odd and quaint and all that. I liked the idea but I said that that man might turn up and object. But Warner said it couldn't

---

[3] Raymond was playing Colonel Sellers in 1876 and along there. About twenty years later Mayo dramatized *Pudd'nhead Wilson* and played the title role delightfully. (M.T.)

happen; that he was doubtless dead by this time and, be he
dead or alive, we must have the name; it was exactly the right
one and we couldn't do without it. So the change was made.
Warner's man was a farmer in a cheap and humble way.
When the book had been out a week, a college-bred gentleman of courtly manners and ducal upholstery arrived in Hartford in a sultry state of mind and with a libel suit in his eye,
and *his* name was Eschol Sellers! He had never heard of the
other one and had never been within a thousand miles of him.
This damaged aristocrat's program was quite definite and
business-like: the American Publishing Company must suppress the edition as far as printed and change the name in the
plates or stand a suit for $10,000. He carried away the com-
pany's promise and many apologies and we changed the name
back to Colonel Mulberry Sellers in the plates. Apparently
there is nothing that cannot happen. Even the existence of
two unrelated men wearing the impossible name of Eschol
Sellers is a possible thing.

James Lampton floated, all his days, in a tinted mist of magnificent dreams and died at last without seeing one of them
realized. I saw him last in 1884, when it had been twenty-six
years since I ate the basin of raw turnips and washed them
down with a bucket of water in his house. He was become old
and white-headed but he entertained me in the same old
breezy way of his earlier life and he was all there yet—not a
detail wanting; the happy light in his eye, the abounding hope
in his heart, the persuasive tongue, the miracle-breeding
imagination—they were all there; and before I could turn
around he was polishing up his Aladdin's lamp and flashing
the secret riches of the world before me. I said to myself: "I
did not overdraw him by a shade, I set him down as he was;
and he is the same man to-day. Cable[4] will recognize him." I
asked him to excuse me a moment and ran into the next room,
which was Cable's. Cable and I were stumping the Union on
a reading tour. I said:

"I am going to leave your door open so that you can listen.
There is a man in there who is interesting."

I went back and asked Lampton what he was doing now.
He began to tell me of a "small venture" he had begun in
New Mexico through his son; "only a little thing—a mere trifle
—partly to amuse my leisure, partly to keep my capital from
lying idle, but mainly to develop the boy—develop the boy.

[4] George Washington Cable.

Fortune's wheel is ever revolving; he may have to work for his living some day—as strange things have happened in this world. But it's only a little thing—a mere trifle, as I said."

And so it was—as he began it. But under his deft hands it grew and blossomed and spread—oh, beyond imagination. At the end of half an hour he finished; finished with the remark, uttered in an adorably languid manner:

"Yes, it is but a trifle, as things go nowadays—a bagatelle—but amusing. It passes the time. The boy thinks great things of it but he is young, you know, and imaginative; lacks the experience which comes of handling large affairs and which tempers the fancy and perfects the judgment. I suppose there's a couple of millions in it, possibly three, but not more, I think; still, for a boy, you know, just starting in life, it is not bad. I should not want him to make a fortune—let that come later. It could turn his head at his time of life and in many ways be a damage to him."

Then he said something about his having left his pocket-book lying on the table in the main drawing room at home and about its being after banking hours now, and—

I stopped him there and begged him to honor Cable and me by being our guest at the lecture—with as many friends as might be willing to do us the like honor. He accepted. And he thanked me as a prince might who had granted us a grace. The reason I stopped his speech about the tickets was because I saw that he was going to ask me to furnish them to him and let him pay next day; and I knew that if he made the debt he would pay it if he had to pawn his clothes. After a little further chat he shook hands heartily and affectionately and took his leave. Cable put his head in at the door and said:

"That was Colonel Sellers."

◆◇◆◇◆◇◆◇◆◇◆◇◆◇◆◇◆◇◆

CHAPTER 6

My father bought the enormous area of around 100,000 acres at one purchase. The entire lot must have cost him somewhere in the neighborhood of four hundred dollars. That was a good deal of money to pass over at one payment in those days—at least it was considered so away up there in the pineries and the "Knobs" of the Cumberland Mountains of Fentress County, East Tennessee. When my father paid down that great sum and turned and stood in the courthouse door of Jamestown and looked abroad over his vast possessions, he said, "Whatever befalls me, my heirs are secure; I shall not live to see these acres turn to silver and gold but my children will." Thus with the very kindest intentions in the world toward us he laid the heavy curse of prospective wealth upon our shoulders. He went to his grave in the full belief that he had done us a kindness. It was a woeful mistake but fortunately he never knew it.

He further said: "Iron ore is abundant in this tract, and there are other minerals; there are thousands of acres of the finest yellow-pine timber in America, and it can be rafted down Obeds River to the Cumberland, down the Cumberland to the Ohio, down the Ohio to the Mississippi, and down the Mississippi to any community that wants it. There is no end to the tar, pitch and turpentine which these vast pineries will yield. This is a natural wine district, too; there are no vines elsewhere in America, cultivated or otherwise, that yield such grapes as grow wild here. There are grazing lands, corn lands, wheat lands, potato lands, there are all species of timber—there is everything in and on this great tract of land that can make land valuable. The United States contain fourteen millions of inhabitants; the population has increased eleven millions in forty years and will henceforth increase faster than ever; my children will see the day that immigration will push its way to Fentress County, Tennessee, and then, with 100,000 acres of excellent land in their hands, they will become fabulously wealthy."

Everything my father said about the capabilities of the land was perfectly true—and he could have added, with like truth, that there were inexhaustible mines of coal on the land, but the chances are that he knew very little about the article, for the innocent Tennesseeans were not accustomed to digging in the earth for their fuel. And my father might have added to the list of eligibilities that the land was only a hundred miles from Knoxville and right where some future line of railway leading south from Cincinnati could not help but pass through it. But he never had seen a railway and it is barely possible that he had not even heard of such a thing. Curious as it may seem, as late as around 1860 there were people living close to Jamestown who never had heard of a railroad and could not be brought to believe in steamboats. They do not vote for Jackson in Fentress County; they vote for Washington. A venerable lady of that locality said of her son: "Jim's come back from Kaintuck and fotch a stuck-up gal with him from up thar; and bless you they've got more newfangled notions, massy *on* us! Common log house ain't good enough for *them* —no indeedy!—but they've tuck 'n' gaumed the inside of theirn all over with some kind of nasty disgustin' truck which they say is all the go in Kaintuck amongst the upper hunky and which they calls it plarsterin'!"

My eldest brother was four or five years old when the great purchase was made, and my eldest sister was an infant in arms. The rest of us—and we formed the great bulk of the family—came afterward and were born along from time to time during the next ten years. Four years after the purchase came the great financial crash of '34, and in that storm my father's fortunes were wrecked. From being honored and envied as the most opulent citizen of Fentress County—for outside of his great land possessions he was considered to be worth not less than three thousand five hundred dollars—he suddenly woke up and found himself reduced to less than one-fourth of that amount. He was a proud man, a silent, austere man, and not a person likely to abide among the scenes of his vanished grandeur and be the target for public commiseration. He gathered together his household and journeyed many tedious days through wilderness solitudes toward what was then the "Far West," and at last pitched his tent in the little town of Florida, Missouri. He "kept store" there several years but had no luck, except that I was born to him. He presently removed to Hannibal and prospered somewhat; rose to the dignity of justice of the peace and had been elected to the clerkship of the Surrogate Court when the summons came which no man may disregard. He had been doing tolerably well, for that age of the world, during the first years of his residence in Hannibal, but ill fortune tripped him once more. He did the friendly office of "going security" for Ira Stout, and Ira walked off and deliberately took the benefit of the new bankrupt law—a deed which enabled him to live easily and comfortably along till death called for him, but a deed which ruined my father, sent him poor to his grave and condemned his heirs to a long and discouraging struggle with the world for a livelihood. But my father would brighten up and gather heart, even upon his deathbed, when he thought of the Tennessee land. He said that it would soon make us all rich and happy. And so believing, he died.

We straightway turned our waiting eyes upon Tennessee. Through all our wanderings and all our ups and downs they gazed thitherward, over intervening continents and seas, with the hope of old habit and a faith that rises and falls but never dies.

After my father's death we reorganized the domestic establishment but on a temporary basis, intending to arrange it permanently after the land was sold. My brother borrowed five hundred dollars and bought a worthless weekly newspaper, believing, as we all did, that it was not worth while to go at anything in serious earnest until the land was disposed of and we could embark intelligently in something. We rented a large house to live in, at first, but we were disappointed in a sale we had expected to make (the man wanted only a part of the land and we talked it over and decided to sell all or none) and we were obliged to move to a less expensive one.

As I have said, that vast plot of Tennessee land was held by my father twenty years—intact. When he died in 1847 we began to manage it ourselves. Forty years afterward we had managed it all away except 10,000 acres and gotten nothing to remember the sales by. About 1887—possibly it was earlier —the 10,000 went. My brother found a chance to trade it for a house and lot in the town of Corry, in the oil regions of Pennsylvania. About 1894 he sold this property for $250. That ended the Tennessee land.

If any penny of cash ever came out of my father's wise investment but that, I have no recollection of it. No, I am overlooking a detail. It furnished me a field for Sellers and a book. Out of my half of the book I got $15,000 or $20,000; out of the play I got $75,000 or $80,000—just about a dollar an acre. It is curious; I was not alive when my father made the investment, therefore he was not intending any partiality; yet I was the only member of the family that ever profited by it. I shall have occasion to mention this land again now and then, as I go along, for it influenced our life in one way or another during more than a generation. Whenever things grew dark it rose and put out its hopeful Sellers hand and cheered us up and said, "Do not be afraid—trust in me—wait." It kept us hoping and hoping during forty years and forsook us at last. It put our energies to sleep and made visionaries of us—dreamers and indolent. We were always going to be rich next year—no

occasion to work. It is good to begin life poor; it is good to begin life rich—these are wholesome; but to begin it poor and
prospectively rich! The man who has not experienced it cannot imagine the curse of it.

◇◇◇◇◇◇◇◇◇◇◇◇◇◇◇◇◇◇

CHAPTER 7

When my mother died in October 1890 she was well along in
her eighty-eighth year, a mighty age, a well-contested fight
for life for one who at forty was so delicate of body as to be
accounted a confirmed invalid and destined to pass soon
away. I knew her well during the first twenty-five years of my
life; but after that I saw her only at wide intervals, for we
lived many days' journey apart. I am not proposing to write
about her but merely to talk about her; not give her formal
history but merely make illustrative extracts from it, so to
speak; furnish flashlight glimpses of her character, not a pro-
cessional view of her career. Technically speaking, she had
no career; but she had a character and it was of a fine and
striking and lovable sort.

What becomes of the multitudinous photographs which
one's mind takes of people? Out of the million which my
mental camera must have taken of this first and closest friend,
only one clear and strongly defined one of early date remains.
It dates back forty-seven years; she was forty years old then,
and I was eight.[1] She held me by the hand and we were kneeling by the bedside of my brother, two years older than I, who
lay dead, and the tears were flowing down her cheeks un-
checked. And she was moaning. That dumb sign of anguish
was perhaps new to me, since it made upon me a very strong
impression—an impression which holds its place still with the
picture which it helped to intensify and make memorable.

She had a slender, small body but a large heart—a heart so
large that everybody's grief and everybody's joys found welcome in it and hospitable accommodation. The greatest difference which I find between her and the rest of the people
whom I have known is this, and it is a remarkable one: those
others felt a strong interest in a few things, whereas to the

[1] Written in 1890.

very day of her death she felt a strong interest in the whole
world and everything and everybody in it. In all her life she
never knew such a thing as a half-hearted interest in affairs
and people, or an interest which drew a line and left out certain affairs and was indifferent to certain people. The invalid
who takes a strenuous and indestructible interest in everything and everybody but himself, and to whom a dull moment
is an unknown thing and an impossibility, is a formidable
adversary for disease and a hard invalid to vanquish. I am
certain that it was this feature of my mother's makeup that
carried her so far toward ninety.

Her interest in people and other animals was warm, personal, friendly. She always found something to excuse, and as
a rule to love, in the toughest of them—even if she had to put
it there herself. She was the natural ally and friend of the
friendless. It was believed that, Presbyterian as she was, she
could be beguiled into saying a soft word for the devil himself, and so the experiment was tried. The abuse of Satan began; one conspirator after another added his bitter word, his
malign reproach, his pitiless censure, till at last, sure enough,
the unsuspecting subject of the trick walked into the trap.
She admitted that the indictment was sound, that Satan was
utterly wicked and abandoned, just as these people had said;
but would any claim that he had been treated fairly? A sinner
was but a sinner; Satan was just that, like the rest. What saves
the rest?—their own efforts alone? No—or none might ever be
saved. To their feeble efforts is added the mighty help of
pathetic, appealing, imploring prayers that go up daily out of
all the churches in Christendom and out of myriads upon
myriads of pitying hearts. But who prays for Satan? Who, in
eighteen centuries, has had the common humanity to pray for
the one sinner that needed it most, our one fellow and brother
who most needed a friend yet had not a single one, the one
sinner among us all who had the highest and clearest *right* to
every Christian's daily and nightly prayers, for the plain and
unassailable reason that his was the first and greatest need,
he being among sinners the supremest?

This friend of Satan was a most gentle spirit and an un-
studied and unconscious pathos was her native speech. When
her pity or her indignation was stirred by hurt or shame inflicted upon some defenseless person or creature, she was the
most eloquent person I have heard speak. It was seldom eloquence of a fiery or violent sort, but gentle, pitying, persua-

sive, appealing; and so genuine and so nobly and simply worded and so touchingly uttered, that many times I have seen it win the reluctant and splendid applause of tears. Whenever anybody or any creature was being oppressed, the fears that belonged to her sex and her small stature retired to the rear and her soldierly qualities came promptly to the front. One day in our village I saw a vicious devil of a Corsican, a common terror in the town, chasing his grown daughter past cautious male citizens with a heavy rope in his hand and declaring he would wear it out on her. My mother spread her door wide to the refugee and then, instead of closing and locking it after her, stood in it and stretched her arms across it, barring the way. The man swore, cursed, threatened her with his rope; but she did not flinch or show any sign of fear; she only stood straight and fine and lashed him, shamed him, derided him, defied him in tones not audible to the middle of the street but audible to the man's conscience and dormant manhood; and he asked her pardon and gave her his rope and said with a most great and blasphemous oath that she was the bravest woman he ever saw; and so went his way without another word and troubled her no more. He and she were always good friends after that, for in her he had found a long-felt want—somebody who was not afraid of him.

One day in St. Louis she walked out into the street and greatly surprised a burly cartman who was beating his horse over the head with the butt of his heavy whip; for she took the whip away from him and then made such a persuasive appeal in behalf of the ignorantly offending horse that he was tripped into saying he was to blame; and also into volunteering a promise which of course he couldn't keep, for he was not built in that way—a promise that he wouldn't ever abuse a horse again.

That sort of interference in behalf of abused animals was a common thing with her all her life; and her manner must have been without offense and her good intent transparent, for she always carried her point and also won the courtesy and often the friendly applause of the adversary. All the race of dumb animals had a friend in her. By some subtle sign the homeless, hunted, bedraggled and disreputable cat recognized her at a glance as the born refuge and champion of his sort—and followed her home. His instinct was right, he was as welcome as the prodigal son. We had nineteen cats at one time, in 1845. And there wasn't one in the lot that had any character, not

one that had any merit, except the cheap and tawdry merit of
being unfortunate. They were a vast burden to us all—including
my mother—but they were out of luck and that was
enough; they had to stay. However, better these than no pets
at all; children must have pets and we were not allowed to
have caged ones. An imprisoned creature was out of the question—my
mother would not have allowed a rat to be restrained
of its liberty.

In the small town of Hannibal, Missouri, when I was a boy
everybody was poor but didn't know it; and everybody was
comfortable and did know it. And there were grades of society—people
of good family, people of unclassified family,
people of no family. Everybody knew everybody and was
affable to everybody and nobody put on any visible airs; yet
the class lines were quite clearly drawn and the familiar social
life of each class was restricted to that class. It was a little
democracy which was full of liberty, equality and Fourth of
July, and sincerely so, too; yet you perceived that the aristocratic
taint was there. It was there and nobody found fault
with the fact or ever stopped to reflect that its presence was
an inconsistency.

I suppose that this state of things was mainly due to the circumstance
that the town's population had come from slave
states and still had the institution of slavery with them in their
new home. My mother, with her large nature and liberal sympathies,
was not intended for an aristocrat, yet through her
breeding she was one. Few people knew it, perhaps, for it was
an instinct, I think, rather than a principle. So its outward
manifestation was likely to be accidental, not intentional, and
also not frequent. But I knew of that weak spot. I knew that
privately she was proud that the Lambtons, now Earls of Durham,
had occupied the family lands for nine hundred years;
that they were feudal lords of Lambton Castle and holding
the high position of ancestors of hers when the Norman Conqueror
came over to divert the Englishry. I argued—cautiously
and with mollifying circumlocutions, for one had to be careful
when he was on that holy ground, and mustn't cavort—
that there was no particular merit in occupying a piece of land
for nine hundred years with the friendly assistance of an entail;
anybody could do it, with intellect or without; therefore
the entail was the thing to be proud of, just the entail and
nothing else; consequently, she was merely descended from
an entail and she might as well be proud of being de-

scended from a mortgage. Whereas my own ancestry was quite a different and superior thing, because it had the addition of an ancestor—one Clemens—who *did* something; something which was very creditable to him and satisfactory to me, in that he was a member of the court that tried Charles I and delivered him over to the executioner.

Ostensibly this was chaff but at the bottom it was not. I had a very real respect for that ancestor and this respect has increased with the years, not diminished. He did what he could toward reducing the list of crowned shams of his day. However, I can say this for my mother, that I never heard her refer in any way to her gilded ancestry when any person not a member of the family was present, for she had good American sense. But with other Lamptons whom I have known, it was different. "Colonel Sellers" was a Lampton and a tolerably near relative of my mother's; and when he was alive, poor old airy soul, one of the earliest things a stranger was likely to hear from his lips was some reference to the "head of our line," flung off with a painful casualness that was wholly beneath criticism as a work of art. It compelled inquiry, of course; it was intended to compel it. Then followed the whole disastrous history of how the Lambton heir came to this country a hundred and fifty years or so ago, disgusted with that foolish fraud, hereditary aristocracy, and married, and shut himself away from the world in the remotenesses of the wilderness, and went to breeding ancestors of future American claimants, while at home in England he was given up as dead and his titles and estates turned over to his younger brother, usurper and personally responsible for the perverse and unseatable usurpers of our day. And the colonel always spoke with studied and courtly deference of the claimant of his day—a second cousin of his—and referred to him with entire seriousness as "the earl."

"The earl" was a man of parts and might have accomplished something for himself but for the calamitous accident of his birth. He was a Kentuckian and a well-meaning man; but he had no money and no time to earn any; for all his time was taken up in trying to get me and others of the tribe to furnish him capital to fight his claim through the House of Lords with. He had all the documents, all the proofs; he knew he could win. And so he dreamed his life away, always in poverty, sometimes in actual want, and died at last, far from home, and was buried from a hospital by strangers who did not know he was an earl, for he did not look it. That poor fellow used to sign his letters "Durham," and in them he would find fault with me for voting the Republican ticket, for the reason that it was unaristocratic and by consequence un-Lamptonian. And presently along would come a letter from some red-hot Virginian, son of my other branch, and abuse me bitterly for the same vote—on the ground that the Republican was an aristocratic party and it was not becoming in the descendant of a regicide to train with that kind of animals. And so I used to almost wish I hadn't had any ancestors, they were so much trouble to me.

As I have said, we lived in a slaveholding community; indeed, when slavery perished, my mother had been in daily touch with it for sixty years. Yet, kindhearted and compassionate as she was, I think she was not conscious that slavery was a bald, grotesque and unwarrantable usurpation. She had never heard it assailed in any pulpit but had heard it defended and sanctified in a thousand; her ears were familiar with Bible texts that approved it but if there were any that disapproved it they had not been quoted by her pastors; as far as her experience went, the wise and the good and the holy were unanimous in the conviction that slavery was right, righteous, sacred, the peculiar pet of the Deity and a condition which the slave himself ought to be daily and nightly thankful for. Manifestly, training and association can accomplish strange miracles. As a rule our slaves were convinced and content. So doubtless are the far more intelligent slaves of a monarchy; they revere and approve their masters, the monarch and the noble, and recognize no degradation in the fact that they are slaves—slaves with the name blinked, and less respectworthy than were our black ones, if to be a slave by meek consent is baser than to be a slave by compulsion—and doubtless it is.

However, there was nothing about the slavery of the Hannibal region to rouse one's dozing humane instincts to activity. It was the mild domestic slavery, not the brutal plantation article. Cruelties were very rare and exceedingly and wholesomely unpopular. To separate and sell the members of a slave family to different masters was a thing not well liked by the people and so it was not often done, except in the settling of estates. I have no recollection of ever seeing a slave auction in that town; but I am suspicious that that is because the thing was a common and commonplace spectacle, not an uncommon and impressive one. I vividly remember seeing a dozen black men and women chained to one another, once, and lying in a group on the pavement, awaiting shipment to the southern slave market. Those were the saddest faces I have ever seen. Chained slaves could not have been a common sight or this picture would not have made so strong and lasting an impression upon me.

The "nigger trader" was loathed by everybody. He was regarded as a sort of human devil who bought and conveyed poor helpless creatures to hell—for to our whites and blacks alike the southern plantation was simply hell; no milder name could describe it. If the threat to sell an incorrigible slave "down the river" would not reform him, nothing would—his case was past cure. Yet I remember that once when a white man killed a Negro man for a trifling little offence everybody seemed indifferent about it—as regarded the slave—though considerable sympathy was felt for the slave's owner, who had been bereft of valuable property by a worthless person who was not able to pay for it.

It is commonly believed that an infallible effect of slavery was to make such as lived in its midst hardhearted. I think it had no such effect—speaking in general terms. I think it stupefied everybody's humanity as regarded the slave, but stopped there. There were no hardhearted people in our town—I mean there were no more than would be found in any other town of the same size in any other country; and in my experience hardhearted people are very rare everywhere.

CHAPTER 8

My school days began when I was four years and a half old. There were no public schools in Missouri in those early days but there were two private schools—terms twenty-five cents per week per pupil and collect it if you can. Mrs. Horr taught the children in a small log house at the southern end of Main Street. Mr. Sam Cross taught the young people of larger growth in a frame schoolhouse on the hill. I was sent to Mrs. Horr's school and I remember my first day in that little log house with perfect clearness, after these sixty-five years and upwards[1]—at least I remember an episode of that first day. I broke one of the rules and was warned not to do it again and was told that the penalty for a second breach was a whipping. I presently broke the rule again and Mrs. Horr told me to go out and find a switch and fetch it. I was glad she appointed me, for I believed I could select a switch suitable to the occasion with more judiciousness than anybody else.

In the mud I found a cooper's shaving of the old-time pattern, oak, two inches broad, a quarter of an inch thick, and rising in a shallow curve at one end. There were nice new shavings of the same breed close by but I took this one, although it was rotten. I carried it to Mrs. Horr, presented it and stood before her in an attitude of meekness and resignation which seemed to me calculated to win favor and sympathy, but it did not happen. She divided a long look of strong disapprobation equally between me and the shaving; then she called me by my entire name, Samuel Langhorne Clemens—probably the first time I had ever heard it all strung together in one procession—and said she was ashamed of me. I was to learn later that when a teacher calls a boy by his entire name it means trouble. She said she would try and appoint a boy with a better judgment than mine in the matter of switches, and it saddens me yet to remember how many faces lighted up with the hope of getting that appointment. Jim Dunlap got it and when he returned with the switch of his choice I recognized that he was an expert.

Mrs. Horr was a New England lady of middle age with New England ways and principles and she always opened school with prayer and a chapter from the New Testament; also she explained the chapter with a brief talk. In one of these talks she dwelt upon the text, "Ask and ye shall receive," and said that whosoever prayed for a thing with earnestness and strong desire need not doubt that his prayer would be answered.

I was so forcibly struck by this information and so gratified by the opportunities which it offered that this was probably the first time I had heard of it. I thought I would give it a trial. I believed in Mrs. Horr thoroughly and I had no doubts as to the result. I prayed for gingerbread. Margaret Kooneman, who was the baker's daughter, brought a slab of gingerbread to school every morning; she had always kept it out of sight before but when I finished my prayer and glanced up,

[1] Written in 1906.

there it was in easy reach and she was looking the other way. In all my life I believe I never enjoyed an answer to prayer more than I enjoyed that one; and I was a convert, too. I had no end of wants and they had always remained unsatisfied up to that time, but I meant to supply them and extend them now that I had found out how to do it.

But this dream was like almost all the other dreams we indulge in in life, there was nothing in it. I did as much praying during the next two or three days as any one in that town, I suppose, and I was very sincere and earnest about it too, but nothing came of it. I found that not even the most powerful prayer was competent to lift that gingerbread again, and I came to the conclusion that if a person remains faithful to his gingerbread and keeps his eye on it he need not trouble himself about your prayers.

Something about my conduct and bearing troubled my mother and she took me aside and questioned me concerning it with much solicitude. I was reluctant to reveal to her the change that had come over me, for it would grieve me to distress her kind heart, but at last I confessed, with many tears, that I had ceased to be a Christian. She was heartbroken and asked me why.

I said it was because I had found out that I was a Christian for revenue only and I could not bear the thought of that, it was so ignoble.

She gathered me to her breast and comforted me. I had gathered from what she said that if I would continue in that condition I would never be lonesome.

My mother had a good deal of trouble with me but I think she enjoyed it. She had none at all with my brother Henry, who was two years younger than I, and I think that the unbroken monotony of his goodness and truthfulness and obedience would have been a burden to her but for the relief and variety which I furnished in the other direction. I was a tonic. I was valuable to her. I never thought of it before but now I see it. I never knew Henry to do a vicious thing toward me or toward anyone else—but he frequently did righteous ones that cost me as heavily. It was his duty to report me, when I needed reporting and neglected to do it myself, and he was very faithful in discharging that duty. He is Sid in *Tom Sawyer*. But Sid was not Henry. Henry was a very much finer and better boy than ever Sid was.

It was Henry who called my mother's attention to the fact

that the thread with which she had sewed my collar together to keep me from going in swimming had changed color. My mother would not have discovered it but for that, and she was manifestly piqued when she recognized that that prominent bit of circumstantial evidence had escaped her sharp eye. That detail probably added a detail to my punishment. It is human. We generally visit our shortcomings on somebody else when there is a possible excuse for it—but no matter. I took it out of Henry. There is always compensation for such as are unjustly used. I often took it out of him—sometimes as an advance payment for something which I hadn't yet done. These were occasions when the opportunity was too strong a temptation, and I had to draw on the future. I did not need to copy this idea from my mother and probably didn't. It is most likely that I invented it for myself. Still, she wrought upon that principle upon occasion.

If the incident of the broken sugar bowl is in *Tom Sawyer*— I don't remember whether it is or not—that is an example of it. Henry never stole sugar. He took it openly from the bowl. His mother knew he wouldn't take sugar when she wasn't looking, but she had her doubts about me. Not exactly doubts, either. She knew very well I *would*. One day when she was not present Henry took sugar from her prized and precious old-English sugar bowl, which was an heirloom in the family—and he managed to break the bowl. It was the first time I had ever had a chance to tell anything on him and I was inexpressibly glad. I told him I was going to tell on him but he was not disturbed. When my mother came in and saw the bowl lying on the floor in fragments she was speechless for a minute. I allowed that silence to work; I judged it would increase the effect. I was waiting for her to ask, "Who did that?" —so that I could fetch out my news. But it was an error of calculation. When she got through with her silence she didn't ask anything about it—she merely gave me a crack on the skull with her thimble that I felt all the way down to my heels. Then I broke out with my injured innocence, expecting to make her very sorry that she had punished the wrong one. I expected her to do something remorseful and pathetic. I told her that I was not the one—it was Henry. But there was no upheaval. She said, without emotion: "It's all right. It isn't any matter. You deserve it for something that you are going to do that I shan't hear about."

There was a stairway outside the house, which led up to

the rear part of the second story. One day Henry was sent on an errand and he took a tin bucket along. I knew he would have to ascend those stairs, so I went up and locked the door on the inside and came down into the garden, which had been newly plowed and was rich in choice, firm clods of black mold. I gathered a generous equipment of these and ambushed him. I waited till he had climbed the stairs and was near the landing and couldn't escape. Then I bombarded him with clods, which he warded off with his tin bucket the best he could, but without much success, for I was a good marksman. The clods smashing against the weather boarding fetched my mother out to see what was the matter and I tried to explain that I was amusing Henry. Both of them were after me in a minute but I knew the way over that high board fence and escaped for that time. After an hour or two, when I ventured back, there was no one around and I thought the incident was closed. But it was not so. Henry was ambushing me. With an unusually competent aim for him, he landed a stone on the side of my head which raised a bump there which felt like the Matterhorn. I carried it to my mother straightway for sympathy but she was not strongly moved. It seemed to be her idea that incidents like this would eventually reform me if I harvested enough of them. So the matter was only educational. I had had a sterner view of it than that before.

It was not right to give the cat the "Pain-Killer"; I realize it now. I would not repeat it in these days. But in those "Tom Sawyer" days it was a great and sincere satisfaction to me to see Peter perform under its influence—and if actions *do* speak as loud as words, he took as much interest in it as I did. It was a most detestable medicine, Perry Davis's Pain-Killer. Mr. Pavey's Negro man, who was a person of good judgment and considerable curiosity, wanted to sample it and I let him. It was his opinion that it was made of hell-fire.

Those were the cholera days of '49. The people along the Mississippi were paralyzed with fright. Those who could run away did it. And many died of fright in the flight. Fright killed three persons where the cholera killed one. Those who couldn't flee kept themselves drenched with cholera preventives and my mother chose Perry Davis's Pain-Killer for me. She was not distressed about herself. She avoided that kind of preventive. But she made me promise to take a teaspoonful of Pain-Killer every day. Originally it was my intention to keep the promise but at that time I didn't know as much about Pain-Killer as I knew after my first experiment with it. She didn't watch Henry's bottle—she could trust Henry. But she marked my bottle with a pencil on the label every day, and examined it to see if the teaspoonful had been removed. The floor was not carpeted. It had cracks in it and I fed the Pain-Killer to the cracks with very good results—no cholera occurred down below.

It was upon one of these occasions that that friendly cat came waving his tail and supplicating for Pain-Killer—which he got—and then went into those hysterics which ended with his colliding with all the furniture in the room and finally going out of the open window and carrying the flowerpots with him, just in time for my mother to arrive and look over her glasses in petrified astonishment and say, "What in the world is the matter with Peter?"

I don't remember what my explanation was but if it is recorded in that book[2] it may not be the right one.

Whenever my conduct was of such exaggerated impropriety that my mother's extemporary punishments were inadequate, she saved the matter up for Sunday and made me go to church Sunday night—which was a penalty sometimes bearable, perhaps, but as a rule it was not and I avoided it for the sake of my constitution. She would never believe that I had been to church until she had applied her test. She made me tell her what the text was. That was a simple matter—caused me no trouble. I didn't have to go to church to get a text. I selected one for myself. This worked very well until one time when my text and the one furnished by a neighbor, who had been to church, didn't tally. After that my mother took other methods. I don't know what they were now.

In those days men and boys wore rather long cloaks in the wintertime. They were black and were lined with very bright and showy Scotch plaids. One winter's night when I was starting to church to square a crime of some kind committed during the week, I hid my cloak near the gate and went off and played with the other boys until church was over. Then I returned home. But in the dark I put the cloak on wrong side out, entered the room, threw the cloak aside, and then stood the usual examination. I got along very well until the temperature of the church was mentioned. My mother said,

[2] *Tom Sawyer.*

"It must have been impossible to keep warm there on such a night."

I didn't see the art of that remark and was foolish enough to explain that I wore my cloak all the time that I was in church. She asked if I kept it on from church home too. I didn't see the bearing of that remark. I said that that was what I had done. She said: "You wore it with that red Scotch plaid outside and glaring? Didn't that attract any attention?"

Of course to continue such a dialogue would have been tedious and unprofitable and I let it go and took the consequences.

That was about 1849. Tom Nash was a boy of my own age —the postmaster's son. The Mississippi was frozen across and he and I went skating one night, probably without permission. I cannot see why we should go skating in the night unless without permission, for there could be no considerable amusement to be gotten out of skating at midnight if nobody was going to object to it. About midnight, when we were more than half a mile out toward the Illinois shore, we heard some ominous rumbling and grinding and crashing going on between us and the home side of the river, and we knew what it meant—the river was breaking up. We started for home, pretty badly scared. We flew along at full speed whenever the moonlight sifting down between the clouds enabled us to tell which was ice and which was water. In the pauses we waited, started again whenever there was a good bridge of ice, paused again when we came to naked water, and waited in distress until a floating vast cake should bridge that place. It took us an hour to make the trip—a trip which we made in a misery of apprehension all the time. But at last we arrived within a very brief distance of the shore. We waited again. There was another place that needed bridging. All about us the ice was plunging and grinding along and piling itself up in mountains on the shore and the dangers were increasing, not diminishing. We grew very impatient to get to solid ground, so we started too early and went springing from cake to cake. Tom made a miscalculation and fell short. He got a bitter bath but he was so close to shore that he only had to swim a stroke or two—then his feet struck hard bottom and he crawled out. I arrived a little later, without accident. We had been in a drenching perspiration and Tom's bath was a disaster for him. He took to his bed, sick, and had a procession of diseases. The closing one was scarlet fever and he came out of it stone deaf. Within a year or two speech departed, of course. But some years later he was taught to talk, after a fashion—one couldn't always make out what it was he was trying to say. Of course he could not modulate his voice, since he couldn't hear himself talk. When he supposed he was talking low and confidentially, you could hear him in Illinois.

Four years ago[2] I was invited by the University of Missouri to come out there and receive the honorary degree of LL.D. I took that opportunity to spend a week in Hannibal—a city now, a village in my day. It had been fifty-five years since Tom Nash and I had had that adventure. When I was at the railway station ready to leave Hannibal, there was a great crowd of citizens there. I saw Tom Nash approaching me across a vacant space and I walked toward him, for I recognized him at once. He was old and whiteheaded, but the boy of fifteen was still visible in him. He came up to me, made a trumpet of his hands at my ear, nodded his head toward the citizens and said confidentially—in a yell like a fog horn— "Same damned fools, Sam."

◇◇◇◇◇◇◇◇◇◇◇◇◇◇◇◇◇◇◇◇

CHAPTER 9

In 1849, when I was fourteen years old, we were still living in Hannibal, on the banks of the Mississippi, in the new "frame" house built by my father five years before. That is, some of us lived in the new part, the rest in the old part back of it and attached to it. In the autumn my sister gave a party and invited all the marriageable young people of the village. I was too young for this society and was too bashful to mingle with young ladies, anyway, therefore I was not invited—at least not for the whole evening. Ten minutes of it was to be my whole share. I was to do the part of a bear in a small fairy play. I was to be disguised all over in a close-fitting brown hairy stuff proper for a bear. About half past ten I was told to go to my room and put on this disguise and be ready in half an hour. I started but changed my mind, for I wanted to practice a little and that room was very small. I crossed over to the large unoccupied house on the corner of Main Street, unaware that a dozen of the young people were also going there to dress for their parts. I took the little black boy, Sandy, with me and we selected a roomy and empty chamber on the second floor. We entered it talking and this gave a couple of half-dressed young ladies an opportunity to take refuge behind a screen undiscovered. Their gowns and things were hanging on hooks behind the door but I did not see them; it was Sandy that shut the door but all his heart was in the theatricals and he was as unlikely to notice them as I was myself.

That was a rickety screen with many holes in it but as I did not know there were girls behind it I was not disturbed by that detail. If I had known, I could not have undressed in the flood of cruel moonlight that was pouring in at the curtainless windows; I should have died of shame. Untroubled by apprehensions, I stripped to the skin and began my practice. I was full of ambition, I was determined to make a hit, I was burning to establish a reputation as a bear and get further engagements; so I threw myself into my work with an abandon that promised great things. I capered back and forth from one end of the room to the other on all fours, Sandy applauding with enthusiasm; I walked upright and growled and snapped and snarled, I stood on my head, I flung handsprings, I danced a lubberly dance with my paws bent and my imaginary snout sniffing from side to side, I did everything a bear could do and many things which no bear could ever do and no bear with any dignity would want to do, anyway; and of course I never suspected that I was making a spectacle of myself to anyone but Sandy. At last, standing on my head, I paused in that attitude to take a minute's rest. There was a moment's silence, then Sandy spoke up with excited interest and said:

"Mars Sam, has you ever seed a dried herring?"

"No. What is that?"

"It's a fish."

"Well, what of it? Anything peculiar about it?"

"Yes, suh, you bet you dey is. *Dey* eats 'em innards and all!"

There was a smothered burst of feminine snickers from behind the screen! All the strength went out of me and I toppled forward like an undermined tower and brought the screen down with my weight, burying the young ladies under it. In their fright they discharged a couple of piercing screams—

and possibly others—but I did not wait to count. I snatched my clothes and fled to the dark hall below, Sandy following. I was dressed in half a minute and out the back way. I swore Sandy to eternal silence, then we went away and hid until the party was over. The ambition was all out of me. I could not have faced that giddy company after my adventure, for there would be two performers there who knew my secret and would be privately laughing at me all the time. I was searched for but not found, and the bear had to be played by a young gentleman in his civilized clothes. The house was still and everybody asleep when I finally ventured home. I was very heavyhearted and full of a bitter sense of disgrace. Pinned to my pillow I found a slip of paper which bore a line which did not lighten my heart but only made my face burn. It was written in a laboriously disguised hand and these were its mocking terms:

You probably couldn't have played bear but you played bare very well—oh, very *very* well!

We think boys are rude, unsensitive animals but it is not so in all cases. Each boy has one or two sensitive spots and if you can find out where they are located you have only to touch them and you can scorch him as with fire. I suffered miserably over that episode. I expected that the facts would be all over the village in the morning but it was not so. The secret remained confined to the two girls and Sandy and me. That was some appeasement of my pain but it was far from sufficient—the main trouble remained: I was under four mocking eyes and it might as well have been a thousand, for I suspected all girls' eyes of being the ones I so dreaded. During several weeks I could not look any young lady in the face; I dropped my eyes in confusion when any one of them smiled upon me and gave me greeting; I said to myself, "That is one of them," and got quickly away. Of course I was meeting the right girls everywhere but if they ever let slip any betraying sign I was not bright enough to catch it. When I left Hannibal four years later the secret was still a secret; I had never guessed those girls out and was no longer hoping or expecting to do it.

One of the dearest and prettiest girls in the village at the time of my mishap was one whom I will call Mary Wilson, because that was not her name. She was twenty years old;

she was dainty and sweet, peach-blooming and exquisite, gracious and lovely in character. I stood in awe of her, for she seemed to me to be made out of angel clay and rightfully unapproachable by just any unholy ordinary kind of boy like me. I probably never suspected *her*. But—

The scene changes to Calcutta—forty-seven years later. It was in 1896. I arrived there on a lecturing trip. As I entered the hotel a vision passed out of it, clothed in the glory of the Indian sunshine—the Mary Wilson of my long-vanished boyhood! It was a startling thing. Before I could recover from the pleasant shock and speak to her she was gone. I thought maybe I had seen an apparition but it was not so, she was flesh. She was the granddaughter of the other Mary. The other Mary, now a widow, was upstairs and presently sent for me. She was old and gray-haired but she looked young and was very handsome. We sat down and talked. We steeped our thirsty souls in the reviving wine of the past, the pathetic past, the beautiful past, the dear and lamented past; we uttered the names that had been silent upon our lips for fifty years and it was as if they were made of music; with reverent hands we unburied our dead, the mates of our youth, and caressed them with our speech; we searched the dusty chambers of our memories and dragged forth incident after incident, episode after episode, folly after folly, and laughed such good laughs over them, with the tears running down; and finally Mary said, suddenly, and without any leading up:

"Tell me! What is the special peculiarity of dried herrings?"

It seemed a strange question at such a hallowed time as this. And so inconsequential, too. I was a little shocked. And yet I was aware of a stir of some kind away back in the deeps of my memory somewhere. It set me to musing—thinking—searching. Dried herrings? Dried herrings? The peculiarity of dri . . . I glanced up. Her face was grave, but there was a dim and shadowy twinkle in her eye which— All of a sudden I knew and far away down in the hoary past I heard a remembered voice murmur, "Dey eats 'em innards and all!"

"At—last! I've found one of you, anyway! Who was the other girl?"

But she drew the line there. She wouldn't tell me.

But a boy's life is not all comedy; much of the tragic enters into it. The drunken tramp who was burned up in the village jail lay upon my conscience a hundred nights afterward and filled them with hideous dreams—dreams in which I saw his appealing face as I had seen it in the pathetic reality, pressed against the window bars, with the red hell glowing behind him—a face which seemed to say to me, "If you had not given me the matches this would not have happened; you are responsible for my death." I was *not* responsible for it, for I had meant no harm but only good, when I let him have the matches; but no matter, mine was a trained Presbyterian conscience and knew but the one duty—to hunt and harry its slave upon all pretexts and on all occasions, particularly when there was no sense nor reason in it. The tramp—who was to blame—suffered ten minutes; I, who was not to blame, suffered three months.

The shooting down of poor old Smarr in the main street at noonday supplied me with some more dreams; and in them I always saw again the grotesque closing picture—the great family Bible spread open on the profane old man's breast by some thoughtful idiot and rising and sinking to the labored breathings and adding the torture of its leaden weight to the dying struggles. We are curiously made. In all the throng of gaping and sympathetic onlookers there was not one with common sense enough to perceive that an anvil would have been in better taste there than the Bible, less open to sarcastic criticism and swifter in its atrocious work. In my nightmares I gasped and struggled for breath under the crush of that vast book for many a night.

All within the space of a couple of years we had two or three other tragedies and I had the ill luck to be too near by on each occasion. There was the slave man who was struck down with a chunk of slag for some small offense; I saw him die. And the young Californian emigrant who was stabbed with a bowie knife by a drunken comrade; I saw the red life gush from his breast. And the case of the rowdy young brothers and their harmless old uncle; one of them held the old man down with his knees on his breast while the other one tried repeatedly to kill him with an Allen revolver which wouldn't go off. I happened along just then, of course.

Then there was the case of the young Californian emigrant who got drunk and proposed to raid the "Welshman's house" all alone one dark and threatening night. This house stood halfway up Holliday's Hill and its sole occupants were a poor but quite respectable widow and her blameless daughter. The invading ruffian woke the whole village with his ribald yells and coarse challenges and obscenities. I went

up there with a comrade—John Briggs, I think—to look and
listen. The figure of the man was dimly visible; the women
were on their porch, not visible in the deep shadow of its
roof, but we heard the elder woman's voice. She had loaded
an old musket with slugs and she warned the man that if he
stayed where he was while she counted ten it would cost
him his life. She began to count, slowly; he began to laugh.
He stopped laughing at "six"; then through the deep stillness,
in a steady voice, followed the rest of the tale: "Seven . . .
eight . . . nine"—a long pause, we holding our breaths—"ten!"
A red spout of flame gushed out into the night and the man
dropped with his breast riddled to rags. Then the rain and
the thunder burst loose and the waiting town swarmed up
the hill in the glare of the lightning like an invasion of ants.
Those people saw the rest; I had had my share and was satisfied. I went home to dream and was not disappointed.

My teaching and training enabled me to see deeper into
these tragedies than an ignorant person could have done.
I knew what they were for. I tried to disguise it from myself
but down in the secret deeps of my troubled heart I knew
—and I *knew* I knew. They were inventions of Providence to
beguile me to a better life. It sounds curiously innocent
and conceited now, but to me there was nothing strange
about it; it was quite in accordance with the thoughtful and
judicious ways of Providence as I understood them. It would
not have surprised me nor even overflattered me if Providence
had killed off that whole community in trying to save an
asset like me. Educated as I had been, it would have seemed
just the thing and well worth the expense. *Why* Providence
should take such an anxious interest in such a property,
that idea never entered my head, and there was no one in
that simple hamlet who would have dreamed of putting it
there. For one thing, no one was equipped with it.

It is quite true, I took all the tragedies to myself and
tallied them off in turn as they happened, saying to myself
in each case, with a sigh, "Another one gone—and on my
account; this ought to bring me to repentance; the patience of
God will not always endure." And yet privately I believed it
would. That is, I believed it in the daytime; but not in the
night. With the going down of the sun my faith failed and the
clammy fears gathered about my heart. It was then that I repented. Those were awful nights, nights of despair, nights
charged with the bitterness of death. After each tragedy I

recognized the warning and repented; repented and begged; begged like a coward, begged like a dog; and not in the interest of those poor people who had been extinguished for my sake but only in my *own* interest. It seems selfish when I look back on it now.

My repentances were very real, very earnest; and after each tragedy they happened every night for a long time. But as a rule they could not stand the daylight. They faded out and shredded away and disappeared in the glad splendor of the sun. They were the creatures of fear and darkness and they could not live out of their own place. The day gave me cheer and peace and at night I repented again. In all my boyhood life I am not sure that I ever tried to lead a better life in the daytime—or wanted to. In my age I should never think of wishing to do such a thing. But in my age, as in my youth, night brings me many a deep remorse. I realize that from the cradle up I have been like the rest of the race —never quite sane in the night. When "Injun Joe" died . . . But never mind. Somewhere I have already described what a raging hell of repentance I passed through then. I believe that for months I was as pure as the driven snow. After dark.

◇◇◇◇◇◇◇◇◇◇◇◇◇◇◇◇◇◇◇◇

CHAPTER 10

In Hannibal when I was about fifteen I was for a short time a Cadet of Temperance, an organization which probably covered the whole United States during as much as a year— possibly even longer. It consisted in a pledge to refrain, during membership, from the use of tobacco; I mean it consisted partly in that pledge and partly in a red merino sash, but the red merino sash was the main part. The boys joined in order to be privileged to wear it—the pledge part of the matter was of no consequence. It was so small in importance that, contrasted with the sash, it was in effect nonexistent. The organization was weak and impermanent because there were not enough holidays to support it. We could turn out and march and show the red sashes on May Day with the Sunday schools and on the Fourth of July with the Sunday schools, the independent fire company and the militia company. But you can't keep a juvenile moral institution alive on two displays of its sash per year. As a private I could not have held out beyond one procession but I was Illustrious Grand Worthy Secretary and Royal Inside Sentinel and had the privilege of inventing the passwords and of wearing a rosette on my sash. Under these conditions I was enabled to remain steadfast until I had gathered the glory of two displays—May Day and the Fourth of July. Then I resigned straightway and straightway left the lodge.

I had not smoked for three full months and no words can adequately describe the smoke appetite that was consuming me. I had been a smoker from my ninth year—a private one during the first two years but a public one after that—that is to say, after my father's death. I was smoking and utterly happy before I was thirty steps from the lodge door. I do not now know what the brand of the cigar was. It was probably not choice, or the previous smoker would not have thrown it away so soon. But I realized that it was the best cigar that was ever made. The previous smoker would have thought the same if he had been without a smoke for three months. I smoked that stub without shame. I could not do it now without shame because now I am more refined than I was then. But I would smoke it just the same. I know myself and I know the human race well enough to know that.

In those days the native cigar was so cheap that a person who could afford anything could afford cigars. Mr. Garth had a great tobacco factory and he also had a small shop in the village for the retail sale of his products. He had one brand of cigars which even poverty itself was able to buy. He had had these in stock a good many years and although they looked well enough on the outside, their insides had decayed to dust and would fly out like a puff of vapor when they were broken in two. This brand was very popular on account of its extreme cheapness. Mr. Garth had other brands which were cheap and some that were bad, but the supremacy over them enjoyed by this brand was indicated by its name. It was called "Garth's damnedest." We used to trade old newspapers (exchanges) for that brand.

There was another shop in the village where the conditions were friendly to penniless boys. It was kept by a lonely and melancholy little hunchback and we could always get a supply of cigars by fetching a bucket of water for him from the village pump, whether he needed water or not. One day we found him asleep in his chair—a custom of his—and we waited patiently for him to wake up, which was a custom of ours. But he slept so long this time that at last our patience was exhausted and we tried to wake him—but he was dead. I remember the shock of it yet.

In my early manhood and in middle life I used to vex myself with reforms every now and then. And I never had occasion to regret these divergencies for, whether the resulting deprivations were long or short, the rewarding pleasure which I got out of the vice when I returned to it always paid me for all that it cost.

It was back in those far-distant days that Jim Wolf came to us. He was from Shelbyville, a hamlet thirty or forty miles back in the country, and he brought all his native sweetness and gentlenesses and simplicities with him. He was approaching seventeen, a grave and slender lad, trustful, honest, honorable, a creature to love and cling to. And he was incredibly bashful. He was with us a good while but he could never conquer that peculiarity; he could not be at ease in the presence of any woman, not even in my good and gentle mother's; and as to speaking to any girl, it was wholly impossible.

It is to this kind that untoward things happen. My sister gave a "candy-pull" on a winter's night. I was too young to be of the company and Jim was too diffident. I was sent up to bed early and Jim followed of his own motion. His room was in the new part of the house and his window looked out on the roof of the L annex. That roof was six inches deep in snow and the snow had an ice crust upon it which was as slick as glass. Out of the comb of the roof projected a short chimney, a common resort for sentimental cats on moonlight nights—and this was a moonlight night. Down at the eaves, below the chimney, a canopy of dead vines spread away to some posts, making a cozy shelter, and after an hour or two the rollicking crowd of young ladies and gentlemen grouped themselves in its shade, with their saucers of liquid and piping-hot candy disposed about them on the frozen ground to cool. There was joyous chaffing and joking and laughter—peal upon peal of it.

About this time a couple of old, disreputable tomcats got up on the chimney and started a heated argument about something; also about this time I gave up trying to get to sleep and went visiting to Jim's room. He was awake and fuming about the cats and their intolerable yowling. I asked him, mockingly, why he didn't climb out and drive them away. He was nettled and said overboldly that for two cents he *would*.

It was a rash remark and was probably repented of before it was fairly out of his mouth. But it was too late—he was committed. I knew him; and I knew he would rather break his neck than back down, if I egged him on judiciously.

"Oh, of course you would! Who's doubting it?"

It galled him and he burst out, with sharp irritation, "Maybe *you* doubt it!"

"I? Oh no! I shouldn't think of such a thing. You are always doing wonderful things, with your mouth."

He was in a passion now. He snatched on his yarn socks and began to raise the window, saying in a voice quivering with anger:

"*You* think I dasn't—you do! Think what you blame please. *I* don't care what you think. I'll show you!"

The window made him rage; it wouldn't stay up.

I said, "Never mind, I'll hold it."

Indeed, I would have done anything to help. I was only a boy and was already in a radiant heaven of anticipation. He climbed carefully out, clung to the window sill until his feet were safely placed, then began to pick his perilous way on all fours along the glassy comb, a foot and a hand on each side of it. I believe I enjoy it now as much as I did then; yet it is nearly fifty years ago. The frosty breeze flapped his short shirt about his lean legs; the crystal roof shone like polished marble in the intense glory of the moon; the unconscious cats sat erect upon the chimney, alertly watching each other, lashing their tails and pouring out their hollow grievances; and slowly and cautiously Jim crept on, flapping as he went, the gay and frolicsome young creatures under the vine canopy unaware, and outraging these solemnities with their misplaced laughter. Every time Jim slipped I had a hope; but always on he crept and disappointed it. At last he was within reaching distance. He paused, raised himself carefully up, measured his distance deliberately, then made a frantic grab at the nearest cat—and missed it. Of course he lost his balance. His heels flew up, he struck on his back, and like a rocket he darted down the roof feet first, crashed through the dead vines and landed in a sitting position in fourteen saucers of red-hot candy in the midst of all that party—and dressed as *he* was—this lad who could not look a girl in the face with his clothes on. There was a wild scramble and a storm of shrieks and Jim fled up the stairs, dripping broken crockery all the way.

The incident was ended. But I was not done with it yet, though I supposed I was. Eighteen or twenty years later I arrived in New York from California, and by that time I had failed in all my other undertakings and had stumbled into literature without intending it. This was early in 1867. I was offered a large sum to write something for the *Sunday Mercury* and I answered with the tale of "Jim Wolf and the Cats." I also collected the money for it—twenty-five dollars. It seemed overpay but I did not say anything about that, for I was not so scrupulous then as I am now.

A year or two later "Jim Wolf and the Cats" appeared in a Tennessee paper in a new dress—as to spelling; it was masquerading in a Southern dialect. The appropriator of the tale had a wide reputation in the West and was exceedingly popular. Deservedly so, I think. He wrote some of the breeziest and funniest things I have ever read and did his work with distinguished ease and fluency. His name has passed out of my memory.

A couple of years went by; then the original story cropped up again and went floating around in the original spelling and with my name to it. Soon, first one paper and then another fell upon me vigorously for "stealing" "Jim Wolf and the Cats" from the Tennessee man. I got a merciless basting but I did not mind it. It's all in the game. Besides, I had learned, a good while before that, that it is not wise to keep the fires going under a slander unless you can get some large advantage out of keeping it alive. Few slanders can stand the wear of silence.

Uncle Remus still lives, and must be over a thousand years old. Indeed I know that this must be so, because I have seen a new photograph of him in the public prints within the last month or so[1] and in that picture his aspects are distinctly and strikingly geological and one can see that he is thinking about the mastodons and the plesiosaurs that he used to play with when he was young.

---

[1] Written October 16, 1906.

It is just a quarter of a century since I have seen Uncle Remus. He visited us in our home in Hartford and was reverently devoured by the big eyes of Susy and Clara, for I made a deep and awful impression upon the little creatures—who knew his book by heart through my nightly declamation of its tales to them—by revealing to them privately that he was the real Uncle Remus whitewashed so that he could come into people's houses the front way.

He was the bashfulest grown person I have ever met. When there were people about he stayed silent and seemed to suffer until they were gone. But he was lovely nevertheless, for the sweetness and benignity of the immortal Remus looked out from his eyes and the graces and sincerities of his character shone in his face.

It may be that Jim Wolf was as bashful as Harris. It hardly seems possible, yet as I look back fifty-six years and consider Jim Wolf I am almost persuaded that he was. He was seventeen and yet he was as much as four times as bashful as I was, though I was only fourteen. He boarded and slept in the house but he was always tongue-tied in the presence of my sister, and when even my gentle mother spoke to him he could not answer save in frightened monosyllables. He would not enter a room where a girl was; nothing could persuade him to do such a thing.

Once when he was in our small parlor alone, two majestic old maids entered and seated themselves in such a way that Jim could not escape without passing by them. He would as soon have thought of passing by one of Harris's plesiosaurs, ninety feet long. I came in presently, was charmed with the situation and sat down in a corner to watch Jim suffer and to enjoy it. My mother followed a minute later and sat down with the visitors and began to talk. Jim sat upright in his chair, and during a quarter of an hour he did not change his position by a shade—neither General Grant nor a bronze image could have maintained that immovable pose more successfully. I mean as to body and limbs; with the face there was a difference. By fleeting revealments of the face I saw that something was happening—something out of the common. There would be a sudden twitch of the muscles of the face, an instant distortion which in the next instant had passed and left no trace. These twitches gradually grew in frequency but no muscle outside of the face lost any of its rigidity or betrayed any interest in what was happening to

Jim. I mean if something *was* happening to him, and I knew perfectly well that that was the case. At last a pair of tears began to swim slowly down his cheeks amongst the twitchings, but Jim sat still and let them run; then I saw his right hand steal along his thigh until halfway to his knee, then take a vigorous grip upon the cloth.

That was a wasp that he was grabbing. A colony of them were climbing up his legs and prospecting around, and every time he winced they stabbed him to the hilt—so for a quarter of an hour one group of excursionists after another climbed up Jim's legs and resented even the slightest wince or squirm that he indulged himself with in his misery. When the entertainment had become nearly unbearable he conceived the idea of gripping them between his fingers and putting them out of commission. He succeeded with many of them but at great cost, for as he couldn't see the wasp he was as likely to take hold of the wrong end of him as he was the right; then the dying wasp gave him a punch to remember the incident by.

If those ladies had stayed all day and if all the wasps in Missouri had come and climbed up Jim's legs nobody there would ever have known it but Jim and the wasps and me. There he would have sat until the ladies left. When they were gone we went upstairs and he took his clothes off and his legs were a picture to look at. They looked as if they were nailed all over with shirt buttons, each with a single red hole in the center. The pain was intolerable—no, would have been intolerable, but the pain of the presence of those ladies had been so much harder to bear that the pain of the wasps' stings was quite pleasant and enjoyable by comparison.

Jim never could enjoy wasps. I remember a circumstance in support of this conviction of mine; it preceded the episode which I have just recorded. In those extremely youthful days I was not aware that practical joking was a thing which, aside from being as a rule witless, is a base pastime and disreputable. In those early days I gave the matter no thought but indulged freely in practical joking without stopping to consider its moral aspects. During three-fourths of my life I have held the practical joker in limitless contempt and detestation; I have despised him as I have despised no other criminal, and when I am delivering my opinion about him the reflection that I have been a practical joker myself seems to increase my bitterness rather than to modify it.

One afternoon I found the upper part of the window in Jim's bedroom thickly cushioned with wasps. Jim always slept on the side of his bed that was against the window. I had what seemed to me a happy inspiration: I turned back the bedclothes and, at cost of one or two stings, brushed the wasps down and collected a few hundred of them on the sheet on that side of the bed, then turned the covers over them and made prisoners of them. I made a deep crease down the center of the bed to protect the front side from invasion by them and then at night I offered to sleep with Jim. He was willing.

I made it a point to be in bed first to see if my side of it was still a safe place to rest in. It was. None of the wasps had passed the frontier. As soon as Jim was ready for bed I blew out the candle and let him climb in in the dark. He was talking as usual but I couldn't answer, because by anticipation I was suffocating with laughter, and although I gagged myself with a hatful of the sheet, I was on the point of exploding all the time. Jim stretched himself out comfortably, still pleasantly chatting; then his talk began to break and become disjointed; separations intervened between his words, and each separation was emphasized by a more or less sudden and violent twitch of his body, and I knew that the immigrants were getting in their work. I knew I ought to evince some sympathy and ask what was the matter but I couldn't do it because I should laugh if I tried. Presently he stopped talking altogether—that is, on the subject which he had been pursuing, and he said, "There is something in this bed."

I knew it but held my peace.

He said, "There's thousands of them."

Then he said he was going to find out what it was. He reached down and began to explore. The wasps resented this intrusion and began to stab him all over and everywhere. Then he said he had captured one of them and asked me to strike a light. I did it, and when he climbed out of bed his shirt was black with half-crushed wasps dangling by one hind leg, and in his two hands he held a dozen prisoners that were stinging and stabbing him with energy, but his grit was good and he held them fast. By the light of the candle he identified them and said, "Wasps!"

It was his last remark for the night. He added nothing to it.

In silence he uncovered his side of the bed and, dozen by dozen, he removed the wasps to the floor and beat them to a pulp with the bootjack, with earnest and vindictive satisfaction, while I shook the bed with mute laughter—laughter which was not all a pleasure to me, for I had the sense that his silence was ominous. The work of extermination being finally completed, he blew out the light and returned to bed and seemed to compose himself to sleep—in fact he did lie stiller than anybody else could have done in the circumstances.

I remained awake as long as I could and did what I could to keep my laughter from shaking the bed and provoking suspicion, but even my fears could not keep me awake forever and I finally fell asleep and presently woke again—under persuasion of circumstances. Jim was kneeling on my breast and pounding me in the face with both fists. It hurt—but he was knocking all the restraints of my laughter loose; I could not contain it any longer and I laughed until all my body was exhausted and my face, as I believed, battered to a pulp.

Jim never afterward referred to that episode and I had better judgment than to do it myself, for he was a third longer than I was, although not any wider.

I played many practical jokes upon him but they were all cruel and all barren of wit. Any brainless swindler could have invented them. When a person of mature age perpetrates a practical joke it is fair evidence, I think, that he is weak in the head and hasn't enough heart to signify.

◇◇◇◇◇◇◇◇◇◇◇◇◇◇◇◇◇◇◇◇

CHAPTER 11

An exciting event in our village was the arrival of the mesmerizer. I think the year was 1850. As to that I am not sure but I know the month—it was May; that detail has survived the wear of fifty years. A pair of connected little incidents of that month have served to keep the memory of it green for me all this time; incidents of no consequence and not worth embalming, yet my memory has preserved them carefully and flung away things of real value to give them space and make them comfortable. The truth is, a person's memory has no more sense than his conscience and no appreciation whatever of values and proportions. However, never mind those trifling incidents; my subject is the mesmerizer now.

He advertised his show and promised marvels. Admission as usual: 25 cents, children and Negroes half price. The village had heard of mesmerism in a general way but had not encountered it yet. Not many people attended the first night but next day they had so many wonders to tell that everybody's curiosity was fired and after that for a fortnight the magician had prosperous times. I was fourteen or fifteen years old, the age at which a boy is willing to endure all things, suffer all things short of death by fire, if thereby he may be conspicuous and show off before the public; and so, when I saw the "subjects" perform their foolish antics on the platform and make the people laugh and shout and admire I had a burning desire to be a subject myself.

Every night for three nights I sat in the row of candidates on the platform and held the magic disk in the palm of my hand and gazed at it and tried to get sleepy, but it was a failure; I remained wide awake and had to retire defeated, like the majority. Also, I had to sit there and be gnawed with envy of Hicks, our journeyman; I had to sit there and see him scamper and jump when Simmons the enchanter exclaimed, "See the snake! See the snake!" and hear him say, "My, how beautiful!" in response to the suggestion that he was observing a splendid sunset; and so on—the whole insane business. I couldn't laugh, I couldn't applaud; it filled me with bitterness to have others do it and to have people make a hero of Hicks and crowd around him when the show was over and ask him for more and more particulars of the wonders he had seen in his visions and manifest in many ways that they were proud to be acquainted with him. Hicks —the idea! I couldn't stand it; I was getting boiled to death in my own bile.

On the fourth night temptation came and I was not strong enough to resist. When I had gazed at the disk a while I pretended to be sleepy and began to nod. Straightway came the professor and made passes over my head and down my body and legs and arms, finishing each pass with a snap of his fingers in the air to discharge the surplus electricity; then he began to "draw" me with the disk, holding it in his fingers and telling me I could not take my eyes off it, try as I might; so I rose slowly, bent and gazing, and followed that disk all over the place, just as I had seen the others do. Then I was put through the other paces. Upon suggestion I fled from snakes, passed buckets at a fire, became excited over hot steamboat races, made love to imaginary girls and kissed them, fished from the platform and landed mud cats that outweighed me—and so on, all the customary marvels. But not in the customary way. I was cautious at first and watchful, being afraid the professor would discover that I was an impostor and drive me from the platform in disgrace; but as soon as I realized that I was not in danger, I set myself the task of terminating Hicks's usefulness as a subject and of usurping his place.

It was a sufficiently easy task. Hicks was born honest, I without that incumbrance—so some people said. Hicks saw what he saw and reported accordingly, I saw more than was visible and added to it such details as could help. Hicks had no imagination; I had a double supply. He was born calm, I was born excited. No vision could start a rapture in him and he was constipated as to language, anyway; but if I saw a vision I emptied the dictionary onto it and lost the remnant of my mind into the bargain.

At the end of my first half hour Hicks was a thing of the past, a fallen hero, a broken idol, and I knew it and was glad and said in my heart, "Success to crime!" Hicks could never have been mesmerized to the point where he could kiss an imaginary girl in public or a real one either, but I was competent. Whatever Hicks had failed in, I made it a point to succeed in, let the cost be what it might, physically or morally. He had shown several bad defects and I had made a note of them. For instance, if the magician asked, "What do you see?" and left him to invent a vision for himself, Hicks was dumb and blind, he couldn't see a thing nor say a word, whereas the magician soon found out that when it came to seeing visions of a stunning and marketable sort I could get along better without his help than with it.

Then there was another thing: Hicks wasn't worth a tallow dip on mute mental suggestion. Whenever Simmons stood behind him and gazed at the back of his skull and tried to drive a mental suggestion into it, Hicks sat with vacant face and never suspected. If he had been noticing he could have seen by the rapt faces of the audience that something was going on behind his back that required a response. Inasmuch as I was an imposter I dreaded to have this test put

upon me, for I knew the professor would be "willing" me to
do something, and as I couldn't know what it was, I should
be exposed and denounced. However, when my time came, I
took my chance. I perceived by the tense and expectant faces
of the people that Simmons was behind me willing me with
all his might. I tried my best to imagine what he wanted but
nothing suggested itself. I felt ashamed and miserable then.
I believed that the hour of my disgrace was come and that
in another moment I should go out of that place disgraced. I
ought to be ashamed to confess it but my next thought was
not how I could win the compassion of kindly hearts by
going out humbly and in sorrow for my misdoings, but how
I could go out most sensationally and spectacularly.

There was a rusty and empty old revolver lying on the table
among the "properties" employed in the performances. On
May Day two or three weeks before there had been a celebration by the schools and I had had a quarrel with a big
boy who was the school bully and I had not come out of it
with credit. That boy was now seated in the middle of the
house, halfway down the main aisle. I crept stealthily and
impressively toward the table, with a dark and murderous
scowl on my face, copied from a popular romance, seized
the revolver suddenly, flourished it, shouted the bully's
name, jumped off the platform and made a rush for him and
chased him out of the house before the paralyzed people
could interfere to save him. There was a storm of applause,
and the magician, addressing the house, said, most impressively—

"That you may know how really remarkable this is and
how wonderfully developed a subject we have in this boy, I
assure you that without a single spoken word to guide him he
has carried out what I mentally commanded him to do, to the
minutest detail. I could have stopped him at a moment in
his vengeful career by a mere exertion of my will, therefore
the poor fellow who has escaped was at no time in danger."

So I was not in disgrace. I returned to the platform a hero
and happier than I have ever been in this world since. As
regards mental suggestion, my fears of it were gone. I judged
that in case I failed to guess what the professor might be
willing me to do, I could count on putting up something that
would answer just as well. I was right, and exhibitions of unspoken suggestion became a favorite with the public. Whenever I perceived that I was being willed to do something I

got up and did something—anything that occurred to me—and the magician, not being a fool, always ratified it. When people asked me, "How *can* you tell what he is willing you to do?" I said, "It's just as easy," and they always said admiringly, "Well, it beats *me* how you can do it."

Hicks was weak in another detail. When the professor made passes over him and said "his whole body is without sensation now—come forward and test him, ladies and gentlemen," the ladies and gentlemen always complied eagerly and stuck pins into Hicks, and if they went deep Hicks was sure to wince, then that poor professor would have to explain that Hicks "wasn't sufficiently under the influence." But I didn't wince; I only suffered and shed tears on the inside. The miseries that a conceited boy will endure to keep up his "reputation"! And so will a conceited man; I know it in my own person and have seen it in a hundred thousand others. That professor ought to have protected me and I often hoped he would, when the tests were unusually severe, but he didn't. It may be that he was deceived as well as the others, though I did not believe it nor think it possible. Those were dear good people but they must have carried simplicity and credulity to the limit. They would stick a pin in my arm and bear on it until they drove it a third of its length in, and then be lost in wonder that by a mere exercise of will power the professor could turn my arm to iron and make it insensible to pain. Whereas it was not insensible at all; I was suffering agonies of pain.

After that fourth night, that proud night, that triumphant night, I was the only subject. Simmons invited no more candidates to the platform. I performed alone every night the rest of the fortnight. Up to that time a dozen wise old heads, the intellectual aristocracy of the town, had held out as implacable unbelievers. I was as hurt by this as if I were engaged in some honest occupation. There is nothing surprising about this. Human beings feel dishonor the most, sometimes, when they most deserve it. That handful of over-wise gentlemen kept on shaking their heads all the first week and saying they had seen no marvels there that could not have been produced by collusion; and they were pretty vain of their unbelief too and liked to show it and air it and be superior to the ignorant and the gullible. Particularly old Dr. Peake, who was the ringleader of the irreconcilables and very formidable; for he was an F.F.V., he was learned, white-

haired and venerable, nobly and richly clad in the fashions
of an earlier and a courtlier day, he was large and stately,
and he not only seemed wise but was what he seemed in that
regard. He had great influence and his opinion upon any
matter was worth much more than that of any other person
in the community. When I conquered him at last, I knew I
was undisputed master of the field; and now after more than
fifty years I acknowledge with a few dry old tears that I rejoiced without shame.

In 1847 we were living in a large white house on the corner
of Hill and Main Streets—a house that still stands but isn't
large now although it hasn't lost a plank; I saw it a year ago
and noticed that shrinkage.[1] My father died in it in March of
the year mentioned but our family did not move out of it
until some months afterward. Ours was not the only family in
the house; there was another, Dr. Grant's. One day Dr.
Grant and Dr. Reyburn argued a matter on the street with
sword canes and Grant was brought home multifariously
punctured. Old Dr. Peake calked the leaks and came every
day for a while to look after him.

The Grants were Virginians, like Peake, and one day when
Grant was getting well enough to be on his feet and sit
around in the parlor and talk, the conversation fell upon
Virginia and old times. I was present but the group were
probably unconscious of me, I being only a lad and a negligi-
ble quantity. Two of the group—Dr. Peake and Mrs. Crawford,
Mrs. Grant's mother—had been of the audience when the
Richmond theater burned down thirty-six years before, and
they talked over the frightful details of that memorable
tragedy. These were eyewitnesses, and with their eyes I saw
it all with an intolerable vividness: I saw the black smoke
rolling and tumbling toward the sky, I saw the flames burst
through it and turn red, I heard the shrieks of the despairing,
I glimpsed their faces at the windows, caught fitfully through
the veiling smoke, I saw them jump to their death or to muti-
lation worse than death. The picture is before me yet and can
never fade.

In due course they talked of the colonial mansion of the
Peakes, with its stately columns and its spacious grounds,
and by odds and ends I picked up a clearly defined idea of

[1] Written in 1903.

the place. I was strongly interested, for I had not before heard of such palatial things from the lips of people who had seen them with their own eyes. One detail, casually dropped, hit my imagination hard. In the wall by the great front door there was a round hole as big as a saucer—a British cannon ball had made it in the war of the Revolution. It was breathtaking; it made history real; history had never been real to me before.

Very well, three or four years later, as already mentioned, I was king bee and sole "subject" in the mesmeric show; it was the beginning of the second week; the performance was half over; just then the majestic Dr. Peake with his ruffled bosom and wristbands and his gold-headed cane entered, and a deferential citizen vacated his seat beside the Grants and made the great chief take it. This happened while I was trying to invent something fresh in the way of vision, in response to the professor's remark—

"Concentrate your powers. Look—look attentively. There—don't you see something? Concentrate—concentrate! Now then —describe it."

Without suspecting it, Dr. Peake, by entering the place, had reminded me of the talk of three years before. He had also furnished me capital and was become my confederate, an accomplice in my frauds. I began on a vision, a vague and dim one (that was part of the game at the beginning of a vision; it isn't best to see it too clearly at first, it might look as if you had come loaded with it). The vision developed by degrees and gathered swing, momentum, energy. It was the Richmond fire. Dr. Peake was cold at first and his fine face had a trace of polite scorn in it; but when he began to recognize that fire, that expression changed and his eyes began to light up. As soon as I saw that, I threw the valves wide open and turned on all the steam and gave those people a supper of fire and horrors that was calculated to last them one while! They couldn't gasp when I got through—they were petrified. Dr. Peake had risen and was standing—and breathing hard. He said, in a great voice:

"My doubts are ended. No collusion could produce that miracle. It was totally impossible for him to know those details, yet he has described them with the clarity of an eyewitness—and with what unassailable truthfulness God knows I know!"

I saved the colonial mansion for the last night and solidified and perpetuated Dr. Peake's conversion with the cannon-ball hole. He explained to the house that I could never have heard of that small detail, which differentiated this mansion from all other Virginian mansions and perfectly identified it, therefore the fact stood proven that I had *seen* it in my vision. Lawks!

It is curious. When the magician's engagement closed there was but one person in the village who did not believe in mesmerism and I was the one. All the others were converted but I was to remain an implacable and unpersuadable disbeliever in mesmerism and hypnotism for close upon fifty years. This was because I never would examine them, in after life. I couldn't. The subject revolted me. Perhaps it brought back to me a passage in my life which for pride's sake I wished to forget; though I thought, or persuaded myself I thought, I should never come across a "proof" which wasn't thin and cheap and probably had a fraud like me behind it.

The truth is I did not have to wait long to get tired of my triumphs. Not thirty days, I think. The glory which is built upon a lie soon becomes a most unpleasant incumbrance. No doubt for a while I enjoyed having my exploits told and retold and told again in my presence and wondered over and exclaimed about, but I quite distinctly remember that there presently came a time when the subject was wearisome and odious to me and I could not endure the disgusting discomfort of it. I am well aware that the world-glorified doer of a deed of great and real splendor has just my experience; I know that he deliciously enjoys hearing about it for three or four weeks and that pretty soon after that he begins to dread the mention of it and by and by wishes he had been with the damned before he ever thought of doing that deed. I remember how General Sherman used to rage and swear over "While we were marching through Georgia," which was played at him and sung at him everywhere he went; still, I think I suffered a shade more than the legitimate hero does, he being privileged to soften his misery with the reflection that his glory was at any rate golden and reproachless in its origin, whereas I had no such privilege, there being no possible way to make mine respectable.

How easy it is to make people believe a lie and how hard it is to undo that work again! Thirty-five years after those evil exploits of mine I visited my old mother, whom I had not seen for ten years; and being moved by what seemed to me a rather noble and perhaps heroic impulse, I thought I would humble myself and confess my ancient fault. It cost me a great effort to make up my mind; I dreaded the sorrow that would rise in her face and the shame that would look out of her eyes; but after long and troubled reflection, the sacrifice seemed due and right and I gathered my resolution together and made the confession.

To my astonishment there were no sentimentalities, no dramatics, no George Washington effects; she was not moved in the least degree; she simply did not believe me and said so! I was not merely disappointed, I was nettled to have my costly truthfulness flung out of the market in this placid and confident way when I was expecting to get a profit out of it. I asserted and reasserted, with rising heat, my statement that every single thing I had done on those long-vanished nights was a lie and a swindle; and when she shook her head tranquilly and said she knew better, I put up my hand and *swore* to it—adding a triumphant, "*Now* what do you say?"

It did not affect her at all; it did not budge her the fraction of an inch from her position. If this was hard for me to endure, it did not begin with the blister she put upon the raw when she began to put my sworn oath out of court with *arguments* to prove that I was under a delusion and did not know what I was talking about. Arguments! Arguments to show that a person on a man's outside can know better what is on his inside than he does himself. I had cherished some contempt for arguments before, I have not enlarged my respect for them since. She refused to believe that I had invented my visions myself; she said it was folly: that I was only a child at the time and could not have done it. She cited the Richmond fire and the colonial mansion and said they were quite beyond my capacities. Then I saw my chance! I said she was right—I didn't invent those, I got them from Dr. Peake. Even this great shot did not damage. She said Dr. Peake's evidence was better than mine, and he had said in plain words that it was impossible for me to have heard about those things. Dear, dear, what a grotesque and unthinkable situation: a confessed swindler convicted of honesty and condemned to acquittal by circumstantial evidence furnished by the swindled!

I realized with shame and with impotent vexation that I was defeated all along the line. I had but one card left but it was a formidable one. I played it and stood from under. It seemed ignoble to demolish her fortress after she had defended it so valiantly but the defeated know not mercy. I played that master card. It was the pin-sticking. I said solemnly—

"I give you my honor, a pin was never stuck into me without causing me cruel pain."

She only said—

"It is thirty-five years. I believe you do think that now but I was there and I know better. You never winced."

She was so calm! and I was so far from it, so nearly frantic.

"Oh, my goodness!" I said, "let me *show* you that I am speaking the truth. Here is my arm; drive a pin into it—drive it to the head—I shall not wince."

She only shook her gray head and said with simplicity and conviction—

"You are a man now and could dissemble the hurt; but you were only a child then and could not have done it."

And so the lie which I played upon her in my youth remained with her as an unchallengeable truth to the day of her death. Carlyle said "a lie cannot live." It shows that he did not know how to tell them. If I had taken out a life policy on this one the premiums would have bankrupted me ages ago.

◇◇◇◇~◇◇◇◇◇◇◇◇◇◇◇◇◇

CHAPTER 12

Where now is Billy Rice? He was a joy to me and so were the other stars of the nigger show—Billy Birch, David Wambold, Backus and a delightful dozen of their brethren who made life a pleasure to me forty years ago and later. Birch, Wambold and Backus are gone years ago; and with them departed to return no more forever, I suppose, the real nigger show— the genuine nigger show, the extravagant nigger show—the show which to me had no peer and whose peer has not yet arrived, in my experience. We have the grand opera; and I have witnessed and greatly enjoyed the first act of everything which Wagner created, but the effect on me has always been

so powerful that one act was quite sufficient; whenever I have
witnessed two acts I have gone away physically exhausted;
and whenever I have ventured an entire opera the result has
been the next thing to suicide. But if I could have the nigger
show back again in its pristine purity and perfection I should
have but little further use for opera. It seems to me that to the
elevated mind and the sensitive spirit the hand organ and the
nigger show are a standard and a summit to whose rarefied
altitude the other forms of musical art may not hope to reach.

I remember the first Negro musical show I ever saw. It
must have been in the early forties. It was a new institution.
In our village of Hannibal we had not heard of it before and
it burst upon us as a glad and stunning surprise.

The show remained a week and gave a performance every
night. Church members did not attend these performances,
but all the worldlings flocked to them and were enchanted.
Church members did not attend shows out there in those days.
The minstrels appeared with coal-black hands and faces and
their clothing was a loud and extravagant burlesque of the
clothing worn by the plantation slave of the time; not that the
rags of the poor slave were burlesqued, for that would not
have been possible; burlesque could have added nothing in
the way of extravagance to the sorrowful accumulation of rags
and patches which constituted his costume; it was the form
and color of his dress that was burlesqued. Standing collars
were in fashion in that day and the minstrel appeared in a
collar which engulfed and hid half of his head and projected
so far forward that he could hardly see sideways over its
points. His coat was sometimes made of curtain calico with a
swallowtail that hung nearly to his heels and had buttons as
big as a blacking box. His shoes were rusty and clumsy and
cumbersome and five or six sizes too large for him. There were
many variations upon this costume and they were all extravagant and were by many believed to be funny.

The minstrel used a very broad Negro dialect; he used it
competently and with easy facility and it was funny—delightfully and satisfyingly funny. However, there was one member
of the minstrel troupe of those early days who was not extravagantly dressed and did not use the Negro dialect. He was
clothed in the faultless evening costume of the white society
gentleman and used a stilted, courtly, artificial and painfully
grammatical form of speech, which the innocent villagers took
for the real thing as exhibited in high and citified society, and

they vastly admired it and envied the man who could frame it on the spot without reflection and deliver it in this easy and fluent and artistic fashion. "Bones" sat at one end of the row of minstrels, "Banjo" sat at the other end, and the dainty gentleman just described sat in the middle. This middleman was the spokesman of the show. The neatness and elegance of his dress, the studied courtliness of his manners and speech and the shapeliness of his undoctored features made him a contrast to the rest of the troupe and particularly to "Bones" and "Banjo." "Bones" and "Banjo" were the prime jokers and whatever funniness was to be gotten out of paint and exaggerated clothing they utilized to the limit. Their lips were thickened and lengthened with bright red paint to such a degree that their mouths resembled slices cut in a ripe watermelon.

The original ground plan of the minstrel show was maintained without change for a good many years. There was no curtain to the stage in the beginning; while the audience waited they had nothing to look at except the row of empty chairs back of the footlights; presently the minstrels filed in and were received with a wholehearted welcome; they took their seats, each with his musical instrument in his hand; then the aristocrat in the middle began with a remark like this:

"I hope, gentlemen, I have the pleasure of seeing you in your accustomed excellent health and that everything has proceeded prosperously with you since last we had the good fortune to meet."

"Bones" would reply for himself and go on and tell about something in the nature of peculiarly good fortune that had lately fallen to his share; but in the midst of it he would be interrupted by "Banjo" who would throw doubt upon his statement of the matter; then a delightful jangle of assertion and contradiction would break out between the two; the quarrel would gather emphasis, the voices would grow louder and louder and more and more energetic and vindictive, and the two would rise and approach each other, shaking fists and instruments and threatening bloodshed, the courtly middleman meantime imploring them to preserve the peace and observe the proprieties—but all in vain, of course. Sometimes the quarrel would last five minutes, the two contestants shouting deadly threats in each other's faces with their noses not six inches apart, the house shrieking with laughter all the while at this happy and accurate imitation of the usual and familiar Negro quarrel, then finally the pair of malignants would gradually

back away from each other, each making impressive threats
as to what was going to happen the "next time" each should
have the misfortune to cross the other's path; then they would
sink into their chairs and growl back and forth at each other
across the front of the line until the house had had time to
recover from its convulsions and hysterics and quiet down.

The aristocrat in the middle of the row would now make a
remark which was surreptitiously intended to remind one of
the end men of an experience of his of a humorous nature and
fetch it out of him—which it always did. It was usually an experience of a stale and moldy sort and as old as America. One
of these things, which always delighted the audience of those
days until the minstrels wore it threadbare, was "Bones's" account of the perils which he had once endured during a storm
at sea. The storm lasted so long that in the course of time all
the provisions were consumed. Then the middleman would
inquire anxiously how the people managed to survive.

"Bones" would reply, "We lived on eggs."

"You lived on eggs! Where did you get eggs?"

"Every day, when the storm was so bad, the Captain laid
to."

During the first five years that joke convulsed the house,
but after that the population of the United States had heard
it so many times that they respected it no longer and always
received it in a deep and reproachful and indignant silence,
along with others of its caliber which had achieved disfavor
by long service.

The minstrel troupes had good voices and both their solos
and their choruses were a delight to me as long as the Negro
show continued in existence. In the beginning the songs were
rudely comic, such as "Buffalo Gals," "Camptown Races,"
"Old Dan Tucker," and so on; but a little later sentimental
songs were introduced, such as "The Blue Juniata," "Sweet
Ellen Bayne," "Nelly Bly," "A Life on the Ocean Wave," "The
Larboard Watch," etc.

The minstrel show was born in the early forties and it had a
prosperous career for about thirty-five years; then it degen-
erated into a variety show and was nearly all variety show
with a Negro act or two thrown in incidentally. The real
Negro show has been stone dead for thirty years. To my mind
it was a thoroughly delightful thing and a most competent
laughter-compeller and I am sorry it is gone.

As I have said, it was the worldlings that attended that first minstrel show in Hannibal. Ten or twelve years later the minstrel show was as common in America as the Fourth of July but my mother had never seen one. She was about sixty years old by this time and she came down to St. Louis with a dear and lovely lady of her own age, an old citizen of Hannibal, Aunt Betsey Smith. She wasn't anybody's aunt in particular, she was aunt to the whole town of Hannibal; this was because of her sweet and generous and benevolent nature and the winning simplicity of her character.

Like my mother, Aunt Betsey Smith had never seen a Negro show. She and my mother were very much alive; their age counted for nothing; they were fond of excitement, fond of novelties, fond of anything going that was of a sort proper for members of the church to indulge in. They were always up early to see the circus procession enter the town and to grieve because their principles did not allow them to follow it into the tent; they were always ready for Fourth of July processions, Sunday-school processions, lectures, conventions, camp meetings, revivals in the church—in fact, for any and every kind of dissipation that could not be proven to have anything irreligious about it—and they never missed a funeral.

In St. Louis they were eager for novelties and they applied to me for help. They wanted something exciting and proper. I told them I knew of nothing in their line except a Convention which was to meet in the great hall of the Mercantile Library and listen to an exhibition and illustration of native African music by fourteen missionaries who had just returned from that dark continent. I said that if they actually and earnestly desired something instructive and elevating, I would recommend the Convention, but that if at bottom they really wanted something frivolous I would look further. But no, they were charmed with the idea of the Convention and eager to go. I was not telling them the strict truth and I knew it at the time, but it was no great matter; it is not worth while to strain one's self to tell the truth to people who habitually discount everything you tell them, whether it is true or isn't.

The alleged missionaries were the Christy minstrel troupe, in that day one of the most celebrated of such troupes and also one of the best. We went early and got seats in the front bench. By and by when all the seats on that spacious floor were occupied, there were sixteen hundred persons present. When the grotesque Negroes came filing out on the stage in their extravagant costumes, the old ladies were almost speechless with astonishment. I explained to them that the missionaries always dressed like that in Africa.

But Aunt Betsey said, reproachfully, "But they're niggers."

I said, "That is no matter; they are Americans in a sense, for they are employed by the American Missionary Society."

Then both the ladies began to question the propriety of their countenancing the industries of a company of Negroes, no matter what their trade might be, but I said that they could see by looking around that the best people in St. Louis were present and that certainly they would not be present if the show were not a proper sort.

They were comforted and also quite shamelessly glad to be there. They were happy now and enchanted with the novelty of the situation; all that they had needed was a pretext of some kind or other to quiet their consciences, and their consciences were quiet now; quiet enough to be dead. They gazed on that long curved line of artistic mountebanks with devouring eyes. The middleman began. Presently he led up to that old joke which I was telling about a while ago. Everybody in the house except my novices had heard it a hundred times; a frozen and solemn and indignant silence settled down upon the sixteen hundred, and poor "Bones" sat there in that depressing atmosphere and went through with his joke. It was brand new to my venerable novices and when he got to the end and said, "We lived on eggs," and followed it by explaining that every day during the storm the Captain "laid *to*," they threw their heads back and went off into heart-whole cackles and convulsions of laughter that so astonished and delighted that great audience that it rose in a solid body to look and see who it might be that had not heard that joke before. The laughter of my novices went on and on till their hilarity became contagious and the whole sixteen hundred joined in and shook the place with the thunders of their joy.

Aunt Betsey and my mother achieved a brilliant success for the Christy minstrels that night, for all the jokes were as new to them as they were old to the rest of the house. They received them with screams of laughter and passed the hilarity on, and the audience left the place sore and weary with laughter and full of gratitude to the innocent pair that had furnished to their jaded souls that rare and precious pleasure.

CHAPTER 13

I lately received a letter from England from a gentleman whose belief in phrenology is strong and who wonders why phrenology has apparently never interested me enough to move me to write about it.[1] I have explained as follows:

DEAR SIR:

I never did profoundly study phrenology; therefore I am neither qualified to express an opinion about it nor entitled to do so. In London, 33 or 34 years ago, I made a small test of phrenology for my better information. I went to Fowler under an assumed name and he examined my elevations and depressions and gave me a chart which I carried home to the Langham Hotel and studied with great interest and amusement—the same interest and amusement which I should have found in the chart of an impostor who had been passing himself off for me and who did not resemble me in a single sharply defined detail. I waited 3 months and went to Mr. Fowler again, heralding my arrival with a card bearing both my name and my nom de guerre. Again I carried away an elaborate chart. It contained several sharply defined details of my character, but it bore no recognizable resemblance to the earlier chart. These experiences gave me a prejudice against phrenology which has lasted until now. I am aware that the prejudice should have been against Fowler, instead of against the art; but I am human and that is not the way that prejudices act.

In America, forty or fifty years ago, Fowler and Wells stood at the head of the phrenological industry, and the firm's name was familiar in all ears. Their publications had a wide currency and were read and studied and discussed by truth seek-

[1] Written December 26, 1906.

ers and by converts all over the land. One of the most frequent arrivals in our village of Hannibal was the peripatetic phrenologist and he was popular and always welcome. He gathered the people together and gave them a gratis lecture on the marvels of phrenology, then felt their bumps and made an estimate of the result, at twenty-five cents per head. I think the people were almost always satisfied with these translations of their characters—if one may properly use that word in this connection; and indeed the word is right enough, for the estimates really were translations, since they conveyed seeming facts out of apparent simplicities into unsimple technical forms of expression, although as a rule their meanings got left behind on the journey. Phrenology found many a bump on a man's head and it labeled each bump with a formidable and outlandish name of its own. The phrenologist took delight in mouthing these great names; they gurgled from his lips in an easy and unembarrassed stream, and this exhibition of cultivated facility compelled the envy and admiration of everybody. By and by the people became familiar with these strange names and addicted to the use of them and they batted them back and forth in conversation with deep satisfaction—a satisfaction which could hardly have been more contenting if they had known for certain what the words meant.

It is not at all likely, I think, that the traveling expert ever got any villager's character quite right, but it is a safe guess that he was always wise enough to furnish his clients character-charts that would compare favorably with George Washington's. It was a long time ago and yet I think I still remember that no phrenologist ever came across a skull in our town that fell much short of the Washington standard. This general and close approach to perfection ought to have roused suspicion, perhaps, but I do not remember that it did. It is my impression that the people admired phrenology and believed in it and that the voice of the doubter was not heard in the land.

I was reared in this atmosphere of faith and belief and trust, and I think its influence was still upon me, so many years afterward, when I encountered Fowler's advertisements in London. I was glad to see his name and glad of an opportunity to personally test his art. The fact that I went to him under a fictitious name is an indication that not the whole bulk of the faith of my boyhood was still with me; it looks like circumstantial evidence that in some way my faith had suffered impairment in the course of the years. I found Fowler on duty, in the midst of the impressive symbols of his trade. On brackets, on tables, on shelves, all about the room, stood marble-white busts, hairless, every inch of the skull occupied by a shallow bump, and every bump labeled with its imposing name, in black letters.

Fowler received me with indifference, fingered my head in an uninterested way and named and estimated my qualities in a bored and monotonous voice. He said I possessed amazing courage, an abnormal spirit of daring, a pluck, a stern will, a fearlessness that were without limit. I was astonished at this, and gratified, too; I had not suspected it before; but then he foraged over on the other side of my skull and found a hump there which he called "caution." This hump was so tall, so mountainous, that it reduced my courage-bump to a mere hillock by comparison, although the courage-bump had been so prominent up to that time—according to his description of it—that it ought to have been a capable thing to hang my hat on; but it amounted to nothing, now, in the presence of that Matterhorn which he called my Caution. He explained that if that Matterhorn had been left out of my scheme of character I would have been one of the bravest men that ever lived—possibly the bravest—but that my cautiousness was so prodigiously superior to it that it abolished my courage and made me almost spectacularly timid. He continued his discoveries, with the result that I came out safe and sound, at the end, with a hundred great and shining qualities; but which lost their value and amounted to nothing because each of the hundred was coupled up with an opposing defect which took the effectiveness all out of it.

However, he found a *cavity*, in one place; a cavity where a bump would have been in anybody else's skull. That cavity, he said, was all alone, all by itself, occupying a solitude, and had no opposing bump, however slight in elevation, to modify and ameliorate its perfect completeness and isolation. He startled me by saying that that cavity represented the total absence of the sense of humor! He now became almost interested. Some of his indifference disappeared. He almost grew eloquent over this America which he had discovered. He said he often found bumps of humor which were so small that they were hardly noticeable, but that in his long experience this was the first time he had ever come across a *cavity* where that bump ought to be.

I was hurt, humiliated, resentful, but I kept these feelings to myself; at bottom I believed his diagnosis was wrong, but I was not certain. In order to make sure, I thought I would wait until he should have forgotten my face and the peculiarities of my skull, and then come back and try again and see if he had really known what he had been talking about, or had only been guessing. After three months I went to him again, but under my own name this time. Once more he made a striking discovery—the cavity was gone, and in its place was a Mount Everest—figuratively speaking—31,000 feet high, the loftiest bump of humor he had ever encountered in his lifelong experience! I went from his presence prejudiced against phrenology, but it may be, as I have said to the English gentleman, that I ought to have conferred the prejudice upon Fowler and not upon the art which he was exploiting.[2]

Eleven years ago, on board a ship bound for Europe, William T. Stead made a photograph of my right hand, and afterwards, in London, sent replicas of it to twelve palmists, concealing from them my name and asking them to make and send to him estimates of the character of the owner of the hand. The estimates were furnished and Stead published six or seven of them in his magazine. By those estimates I found that my make up was about like anybody else's; I did not seem to differ much from other people; certainly in no prominent and striking way—except in a single detail. In none of the estimates was the word humor mentioned—if my memory is not mistreating me—except in one; in that one the palmist said that the possessor of that hand was totally destitute of the sense of humor.

Two years ago Col. Harvey[3] took prints of my two hands and sent them to six professional palmists of distinguished reputation here in New York City; and he, also, withheld my name and asked for estimates. History repeated itself. The word humor occurred only once in the six estimates and then it was accompanied by the definite remark that the possessor of the hands was destitute of the sense of humor. Now then, I have Fowler's estimate; I have the estimates of Stead's six or

[2] Feb. 10, 1907. The English gentleman was not really a gentleman: he sold my private letter to a newspaper. (M.T.)

[3] George Harvey, at that time president of Harper & Brothers, Mark Twain's publishers.

seven palmists; I have the estimates of Harvey's half-dozen: the evidence that I do not possess the sense of humor is overwhelming, satisfying, convincing, incontrovertible—and at last I believe it myself.

◇◇◇◇◇◇◇◇◇◇◇◇◇◇◇◇◇◇

CHAPTER 14

For thirty years I have received an average of a dozen letters a year from strangers who remember me or whose fathers remember me as a boy and young man. But these letters are almost always disappointing. I have not known these strangers nor their fathers. I have not heard of the names they mention; the reminiscences to which they call my attention have had no part in my experience; all of which means that these strangers have been mistaking me for somebody else. But at last I have the refreshment, this morning,[1] of a letter from a man who deals in names that were familiar to me in my boyhood. The writer incloses a newspaper clipping which has been wandering through the press for four or five weeks, and he wants to know if his brother, Captain Tonkray, was really the original of "Huckleberry Finn."

I have replied that "Huckleberry Finn" was Tom Blankenship. As this writer evidently knew the Hannibal of the 'forties, he will easily recall Tom Blankenship. Tom's father was at one time Town Drunkard, an exceedingly well-defined and unofficial office of those days. He succeeded General—(I forget the General's name)[2] and for a time he was sole and only incumbent of the office; but afterward Jimmy Finn proved competency and disputed the place with him, so we had two town drunkards at one time—and it made as much trouble in that village as Christendom experienced in the fourteenth century, when there were two Popes at the same time.

In *Huckleberry Finn* I have drawn Tom Blankenship exactly as he was. He was ignorant, unwashed, insufficiently fed; but he had as good a heart as ever any boy had. His liberties were totally unrestricted. He was the only really independent person—boy or man—in the community, and by consequence

---

[1] Written March 8, 1906.
[2] Gaines.

he was tranquilly and continuously happy and was envied by all the rest of us. We liked him; we enjoyed his society. And as his society was forbidden us by our parents the prohibition trebled and quadrupled its value, and therefore we sought and got more of his society than of any other boy's. I heard, four years ago, that he was justice of the peace in a remote village in Montana and was a good citizen and greatly respected.

During Jimmy Finn's term he was not exclusive; he was not finical; he was not hypercritical; he was largely and handsomely democratic—and slept in the deserted tanyard with the hogs. My father tried to reform him once but did not succeed. My father was not a professional reformer. In him the spirit of reform was spasmodic. It only broke out now and then, with considerable intervals between. Once he tried to reform Injun Joe. That also was a failure. It was a failure and we boys were glad. For Injun Joe, drunk, was interesting and a benefaction to us, but Injun Joe sober was a dreary spectacle. We watched my father's experiments upon him with a good deal of anxiety but it came out all right and we were satisfied. Injun Joe got drunk oftener than before and became intolerably interesting.

I think that in *Tom Sawyer* I starved Injun Joe to death in the cave. But that may have been to meet the exigencies of romantic literature. I can't remember now whether the real Injun Joe died in the cave or out of it but I do remember that the news of his death reached me at a most unhappy time— that is to say, just at bedtime on a summer night, when a prodigious storm of thunder and lightning accompanied by a deluging rain that turned the streets and lanes into rivers caused me to repent and resolve to lead a better life. I can remember those awful thunderbursts and the white glare of the lightning yet and the wild lashing of the rain against the windowpanes. By my teachings I perfectly well knew what all that wild rumpus was for—Satan had come to get Injun Joe. I had no shadow of doubt about it. It was the proper thing when a person like Injun Joe was required in the under world and I should have thought it strange and unaccountable if Satan had come for him in a less spectacular way. With every glare of lightning I shriveled and shrank together in mortal terror, and in the interval of black darkness that followed I poured out my lamentings over my lost condition, and my supplications for just one more chance, with an energy and feeling and sincerity quite foreign to my nature.

But in the morning I saw that it was a false alarm and concluded to resume business at the old stand and wait for another reminder.

Now I will quote a brief paragraph from this letter which I have received from Mr. Tonkray. He says:

> You no doubt are at a loss to know who I am. I will tell you. In my younger days I was a resident of Hannibal, Mo., and you and I were schoolmates attending Mr. Dawson's school along with Sam and Will Bowen and Andy Fuqua and others whose names I have forgotten. I was then about the smallest boy in school, for my age, and they called me little Aleck Tonkray for short.

I don't remember Aleck Tonkray but I knew those other people as well as I knew the town drunkards. I remember Dawson's schoolhouse perfectly. If I wanted to describe it I could save myself the trouble by conveying the description of it to these pages from *Tom Sawyer*. I can remember the drowsy and inviting summer sounds that used to float in through the open windows from that distant boy-Paradise, Cardiff Hill, and mingle with the murmurs of the studying pupils and make them the more dreary by the contrast. I remember Andy Fuqua, the oldest pupil—a man of twenty-five. I remember the youngest pupil, Nannie Owsley, a child of seven. I remember George RoBards, eighteen or twenty years old, the only pupil who studied Latin. I remember vaguely the rest of the twenty-five boys and girls. I remember Mr. Dawson very well. I remember his boy, Theodore, who was as good as he could be. In fact he was inordinately good, extravagantly good, offensively good, detestably good—and he had popeyes—and I would have drowned him if I had had a chance. In that school we were all about on an equality and, so far as I remember, the passion of envy had no place in our hearts except in the case of Arch Fuqua—the other one's brother. Of course we all went barefoot in the summertime. Arch Fuqua was about my own age—ten or eleven. In the winter we could stand him, because he wore shoes then, and his great gift was hidden from our sight and we were enabled to forget it. But in the summertime he was a bitterness to us. He was our envy, for he could double back his big toe and let it fly and you could hear it snap thirty yards. There was not another boy in the school that could approach this feat. He had not a rival as regards a physical distinction—except in Theodore Eddy, who could work his ears like a horse. But he was no real rival, because you couldn't hear him work his ears; so all the advantage lay with Arch Fuqua.

I am talking of a time sixty years ago and upward. I remember the names of some of those schoolmates and, by fitful glimpses, even their faces rise dimly before me for a moment —only just long enough to be recognized; then they vanish. I catch glimpses of George RoBards, the Latin pupil—slender, pale, studious, bending over his book and absorbed in it, his long straight black hair hanging down below his jaws like a pair of curtains on the sides of his face. I can see him give his head a toss and flirt one of the curtains back around his head —to get it out of his way, apparently; really to show off. In that day it was a great thing among the boys to have hair of so flexible a sort that it could be flung back in that way, with a flirt of the head. George RoBards was the envy of us all. For there was no hair among us that was so competent for this exhibition as his—except, perhaps, the yellow locks of Will Bowen and John RoBards. My hair was a dense ruck of short curls and so was my brother Henry's. We tried all kinds of devices to get these crooks straightened out so that they would flirt but we never succeeded. Sometimes, by soaking our heads and then combing and brushing our hair down tight and flat to our skulls, we could get it straight, temporarily, and this gave us a comforting moment of joy. But the first time we gave it a flirt it all shriveled into curls again and our happiness was gone.

George was a fine young fellow in all ways. He and Mary Moss were sweethearts and pledged to eternal constancy, from a time when they were merely children. But Mr. Lakenan arrived now and became a resident. He took an important position in the little town at once and maintained it. He brought with him a distinguished reputation as a lawyer. He was educated, cultured; he was grave even to austerity; he was dignified in his conversation and deportment. He was a rather oldish bachelor—as bachelor oldishness was estimated in that day. He was a rising man. He was contemplated with considerable awe by the community, and as a catch he stood at the top of the market. That blooming and beautiful thing, Mary Moss, attracted his favor. He laid siege to her and won. Everybody said she accepted him to please her parents, not herself. They were married. And everybody again, testifying, said he continued her schooling all by himself, proposing to educate her up to standard and make her a meet companion for him. These things may have been true. They may not have been true. But they were interesting. This is the main requirement in a village like that. George went away, presently, to some far-off region and there he died—of a broken heart, everybody said. That could be true, for he had good cause. He would go far before he would find another Mary Moss.

How long ago that little tragedy happened! None but the white heads know about it now. Lakenan is dead these many years but Mary still lives and is still beautiful, although she has grandchildren.

John RoBards was the little brother of George; he was a wee chap with silky golden curtains to his face which dangled to his shoulders and below and could be flung back ravishingly. When he was twelve years old he crossed the plains with his father amid the rush of the gold seekers of '49; and I remember the departure of the cavalcade when it spurred westward. We were all there to see and to envy. And I can still see that proud little chap sailing by on a great horse, with his long locks streaming out behind. We were all on hand to gaze and envy when he returned two years later in unimaginable glory —*for he had traveled!* None of us had ever been forty miles from home. But he had crossed the continent. He had been in the gold mines, that fairyland of our imagination. And he had done a still more wonderful thing. He had been in ships—in ships on the actual ocean; in ships on three actual oceans. For he had sailed down the Pacific and round the Horn among icebergs and through snowstorm and wild wintry gales and had sailed on and turned the corner and flown northward in the trades and up through the blistering equatorial waters— and there in his brown face were the proofs of what he had been through. We would have sold our souls to Satan for the privilege of trading places with him.

I saw him when I was out on that Missouri trip four years ago. He was old then—though not quite so old as I—and the burden of life was upon him. He said his granddaughter, twelve years old, had read my books and would like to see me. It was a pathetic time, for she was a prisoner in her room and marked for death. And John knew that she was passing swiftly away. Twelve years old—just her grandfather's age when he rode away on that great journey. In her I seemed to see that boy again. It was as if he had come back out of that remote past and was present before me in his golden youth. Her malady was heart disease and her brief life came to a close a few days later.

Another of those schoolboys was John Garth. And one of the prettiest of the schoolgirls was Helen Kercheval. They grew up and married. He became a prosperous banker and a prominent and valued citizen; and a few years ago he died, rich and honored. *He died.* It is what I have to say about so many of those boys and girls. The widow still lives, and there are grandchildren. In her pantalette days and my barefoot days she was a schoolmate of mine. I saw John's tomb when I made that Missouri visit.

Her father, Mr. Kercheval, had an apprentice in the early days when I was nine years old, and he had also a slave woman who had many merits. But I can't feel very kindly or forgivingly toward either that good apprentice boy or that good slave woman, for they saved my life. One day when I was playing on a loose log which I supposed was attached to a raft —but it wasn't—it tilted me into Bear Creek. And when I had been under water twice and was coming up to make the third and fatal descent, my fingers appeared above the water and that slave woman seized them and pulled me out. Within a week I was in again and that apprentice had to come along just at the wrong time, and he plunged in and dived, pawed around on the bottom and found me and dragged me out and emptied the water out of me and I was saved again. I was drowned seven times after that before I learned to swim—once in Bear Creek and six times in the Mississippi. I do not now know who the people were who interfered with the intentions of a Providence wiser than themselves but I hold a grudge against them yet. When I told the tale of these remarkable happenings to Rev. Dr. Burton of Hartford, he said he did not believe it. *He slipped on the ice the very next year and sprained his ankle.*

Another schoolmate was John Meredith, a boy of a quite uncommonly sweet and gentle disposition. He grew up and when the Civil War broke out he became a sort of guerrilla chief on the Confederate side, and I was told that in his raids upon Union families in the country parts of Monroe County— in earlier times the friends and familiars of his father—he was remorseless in his devastations and sheddings of blood. It seems almost incredible that this could have been that gentle comrade of my school days; yet it can be true, for Robespierre when he was young was like that. John has been in his grave many and many a year.

Will Bowen was another schoolmate and so was his brother, Sam, who was his junior by a couple of years. Before the Civil War broke out both became St. Louis and New Orleans pilots. Both are dead, long ago. While Sam was still very young he had a curious adventure. He fell in love with a girl of sixteen, only child of a very wealthy German brewer. He wanted to marry her but he and she both thought that the papa would not only not consent but would shut his door against Sam. The old man was not so disposed but they were not aware of that. He had his eye upon them and it was not a hostile eye. This indiscreet young couple got to living together surreptitiously. Before long the old man died. When the will was examined it was found that he had left the whole of his wealth to Mrs. Samuel A. Bowen. Then the poor things made another mistake. They rushed down to the French suburb, Carondelet, and got a magistrate to marry them and date the marriage back a few months. The old brewer had some nieces and nephews and cousins, and different kinds of assets of that sort, and they traced out the fraud and proved it and got the property. This left Sam with a girl wife on his hands and the necessity of earning a living for her at the pilot wheel. After a few years Sam and another pilot were bringing a boat up from New Orleans when the yellow fever broke out among the few passengers and the crew. Both pilots were stricken with it and there was nobody to take their place at the wheel. The boat was landed at the head of Island 82 to wait for succor. Death came swiftly to both pilots—and there they lie buried, unless the river has cut the graves away and washed the bones into the stream, a thing which probably happened long ago.

◇◇◇◇◇◇◇◇◇◇◇◇◇◇◇◇◇◇

CHAPTER 15

I recall Mary Miller. She was not my first sweetheart but I think she was the first one that furnished me a broken heart. I fell in love with her when she was eighteen and I nine—but she scorned me and I recognized that this was a cold world. I had not noticed that temperature before. I believe I was as miserable as even a grown man could be. But I think that this sorrow did not remain with me long. As I remember it I soon transferred my worship to Artimisia Briggs, who was a year older than Mary Miller. When I revealed my passion to her she did not scoff at it. She did not make fun of it. She was very kind and gentle about it. But she was also firm, and said she did not want to be pestered by children.

And there was Mary Lacy. She was a schoolmate. But she also was out of my class because of her advanced age. She was pretty wild and determined and independent. She was ungovernable and was considered incorrigible. But that was all a mistake. She married and at once settled down and became in all ways a model matron and was as highly respected as any matron in the town. Four years ago[1] she was still living, and had been married fifty years.

Jimmie McDaniel was another schoolmate. His age and mine about tallied. His father kept the candy shop and he was the most envied little chap in the town—after Tom Blankenship —for, although we never saw him eating candy, we supposed that it was, nevertheless, his ordinary diet. He pretended that he never ate it, didn't care for it because there was nothing forbidden about it—there was plenty of it and he could have as much of it as he wanted. Still, there was circumstantial evidence that suggested that he only scorned candy in public to show off, for he had the worst teeth in town. He was the first human being to whom I ever told a humorous story, so far as I can remember. This was about Jim Wolf and the cats; and I gave him that tale the morning after that memorable episode. I thought he would laugh his teeth out. I had never been so proud and happy before and I have seldom been so proud and happy since. I saw him four years ago when I was out there. He was working in a cigar-making shop. He wore an apron that came down to his knees and a beard that came nearly half as far, and yet it was not difficult for me to recognize him. He had been married fifty-four years. He had many children and grandchildren and great-grandchildren, and also even posterity, they all said—thousands—yet the boy to whom I had told the cat story when we were callow juveniles was still present in that cheerful little old man.

Artimisia Briggs got married not long after refusing me. She married Richmond, the stone mason, who was my Methodist

[1] A reference to the visit to Missouri in 1902.

Sunday-school teacher in the earliest days and he had one distinction which I envied him: at some time or other he had hit his thumb with his hammer and the result was a thumbnail which remained permanently twisted and distorted and curved and pointed, like a parrot's beak. I should not consider it an ornament now, I suppose, but it had a fascination for me then and a vast value, because it was the only one in the town. He was a very kindly and considerate Sunday-school teacher, and patient and compassionate, so he was the favorite teacher with us little chaps. In that school they had slender oblong pasteboard blue tickets, each with a verse from the Testament printed on it, and you could get a blue ticket by reciting two verses. By reciting five verses you could get three blue tickets, and you could trade these at the bookcase and borrow a book for a week. I was under Mr. Richmond's spiritual care every now and then for two or three years and he was never hard upon me. I always recited the same five verses every Sunday. He was always satisfied with the performance. He never seemed to notice that these were the same five foolish virgins that he had been hearing about every Sunday for months. I always got my tickets and exchanged them for a book. They were pretty dreary books, for there was not a bad boy in the entire bookcase. They were *all* good boys and good girls and drearily uninteresting but they were better society than none and I was glad to have their company and disapprove of it.

Twenty years ago Mr. Richmond had become possessed of Tom Sawyer's cave in the hills three miles from town and had made a tourist resort of it. In 1849, when the gold seekers were streaming through our little town of Hannibal, many of our grown men got the gold fever and I think that all the boys had it. On the Saturday holidays in summertime we used to borrow skiffs whose owners were not present and go down the river three miles to the cave hollow (Missourian for "valley"), and there we staked out claims and pretended to dig gold, panning out half a dollar a day at first; two or three times as much, later, and by and by whole fortunes, as our imaginations became inured to the work. Stupid and unprophetic lads! We were doing this in play and never suspecting. Why, that cave hollow and all the adjacent hills were made of gold! —but we did not know it. We took it for dirt. We left its rich secret in its own peaceful possession and grew up in poverty and went wandering about the world struggling for bread— and this because we had not the gift of prophecy. That region was all dirt and rocks to us, yet all it needed was to be ground up and scientifically handled and it was gold. That is to say, the whole region was a cement mine—and they make the finest kind of Portland cement there now, five thousand barrels a day, with a plant that cost $2,000,000.

Several months ago[2] a telegram came to me from there saying that Tom Sawyer's cave was now being ground into cement. Would I like to say anything about it in public? But I had nothing to say. I was sorry we lost our cement mine but it was not worth while to talk about it at this late day and, to take it all around, it was a painful subject anyway. There are seven miles of Tom Sawyer's cave—that is to say, the lofty ridge which conceals that cave stretches down the bank of the Mississippi seven miles to the town of Saverton.

For a little while Reuel Gridley attended that school of ours. He was an elderly pupil; he was perhaps twenty-two or twenty-three years old. Then came the Mexican War and he volunteered. A company of infantry was raised in our town and Mr. Hickman, a tall, straight, handsome athlete of twenty-five, was made captain of it and had a sword by his side and a broad yellow stripe down the leg of his gray uniform pants. And when that company marched back and forth through the streets in its smart uniform—which it did several times a day for drill—its evolutions were attended by all the boys whenever the school hours permitted. I can see that marching company yet and I can almost feel again the consuming desire that I had to join it. But they had no use for boys of twelve and thirteen, and before I had a chance in another war, the desire to kill people to whom I had not been introduced had passed away.

I saw the splendid Hickman in his old age. He seemed about the oldest man I had ever seen—an amazing and melancholy contrast with the showy young captain I had seen preparing his warriors for carnage so many, many years before. Hickman is dead—it is the old story. As Susy[3] said, "What is it all for?"

Reuel Gridley went away to the wars and we heard of him no more for fifteen or sixteen years. Then one day in Carson City, while I was having a difficulty with an editor on the sidewalk—an editor better built for war than I was—I heard a voice say: "Give him the best you've got, Sam. I'm at your

[2] Written in March, 1906.
[3] Mark Twain's daughter, who had died some ten years before.

back." It was Reuel Gridley. He said he had not recognized me by my face but by my drawling style of speech.

He went down to the Reese River mines about that time and presently he lost an election bet in his mining camp, and by the terms of it he was obliged to buy a fifty-pound sack of self-rising flour and carry it through the town, preceded by music, and deliver it to the winner of the bet. Of course the whole camp was present and full of fluid and enthusiasm. The winner of the bet put up the sack at auction for the benefit of the United States Sanitary Fund and sold it. The purchaser put it up for the Fund and sold it. The excitement grew and grew. The sack was sold over and over again for the benefit of the Fund. The news of it came to Virginia City by telegraph. It produced great enthusiasm and Reuel Gridley was begged by telegraph to bring the sack and have an auction in Virginia City. He brought it. An open barouche was provided, also a brass band. The sack was sold over and over again at Gold Hill, then was brought up to Virginia City toward night and sold—and sold again and again, and still again, netting twenty or thirty thousand dollars for the Sanitary Fund. Gridley carried it across California and sold it at various towns. He sold it for large sums in Sacramento and in San Francisco. He brought it East, sold it in New York and in various other cities, then carried it out to a great fair at St. Louis, went on selling it, finally made it up into small cakes and sold those at a dollar apiece. First and last, the sack of flour which had originally cost ten dollars, perhaps, netted more than two hundred thousand dollars for the Sanitary Fund. Reuel Gridley has been dead these many, many years—it is the old story.

In that school were the first Jews I had ever seen. It took me a good while to get over the awe of it. To my fancy they were clothed invisibly in the damp and cobwebby mold of antiquity. They carried me back to Egypt, and in imagination I moved among the Pharaohs and all the shadowy celebrities of that remote age. The name of the boys was Levin. We had a collective name for them which was the only really large and handsome witticism that was ever born in that Congressional district. We called them "Twenty-two"—and even when the joke was old and had been worn threadbare we always followed it with the explanation, to make sure that it would be understood, "Twice Levin—twenty-two."

There were other boys whose names remain with me. Irving Ayres—but no matter; he's dead. Then there was George

Butler, whom I remember as a child of seven wearing a blue leather belt with a brass buckle, and hated and envied by all the boys on account of it. He was a nephew of General Ben Butler and fought gallantly at Ball's Bluff and in several other actions of the Civil War. He is dead, long and long ago.

Will Bowen (dead long ago), Ed Stevens (dead long ago) and John Briggs were special mates of mine. John is still living.

In 1845, when I was ten years old, there was an epidemic of measles in the town and it made a most alarming slaughter among the little people. There was a funeral almost daily and the mothers of the town were nearly demented with fright. My mother was greatly troubled. She worried over Pamela and Henry and me and took constant and extraordinary pains to keep us from coming into contact with the contagion. But upon reflection I believed that her judgment was at fault. It seemed to me that I could improve upon it if left to my own devices. I cannot remember now whether I was frightened about the measles or not but I clearly remember that I grew very tired of the suspense I suffered on account of being continually under the threat of death. I remember that I got so weary of it and so anxious to have the matter settled one way or the other, and promptly, that this anxiety spoiled my days and my nights. I had no pleasure in them. I made up my mind to end this suspense and settle this matter one way or the other and be done with it.

Will Bowen was dangerously ill with the measles and I thought I would go down there and catch them. I entered the house by the front way and slipped along through rooms and halls, keeping sharp watch against discovery, and at last I reached Will's bedroom in the rear of the house on the second floor and got into it uncaptured. But that was as far as my victory reached. His mother caught me there a moment later and snatched me out of the house and gave me a most competent scolding and drove me away. She was so scared that she could hardly get her words out and her face was white. I saw that I must manage better next time and I did. I hung about the lane at the rear of the house and watched through cracks in the fence until I was convinced that the conditions were favorable. Then I slipped through the back yard and up the back way and got into the room and into the bed with Will Bowen without being observed. I don't know how long I was in the bed. I only remember that Will Bowen, as society, had no value for me, for he was too sick to even notice that

I was there. When I heard his mother coming I covered up
my head, but that device was a failure. It was dead summertime—the cover was nothing more than a limp blanket or sheet,
and anybody could see that there were two of us under it. It
didn't remain two very long. Mrs. Bowen snatched me out
of that bed and conducted me home herself, with a grip on
my collar which she never loosened until she delivered me
into my mother's hands along with her opinion of that kind
of a boy.

It was a good case of measles that resulted. It brought me
within a shade of death's door. It brought me to where I no
longer felt any interest in anything, but, on the contrary, felt
a total absence of interest—which was most placid and tranquil
and sweet and delightful and enchanting. I have never enjoyed anything in my life any more than I enjoyed dying that
time. I was, in effect, dying. The word had been passed and
the family notified to assemble around the bed and see me
off. I knew them all. There was no doubtfulness in my vision.
They were all crying, but that did not affect me. I took but
the vaguest interest in it and that merely because I was the
center of all this emotional attention and was gratified by it
and vain of it.

When Doctor Cunningham had made up his mind that
nothing more could be done for me he put bags of hot ashes
all over me. He put them on my breast, on my wrists, on my
ankles; and so, very much to his astonishment—and doubtless
to my regret—he dragged me back into this world and set me
going again.

◇◇◇◇◇◇◇◇◇◇◇◇◇◇◇◇◇◇◇

CHAPTER 16

One day recently[1] a chance remark called to my mind an early
sweetheart of mine and I fell to talking about her. I hadn't
seen her for forty-eight years; but no matter, I found that I
remembered her quite vividly and that she possessed a lively
interest for me notwithstanding that prodigious interval of
time that had spread its vacancy between her and me. She
wasn't yet fifteen when I knew her. It was in the summertime

[1] Written July 30, 1906.

and she had gone down the Mississippi from St. Louis to New Orleans as guest of a relative of hers who was a pilot on the *John J. Roe*, a steamboat whose officers I knew very well, as I had served a term as steersman in that boat's pilothouse. She was a freighter. She was not licensed to carry passengers but she always had a dozen on board and they were privileged to be there because they were not registered; they paid no fare; they were guests of the Captain and nobody was responsible for them if anything of a fatal nature happened to them.

It was a delightful old tug and she had a very spacious boiler-deck—just the place for moonlight dancing and daylight frolics, and such things were always happening. She was a charmingly leisurely boat and the slowest one on the planet. Up-stream she couldn't even beat an island; down-stream she was never able to overtake the current. But she was a love of a steamboat. Mark Leavenworth, her captain, was a giant, and hospitable and good-natured, which is the way of giants. Zeb, his brother, was another giant, possessed of the same qualities, and of a laugh which could be heard from Vicksburg to Nebraska. He was one of the pilots and Beck Jolly was another.

Jolly was very handsome, very graceful, very intelligent, companionable—a fine character—and he had the manners of a duke. If that is too strong I will say a viscount. Beck Jolly was a beautiful creature to look at. But it's different now. I saw him four years ago and he had white hair, and not much of it; two sets of cheeks; a cataract of chins; and by and large he looked like a gasometer.

The clerks, the mates, the chief steward and all officials, big and little, of the *John J. Roe*, were simple-hearted folk and overflowing with good-fellowship and the milk of human kindness. They had all been reared on farms in the interior of Indiana and they had brought the simple farm ways and farm spirit to that steamboat and had domesticated it there. When she was on a voyage there was nothing in her to suggest a steamboat. One didn't seem to be on board a steamboat at all. He was floating around on a farm. Nothing in this world pleasanter than this can be imagined.

At the time I speak of I had fallen out of the heaven of the *John J. Roe* and was steering for Brown, on the swift passenger packet, the *Pennsylvania*, a boat which presently blew up and killed my brother Henry. On a memorable trip, the

Pennsylvania arrived at New Orleans, and when she was berthed I discovered that her stern lapped the fo'castle of the *John J. Roe*. I went aft, climbed over the rail of the ladies' cabin and from that point jumped aboard the *Roe*, landing on that spacious boiler-deck of hers. It was like arriving at home at the farmhouse after a long absence. It was the same delight to me to meet and shake hands with the Leavenworths and the rest of that dear family of steamboating backwoodsmen and hayseeds as if they had all been blood kin to me. As usual, there were a dozen passengers, male and female, young and old; and as usual they were of the hearty and likeable sort affected by the *John J. Roe* farmers. Now, out of their midst, floating upon my enchanted vision, came that slip of a girl of whom I have spoken—that instantly elected sweetheart out of the remotenesses of interior Missouri—a frank and simple and winsome child who had never been away from home in her life before, and had brought with her to these distant regions the freshness and the fragrance of her own prairies.

I can state the rest, I think, in a very few words. I was not four inches from that girl's elbow during our waking hours for the next three days. Then there came a sudden interruption. Zeb Leavenworth came flying aft shouting, "The *Pennsylvania* is backing out." I fled at my best speed, and as I broke out upon that great boiler-deck the *Pennsylvania* was gliding sternward past it. I made a flying leap and just did manage to make the connection, and nothing to spare. My toes found room on the guard; my finger-ends hooked themselves upon the guard-rail, and a quartermaster made a snatch for me and hauled me aboard.

That comely child, that charming child, was Laura M. Wright, and I could see her with perfect distinctness in the unfaded bloom of her youth, with her plaited tails dangling from her young head and her white summer frock puffing about in the wind of that ancient Mississippi time—I could see all this with perfect distinctness when I was telling about it last Saturday. And I finished with the remark, "I never saw her afterward. It is now forty-eight years, one month and twenty-seven days since that parting, and no word has ever passed between us since."

I reached home from Fairhaven last Wednesday and found a letter from Laura Wright. It shook me to the foundations. The plaited tails fell away; the peachy young face vanished; the fluffy short frock along with it; and in the place of that carefree little girl of forty-eight years ago, I imagined the world-worn and trouble-worn widow of sixty-two. Laura's letter was an appeal to me for pecuniary help for herself and for her disabled son, who, as she incidentally mentioned, is thirty-seven years old. She is a school teacher. She is in need of a thousand dollars and I sent it.

It is an awful world—it is a fiendish world. When I knew that child her father was an honored Judge of a high court in the middle of Missouri and was a rich man, as riches were estimated in that day and region. What had that girl done, what crime had she committed that she must be punished with poverty and drudgery in her old age? However, let me get right away from this subject before I get warmed up and say indiscreet things— Be Jesus!

At last we have heard again from my long vanished little fourteen-year-old sweetheart of nearly fifty years ago.[2] It had begun to look very much as if we had lost her again. She was drifting about among old friends in Missouri and we couldn't get upon her track. We supposed that she had returned to her home in California, where she teaches school, and we sent the check there. It traveled around during two months and finally found her, three or four days ago, in Columbia, Missouri. She has written a charming letter and it is full of character. Because of the character exhibited, I find in her, once more at sixty-two, the little girl of fourteen of so long ago.

When she went back up the river, on board the *John J. Roe,* the boat struck a snag in the night and was apparently booked to find the bottom of the Mississippi in a few minutes. She was rushed to the shore and there was great excitement and much noise. Everybody was commanded to vacate the vessel instantly. This was done; at least for the moment no one seemed to be missing. Then Youngblood, one of the pilots, discovered that his little niece was not among the rescued. He and old Davis, the mate, rushed aboard the sinking boat and hammered on Laura's door, which they found locked, and shouted to her to come out—that there was not a moment to lose.

She replied quite calmly that there was something the matter with her hoop skirt, and she couldn't come yet. They said,

[2] Written August 31, 1906.

"Never mind the hoop skirt. Come without it. There is no time to waste upon trifles."

But she answered, just as calmly, that she wasn't going to come until the skirt was repaired and she was in it. She kept her word and came ashore at her leisure, completely dressed.

I was thinking of this when I was reading her letter this morning, and the thought carried me so far back into the hoary past that for the moment I was living it over again and was again a heedless and giddy lad, with all the vast intervening stretch of years abolished—and along with it my present condition and my white head. And so, when I presently came upon the following passage in her letter it hit me with an astonishing surprise and seemed to be referring to somebody else:

> But I must not weary you nor take up your valuable time with my chatter. I really forget that I am writing to one of the world's most famous and sought-after men, which shows you that I am still roaming in the Forest of Arden.

And so I am a hero to Laura Wright! It is wholly unthinkable. One can be a hero to other folk, and in a sort of vague way understand it, or at least believe it, but that a person can really be a hero to a near and familiar friend is a thing which no hero has ever yet been able to realize, I am sure.

She has been visiting the Youngbloods. It revives in me some ancient and tragic memories. Youngblood was as fine a man as I have known. In that day he was young and had a young wife and two small children—a most happy and contented family. He was a good pilot and he fully appreciated the responsibilities of that great position. Once when a passenger boat upon which he was standing a pilot's watch was burned on the Mississippi, he landed the boat and stood to his post at the wheel until everybody was ashore and the entire after part of the boat, including the after part of the pilot-house, was a mass of flame; then he climbed out over the breast-board and escaped with his life, though badly scorched and blistered by the fire. A year or two later, in New Orleans, he went out one night to do an errand for the family and was never heard of again. It was supposed that he was murdered and that was doubtless the case, but the matter remains a mystery yet.

That old mate, Davis, was a very interesting man. He was past sixty, and his bush of hair and whiskers would have been white if he had allowed them to have their own way, but he didn't. He dyed them, and as he only dyed them four times a year he was generally a curious spectacle. When the process was successful his hair and whiskers were sometimes a bright and attractive green; at other times they were a deep and agreeable purple; at still other times they would grow out and expose half an inch of white hair. Then the effect was striking, particularly as regards his whiskers, because in certain lights the belt of white hair next to his face would become nearly invisible; then his brush of whiskers did not seem to be connected with his face at all, but quite separated from it and independent of it. Being a chief mate, he was a prodigious and competent swearer, a thing which the office requires. But he had an auxiliary vocabulary which no other mate on the river possessed and it made him able to persuade indolent roustabouts more effectively than did the swearing of any other mate in the business, because while it was not profane it was of so mysterious and formidable and terrifying a nature that it sounded five or six times as profane as any language to be found on the fo'castle anywhere in the river service.

Davis had no education beyond reading and something which so nearly resembled writing that it was reasonably well calculated to deceive. He read, and he read a great deal, and diligently, but his whole library consisted of a single book. It was Lyell's Geology, and he had stuck to it until all its grim and rugged scientific terminology was familiar in his mouth, though he hadn't the least idea of what the words meant, and didn't care what they meant. All he wanted out of those great words was the energy they stirred up in his roustabouts. In times of extreme emergency he would let fly a volcanic irruption of the old regular orthodox profanity mixed up and seasoned all through with imposing geological terms, then formally charge his roustabouts with being Old Silurian Invertebrates out of the Incandescent Anisodactylous Post-Pliocene Period, and damn the whole gang in a body to perdition.

CHAPTER 17

I was educated not only in the common school at Hannibal but also in my brother Orion's newspaper office, where I served in all capacities, including staff work. My literature attracted the town's attention "but not its admiration" (my brother's testimony).

Orion Clemens was born in Jamestown, Tennessee, in 1825. He was the family's first-born. Between him and me came a sister, Margaret, who died aged nine in 1839 in that village of Florida, Missouri, where I was born; and Pamela, mother of Samuel E. Moffett, who was an invalid all her life and died in the neighborhood of New York a year ago,[1] aged about seventy-five. Also there was a brother, Benjamin, who died in 1842, aged ten.

Orion's boyhood was spent in that wee little log hamlet of Jamestown up there among the knobs—so called—of East Tennessee, among a very sparse population of primitives who were as ignorant of the outside world and as unconscious of it as the other wild animals were that inhabited the forest around. The family migrated to Florida, then moved to Hannibal when Orion was ten years old. When he was fifteen or sixteen he was sent to St. Louis and there he learned the printer's trade. One of his characteristics was eagerness. He woke with an eagerness about some matter or other every morning; it consumed him all day; it perished in the night and he was on fire with a fresh new interest next morning before he could get his clothes on. He exploited in this way three hundred and sixty-five red-hot new eagernesses every year of his life—until he died sitting at a table with a pen in his hand, in the early morning, jotting down the conflagration for that day and preparing to enjoy the fire and smoke of it until night should extinguish it. He was then seventy-two years old. But I am forgetting another characteristic, a very pronounced one. That was his deep glooms, his de-

[1] Written March 28, 1906.

spondencies, his despairs; these had their place in each and every day along with the eagernesses. Thus his day was divided—no, not divided, mottled—from sunrise to midnight with alternating brilliant sunshine and black cloud. Every day he was the most joyous and hopeful man that ever was, I think, and also every day he was the most miserable man that ever was.

While he was in his apprenticeship in St. Louis he got well acquainted with Edward Bates, who was afterward in Mr. Lincoln's first Cabinet. Bates was a very fine man, an honorable and upright man, and a distinguished lawyer. He patiently allowed Orion to bring to him each new project; he discussed it with him and extinguished it by argument and irresistible logic—at first. But after a few weeks he found that this labor was not necessary; that he could leave the new project alone and it would extinguish itself the same night. Orion thought he would like to become a lawyer. Mr. Bates encouraged him, and he studied law nearly a week, then of course laid it aside to try something new. He wanted to become an orator. Mr. Bates gave him lessons. Mr. Bates walked the floor reading from an English book aloud and rapidly turning the English into French, and he recommended this exercise to Orion. But as Orion knew no French, he took up that study and wrought at it with enthusiasm two or three days; then gave it up.

During his apprenticeship in St. Louis he joined a number of churches, one after another, and taught in the Sunday schools—changing his Sunday school every time he changed his religion. He was correspondingly erratic in his politics— Whig today, Democrat next week, and anything fresh that he could find in the political market the week after. I may remark here that throughout his long life he was always trading religions and enjoying the change of scenery. I will also remark that his sincerity was never doubted; his truthfulness was never doubted; and in matters of business and money his honesty was never questioned. Notwithstanding his forever-recurring caprices and changes, his principles were high, always high, and absolutely unshakable. He was the strangest compound that ever got mixed in a human mold. Such a person as that is given to acting upon impulse and without reflection; that was Orion's way. Everything he did he did with conviction and enthusiasm and with a vainglorious pride in the thing he was doing—and no matter what that thing was, whether good, bad or indifferent, he repented of it every time in sackcloth and ashes before twenty-four hours had sped. Pessimists are born, not made. Optimists are born, not made. But I think he was the only person I have ever known in whom pessimism and optimism were lodged in exactly equal proportions. Except in the matter of grounded principle, he was as unstable as water. You could dash his spirits with a single word; you could raise them into the sky again with another one. You could break his heart with a word of disapproval; you could make him as happy as an angel with a word of approval. And there was no occasion to put any sense or any vestige of mentality of any kind into these miracles; anything you might say would answer.

He had another conspicuous characteristic and it was the father of those which I have just spoken of. This was an intense lust for approval. He was so eager to be approved, so girlishly anxious to be approved by anybody and everybody, without discrimination, that he was commonly ready to forsake his notions, opinions and convictions at a moment's notice in order to get the approval of any person who disagreed with them. I wish to be understood as reserving his fundamental principles all the time. He never forsook those to please anybody. Born and reared among slaves and slaveholders, he was yet an abolitionist from his boyhood to his death. He was always truthful; he was always sincere; he was always honest and honorable. But in light matters—matters of small consequence, like religion and politics and such things—he never acquired a conviction that could survive a disapproving remark from a cat.

He was always dreaming; he was a dreamer from birth and this characteristic got him into trouble now and then. Once when he was twenty-three or twenty-four years old and was become a journeyman he conceived the romantic idea of coming to Hannibal without giving us notice, in order that he might furnish to the family a pleasant surprise. If he had given notice he would have been informed that we had changed our residence and that that gruff old bass-voiced sailorman, Doctor Meredith, our family physician, was living in the house which we had formerly occupied and that Orion's former room in that house was now occupied by Doctor Meredith's two ripe old-maid sisters. Orion arrived at Hannibal per steamboat in the middle of the night and started with his customary eagerness on his excursion, his mind all on fire

with his romantic project and building and enjoying his surprise in advance. He was always enjoying things in advance;
it was the make of him. He never could wait for the event,
but he must build it out of dream-stuff and enjoy it beforehand—consequently sometimes when the event happened he
saw that it was not as good as the one he had invented in
his imagination and so he had lost profit by not keeping the
imaginary one and letting the reality go.

When he arrived at the house he went around to the back
door and slipped off his boots and crept upstairs and arrived
at the room of those old maids without having wakened any
sleepers. He undressed in the dark and got into bed and
snuggled up against somebody. He was a little surprised, but
not much, for he thought it was our brother Ben. It was winter
and the bed was comfortable and the supposed Ben added to
the comfort—and so he was dropping off to sleep very well
satisfied with his progress so far and full of happy dreams of
what was going to happen in the morning. But something
else was going to happen sooner than that, and it happened
now. The old maid that was being crowded squirmed and
struggled and presently came to a half-waking condition and
protested against the crowding. That voice paralyzed Orion.
He couldn't move a limb; he couldn't get his breath; and
the crowded one began to paw around, found Orion's new
whiskers, and screamed, "Why, it's a man!" This removed the
paralysis, and Orion was out of the bed and clawing around
in the dark for his clothes in a fraction of a second. Both
maids began to scream, so Orion did not wait to get his
whole outfit. He started with such parts of it as he could
grab. He flew to the head of the stairs and started down,
and he was paralyzed again at that point, because he saw
the faint yellow flame of a candle soaring up the stairs from
below and he judged that Doctor Meredith was behind it,
and he was. He had no clothes on to speak of, but no matter,
he was well enough fixed for an occasion like this, because
he had a butcher knife in his hand. Orion shouted to him and
this saved his life, for the doctor recognized his voice. Then,
in those deep sea-going bass tones of his that I used to admire so much when I was a little boy, he explained to Orion
the change that had been made, told him where to find the
Clemens family, and closed with some quite unnecessary
advice about posting himself before he undertook another

adventure like that—advice which Orion probably never needed again as long as he lived.

CHAPTER 18

When my father died, in 1847, the disaster happened—as is the customary way with such things—just at the very moment when our fortunes had changed and we were about to be comfortable once more after several years of grinding poverty and privation which had been inflicted upon us by the dishonest act of one Ira Stout, to whom my father had lent several thousand dollars—a fortune in those days and in that region. My father had just been elected clerk of the Surrogate Court. This modest prosperity was not only quite sufficient for us and for our ambitions, but he was so esteemed —held in such high regard and honor throughout the county— that his occupancy of that dignified office would, in the opinion of everybody, be his possession as long as he might live. He went to Palmyra, the county-seat, to be sworn in about the end of February. In returning home horseback twelve miles a storm of sleet and rain assailed him and he arrived at the house in a half-frozen condition. Pleurisy followed and he died on the 24th of March.

Thus our splendid new fortune was snatched from us and we were in the depths of poverty again. It is the way such things are accustomed to happen. The Clemens family was penniless again.

Orion did not come to Hannibal until two or three years after my father's death. He remained in St. Louis. He was a journeyman printer and earning wages. Out of his wage he supported my mother and my brother Henry, who was two years younger than I. My sister Pamela helped in this support by taking piano pupils. Thus we got along, but it was pretty hard sledding. I was not one of the burdens, because I was taken from school at once upon my father's death and placed in the office of the Hannibal *Courier* as printer's apprentice, and Mr. Ament, the editor and proprietor of the paper, allowed me the usual emolument of the office of apprentice— that is to say, board and clothes but no money. The clothes

consisted of two suits a year but one of the suits always failed
to materialize and the other suit was not purchased so long
as Mr. Ament's old clothes held out. I was only about half
as big as Ament, consequently his shirts gave me the uncomfortable sense of living in a circus tent, and I had to turn
up his pants to my ears to make them short enough.

There were two other apprentices. One was Wales McCor-
mick, seventeen or eighteen years old and a giant. When he
was in Ament's clothes they fitted him as the candle mold fits
the candle—thus he was generally in a suffocated condition,
particularly in the summertime. He was a reckless, hilarious,
admirable creature; he had no principles and was delightful
company. At first we three apprentices had to feed in the
kitchen with the old slave cook and her very handsome and
bright and well-behaved young mulatto daughter. For
his own amusement—for he was not generally laboring for
other people's amusement—Wales was constantly and persistently and loudly and elaborately making love to that
mulatto girl and distressing the life out of her and worrying
the old mother to death. She would say, "Now, Marse Wales,
Marse Wales, can't you behave yourself?" With encouragement like that, Wales would naturally renew his attentions
and emphasize them. It was killingly funny to Ralph and me.
And, to speak truly, the old mother's distress about it was
merely a pretense. She quite well understood that by the
customs of slaveholding communities it was Wales's right to
make love to that girl if he wanted to. But the girl's distress
was very real. She had a refined nature and she took all
Wales's extravagant love-making in earnest.

We got but little variety in the way of food at that kitchen
table and there wasn't enough of it anyway. So we apprentices
used to keep alive by arts of our own—that is to say, we crept
into the cellar nearly every night by a private entrance which
we had discovered and we robbed the cellar of potatoes and
onions and such things and carried them downtown to the
printing-office, where we slept on pallets on the floor and
cooked them at the stove and had very good times. Wales
had a secret of cooking a potato which was noble and wonderful and all his own. Since Wales's day I have seen a potato
cooked in that way only once. It was when Wilhelm II,
Emperor of Germany, commanded my presence at a private
feed toward the end of the year 1891. And when that potato
appeared on the table it surprised me out of my discretion and

made me commit the unforgivable sin, before I could get
a grip on my discretion again—that is to say, I made a joyful
exclamation of welcome over the potato, addressing my remark
to the Emperor at my side without waiting for him to take
the first innings. I think he honestly tried to pretend that he
was not shocked and outraged but he plainly was; and so
were the other half-dozen grandees who were present. They
were all petrified and nobody could have said a word if he
had tried. The ghastly silence endured for as much as half a
minute and would have lasted until now, of course, if the
Emperor hadn't broken it himself, for no one else there would
have ventured that. It was at half past six in the evening
and the frost did not get out of the atmosphere entirely until
close upon midnight, when it did finally melt away—or wash
away—under generous floods of beer.

As I have indicated, Mr. Ament's economies were of a
pretty close and rigid kind. By and by, when we apprentices
were promoted from the basement to the ground floor and
allowed to sit at the family table, along with the one journeyman, Pet MacMurray, the economies continued. Mrs. Ament
was a bride. She had attained to that distinction very recently,
after waiting a good part of a lifetime for it, and she was the
right woman in the right place, according to the Amentian
idea, for she did not trust the sugar bowl to us but sweetened
our coffee herself. That is, she went through the motions.
She didn't really sweeten it. She seemed to put one heaping
teaspoonful of brown sugar into each cup but, according to
Wales, that was a deceit. He said she dipped the spoon in
the coffee first to make the sugar stick and then scooped the
sugar out of the bowl with the spoon upside down, so that
the effect to the eye was a heaped-up spoon, whereas the
sugar on it was nothing but a layer. This all seems perfectly
true to me and yet that thing would be so difficult to perform
that I suppose it really didn't happen but was one of Wales's
lies.

I have said that Wales was reckless, and he was. It was the
recklessness of ever-bubbling and indestructible good spirits
flowing from the joy of youth. I think there wasn't anything
that that vast boy wouldn't do to procure five minutes' entertainment for himself. One never knew where he would
break out next. Among his shining characteristics was the most
limitless and adorable irreverence. There didn't seem to be

anything serious in life for him; there didn't seem to be anything that he revered.

Once the celebrated founder of the at that time new and widespread sect called Campbellites arrived in our village from Kentucky and it made a prodigious excitement. The farmers and their families drove or tramped into the village from miles around to get a sight of the illustrious Alexander Campbell and to have a chance to hear him preach. When he preached in a church many had to be disappointed, for there was no church that would begin to hold all the applicants; so in order to accommodate all, he preached in the open air in the public square and that was the first time in my life that I had realized what a mighty population this planet contains when you get them all together.

He preached a sermon on one of these occasions which he had written especially for that occasion. All the Campbellites wanted it printed, so that they could save it and read it over and over again and get it by heart. So they drummed up sixteen dollars, which was a large sum then, and for this great sum Mr. Ament contracted to print five hundred copies of that sermon and put them in yellow paper covers. It was a sixteen-page duodecimo pamphlet and it was a great event in our office. As we regarded it, it was a book, and it promoted us to the dignity of book printers. Moreover, no such mass of actual money as sixteen dollars, in one bunch, had ever entered that office on any previous occasion. People didn't pay for their paper and for their advertising in money; they paid in drygoods, sugar, coffee, hickory wood, oak wood, turnips, pumpkins, onions, watermelons—and it was very seldom indeed that a man paid in money, and when that happened we thought there was something the matter with him.

We set up the great book in pages—eight pages to a form—and by help of a printer's manual we managed to get the pages in their apparently crazy but really sane places on the imposing-stone. We printed that form on a Thursday. Then we set up the remaining eight pages, locked them into a form and struck a proof. Wales read the proof and presently was aghast, for he had struck a snag. And it was a bad time to strike a snag, because it was Saturday; it was approaching noon; Saturday afternoon was our holiday and we wanted to get away and go fishing. At such a time as this Wales struck that snag and showed us what had happened. He had

left out a couple of words in a thin-spaced page of solid
matter and there wasn't another breakline for two or three
pages ahead. What in the world was to be done? Overrun
all those pages in order to get in the two missing words?
Apparently there was no other way. It would take an hour
to do it. Then a revise must be sent to the great minister;
we must wait for him to read the revise; if he encountered
any errors we must correct them. It looked as if we might lose
half the afternoon before we could get away.

Then Wales had one of his brilliant ideas. In the line in
which the "out" had been made occurred the name Jesus
Christ. Wales reduced it in the French way to J. C. It made
room for the missing words but it took 99 per cent of the
solemnity out of a particularly solemn sentence. We sent off
the revise and waited. We were not intending to wait long.
In the circumstances we meant to get out and go fishing
before that revise should get back, but we were not speedy
enough. Presently that great Alexander Campbell appeared
at the far end of that sixty-foot room, and his countenance
cast a gloom over the whole place. He strode down to our end
and what he said was brief, but it was very stern and it was
to the point. He read Wales a lecture. He said, "So long as
you live, don't you ever diminish the Saviour's name again.
Put it *all* in." He repeated this admonition a couple of times
to emphasize it, then he went away.

In that day the common swearers of the region had a way
of their own of *emphasizing* the Saviour's name when they
were using it profanely and this fact intruded itself into
Wales's incorrigible mind. It offered him an opportunity for
a momentary entertainment which seemed to him to be more
precious and more valuable than even fishing and swimming
could afford. So he imposed upon himself the long and weary
and dreary task of overrunning all those three pages in order
to improve upon his former work and incidentally and thoughtfully improve upon the great preacher's admonition. He enlarged the offending J. C. into Jesus H. Christ. Wales knew
that that would make prodigious trouble and it did. But it was
not in him to resist it. He had to succumb to the law of his
make. I don't remember what his punishment was but he was
not the person to care for that. He had already collected his
dividend.

CHAPTER 19

It was during my first year's apprenticeship in the *Courier* office that I did a thing which I have been trying to regret for fifty-five years.[1] It was a summer afternoon and just the kind of weather that a boy prizes for river excursions and other frolics, but I was a prisoner. The others were all gone holidaying. I was alone and sad. I had committed a crime of some sort and this was the punishment. I must lose my holiday and spend the afternoon in solitude besides. I had the printing office all to myself, there in the third story. I had one comfort and it was a generous one while it lasted. It was the half of a long and broad watermelon, fresh and red and ripe. I gouged it out with a knife and I found accommodation for the whole of it in my person—though it did crowd me until the juice ran out of my ears. There remained then the shell, the hollow shell. It was big enough to do duty as a cradle. I didn't want to waste it and I couldn't think of anything to do with it which could afford entertainment. I was sitting at the open window which looked out upon the sidewalk of the main street three stories below, when it occurred to me to drop it on somebody's head. I doubted the judiciousness of this and I had some compunctions about it too, because so much of the resulting entertainment would fall to my share and so little to the other person's. But I thought I would chance it.

I watched out of the window for the right person to come along—the safe person—but he didn't come. Every time there was a candidate he or she turned out to be an unsafe one and I had to restrain myself. But at last I saw the right one coming. It was my brother Henry. He was the best boy in the whole region. He never did harm to anybody, he never offended anybody. He was exasperatingly good. He had an overflowing abundance of goodness—but not enough to save him this time. I watched his approach with eager interest.

[1] Written March 29, 1906.

He came strolling along, dreaming his pleasant summer dream and not doubting but that Providence had him in His care. If he had known where I was he would have had less confidence in that superstition. As he approached his form became more and more foreshortened. When he was almost under me he was so foreshortened that nothing of him was visible from my high place except the end of his nose and his alternately approaching feet. Then I poised the watermelon, calculated my distance and let it go, hollow side down.

The accuracy of that gunnery was beyond admiration. He had about six steps to make when I let that canoe go and it was lovely to see those two bodies gradually closing in on each other. If he had had seven steps to make or five steps to make my gunnery would have been a failure. But he had exactly the right number to make and that shell smashed down right on the top of his head and drove him into the earth up to the chin, the chunks of that broken melon flying in every direction like a spray. I wanted to go down there and condole with him but it would not have been safe. He would have suspected me at once. I expected him to suspect me, anyway, but as he said nothing about this adventure for two or three days—I was watching him in the meantime in order to keep out of danger—I was deceived into believing that this time he didn't suspect me.

It was a mistake. He was only waiting for a sure opportunity. Then he landed a cobblestone on the side of my head which raised a bump there so large that I had to wear two hats for a time. I carried this crime to my mother, for I was always anxious to get Henry into trouble with her and could never succeed. I thought that I had a sure case this time when she should come to see that murderous bump. I showed it to her but she said it was no matter. She didn't need to inquire into the circumstances. She knew I had deserved it, and the best way would be for me to accept it as a valuable lesson and thereby get profit out of it.

About 1849 or 1850 Orion severed his connection with the printing house in St. Louis and came up to Hannibal and bought a weekly paper called the Hannibal *Journal*, together with its plant and its good will, for the sum of five hundred dollars cash. He borrowed the cash at ten per cent interest from an old farmer named Johnson who lived five miles out of town. Then he reduced the subscription price of the paper from two dollars to one dollar. He reduced the rates for advertising in about the same proportion and thus he created one absolute and unassailable certainty—to wit: that the business would never pay him a single cent of profit.

He took me out of the *Courier* office and engaged my services in his own at three dollars and a half a week, which was an extravagant wage, but Orion was always generous, always liberal with everybody except himself. It cost him nothing in my case, for he never was able to pay me a single penny as long as I was with him. By the end of the first year he found he must make some economies. The office rent was cheap but it was not cheap enough. He could not afford to pay rent of any kind, so he moved the whole plant into the house we lived in, and it cramped the dwelling place cruelly. He kept that paper alive during four years but I have at this time no idea how he accomplished it. Toward the end of each year he had to turn out and scrape and scratch for the fifty dollars of interest due Mr. Johnson, and that fifty dollars was about the only cash he ever received or paid out, I suppose, while he was proprietor of that newspaper, except for ink and printing paper. The paper was a dead failure. It had to be that from the start.

Finally he handed it over to Mr. Johnson and went up to Muscatine, Iowa, and acquired a small interest in a weekly newspaper there. It was not a sort of property to marry on—but no matter. He came across a winning and pretty girl who lived in Quincy, Illinois, a few miles below Keokuk, and they became engaged. He was always falling in love with girls but by some accident or other he had never gone so far as engagement before. And now he achieved nothing but misfortune by it, because he straightway fell in love with a Keokuk girl—at least he imagined that he was in love with her, whereas I think she did the imagining for him. The first thing he knew he was engaged to her; and he was in a great quandary. He didn't know whether to marry the Keokuk one or the Quincy one, or whether to try to marry both of them and suit every one concerned. But the Keokuk girl soon settled that for him. She was a master spirit and she ordered him to the write the Quincy girl and break off that match, which he did. Then he married the Keokuk girl and they began a struggle for life which turned out to be a difficult enterprise and very unpromising.

To gain a living in Muscatine was plainly impossible, so Orion and his new wife went to Keokuk to live, for she wanted to be near her relatives. He bought a little bit of a job-printing plant—on credit, of course—and at once put prices down to where not even the apprentices could get a living out of it, and this sort of thing went on.

I had not joined the Muscatine migration. Just before that happened (which I think was in 1853) I disappeared one night and fled to St. Louis. There I worked in the composing room of the *Evening News* for a time and then started on my travels to see the world. The world was New York City and there was a little World's Fair there. It had just been opened where the great reservoir afterward was and where the sumptuous public library is now being built[2]—Fifth Avenue and 42d Street. I arrived in New York with two or three dollars in pocket change and a ten-dollar bank bill concealed in the lining of my coat. I got work at villainous wages in the establishment of John A. Gray & Green in Cliff Street and I found board in a sufficiently villainous mechanics' boardinghouse in Duane Street. The firm paid my wages in wildcat money at its face value, and my week's wage merely sufficed to pay board and lodging. By and by I went to Philadelphia and worked there some months as a "sub" on the *Inquirer* and the *Public Ledger*. Finally I made a flying trip to Washington to see the sights there, and in 1854 I went back to the Mississippi Valley, sitting upright in the smoking car two or three days and nights. When I reached St. Louis I was exhausted. I went to bed on board a steamboat that was bound for Muscatine. I fell asleep at once, with my clothes on, and didn't wake again for thirty-six hours.

I worked in that little job office in Keokuk as much as two years, I should say, without ever collecting a cent of wages, for Orion was never able to pay anything—but Dick Higham and I had good times. I don't know what Dick got, but it was probably only uncashable promises.

One day in the midwinter of 1856 or 1857—I think it was 1856—I was coming along the main street of Keokuk in the middle of the forenoon. It was bitter weather—so bitter that that street was deserted, almost. A light dry snow was blowing here and there on the ground and on the pavement, swirling this way and that way and making all sorts of beautiful figures, but very chilly to look at. The wind blew

2 Written in 1906.

a piece of paper past me and it lodged against a wall of a house. Something about the look of it attracted my attention and I gathered it in. It was a fifty-dollar bill, the only one I had ever seen, and the largest assemblage of money I had ever seen in one spot. I advertised it in the papers and suffered more than a thousand dollars' worth of solicitude and fear and distress during the next few days lest the owner should see the advertisement and come and take my fortune away. As many as four days went by without an applicant; then I could endure this kind of misery no longer. I felt sure that another four could not go by in this safe and secure way. I felt that I must take that money out of danger. So I bought a ticket for Cincinnati and went to that city. I worked there several months in the printing office of Wrightson & Company.

Our boardinghouse crew was made up of commonplace people of various ages and both sexes. They were full of bustle, frivolity, chatter and the joy of life and were good-natured, clean-minded and well-meaning; but they were oppressively uninteresting, for all that—with one exception. This was Macfarlane, a Scotchman. He was forty years old—just double my age—but we were opposite in most ways and comrades from the start. I always spent my evenings by the wood fire in his room, listening in comfort to his tireless talk and to the dulled complainings of the winter storms until the clock struck ten. At that hour he grilled a smoked herring, after the fashion of an earlier friend in Philadelphia, the Englishman Sumner. His herring was his nightcap and my signal to go.

He was six feet high and rather lank, a serious and sincere man. He had no humor, nor any comprehension of it. He had a sort of smile, whose office was to express his good nature, but if I ever heard him laugh, the memory of it is gone from me. He was intimate with no one in the house but me, though he was courteous and pleasant with all. He had two or three dozen weighty books—philosophies, histories and scientific works—and at the head of this procession were his Bible and his dictionary. After his herring he always read two or three hours in bed.

Diligent talker as he was, he seldom said anything about himself. To ask him a personal question gave him no offense —nor the asker any information; he merely turned the matter aside and flowed placidly on about other things. He told me once that he had had hardly any schooling and that such learning as he had, he had picked up for himself. That was his sole biographical revelation, I believe. Whether he was bachelor, widower or grass widower remained his own secret. His clothes were cheap but neat and caretakingly preserved. Ours was a cheap boardinghouse; he left the house at six, mornings, and returned to it toward six, evenings; his hands were not soft, so I reasoned that he worked at some mechanical calling ten hours a day for humble wages—but I never knew. As a rule, technicalities of a man's vocation and figures and metaphors drawn from it slip out in his talk and reveal his trade; but if this ever happened in Macfarlane's case I was none the wiser, although I was constantly on the watch during half a year for those very betrayals. It was mere curiosity, for I didn't care what his trade was, but I wanted to detect it in true detective fashion and was annoyed because I couldn't do it. I think he was a remarkable man to be able to keep the shop out of his talk all that time.

There was another noteworthy feature about him: he seemed to know his dictionary from beginning to end. He claimed that he did. He was frankly proud of this accomplishment and said I would not find it possible to challenge him with an English word which he could not promptly spell and define. I lost much time trying to hunt up a word which would beat him but those weeks were spent in vain and I finally gave it up; which made him so proud and happy that I wished I had surrendered earlier.

He seemed to be as familiar with his Bible as he was with his dictionary. It was easy to see that he considered himself a philosopher and a thinker. His talk always ran upon grave and large questions; and I must do him the justice to say that his heart and conscience were in his talk and that there was no appearance of reasoning and arguing for the vain pleasure of hearing himself do it.

Of course his thinking and reasoning and philosophizings were those of a but partly taught and wholly untrained mind, yet he hit by accident upon some curious and striking things. For instance. The time was the early part of 1856—fourteen or fifteen years before Mr. Darwin's *Descent of Man* startled the world—yet here was Macfarlane talking the same idea to me, there in the boardinghouse in Cincinnati.

The same general idea, but with a difference. Macfarlane considered that the animal life in the world was developed in the course of æons of time from a few microscopic seed germs, or perhaps *one* microscopic seed germ deposited upon the globe by the Creator in the dawn of time, and that this development was progressive upon an ascending scale toward ultimate perfection until *man* was reached; and that then the progressive scheme broke pitifully down and went to wreck and ruin!

He said that man's heart was the only bad heart in the animal kingdom; that man was the only animal capable of feeling malice, envy, vindictiveness, revengefulness, hatred, selfishness, the only animal that loved drunkenness, almost the only animal that could endure personal uncleanliness and a filthy habitation, the sole animal in whom was fully developed the base instinct called *patriotism*, the sole animal that robs, persecutes, oppresses and kills members of his own immediate tribe, the sole animal that steals and enslaves the members of any *tribe*.

He claimed that man's intellect was a brutal addition to him and degraded him to a rank far below the plane of the other animals, and that there was never a man who did not use his intellect daily all his life to advantage himself at other people's expense. The divinest divine reduced his domestics to humble servitude under him by advantage of his superior intellect, and those servants in turn were above a still lower grade of people by force of brains that were still a little better than theirs.

◇◇◇◇◇◇◇◇◇◇◇◇◇◇◇◇◇◇

CHAPTER 20

I had been reading Lieutenant Herndon's account of his explorations of the Amazon and had been mightily attracted by what he said of coca. I made up my mind that I would go to the headwaters of the Amazon and collect coca and trade in it and make a fortune. I left for New Orleans in the steamer *Paul Jones* with this great idea filling my mind. One of the pilots of that boat was Horace Bixby. Little by little I got acquainted with him and pretty soon I was doing a lot of steering for him in his daylight watches. When I got to New Orleans I inquired about ships leaving for Pará and discovered that there weren't any and learned that there probably wouldn't be any during that century. It had not occurred to me to inquire about these particulars before leaving Cincinnati, so there I was. I couldn't get to the Amazon. I had no friends in New Orleans and no money to speak of. I went to Horace Bixby and asked him to make a pilot out of me. He said he would do it for five hundred dollars, one hundred dollars cash in advance. So I steered for him up to St. Louis, borrowed the money from my brother-in-law, and closed the bargain. I had acquired this brother-in-law several years before. This was Mr. William A. Moffett, a merchant, a Virginian—a fine man in every way. He had married my sister Pamela. Within eighteen months I was become a competent pilot, and I served that office until the Mississippi River traffic was brought to a standstill by the breaking out of the Civil War.

In 1858 I was a steersman on board the swift and popular New Orleans and St. Louis packet, *Pennsylvania*, Captain Kleinfelter. I had been lent to Mr. Brown, one of the pilots of the *Pennsylvania*, by my owner, Mr. Bixby, and I had been steering for Brown about eighteen months, I think. Then in the early days of May, 1858, came a tragic trip—the last trip of that fleet and famous steamboat. I have told all about it in one of my books, called *Life on the Mississippi*. But it is not likely that I told the dream in that book. It is impossible that I can have published it, I think, because I never wanted my mother to know about that dream, and she lived several years after I published that volume.

I had found a place on the *Pennsylvania* for my brother Henry. It was not a place of profit, it was only a place of promise. He was "mud" clerk. Mud clerks received no salary but they were in the line of promotion. They could become, presently, third clerk and second clerk, then chief clerk—that is to say, purser. The dream begins when Henry had been mud clerk about three months. We were lying in port at St. Louis. Pilots and steersmen had nothing to do during the three days that the boat lay in port in St. Louis and New Orleans, but the mud clerk had to begin his labors at dawn and continue them into the night by the light of pineknot torches. Henry and I, moneyless and unsalaried, had billeted ourselves upon our brother-in-law, Mr. Moffett, as night lodgers while in port. We took our meals on board the boat. No, I mean *I* lodged at the house, not Henry. He spent the *evenings* at the house, from nine until eleven, then went to the boat to be ready for his early duties.

On the night of the dream he started away at eleven, shaking hands with the family, and said good-by according to custom. I may mention that handshaking as a good-by was not merely the custom of that family but the custom of the region—the custom of Missouri, I may say. In all my life up to that time I had never seen one member of the Clemens family kiss another one—except once. When my father lay dying in our home in Hannibal he put his arm around my sister's neck and drew her down and kissed her, saying, "Let me die." I remember that, and I remember the death rattle which swiftly followed those words, which were his last. These good-bys were always executed in the family sitting room on the second floor, and Henry went from that room and downstairs without further ceremony. But this time my mother went with him to the head of the stairs and said good-by again. As I remember it, she was moved to this by something in Henry's manner and she remained at the head of the stairs while he descended. When he reached the door he hesitated and climbed the stairs and shook hands good-by again.

In the morning, when I awoke, I had been dreaming, and the dream was so vivid, so like reality, that it deceived me and I thought it *was* real. In the dream I had seen Henry a corpse. He lay in a metallic burial case. He was dressed in a suit of my clothing and on his breast lay a great bouquet of flowers, mainly white roses, with a red rose in the center. The casket stood upon a couple of chairs. I dressed and moved toward that door, thinking I would go in there and look at it, but I changed my mind. I thought I could not yet bear to meet my mother. I thought I would wait awhile and make some preparation for that ordeal. The house was in Locust Street, a little above Thirteenth, and I walked to Fourteenth and to the middle of the block beyond before it suddenly flashed upon me that there was nothing real about this—it was only a dream. I can still feel something of the grateful upheaval of joy of that moment and I can also still feel the remnant of doubt, the suspicion that maybe it was real after all. I returned to the house almost on a run, flew up the stairs two or three steps at a jump and rushed into that sitting room, and was made glad again, for there was no casket there.

We made the usual eventless trip to New Orleans—no, it was not eventless, for it was on the way down that I had the fight with Mr. Brown[1] which resulted in his requiring that I be left ashore at New Orleans. In New Orleans I always had a job. It was my privilege to watch the freight piles from seven in the evening until seven in the morning, and get three dollars for it. It was a three-night job and occurred every thirty-five days. Henry always joined my watch about nine in the evening, when his own duties were ended, and we often walked my rounds and chatted together until midnight. This time we were to part and so the night before the boat sailed I gave Henry some advice. I said: "In case of disaster to the boat, don't lose your head—leave that unwisdom to the passengers—they are competent—they'll attend to it. But you rush for the hurricane deck, and astern to the solitary lifeboat lashed aft the wheelhouse on the port side, and obey the mate's orders—thus you will be useful. When the boat is launched, give such help as you can in getting the women and children into it, and be sure you don't try to get into it yourself. It is summer weather, the river is only a mile wide as a rule, and you can swim ashore without any trouble." Two or three days afterward the boat's boilers exploded at Ship Island, below Memphis, early one morning —and what happened afterward I have already told in *Life on the Mississippi*. As related there, I followed the *Pennsylvania* about a day later on another boat, and we began to get news of the disaster at every port we touched at, and so by the time we reached Memphis we knew all about it.

I found Henry stretched upon a mattress on the floor of a great building, along with thirty or forty other scalded and wounded persons, and was promptly informed by some indiscreet person that he had inhaled steam, that his body was badly scalded and that he would live but a little while; also, I was told that the physicians and nurses were giving their whole attention to persons who had a chance of being saved. They were shorthanded in the matter of physicians and nurses, and Henry and such others as were considered to be fatally hurt were receiving only such attention as could be spared from time to time from the more urgent cases. But Doctor Peyton, a fine and large-hearted old physician of great reputation in the community, gave me his sympathy

---

[1] See *Life on the Mississippi*.

and took vigorous hold of the case and in about a week he had brought Henry around. He never committed himself with prognostications which might not materialize, but at eleven o'clock one night he told me that Henry was out of danger and would get well. Then he said, "At midnight these poor fellows lying here and there and all over this place will begin to mourn and mutter and lament and make outcries and if this commotion should disturb Henry it will be bad for him; therefore ask the physicians on watch to give him an eighth of a grain of morphine, but this is not to be done unless Henry shall show signs that he is being disturbed."

Oh, well, never mind the rest of it. The physicians on watch were young fellows hardly out of the medical college and they made a mistake—they had no way of measuring the eighth of a grain of morphine, so they guessed at it and gave him a vast quantity heaped on the end of a knife blade, and the fatal effects were soon apparent. I think he died about dawn, I don't remember as to that. He was carried to the dead-room and I went away for a while to a citizen's house and slept off some of my accumulated fatigue—and meantime something was happening. The coffins provided for the dead were of unpainted white pine, but in this instance some of the ladies of Memphis had made up a fund of sixty dollars and bought a metallic case, and when I came back and entered the dead-room Henry lay in that open case and he was dressed in a suit of my clothing. I recognized instantly that my dream of several weeks before was here exactly reproduced, so far as these details went—and I think I missed one detail, but that one was immediately supplied, for just then an elderly lady entered the place with a large bouquet consisting mainly of white roses, and in the center of it was a red rose and she laid it on his breast.

I don't believe that I ever had any doubts whatever concerning the salient points of the dream, for those points are of such a nature that they are *pictures*, and pictures can be remembered, when they are vivid, much better than one can remember remarks and uncreted facts. Although it has been so many years since I have told that dream, I can see those pictures now just as clearly defined as if they were before me in this room. I have not told the entire dream. There was a good deal more of it. I mean I have not told all that happened in the dream's fulfillment. After the incident in the deathroom I may mention one detail, and that is this.

When I arrived in St. Louis with the casket it was about eight o'clock in the morning, and I ran to my brother-in-law's place of business, hoping to find him there, but I missed him, for while I was on the way to his office he was on his way from the house to the boat. When I got back to the boat the casket was gone. He had had it conveyed out to his house. I hastened thither and when I arrived the men were just removing the casket from the vehicle to carry it upstairs. I stopped that procedure, for I did not want my mother to see the dead face, because one side of it was drawn and distorted by the effects of the opium. When I went upstairs there stood the two chairs which I had seen in my dream and if I had arrived there two or three minutes later the casket would have been resting upon those two chairs, just as in my dream of several weeks before.

◇◇◇◇◇◇◇◇◇◇◇◇◇◇◇◇◇◇◇◇

CHAPTER 21

I was in New Orleans when Louisiana went out of the Union, January 26, 1861, and I started North the next day. Every day on the trip a blockade was closed by the boat, and the batteries at Jefferson Barracks (below St. Louis) fired two shots through the chimneys the last night of the voyage. In June I joined the Confederates in Ralls County, Missouri, as a second lieutenant under General Tom Harris and came near having the distinction of being captured by Colonel Ulysses S. Grant. I resigned after two weeks' service in the field, explaining that I was "incapacitated by fatigue" through persistent retreating.

Meantime Orion had been sweating along with his little job office in Keokuk, and he and his wife were living with his wife's family—ostensibly as boarders but it is not likely that Orion was ever able to pay the board. On account of charging nothing for the work done in his job office he had almost nothing to do there. He was never able to get it through his head that work done on a profitless basis deteriorates and is presently not worth anything and that customers are obliged to go where they can get better work, even if they must pay better prices for it. He had plenty of time and he took up Blackstone again. He also put up a sign which offered his services to the public as a lawyer. He never got a case in those days, nor even an applicant, although he was quite willing to transact law business for nothing and furnish the stationery himself. He was always liberal that way.

Presently he moved to a wee little hamlet called Alexandria, two or three miles down the river, and he put up that sign there. He got no bites. He was by this time very hard aground. But by this time I was beginning to earn a wage of two hundred and fifty dollars a month as pilot and so I supported him thenceforth until 1861, when his ancient friend, Edward Bates, then a member of Mr. Lincoln's first Cabinet, got him the place of Secretary of the new Territory of Nevada, and Orion and I cleared for that country in the overland stagecoach, I paying the fares, which were pretty heavy, and carrying with me what money I had been able to save—this was eight hundred dollars, I should say—and it was all in silver coin and a good deal of a nuisance because of its weight. And we had another nuisance, which was an Unabridged Dictionary. It weighed about a thousand pounds and was a ruinous expense, because the stagecoach company charged for extra baggage by the ounce. We could have kept a family for a time on what that dictionary cost in the way of extra freight—and it wasn't a good dictionary, anyway—didn't have any modern words in it—only had obsolete ones that they used to use when Noah Webster was a child.

The government of the new Territory of Nevada was an interesting menagerie. Governor Nye was an old and seasoned politician from New York—politician, not statesman. He had white hair. He was in fine physical condition. He had a winningly friendly face and deep lustrous brown eyes that could talk as a native language the tongue of every feeling, every passion, every emotion. His eyes could outtalk his tongue and this is saying a good deal, for he was a very remarkable talker, both in private and on the stump. He was a shrewd man. He generally saw through surfaces and perceived what might be going on inside without being suspected of having an eye on the matter.

When grown-up persons indulge in practical jokes, the fact gauges them. They have lived narrow, obscure and ignorant lives and at full manhood they still retain and cherish a job lot of leftover standards and ideals that would have been discarded with their boyhood if they had then moved out into the world and a broader life. There were many practical jokers in the new Territory. I do not take pleasure in exposing this fact, for I liked those people; but what I am saying is true. I wish I could say a kindlier thing about them instead. If I could say they were burglars or hatrack thieves or something like that, that wouldn't be utterly uncomplimentary. I would prefer it but I can't say those things. They would not be true. These people were practical jokers and I will not try to disguise it. In other respects they were plenty good enough people; honest people; reputable and likable. They played practical jokes upon each other with success and got the admiration and applause and also the envy of the rest of the community. Naturally they were eager to try their arts on big game and that was what the Governor was. But they were not able to score. They made several efforts but the Governor defeated these efforts without any trouble and went on smiling his pleasant smile as if nothing had happened. Finally the joker chiefs of Carson City and Virginia City conspired together to see if their combined talent couldn't win a victory, for the jokers were getting into a very uncomfortable place. The people were laughing at them, instead of at their proposed victim. They banded themselves together to the number of ten and invited the Governor to what was a most extraordinary attention in those days—pickled-oyster stew and champagne—luxuries very seldom seen in that region and existing rather as fabrics of the imagination than as facts.

The Governor took me with him. He said, disparagingly: "It's a poor invention. It doesn't deceive. Their idea is to get me drunk and leave me under the table and from their standpoint this will be very funny. But they don't know me. I am familiar with champagne and have no prejudices against it."

The fate of the joke was not decided until two o'clock in the morning. At that hour the Governor was serene, genial, comfortable, contented, happy and sober, although he was so full that he couldn't laugh without shedding champagne tears. Also, at that hour the last joker joined his comrades under the table, drunk to the last perfection. The Governor remarked: "This is a dry place, Sam. Let's go and get something to drink and go to bed."

The Governor's official menagerie had been drawn from the humblest ranks of his constituents at home—harmless good fellows who had helped in his campaigns, and now they had their reward in petty salaries payable in greenbacks that were worth next to nothing. Those boys had a hard time to make both ends meet. Orion's salary was eighteen hundred dollars a year and he couldn't even support his dictionary on it. But the Irishwoman who had come out on the Governor's staff charged the menagerie only ten dollars a week apiece for board and lodging. Orion and I were of her boarders and lodgers; and so, on these cheap terms the silver I had brought from home held out very well.

At first I roamed about the country seeking silver, but at the end of '62 or the beginning of '63 when I came up from Aurora to begin a journalistic life on the Virginia City *Enterprise* I was presently sent down to Carson City to report the legislative session. I wrote a weekly letter to the paper; it appeared Sundays, and on Mondays the legislative proceedings were obstructed by the complaints of members as a result. They rose to questions of privilege and answered the criticisms of the correspondent with bitterness, customarily describing him with elaborate and uncomplimentary phrases, for lack of a briefer way. To save their time, I presently began to sign the letters, using the Mississippi leadsman's call, "Mark Twain" (two fathoms—twelve feet) for this purpose.

Orion was soon very popular with the members of the legislature because they found that whereas they couldn't usually trust each other, nor anybody else, they could trust him. He easily held the belt for honesty in that country but it didn't do him any good in a pecuniary way because he had no talent for either persuading or scaring legislators. But I was differently situated. I was there every day in the legislature to distribute compliment and censure with evenly balanced justice and spread the same over half a page of the *Enterprise* every morning; consequently I was an influence. I got the legislature to pass a law requiring every corporation doing business in the territory to record its charter in full, without skipping a word, in a record to be kept by the Secretary of the Territory —my brother. All the charters were framed in exactly the same words. For this record service he was authorized to charge forty cents a folio of one hundred words for making the record; five dollars for furnishing a certificate of each record, and so on. Everybody had a toll-road franchise but no toll road. But the franchise had to be recorded and paid for. Everybody was a mining corporation and had to have himself recorded and pay for it. Very well, we prospered. The record service paid an average of one thousand dollars a month in gold.

Governor Nye was often absent from the Territory. He liked to run down to San Francisco every little while and enjoy a rest from Territorial civilization. Nobody complained, for he was prodigiously popular. He had been a stage driver in his early days in New York or New England and had acquired the habit of remembering names and faces and of making himself agreeable to his passengers. As a politician this had been valuable to him and he kept his arts in good condition by practice. By the time he had been Governor a year he had shaken hands with every human being in the Territory of Nevada, and after that he always knew these people instantly at sight and could call them by name. The whole population, of 20,000 persons, were his personal friends and he could do anything he chose to do and count upon their being contented with it. Whenever he was absent from the Territory —which was generally—Orion served his office in his place, as Acting Governor, a title which was soon and easily shortened to "Governor." Mrs. Governor Clemens enjoyed being a Governor's wife. No one on this planet ever enjoyed a distinction more than she enjoyed that one. Her delight in being the head of society was so frank that it disarmed criticism and even envy. Being the Governor's wife and head of society, she looked for a proper kind of house to live in—a house commensurate with these dignities—and she easily persuaded Orion to build that house. Orion could be persuaded to do anything. He built and furnished the house at a cost of twelve thousand dollars and there was no other house in that capital that could approach this property for style and cost.

When Governor Nye's four-year term was drawing to a close, the mystery of why he had ever consented to leave the great State of New York and help inhabit that sage-brush desert was solved. He had gone out there in order to become a United States Senator. All that was now necessary was to turn the Territory into a State. He did it without any difficulty. That patch of sand and that sparse population were not well fitted for the heavy burden of a State government but no matter, the people were willing to have the change and so the Governor's game was made.

Orion's game was made too, apparently, for he was as popular because of his honesty as the Governor was for more substantial reasons. But at the critical moment the inborn capriciousness of his character rose up without warning and disaster followed.

There were several candidates for all the offices in the gift of the new State of Nevada save two—United States Senator (Governor Nye) and Secretary of State (Orion Clemens). Nye was certain to get a Senatorship, and Orion was so sure to get the Secretaryship that no one but him was named for that office. But he was hit with one of his spasms of virtue on the very day that the Republican party was to make its nominations in the convention. Orion refused to go near the convention. He was urged but all persuasions failed. He said his presence there would be an unfair and improper influence and that if he was to be nominated the compliment must come to him as a free and unspotted gift. This attitude would have settled his case for him without further effort, but he had another spasm of virtue on the same day and that made it absolutely sure. It had been his habit for a great many years to change his religion with his shirt, and his ideas about temperance at the same time. He would be a teetotaler for a while and the champion of the cause; then he would change to the other side for a time. On nomination day he suddenly changed from a friendly attitude toward whisky—which was the popular attitude—to uncompromising teetotalism and went absolutely dry. His friends besought and implored but all in vain. He could not be persuaded to cross the threshold of a saloon. The paper next morning contained the list of chosen nominees. His name was not in it. He had not received a vote.

His rich income ceased when the State government came into power. He was without an occupation. Something had to be done. He put up his sign as attorney at law but he got no clients. It was strange. It was difficult to account for. I cannot account for it—but if I were going to guess at a solution I should guess that by the make of him he would examine both sides of a case so diligently and so conscientiously that when he got through with his argument neither he nor a jury would know which side he was on. I think that his client would find out his make in laying his case before him and would take warning and withdraw it in time to save himself from probable disaster.

◇◇◇◇◇◇◇◇◇◇◇◇◇◇◇◇◇◇◇◇

CHAPTER 22

This morning[1] arrives a letter from my ancient silver-mining comrade, Calvin H. Higbie, a man whom I had not seen nor had communication with for forty-four years. Higbie figures in a chapter of mine in *Roughing It*,[2] where the tale is told of how we discovered a rich blind lead in the Wide West Mine in Aurora—or, as we called that region then, Esmeralda—and how, instead of making our ownership of that exceedingly rich property permanent by doing ten days' work on it, as required by the mining laws, he went off on a wild-goose chase to hunt for the mysterious cement mine; and how I went off nine miles to Walker River to nurse Captain John Nye through a violent case of spasmodic rheumatism or blind staggers, or some malady of the kind; and how Cal and I came wandering back into Esmeralda one night just in time to be too late to save our fortune from the jumpers.

I will insert here this letter, and as it will not see the light until Higbie and I are in our graves I shall allow myself the privilege of copying his punctuation and his spelling, for to me they are a part of the man. He is as honest as the day is long. He is utterly simple-minded and straightforward and his spelling and his punctuation are as simple and honest as he is himself. He makes no apology for them and no apology is needed. They plainly state that he is not educated and they as plainly state that he makes no pretense to being educated.

> GREENVILLE, PLUMAS CO., CALIFORNIA
> *March 15—1906.*

SAML. L. CLEMENS.
 NEW YORK CITY, N.Y.
MY DEAR SIR—
 Two or three parties have ben after me to write up my recolections of Our associations in Nevada, in the early 60's and have come to the conclusion to do so, and have

---

[1] March 26, 1906.
[2] *Roughing It* is dedicated to Higbie.

ben jocting down incidents that came to mind, for several years. What I am in dout is, the date you came to Aurora, Nevada—allso, the first trip you made over thee Sieras to California, after coming to Nev. allso as near as possable date, you tended sick man, on, or near Walker River, when our mine was jumped, dont think for a moment that I intend to steal any of your Thunder, but onely to mention some instances that you failed to mention, in any of your articles, Books &c. that I ever saw. I intend to submit the articles to you so that you can see if anything is objectionabl, if so to erase, same, & add anything in its place you saw fit.

I was burned out a few years since, and all old data, went up in smoke, is the reason I ask for above dates. have ben sick more or less for 2 or 3 years, unable to earn anything to speak of, & the finances are getting pretty low, and I will admit that it is mainly for the purpose of Earning a little money, that my first attempt at writing will be made—and I should be so pleased to have your candid opinion, of its merits, and what in your wisdom in such matters, would be its value for publication. I enclose a coppy of Herald in answer to enquiry I made, if such an article was desired.

Hoping to hear from you as soon as convenient, I remain with great respect,

Yours &c
C. H. HIGBIE.

[Copy.]

New York, *Mar.* 6-'06

C. H. HIGBIE,
GREENVILLE—CAL.
DR SIR

I should be glad indeed to receive your account of your experiences with Mark Twain, if they are as interesting as I should imagine they would be the Herald would be quite willing to pay you verry well for them, of course, it would be impassible for me to set a price on the matter until I had an opertunity of examining it. if you will kindly send it on, with the privilege of our authenticating it through Mr. Clemens, I shall be more than pleased, to give you a quick decision and make you an offer as it seems worth to us. however, if you have any particular sum in mind which you think should be the price I would suggest that you communicate with me to that effect.

Yours truly
New York Herald,
By GEO. R. MINER.
Sunday Editor.

I have written Higbie and asked him to let me do his literary trading for him. He can shovel sand better than I can but I can beat him all to pieces in the art of fleecing a publisher.

I have allowed Higbie to assist the *Herald* man's spelling and make it harmonize with his own. He has done it well and liberally and without prejudice. To my mind he has improved it, for I have had an aversion to good spelling for sixty years and more, merely for the reason that when I was a boy there was not a thing I could do creditably except spell according to the book. It was a poor and mean distinction and I early learned to disenjoy it. I suppose that this is because the ability to spell correctly is a talent, not an acquirement. There is some dignity about an acquirement, because it is a product of your own labor. It is wages earned, whereas to be able to do a thing merely by the grace of God and not by your own effort transfers the distinction to our heavenly home—where possibly it is a matter of pride and satisfaction but it leaves you naked and bankrupt.

Higbie was the first person to profit by my great and infallible scheme for finding work for the unemployed. I have tried that scheme now and then for forty-four years. So far as I am aware it has always succeeded and it is one of my high prides that I invented it and that in basing it upon what I conceived to be a fact of human nature I estimated that fact of human nature accurately.

Higbie and I were living in a cotton-domestic lean-to at the base of a mountain. It was very cramped quarters, with barely room for us and the stove—wretched quarters, indeed, for every now and then, between eight in the morning and eight in the evening, the thermometer would make an excursion of fifty degrees. We had a silver-mining claim under the edge of a hill half a mile away in partnership with Bob Howland and Horatio Phillips, and we used to go there every morning, carrying with us our luncheon, and remain all day picking and blasting in our shaft, hoping, despairing, hoping again, and gradually but surely running out of funds. At last, when we were clear out and still had struck nothing, we saw that we must find some other way of earning a living. I secured a place in a nearby quartz mill to screen sand with a long-handled shovel. I hate a long-handled shovel. I never could learn to swing it properly. As often as any other way the sand didn't reach the screen at all but went over my head and down my back, inside of my clothes. It was the most detestable work I have ever engaged in but it paid ten dollars a week and board—and the board was worth while, because it consisted not only of bacon, beans, coffee, bread and molasses, but we had stewed dried apples every day in the week just the same as if it were Sunday. But this palatial life, this gross and luxurious life, had to come to an end and there were two sufficient reasons for it. On my side I could not endure the heavy labor; and on the company's side they did not feel justified in paying me to shovel sand down my back; so I was discharged just at the moment that I was going to resign.

If Higbie had taken that job all would have been well and everybody satisfied, for his great frame would have been competent. He was muscled like a giant. He could handle a long-handled shovel like an emperor and he could work patiently and contentedly twelve hours on a stretch without ever hastening his pulse or his breath. Meantime, he had found nothing to do and was somewhat discouraged. He said, with an outburst of pathetic longing, "If I could only get a job at the Pioneer!"

I said, "What kind of a job do you want at the Pioneer?"

He said, "Why, laborer. They get five dollars a day."

I said, "If that's all you want I can arrange it for you."

Higbie was astonished. He said, "Do you mean to say that you know the foreman there and could get me a job and yet have never said anything about it?"

"No," I said, "I don't know the foreman."

"Well," he said, "who is it you know? How is it you can get me the job?"

"Why," I said, "that's perfectly simple. If you will do as I tell you to do and don't try to improve on my instructions you shall have the job before night."

He said eagerly, "I'll obey the instructions, I don't care what they are."

"Well," I said, "go there and say that you want work as a

laborer; that you are tired of being idle; that you are not used to being idle and can't stand it; that you just merely want the refreshment of work and require nothing in return."

He said, "Nothing?"

I said, "That's it—nothing."

"No wages at all?"

"No, no wages at all."

"Not even board?"

"No, not even board. You are to work for nothing. Make them understand that—that you are perfectly willing to work for nothing. When they look at that figure of yours that foreman will understand that he has drawn a prize. You'll get the job."

Higbie said, indignantly, "Yes, a hell of a job."

I said: "You said you were going to do it and now you are already criticizing. You have said you would obey my instructions. You are always as good as your word. Clear out, now, and get the job."

He said he would.

I was pretty anxious to know what was going to happen—more anxious than I would have wanted him to find out. I preferred to seem entirely confident of the strength of my scheme and I made good show of that confidence. But really I was very anxious. Yet I believed that I knew enough of human nature to know that a man like Higbie would not be flung out of that place without reflection when he was offering those muscles of his for nothing. The hours dragged along and he didn't return. I began to feel better and better. I began to accumulate confidence. At sundown he did at last arrive and I had the joy of knowing that my invention had been a fine inspiration and was successful.

He said the foreman was so astonished at first that he didn't know how to take hold of the proposition but that he soon recovered and was evidently very glad that he was able to accommodate Higbie and furnish him the refreshment he was pining for.

Higbie said, "How long is this to go on?"

I said: "The terms are that you are to stay right there; do your work just as if you were getting the going wages for it. You are never to make any complaint; you are never to indicate that you would like to have wages or board. This will go on one, two, three, four, five, six days, according to the make of that foreman. Some foremen would break down under the strain in a couple of days. There are others who would last a week. It would be difficult to find one who could stand out a whole fortnight without getting ashamed of himself and offering you wages. Now let's suppose that this is a fortnight foreman. In that case you will not be there a fortnight. Because the men will spread it around that the very ablest laborer in this camp is so fond of work that he is willing and glad to do it without pay. You will be regarded as the latest curiosity. Men will come from the other mills to have a look at you. You could charge admission and get it but you mustn't do that. Stick to your colors. When the foremen of the other mills cast their eyes upon this bulk of yours and perceive that you are worth two ordinary men they'll offer you half a man's wages. You are not to accept until you report to your foreman. Give him an opportunity to offer you the same. If he doesn't do it, then you are free to take up with that other man's offer. Higbie, you'll be foreman of a mine or a mill inside of three weeks, and at the best wages going."

It turned out just so—and after that I led an easy life, with nothing to do, for it did not occur to me to take my own medicine. I didn't want a job as long as Higbie had one. One was enough for so small a family—and so during many succeeding weeks I was a gentleman of leisure, with books and newspapers to read and stewed dried apples every day for dinner the same as Sunday, and I wanted no better career than this in this life. Higbie supported me handsomely, never once complained of it, never once suggested that I go out and try for a job at no wages and keep myself.

That would be in 1862. I parted from Higbie about the end of '62—or possibly it could have been the beginning of '63—and went to Virginia City, for I had been invited to come there and take William H. Wright's place as sole reporter on the *Territorial Enterprise* and do Wright's work for three months while he crossed the plains to Iowa to visit his family. However, I have told all about this in *Roughing It.*

I have never seen Higbie since in all these forty-four years.

CHAPTER 23

In those early days dueling suddenly became a fashion in the new territory of Nevada and by 1864 everybody was anxious to have a chance in the new sport, mainly for the reason that he was not able to thoroughly respect himself so long as he had not killed or crippled somebody in a duel or been killed or crippled in one himself.

At that time I had been serving as city editor on Mr. Joe Goodman's Virginia City *Enterprise* for a matter of two years. I was twenty-nine years old. I was ambitious in several ways but I had entirely escaped the seductions of that particular craze. I had had no desire to fight a duel. I had no intention of provoking one. I did not feel respectable but I got a certain amount of satisfaction out of feeling safe. I was ashamed of myself, the rest of the staff were ashamed of me—but I got along well enough. I had always been accustomed to feeling ashamed of myself, for one thing or another, so there was no novelty for me in the situation. I bore it very well.

Plunkett was on the staff. R. M. Daggett was on the staff. These had tried to get into duels but for the present had failed and were waiting. Goodman was the only one of us who had done anything to shed credit upon the paper. The rival paper was the Virginia *Union*. Its editor for a little while was Tom Fitch, called the "silver-tongued orator of Wisconsin"—that was where he came from. He tuned up his oratory in the editorial columns of the *Union* and Mr. Goodman invited him out and modified him with a bullet. I remember the joy of the staff when Goodman's challenge was accepted by Fitch. We ran late that night and made much of Joe Goodman. He was only twenty-four years old; he lacked the wisdom which a person has at twenty-nine and he was as glad of being *it* as I was that I wasn't.

He chose Major Graves for his second (that name is not right but it's close enough, I don't remember the major's name). Graves came over to instruct Joe in the dueling art.

He had been a major under Walker, the "gray-eyed man of destiny," and had fought all through that remarkable man's filibustering campaign in Central America. That fact gauges the major. To say that a man was a major under Walker and came out of that struggle ennobled by Walker's praise is to say that the major was not merely a brave man but that he was brave to the very utmost limit of that word. All of Walker's men were like that.

I knew the Gillis family intimately. The father made the campaign under Walker, and with him one son. They were in the memorable Plaza fight and stood it out to the last against overwhelming odds, as did also all of the Walker men. The son was killed at the father's side. The father received a bullet through the eye. The old man—for he was an old man at the time—wore spectacles, and the bullet and one of the glasses went into his skull, and the bullet remained there. There were some other sons—Steve, George and Jim, very young chaps—the merest lads—who wanted to be in the Walker expedition, for they had their father's dauntless spirit. But Walker wouldn't have them; he said it was a serious expedition and no place for children.

The major was a majestic creature, with a most stately and dignified and impressive military bearing, and he was by nature and training courteous, polite, graceful, winning; and he had that quality which I think I have encountered in only one other man—Bob Howland—a mysterious quality which resides in the eye; and when that eye is turned upon an individual or a squad, in warning, that is enough. The man that has that eye doesn't need to go armed; he can move upon an armed desperado and quell him and take him prisoner without saying a single word. I saw Bob Howland do that once—a slender, good-natured, amiable, gentle, kindly little skeleton of a man, with a sweet blue eye that would win your heart when it smiled upon you, or turn cold and freeze it, according to the nature of the occasion.

The major stood Joe up straight; stood Steve Gillis up fifteen paces away; made Joe turn his right side toward Steve, cock his navy six-shooter—that prodigious weapon—and hold it straight down against his leg; told him that *that* was the correct position for the gun—that the position ordinarily in use at Virginia City (that is to say, the gun straight up in the air, then brought slowly down to your man) was all wrong. At the word *"One,"* you must raise the gun slowly and steadily to the place on the other man's body that you desire to convince. Then, after a pause, *"Two, three—fire—Stop!"* At the word "stop," you may fire—but not earlier. You may give yourself as much time as you please *after* that word. Then, when you fire, you may advance and go on firing at your leisure and pleasure, if you can get any pleasure out of it. And, in the meantime, the other man, if he has been properly instructed and is alive to his privileges, is advancing on *you*, and firing— and it is always likely that more or less trouble will result.

Naturally, when Joe's revolver had risen to a level it was pointing at Steve's breast, but the major said: "No, that is not wise. Take all the risks of getting murdered yourself but don't run any risk of murdering the other man. If you survive a duel you want to survive it in such a way that the memory of it will not linger along with you through the rest of your life and interfere with your sleep. Aim at your man's leg; not at the knee, not above the knee, for those are dangerous spots. Aim below the knee; cripple him but leave the rest of him to his mother."

By grace of these truly wise and excellent instructions, Joe tumbled his man down with a bullet through his lower leg, which furnished him a permanent limp. And Joe lost nothing but a lock of hair, which he could spare better then than he could now. For when I saw him here in New York a year ago his crop was gone; he had nothing much left but a fringe, with a dome rising above.

About a year later I got *my* chance. But I was not hunting for it. Goodman went off to San Francisco for a week's holiday and left me to be chief editor. I had supposed that that was an easy berth, there being nothing to do but write one editorial per day; but I was disappointed in that superstition. I couldn't find anything to write an article about, the first day. Then it occurred to me that inasmuch as it was the 22d of April, 1864, the next morning would be the three-hundredth anniversary of Shakespeare's birthday—and what better theme could I want than that? I got the Cyclopædia and examined it and found out who Shakespeare was and what he had done, and I borrowed all that and laid it before a community that couldn't have been better prepared for instruction about Shakespeare than if they had been prepared by art. There wasn't enough of what Shakespeare had done to make an editorial of the necessary length but I filled it out with what he hadn't done —which in many respects was more important and striking and readable than the handsomest things he had really accomplished.

But next day I was in trouble again. There were no more Shakespeares to work up. There was nothing in past history or in the world's future possibilities to make an editorial out of suitable to that community; so there was but one theme left. That theme was Mr. Laird, proprietor of the Virginia *Union. His* editor had gone off to San Francisco too and Laird was trying his hand at editing. I woke up Mr. Laird with some courtesies of the kind that were fashionable among newspaper editors in that region and he came back at me the next day in a most vitriolic way. So we expected a challenge from Mr. Laird, because according to the rules—according to the etiquette of dueling as reconstructed and reorganized and improved by the duelists of that region—whenever you said a thing about another person that he didn't like, it wasn't sufficient for him to talk back in the same offensive spirit; etiquette required him to send a challenge. So we waited for a challenge—waited all day. It didn't come. And as the day wore along, hour after hour, and no challenge came, the boys grew depressed. They lost heart. But I was cheerful; I felt better and better all the time. They couldn't understand it but *I* could understand it. It was my *make* that enabled me to be cheerful when other people were despondent.

So then it became necessary for us to waive etiquette and challenge Mr. Laird. When we reached that decision, they began to cheer up, but I began to lose some of my animation. However, in enterprises of this kind you are in the hands of your friends; there is nothing for you to do but to abide by what they consider to be the best course. Daggett wrote a challenge for me, for Daggett had the language—the right language—the convincing language—and I lacked it. Daggett poured out a stream of unsavory epithets upon Mr. Laird, charged with a vigor and venom of a strength calculated to persuade him; and Steve Gillis, my second, carried the challenge and came back to wait for the return. It didn't come. The boys were exasperated but I kept my temper. Steve carried another challenge, hotter than the other, and we waited again. Nothing came of it. I began to feel quite comfortable. I began to take an interest in the challenges myself. I had not felt any before; but it seemed to me that I was accumulating a great and valuable reputation at no expense and my delight in this grew and grew as challenge after challenge was declined, until by midnight I was beginning to think that there was nothing in the world so much to be desired as a chance to fight a duel. So I hurried Daggett up; made him keep on sending challenge after challenge. Oh, well, I overdid it: Laird accepted. I might have suspected that that would happen—Laird was a man you couldn't depend on.

The boys were jubilant beyond expression. They helped me make my will, which was another discomfort—and I already had enough. Then they took me home. I didn't sleep any—didn't want to sleep. I had plenty of things to think about and less than four hours to do it in—because five o'clock was the hour appointed for the tragedy and I should have to use up one hour—beginning at four—in practicing with the revolver and finding out which end of it to level at the adversary. At four we went down into a little gorge about a mile from town and borrowed a barn door for a mark—borrowed it of a man who was over in California on a visit—and we set the barn door up and stood a fence rail up against the middle of it to represent Mr. Laird. But the rail was no proper representative of him, for he was longer than a rail and thinner. Nothing would ever fetch him but a line shot, and then, as like as not, he would split the bullet—the worst material for dueling purposes that could be imagined. I began on the rail. I couldn't hit the rail; then I tried the barn door; but I couldn't hit the barn door. There was nobody in danger except stragglers around on the flanks of that mark. I was thoroughly discouraged and I didn't cheer up any when we presently heard pistol shots over in the next little ravine. I knew what that was—that was Laird's gang out practicing him. They would hear my shots and of course they could come up over the ridge to see what kind of a record I was making—see what their chances were against me. Well, I hadn't any record; and I knew that if Laird came over that ridge and saw my barn door without a scratch on it, he would be as anxious to fight as I was—or as I had been at midnight, before that disastrous acceptance came.

Now just as this moment a little bird, no bigger than a sparrow, flew along by and lit on a sagebrush about thirty yards away. Steve whipped out his revolver and shot its head off. Oh, he was a marksman—much better than I was. We ran down there to pick up the bird and just then, sure enough, Mr. Laird and his people came over the ridge and they joined us. And when Laird's second saw that bird with its head shot off he lost color, he faded, and you could see that he was interested.

He said: "Who did that?"

Before I could answer, Steve spoke up and said quite calmly, and in a matter-of-fact way, "Clemens did it."

The second said, "Why, that is wonderful! How far off was that bird?"

Steve said, "Oh, not far—about thirty yards."

The second said, "Well, that is astonishing shooting. How often can he do that?"

Steve said languidly, "Oh, about four times out of five!"

I knew the little rascal was lying but I didn't say anything. The second said:

"Why, that is *amazing* shooting! Why, I supposed he couldn't hit a church!"

He was supposing very sagaciously but I didn't say anything. Well, they said good morning. The second took Mr. Laird home, a little tottery on his legs, and Laird sent back a note in his own hand declining to fight a duel with me on any terms whatever.

Well, my life was saved—saved by that accident. I don't know what the bird thought about that interposition of Providence but I felt very, very comfortable over it—satisfied and content. Now we found out later that Laird had hit *his* mark four times out of six, right along. If the duel had come off he would have so filled my skin with bullet holes that it wouldn't have held my principles.

By breakfast time the news was all over town that I had sent a challenge and Steve Gillis had carried it. Now that would entitle us to two years apiece in the penitentiary, according to the brand-new law. Governor North sent us no message as coming from himself but a message *came* from a close friend of his. He said it would be a good idea for us to leave the territory by the first stagecoach. This would sail next morning at four o'clock—and in the meantime we would be searched for but not with avidity; and if we were in the territory after that stagecoach left we would be the first victims of the new law. Judge North was anxious to have some victims for that law and he would absolutely keep us in the prison the full two years. He wouldn't pardon us out to please anybody.

Well, it seemed to me that our society was no longer desirable in Nevada; so we stayed in our quarters and observed

proper caution all day—except that once Steve went o
the hotel to attend to another customer of mine. That w
Mr. Cutler. You see, Laird was not the only person whom I
had tried to reform during my occupancy of the editorial
chair. I had looked around and selected several other people
and delivered a new zest of life into them through warm
criticism and disapproval—so that when I laid down my editorial pen I had four horsewhippings and two duels owing to
me. We didn't care for the horsewhippings; there was no
glory in them; they were not worth the trouble of collecting.
But honor required that some notice should be taken of that
other duel. Mr. Cutler had come up from Carson City and
had sent a man over with a challenge from the hotel. Steve
went over to pacify him. Steve weighed only ninety-five
pounds but it was well known throughout the territory that
with his fists he could whip anybody that walked on two legs,
let his weight and science be what they might. Steve was a
Gillis, and when a Gillis confronted a man and had a proposition to make the proposition always contained business. When
Cutler found that Steve was my second he cooled down; he
became calm and rational and was ready to listen. Steve gave
him fifteen minutes to get out of the hotel and half an hour to
get out of town or there would be results. So *that* duel went
off successfully, because Mr. Cutler immediately left for Carson a convinced and reformed man.

I have never had anything to do with duels since. I thoroughly disapprove of duels. I consider them unwise and I
know they are dangerous. Also, sinful. If a man should challenge me now I would go to that man and take him kindly
and forgivingly by the hand and lead him to a quiet retired
spot and *kill* him. Still, I have always taken a great interest
in other people's duels. One always feels an abiding interest in
any heroic thing which has entered into his own experience.

◇◇◇◇◇◇◇◇◇◇◇◇◇◇◇◇◇◇◇◇◇

CHAPTER 24

After leaving Nevada I was a reporter on the *Morning Call* of
San Francisco. I was more than that—I was *the* reporter.
There was no other. There was enough work for one and a

little over, but not enough for two—according to Mr. Barnes's idea, and he was the proprietor and therefore better situated to know about it than other people.

By nine in the morning I had to be at the police court for an hour and make a brief history of the squabbles of the night before. They were usually between Irishmen and Irishmen, and Chinamen and Chinamen, with now and then a squabble between the two races for a change. Each day's evidence was substantially a duplicate of the evidence of the day before, therefore the daily performance was killingly monotonous and wearisome. So far as I côuld see there was only one man connected with it who found anything like a compensating interest in it, and that was the court interpreter. He was an Englishman who was glibly familiar with fifty-six Chinese dialects. He had to change from one to another of them every ten minutes and this exercise was so energizing that it kept him always awake, which was not the case with the reporters. Next we visited the higher courts and made notes of the decisions which had been rendered the day before. All the courts came under the head of "regulars." They were sources of reportorial information which never failed. During the rest of the day we raked the town from end to end, gathering such material as we might, wherewith to fill our required column— and if there were no fires to report we started some.

At night we visited the six theaters, one after the other: seven nights a week, three hundred and sixty-five nights in the year. We remained in each of those places five minutes, got the merest passing glimpse of play and opera, and with that for a text we "wrote up" those plays and operas, as the phrase goes, torturing our souls every night from the beginning of the year to the end of it in the effort to find something to say about those performances which we had not said a couple of hundred times before. There has never been a time from that day to this, forty years, that I have been able to look at even the outside of a theater without a spasm of the dry gripes, as "Uncle Remus" calls it—and as for the inside, I know next to nothing about that, for in all this time I have seldom had a sight of it nor ever had a desire in that regard which couldn't have been overcome by argument.

After having been hard at work from nine or ten in the morning until eleven at night scraping material together, I took the pen and spread this muck out in words and phrases and made it cover as much acreage as I could. It was fearful drudgery, soulless drudgery, and almost destitute of interest. It was an awful slavery for a lazy man, and I was born lazy. I am no lazier now than I was forty years ago, but that is because I reached the limit forty years ago. You can't go beyond possibility.

Finally there was an event. One Sunday afternoon I saw some hoodlums chasing and stoning a Chinaman who was heavily laden with the weekly wash of his Christian customers, and I noticed that a policeman was observing this performance with an amused interest—nothing more. He did not interfere. I wrote up the incident with considerable warmth and holy indignation. Usually I didn't want to read in the morning what I had written the night before; it had come from a torpid heart. But this item had come from a live one. There was fire in it and I believed it was literature—and so I sought for it in the paper next morning with eagerness. It wasn't there. It wasn't there the next morning, nor the next. I went up to the composing room and found it tucked away among condemned matter on the standing galley. I asked about it. The foreman said Mr. Barnes had found it in a galley proof and ordered its extinction. And Mr. Barnes furnished his reasons—either to me or to the foreman, I don't remember which; but they were commercially sound. He said that the *Call* was like the New York *Sun* of that day: it was the washerwoman's paper—that is, it was the paper of the poor; it was the only cheap paper. It gathered its livelihood from the poor and must respect their prejudices or perish. The Irish were the poor. They were the stay and support of the *Morning Call;* without them the *Morning Call* could not survive a month—and they hated the Chinamen. Such an assault as I had attempted could rouse the whole Irish hive and seriously damage the paper. The *Call* could not afford to publish articles criticizing the hoodlums for stoning Chinamen.

I was lofty in those days. I have survived it. I was unwise then. I am up-to-date now. Day before yesterday's New York *Sun* has a paragraph or two from its London correspondent which enables me to locate myself. The correspondent mentions a few of our American events of the past twelvemonth, such as the limitless rottenness of our great insurance companies, where theft has been carried on by our most distinguished commercial men as a profession; the exposures of conscienceless graft, colossal graft, in great municipalities like

Philadelphia, St. Louis and other large cities; the recent exposure of millionfold graft in the great Pennsylvania Railway system—with minor uncoverings of commercial swindles from one end of the United States to the other; and finally today's lurid exposure, by Upton Sinclair, of the most titanic and death-dealing swindle of them all, the Beef Trust, an exposure which has moved the President to demand of a reluctant Congress a law which shall protect America and Europe from falling, in a mass, into the hands of the doctor and the undertaker.

According to that correspondent, Europe is beginning to wonder if there is really an honest male human creature left in the United States. A year ago I was satisfied that there was no such person existing upon American soil except myself. That exception has since been rubbed out and now it is my belief that there isn't a single male human being in America who is honest. I held the belt all along, until last January. Then I went down, with Rockefeller and Carnegie and a group of Goulds and Vanderbilts and other professional grafters, and swore off my taxes like the most conscienceless of the lot. It was a great loss to America because I was irreplaceable. It is my belief that it will take fifty years to produce my successor. I believe the entire population of the United States—exclusive of the women—to be rotten, as far as the dollar is concerned. Understand, I am saying these things as a dead person. I should consider it indiscreet in any live one to make these remarks publicly.

But, as I was saying, I was loftier forty years ago than I am now and I felt a deep shame in being situated as I was—slave of such a journal as the *Morning Call*. If I had been still loftier I would have thrown up my berth and gone out and starved, like any other hero. But I had never had any experience. I had *dreamed* heroism, like everybody, but I had had no practice and I didn't know how to begin. I couldn't bear to begin with starving. I had already come near to that once or twice in my life and got no real enjoyment out of remembering about it. I knew I couldn't get another berth if I resigned. I knew it perfectly well. Therefore I swallowed my humiliation and stayed where I was. But whereas there had been little enough interest attaching to my industries before, there was none at all now. I continued my work but I took not the least interest in it, and naturally there were results. I got to neglecting it. As I have said, there was too much of it for one man. The way I was conducting it now, there was apparently work enough in it for two or three. Even Barnes noticed that, and told me to get an assistant, on half wages.

There was a great hulking creature down in the counting room—good-natured, obliging, unintellectual—and he was getting little or nothing a week and boarding himself. A graceless boy of the counting-room force who had no reverence for anybody or anything was always making fun of this beachcomber, and he had a name for him which somehow seemed intensely apt and descriptive—I don't know why. He called him Smiggy McGlural. I offered the berth of assistant to Smiggy and he accepted it with alacrity and gratitude. He went at his work with ten times the energy that was left in me. He was not intellectual but mentality was not required or needed in a *Morning Call* reporter and so he conducted his office to perfection. I gradually got to leaving more and more of the work to McGlural. I grew lazier and lazier and within thirty days he was doing almost the whole of it. It was also plain that he could accomplish the whole of it and more all by himself and therefore had no real need of me.

It was at this crucial moment that that event happened which I mentioned a while ago. Mr. Barnes discharged me. It was the only time in my life that I have ever been discharged and it hurts yet—although I am in my grave. He did not discharge me rudely. It was not in his nature to do that. He was a large, handsome man, with a kindly face and courteous ways, and was faultless in his dress. He could not have said a rude, ungentle thing to anybody. He took me privately aside and advised me to resign. It was like a father advising a son for his good, and I obeyed.

I was on the world now, with nowhere to go. By my Presbyterian training I knew that the *Morning Call* had brought disaster upon itself. I knew the ways of Providence and I knew that this offense would have to be answered for. I could not foresee when the penalty would fall nor what shape it would take but I was as certain that it would come, sooner or later, as I was of my own existence. I could not tell whether it would fall upon Barnes or upon his newspaper. But Barnes was the guilty one and I knew by my training that the punishment always falls upon the innocent one, consequently I felt sure that it was the newspaper that at some future day would suffer for Barnes' crime.

Sure enough! Among the very first pictures that arrived in

the fourth week of April'—there stood the *Morning Call* building towering out of the wrecked city like a Washington Monument; and the body of it was all gone and nothing was left but the iron bones! It was then that I said, "How wonderful are the ways of Providence!" I had known it would happen. I had known it for forty years. I had never lost confidence in Providence during all that time. It was put off longer than I was expecting but it was now comprehensive and satisfactory enough to make up for that. Some people would think it curious that Providence should destroy an entire city of four hundred thousand inhabitants to settle an account of forty years standing, between a mere discharged reporter and a newspaper, but to me there was nothing strange about that, because I was educated, I was trained, I was a Presbyterian and I knew how these things were done. I knew that in Biblical times if a man committed a sin the extermination of the whole surrounding nation—cattle and all—was likely to happen. I knew that Providence was not particular about the rest, so that He got somebody connected with the one He was after. I remembered that in the *Magnalia* a man who went home swearing from prayer meeting one night got his reminder within the next nine months. He had a wife and seven children, and all at once they were attacked by a terrible disease, and one by one they died in agony till at the end of a week there was nothing left but the man himself. I knew that the idea was to punish the man, and I knew that if he had any intelligence he recognized that that intention had been carried out, although mainly at the expense of other people.

◇◇◇◇◇◇◇◇◇◇◇◇◇◇◇◇◇◇

CHAPTER 25

In those ancient times the counting room of the *Morning Call* was on the ground floor; the office of the Superintendent of the United States Mint was on the next floor above, with Bret Harte as private secretary of the Superintendent. The quarters of the editorial staff and the reporter were on the

---

[1] 1906, the year of the great earthquake and the year in which Mark Twain is writing.

third floor, and the composing room on the fourth and final
floor. I spent a good deal of time with Bret Harte in his office
after Smiggy McGlural came, but not before that. Harte was
doing a good deal of writing for the *Californian*—contributing
"Condensed Novels" and sketches to it and also acting as
editor, I think. I was a contributor. So was Charles H. Webb;
also Prentiss Mulford; also a young lawyer named Hastings,
who gave promise of distinguishing himself in literature
some day. Charles Warren Stoddard was a contributor. Am-
brose Bierce, who is still writing acceptably for the magazines
today,[1] was then employed on some paper in San Francisco—
The Golden Era, perhaps. We had very good times together
—very social and pleasant times. But that was after Smiggy
McGlural came to my assistance; there was no leisure before
that. Smiggy was a great advantage to me—during thirty
days. Then he turned into a disaster.

It was Mr. Swain, Superintendent of the Mint, who discovered Bret Harte. Harte had arrived in California in the
fifties, twenty-three or twenty-four years old, and had wandered up into the surface diggings of the camp at Yreka,
a place which had acquired its curious name—when in its
first days it much needed a name—through an accident.
There was a bakeshop with a canvas sign which had not
yet been put up but had been painted and stretched to dry
in such a way that the word BAKERY, all but the B,
showed through and was reversed. A stranger read it wrong
end first, YREKA, and supposed that that was the name of
the camp. The campers were satisfied with it and adopted
it.

Harte taught school in that camp several months. He also
edited the weekly rag which was doing duty as a newspaper.
He spent a little time also in the pocket-mining camp of
Jackass Gulch (where I tarried, some years later, during
three months). It was at Yreka and Jackass Gulch that Harte
learned to accurately observe and put with photographic
exactness on paper the woodland scenery of California and
the general country aspects—the stagecoach, its driver and
its passengers, and the clothing and general style of the
surface miner, the gambler and their women; and it was also
in these places that he learned, without the trouble of observing, all that he didn't know about mining, and how to

[1] 1906.

make it read as if an expert were behind the pen. It was in those places that he also learned how to fascinate Europe and America with the quaint dialect of the miner—a dialect which no man in heaven or earth had ever used until Harte invented it. With Harte it died, but it was no loss. By and by he came to San Francisco. He was a compositor by trade and got work in *The Golden Era* office at ten dollars a week.

Harte was paid for setting type only but he lightened his labors and entertained himself by contributing literature to the paper, uninvited. The editor and proprietor, Joe Lawrence, never saw Harte's manuscripts, because there weren't any. Harte spun his literature out of his head while at work at the case, and set it up as he spun. *The Golden Era* was ostensibly and ostentatiously a literary paper, but its literature was pretty feeble and sloppy and only exhibited the literary forms, without really being literature. Mr. Swain, the Superintendent of the Mint, noticed a new note in that *Golden Era* orchestra—a new and fresh and spirited note that rose above that orchestra's mumbling confusion and was recognizable as music. He asked Joe Lawrence who the performer was and Lawrence told him. It seemed to Mr. Swain a shame that Harte should be wasting himself in such a place and on such a pittance so he took him away, made him his private secretary on a good salary, with little or nothing to do, and told him to follow his own bent and develop his talent. Harte was willing and the development began.

Bret Harte was one of the pleasantest men I have ever known. He was also one of the unpleasantest men I have ever known. He was showy, meretricious, insincere; and he constantly advertised these qualities in his dress. He was distinctly pretty, in spite of the fact that his face was badly pitted with smallpox. In the days when he could afford it— and in the days when he couldn't—his clothes always exceeded the fashion by a shade or two. He was always conspicuously a little more intensely fashionable than the fashionablest of the rest of the community. He had good taste in clothes. With all his conspicuousness there was never anything really loud nor offensive about them. They always had a single smart little accent, effectively located, and that accent would have distinguished Harte from any other of the ultrafashionables. Oftenest it was his necktie. Always it was of a single color, and intense. Most frequently, perhaps, it was crimson—a flash of flame under his chin; or it was indigo blue and as hot and vivid as if one of those splendid and luminous Brazilian butterflies had lighted there. Harte's dainty self-complacencies extended to his carriage and gait. His carriage was graceful and easy, his gait was of the mincing sort but was the right gait for him, for an unaffected one would not have harmonized with the rest of the man and the clothes.

He hadn't a sincere fiber in him. I think he was incapable of emotion, for I think he had nothing to feel with. I think his heart was merely a pump and had no other function. I am almost moved to say I *know* it had no other function. I knew him intimately in the days when he was private secretary on the second floor and I a fading and perishing reporter on the third, with Smiggy McGlural looming doomfully in the near distance. I knew him intimately when he came east five years later in 1870 to take the editorship of the proposed *Lakeside Monthly* in Chicago, and crossed the continent through such a prodigious blaze of national interest and excitement that one might have supposed he was the Viceroy of India on a progress, or Halley's comet come again after seventy-five years of lamented absence.

I knew him pretty intimately thenceforth until he crossed the ocean to be consul, first at Crefeldt in Germany and afterwards in Glasgow. He never returned to America. When he died in London, he had been absent from America and from his wife and daughters twenty-six years.

This is the very Bret Harte whose pathetics, imitated from Dickens, used to be a godsend to the farmers of two hemispheres on account of the freshets of tears they compelled. He said to me once with a cynical chuckle that he thought he had mastered the art of pumping up the tear of sensibility. The idea conveyed was that the tear of sensibility was oil, and that by luck he had struck it.

Harte told me once, when he was spending a business fortnight in my house in Hartford, that his fame was an accident—an accident that he much regretted for a while. He said he had written "The Heathen Chinee" for amusement; then had thrown it into the wastebasket; that presently there was a call for copy to finish out the *Overland Monthly* and let it get to press. He had nothing else, so he fished the "Chinee" out of the basket and sent that. As we all remember, it created an explosion of delight whose reverberations reached the last confines of Christendom, and Harte's name, from being obscure to invisibility in the one week, was as notorious and as visible in the next as if it had been painted on the sky in letters of astronomical magnitude. He regarded this fame as a disaster, because he was already at work on such things as "The Luck of Roaring Camp," a loftier grade of literature, a grade which he had been hoping to presently occupy with distinction in the sight of the world.

"The Heathen Chinee" did obstruct that dream, but not for long. It was presently replaced by the finer glory of "The Luck of Roaring Camp," "Tennessee's Partner," and those other felicitous imitations of Dickens. In the San Franciscan days Bret Harte was by no means ashamed when he was praised as being a successful imitator of Dickens; he was proud of it. I heard him say, myself, that he thought he was the best imitator of Dickens in America, a remark which indicates a fact, to wit: that there were a great many people in America at that time who were ambitiously and undisguisedly imitating Dickens. His long novel, *Gabriel Conroy*, is as much like Dickens as if Dickens had written it himself.

It is a pity that we cannot escape from life when we are young. When Bret Harte started east in his newborn glory thirty-six years ago, with the eyes of the world upon him, he had lived all of his life that was worth living. He had lived all of his life that was to be respectworthy. He had lived all of his life that was to be worthy of his *own* respect. He was entering upon a miserable career of poverty, debt, humiliation, shame, disgrace, bitterness and a world-wide fame which must have often been odious to him, since it made his poverty and the shabbiness of his character conspicuous beyond the power of any art to mercifully hide them.

There was a happy Bret Harte, a contented Bret Harte, an ambitious Bret Harte, a hopeful Bret Harte, a bright, cheerful, easy-laughing Bret Harte, a Bret Harte to whom it was a bubbling and effervescent joy to be alive. That Bret Harte died in San Francisco. It was the corpse of that Bret Harte that swept in splendor across the continent; that refused to go to the Chicago banquet given in its honor because there had been a breach of etiquette—a carriage had not been sent for it; that resumed its eastward journey behind the grand scheme of the *Lakeside Monthly* in sorrowful collapse; that undertook to give all the product of its brain for one year to the *Atlantic Monthly* for ten thousand dollars—a stupendous sum in those days—furnished nothing worth speaking of for the great pay, but collected and spent the money before the year was out and then began a dismal and harassing death-in-life of borrowing from men and living on women which was to cease only at the grave.

He had a curious adventure once, when he was a young chap new to the Pacific Coast and floating around seeking bread and butter. He told me some of his experiences of that early day. For a while he taught a school in the lively gold-mining camp of Yreka, and at the same time he added a trifle to his income by editing the little weekly local journal for the pair of journeymen typesetters who owned it.

His duties as editor required him to read proof. Once a galley slip was laid before him which consisted of one of those old-time obituaries which were so dismally popular all over the United States when we were still a softhearted and sentimental people. There was half a column of the obituary and it was built upon the regulation plan; that is to say, it was made up of superlatives—superlatives wherewith the writer tried to praise Mrs. Thompson, the deceased, to the summit of her merit, the result being a flowery, overheated and most extravagant eulogy, and closing with that remark which was never missing from the regulation obituary: "Our loss is her eternal gain."

In the proof Harte found this observation: "Even in Yreka her chastity was conspicuous." Of course that word was a misprint for "charity," but Harte didn't think of that; he knew a printer's mistake had been made and he also knew that a reference to the manuscript would determine what it was; therefore he followed proofreader custom and with his pen indicated in the usual way that the manuscript must be examined. It was a simple matter and took only a moment of his time; he drew a black line under the word chastity, and in the margin he placed a question mark enclosed in parentheses. It was a brief way of saying, "There is something the matter with this word; examine the manuscript and make the necessary correction." But there is another proofreader law which he overlooked. That law says that when a word is not emphatic enough you must draw a line under it, and this will require the printer to reinforce it by putting it in italics.

When Harte took up the paper in the morning and looked at that obituary he took only one glance; then he levied on a mule that was not being watched and cantered out of town, knowing well that in a very little while there was going to be a visit from the widower, with his gun. In the obituary the derelict observation now stood in this form: "Even in Yreka her *chastity* was conspicuous(?)"—a form which turned the thing into a ghastly and ill-timed sarcasm!

I am reminded in a wide roundabout way of another of Harte's adventures, by a remark in a letter lately received from Tom Fitch, whom Joe Goodman crippled in the duel—for Tom Fitch is still alive, although inhabiting Arizona. After wandering for years and years all about the planet, Fitch has gone back to his early loves, the sand, the sagebrush and the jackass rabbit; and these things and the old-time ways of the natives have refreshed his spirit and restored to him his lost youth. Those friendly people slap him on the shoulder and call him—well, never mind what they call him; it might offend your ears, but it does Fitch's heart good. He knows its deep meanings; he recognizes the affection that is back of it, and so it is music to his spirit and he is grateful.

When "The Luck of Roaring Camp" burst upon the world Harte became instantly famous; his name and his praises were upon every lip. One day he had occasion to go to Sacramento. When he went ashore there he forgot to secure a berth for the return trip. When he came down to the landing, in the late afternoon, he realized that he had made a calamitous blunder; apparently all Sacramento was proposing to go down to San Francisco; there was a queue of men which stretched from the purser's office down the gangplank, across the levee and up the street out of sight.

Harte had one hope: inasmuch as in theaters, operas, steamboats and steamships half a dozen choice places are always reserved to be conferred upon belated clients of distinction, perhaps his name might procure for him one of those reserved places if he could smuggle his card to the purser; so he edged his way along the queue and at last stood shoulder to shoulder with a vast and rugged miner from the mountains, who had his revolvers in his belt, whose great slouch hat overshadowed the whiskered face of a buccaneer and whose raiment was splashed with clay from his chin down to his boot tops. The queue was drifting slowly by the purser's wicket and each member of it was hearing, in his turn, the fatal words: "No berths left; not even floor space." The purser was just saying it to the truculent big miner when Harte passed his card in. The purser exclaimed, passing a key, "Ah, Mr. Bret Harte, glad to see you, sir! Take the whole stateroom, sir."

The bedless miner cast a scowl upon Harte which shed a twilight gloom over the whole region and frightened that author to such a degree that his key and its wooden tag rattled in his quaking hand; then he disappeared from the miner's view and sought seclusion and safety behind the lifeboats and such things on the hurricane deck. But nevertheless the thing happened which he was expecting—the miner soon appeared up there and went peering around; whenever he approached dangerously near, Harte shifted his shelter and hid behind a new one. This went on without unhappy accident for half an hour but at last failure came: Harte made a miscalculation; he crept cautiously out from behind a lifeboat and came face to face with the miner! He felt that it was an awful situation, a fatal situation, but it was not worth while to try to escape, so he stood still and waited for his doom. The miner said, sternly, "Are you Bret Harte?"

Harte confessed it in a feeble voice.

"Did you write that 'Luck of Roaring Camp'?"

Harte confessed again.

"Sure?"

"Yes"—in a whisper.

The miner burst out, fervently and affectionately,

"*Son* of a ——! Put it there!" and he gripped Harte's hand in his mighty talons and mashed it.

Tom Fitch knows that welcome phrase and the love and admiration that purge it of its earthiness and make it divine.

◇◇◇◇◇◇◇◇◇◇◇◇◇◇◇◇◇

CHAPTER 26

The proverb says that Providence protects children and idiots. This is really true. I know it because I have tested it.

I have several times been saved by this mysterious interposition when I was manifestly in extreme peril. It has been common all my life for smart people to perceive in me an easy prey for selfish designs and I have walked without suspicion into the trap set for me, yet have often come out unscathed, against all the likelihoods. More than forty years ago,[1] in San Francisco, the office staff adjourned, upon conclusion of its work at two o'clock in the morning, to a great bowling establishment where there were twelve alleys. I was invited, rather perfunctorily and as a matter of etiquette—by which I mean that I was invited politely but not urgently. But when I diffidently declined, with thanks, and explained that I knew nothing about the game, those lively young fellows became at once eager and anxious and urgent to have my society. This flattered me, for I perceived no trap, and I innocently and gratefully accepted their invitation. I was given an alley all to myself. The boys explained the game to me and they also explained to me that there would be an hour's play and that the player who scored the fewest ten-strikes in the hour would have to provide oysters and beer for the combination. This disturbed me very seriously, since it promised me bankruptcy, and I was sorry that this detail had been overlooked in the beginning. But my pride would not allow me to back out now, so I stayed in and did what I could to look satisfied and glad I had come. It is not likely that I looked as contented as I wanted to, but the others looked glad enough to make up for it, for they were quite unable to hide their evil joy. They showed me how to stand and how to stoop and how to aim the ball and how to let fly; and then the game began.

The results were astonishing. In my ignorance I delivered the balls in apparently every way except the right one; but no matter—during half an hour I never started a ball down the alley that didn't score a ten-strike every time at the other end. The others lost their grip early, and their joy along with it. Now and then one of them got a ten-strike but the occurrence was so rare that it made no show alongside of my giant score. The boys surrendered at the end of the half-hour and put on their coats and gathered around me and in courteous but sufficiently definite language expressed their opinion of an experience-worn and seasoned expert who would stoop to lying and deception in order to rob kind and well-meaning friends who had put their trust in him under the delusion that he was an honest and honorable person. I was not able to convince them that I had not lied, for now my character was gone and they refused to attach any value

---

[1] Written in 1907.

to anything I said. The proprietor of the place stood by for a while saying nothing, then he came to my defense. He said: "It looks like a mystery, gentlemen, but it isn't a mystery after it's explained. That is a *grooved* alley; you've only to start a ball down it any way you please and the groove will do the rest; it will slam the ball against the northeast curve of the head pin every time, and nothing can save the ten from going down."

It was true. The boys made the experiment and they found that there was no art that could send a ball down that alley and fail to score a ten-strike with it. When I had told those boys that I knew nothing about that game I was speaking only the truth; but it was ever thus, all through my life: whenever I have diverged from custom and principle and uttered a truth, the rule has been that the hearer hadn't strength of mind enough to believe it.

A quarter of a century ago I arrived in London to lecture a few weeks under the management of George Dolby, who had conducted the Dickens readings in America five or six years before. He took me to the Albemarle and fed me, and in the course of the dinner he enlarged a good deal and with great satisfaction upon his reputation as a player of fifteen-ball pool, and when he learned by my testimony that I had never seen the game played and knew nothing of the art of pocketing balls he enlarged more and more and still more and kept on enlarging, until I recognized that I was either in the presence of the very father of fifteen-ball pool or in the presence of his most immediate descendant. At the end of the dinner Dolby was eager to introduce me to the game and show me what he could do. We adjourned to the billiard room and he framed the balls in a flat pyramid and told me to fire at the apex ball and then go on and do what I could toward pocketing the fifteen, after which he would take the cue and show me what a past master of the game could do with those balls. I did as required. I began with the diffidence proper to my ignorant estate, and when I had finished my inning all the balls were in the pockets and Dolby was burying me under a volcanic irruption of acid sarcasms.

So I was a liar in Dolby's belief. He thought he had been sold and at a cheap rate; but he divided his sarcasms quite fairly and quite equally between the two of us. He was full of ironical admiration of his childishness and innocence in letting a wandering and characterless and scandalous American load him up with deceptions of so transparent a character that they ought not to have deceived the house cat. On the other hand, he was remorselessly severe upon me for beguiling him, by studied and discreditable artifice, into bragging and boasting about his poor game in the presence of a professional expert disguised in lies and frauds, who could empty more balls in billiard pockets in an hour than he could empty into a basket in a day.

In the matter of fifteen-ball pool I never got Dolby's confidence wholly back, though I got it in other ways and kept it until his death. I have played that game a number of times since, but that first time was the only time in my life that I have ever pocketed all the fifteen in a single inning.

My unsuspicious nature has made it necessary for Providence to save me from traps a number of times. Thirty years ago a couple of Elmira bankers invited me to play the game of "Quaker" with them. I had never heard of the game before and said that if it required intellect I should not be able to entertain them. But they said it was merely a game of chance and required no mentality—so I agreed to make a trial of it. They appointed four in the afternoon for the sacrifice. As the place, they chose a ground-floor room with a large window in it. Then they went treacherously around and advertised the "sell" which they were going to play upon me.

I arrived on time and we began the game—with a large and eager free list to superintend it. These superintendents were outside, with their noses pressed against the windowpane. The bankers described the game to me. So far as I recollect, the pattern of it was this: they had a pile of Mexican dollars on the table; twelve of them were of even date, fifty of them were of odd dates. The bankers were to separate a coin from the pile and hide it under a hand and I must guess "odd" or "even." If I guessed correctly, the coin would be mine; if incorrectly, I lost a dollar. The first guess I made was "even," and was right. I guessed again, "even," and took the money. They fed me another one and I guessed "even," again, and took the money. I guessed "even" the fourth time, and took the money. It seemed to me that "even" was a good guess, and I might as well stay by it, which I did. I guessed "even" twelve times and took the twelve dollars. I was doing as they secretly desired. Their experience of human nature had convinced them that any human being

as innocent as my face proclaimed me to be would repeat his
first guess if it won and would go on repeating it if it should
continue to win. It was their belief that an innocent would
be almost sure at the beginning to guess "even" and not
"odd," and that if an innocent should guess "even" twelve
times in succession and win every time he would go on
guessing "even" to the end—so it was their purpose to let me
win those twelve even dates and then advance the odd dates,
one by one, until I should lose fifty dollars and furnish
those superintendents something to laugh about for a week
to come.

But it did not come out in that way; for by the time I
had won the twelfth dollar and last even date I withdrew from
the game because it was so one-sided that it was monotonous,
and did not entertain me. There was a burst of laughter from
the superintendents at the window when I came out of the
place, but I did not know what they were laughing at nor
whom they were laughing at and it was a matter of no interest to me anyway. Through that incident I acquired an
enviable reputation for smartness and penetration, but it
was not my due, for I had not penetrated anything that the
cow could not have penetrated.

The last quarter of a century of my life has been pretty
constantly and faithfully devoted to the study of the human
race—that is to say, the study of myself, for in my individual
person I am the entire human race compacted together. I
have found that there is no ingredient of the race which I
do not possess in either a small way or a large way. When
it is small, as compared with the same ingredient in somebody else, there is still enough of it for all the purposes of
examination. In my contacts with the species I find no one
who possesses a quality which I do not possess. The shades
of difference between other people and me serve to make
variety and prevent monotony, but that is all; broadly speaking, we are all alike; and so by studying myself carefully and
comparing myself with other people and noting the diver-
gences, I have been enabled to acquire a knowledge of the
human race which I perceive is more accurate and more
comprehensive than that which has been acquired and revealed by any other member of our species. As a result, my
private and concealed opinion of myself is not of a compli-

mentary sort. It follows that my estimate of the human race is the duplicate of my estimate of myself.

I am not proposing to discuss all of the peculiarities of the human race at this time; I only wish to touch lightly upon one or two of them. To begin with, I wonder why a man should prefer a good billiard table to a poor one; and why he should prefer straight cues to crooked ones; and why he should prefer round balls to chipped ones; and why he should prefer a level table to one that slants; and why he should prefer responsive cushions to the dull and unresponsive kind. I wonder at these things, because when we examine the matter we find that the essentials involved in billiards are as competently and exhaustively furnished by a bad billiard outfit as they are by the best one. One of the essentials is amusement. Very well, if there is any more amusement to be gotten out of the one outfit than out of the other, the facts are in favor of the bad outfit. The bad outfit will always furnish thirty per cent more fun for the players and for the spectators than will the good outfit. Another essential of the game is that the outfit shall give the players full opportunity to exercise their best skill and display it in a way to compel the admiration of the spectators. Very well, the bad outfit is nothing behind the good one in this regard. It is a difficult matter to estimate correctly the eccentricities of chipped balls and a slanting table and make the right allowance for them and secure a count; the finest kind of skill is required to accomplish the satisfactory result. Another essential of the game is that it shall add to the interest of the game by furnishing opportunities to bet. Very well, in this regard no good outfit can claim any advantage over a bad one. I know by experience that a bad outfit is as valuable as the best one; that an outfit that couldn't be sold at auction for seven dollars is just as valuable for all the essentials of the game as an outfit that is worth a thousand.

I acquired some of this learning in Jackass Gulch, California, more than forty years ago. Jackass Gulch had once been a rich and thriving surface-mining camp. By and by its gold deposits were exhausted; then the people began to go away and the town began to decay, and rapidly; in my time it had disappeared. Where the bank and the city hall and the church and the gambling dens and the newspaper office and the streets of brick blocks had been, was nothing now but a wide and beautiful expanse of green grass, a peaceful and charming solitude. Half a dozen scattered dwellings were still inhabited and there was still one saloon of a ruined and rickety character struggling for life, but doomed. In its bar was a billiard outfit that was the counterpart of the one in my father-in-law's garret. The balls were chipped, the cloth was darned and patched, the table's surface was undulating and the cues were headless and had the curve of a parenthesis—but the forlorn remnant of marooned miners played games there and those games were more entertaining to look at than a circus and a grand opera combined. Nothing but a quite extraordinary skill could score a carom on that table—a skill that required the nicest estimate of force, distance and how much to allow for the various slants of the table and the other formidable peculiarities and idiosyncrasies furnished by the contradictions of the outfit. Last winter,[2] here in New York, I saw Hoppe and Schaefer and Sutton and the three or four other billiard champions of world-wide fame contend against each other, and certainly the art and science displayed were a wonder to see; yet I saw nothing there in the way of science and art that was more wonderful than shots which I had seen Texas Tom make on the wavy surface of that poor old wreck in the perishing saloon at Jackass Gulch forty years before. Once I saw Texas Tom make a string of seven points on a single inning!—all calculated shots, and not a fluke or a scratch among them. I often saw him make runs of four, but when he made his great string of seven the boys went wild with enthusiasm and admiration. The joy and the noise exceeded that which the great gathering at Madison Square produced when Sutton scored five hundred points at the eighteen-inch game, on a world-famous night last winter. With practice, that champion could score nineteen or twenty on the Jackass Gulch table; but to start with, Texas Tom would show him miracles that would astonish him; also it might have another handsome result: it might persuade the great experts to discard their own trifling game and bring the Jackass Gulch outfit here and exhibit their skill in a game worth a hundred of the discarded one for profound and breathless interest and for displays of almost superhuman skill.

In my experience, games played with a fiendish outfit furnish ecstasies of delight which games played with the

[2] Written October 12, 1906.

other kind cannot match. Twenty-seven years ago my budding little family spent the summer at Bateman's Point, near Newport, Rhode Island. It was a comfortable boarding place, well stocked with sweet mothers and little children, but the male sex was scarce; however, there was another young fellow besides myself, and he and I had good times—Higgins was his name, but that was not his fault. He was a very pleasant and companionable person. On the premises there was what had once been a bowling alley. It was a single alley and it was estimated that it had been out of repair for sixty years— but not the balls, the balls were in good condition; there were forty-one of them and they ranged in size from a grapefruit up to a lignum-vitae sphere that you could hardly lift. Higgins and I played on that alley day after day. At first, one of us located himself at the bottom end to set up the pins in case anything should happen to them, but nothing happened. The surface of that alley consisted of a rolling stretch of elevations and depressions, and neither of us could, by any art known to us, persuade a ball to stay on the alley until it should accomplish something. Little balls and big, the same thing always happened—the ball left the alley before it was halfway home and went thundering down alongside of it the rest of the way and made the gamekeeper climb out and take care of himself. No matter, we persevered and were rewarded. We examined the alley, noted and located a lot of its peculiarities, and little by little we learned how to deliver a ball in such a way that it would travel home and knock down a pin or two. By and by we succeeded in improving our game to a point where we were able to get all of the pins with thirty-five balls—so we made it a thirty-five-ball game. If the player did not succeed with thirty-five, he had lost the game. I suppose that all the balls, taken together, weighed five hundred pounds, or maybe a ton—or along there somewhere—but anyway it was hot weather, and by the time that a player had sent thirty-five of them home he was in a drench of perspiration and physically exhausted.

Next, we started cocked hat—that is to say, a triangle of three pins, the other seven being discarded. In this game we used the three smallest balls and kept on delivering them until we got the three pins down. After a day or two of practice we were able to get the chief pin with an output of four balls, but it cost us a great many deliveries to get the other two; but by and by we succeeded in perfecting our art—at least we perfected it to our limit. We reached a scientific excellence where we could get the three pins down with twelve deliveries of the three small balls, making thirty-six shots to conquer the cocked hat.

Having reached our limit for daylight work, we set up a couple of candles and played at night. As the alley was fifty or sixty feet long, we couldn't see the pins, but the candles indicated their locality. We continued this game until we were able to knock down the invisible pins with thirty-six shots. Having now reached the limit of the candle game, we changed and played it left-handed. We continued the left-handed game until we conquered its limit, which was fifty-four shots. Sometimes we sent down a succession of fifteen balls without getting anything at all. We easily got out of that old alley five times the fun that anybody could have gotten out of the best alley in New York.

One blazing hot day a modest and courteous officer of the regular army appeared in our den and introduced himself. He was about thirty-five years old, well built and militarily erect and straight, and he was hermetically sealed up in the uniform of that ignorant old day—a uniform made of heavy material, and much properer for January than July. When he saw the venerable alley and glanced from that to the long procession of shining balls in the trough, his eye lit with desire and we judged that he was our meat. We politely invited him to take a hand and he could not conceal his gratitude; though his breeding and the etiquette of his profession made him try. We explained the game to him and said that there were forty-one balls and that the player was privileged to extend his inning and keep on playing until he had used them all up—repeatedly—and that for every ten-strike he got a prize. We didn't name the prize—it wasn't necessary, as no prize would ever be needed or called for. He started a sarcastic smile but quenched it, according to the etiquette of his profession. He merely remarked that he would like to select a couple of medium balls and one small one, adding that he didn't think he would need the rest.

Then he began, and he was an astonished man. He couldn't get a ball to stay on the alley. When he had fired about fifteen balls and hadn't yet reached the cluster of pins, his annoyance began to show out through his clothes. He wouldn't let it show in his face; but after another fifteen balls he was not able to control his face; he didn't utter a word, but he exuded mute blasphemy from every pore. He asked permission to take off his coat, which was granted; then he turned himself loose with bitter determination, and although he was only an infantry officer he could have been mistaken for a battery, he got up such a volleying thunder with those balls. Presently he removed his cravat; after a little he took off his vest; and still he went bravely on. Higgins was suffocating. My condition was the same, but it would not be courteous to laugh; it would be better to burst, and we came near it. That officer was good pluck. He stood to his work without uttering a word and kept the balls going until he had expended the outfit four times, making four times forty-one shots; then he had to give it up and he did; for he was no longer able to stand without wobbling. He put on his clothes, bade us a courteous good-by, invited us to call at the Fort and started away. Then he came back and said,

"What is the prize for the ten-strike?"

We had to confess that we had not selected it yet.

He said gravely that he thought there was no occasion for hurry about it.

I believe Bateman's alley was a better one than any other in America in the matter of the essentials of the game. It compelled skill; it provided opportunity for bets; and if you could get a stranger to do the bowling for you there was more and wholesomer and delightfuler entertainment to be gotten out of his industries than out of the finest game by the best expert and played upon the best alley elsewhere in existence.

◇◇◇◇◇◇◇◇◇◇◇◇◇◇◇◇◇◇◇◇

CHAPTER 27

Through Mr. Paine[1] I learn that Jim Gillis is dead.[2] He died, aged seventy-seven, in California about two weeks ago, after a long illness. Mr. Paine went with Mr. Goodman to see him but Jim was too ill to see anyone. Steve Gillis's end is also near at hand and he lies cheerfully and tranquilly waiting. He is up in the sylvan Jackass Gulch country, among the other

---

[1] Albert Bigelow Paine.
[2] Written May 26, 1907.

Gillises whom I knew so well something more than forty years ago—George and Billy, brothers of Steve and Jim.[3] Steve and George and Billy have large crops of grandchildren but Jim remained a bachelor to the end.

I think Jim Gillis was a much more remarkable person than his family and his intimates ever suspected. He had a bright and smart imagination and it was of the kind that turns out impromptu work and does it well, does it with easy facility and without previous preparation, just builds a story as it goes along, careless of whither it is proceeding, enjoying each fresh fancy as it flashes from the brain and caring not at all whether the story shall ever end brilliantly and satisfactorily or shan't end at all. Jim was born a humorist and a very competent one. When I remember how felicitous were his untrained efforts, I feel a conviction that he would have been a star performer if he had been discovered and had been subjected to a few years of training with a pen. A genius is not very likely to ever discover himself; neither is he very likely to be discovered by his intimates; in fact I think I may put it in stronger words and say it is impossible that a genius —at least a literary genius—can ever be discovered by his intimates; they are so close to him that he is out of focus to them and they can't get at his proportions; they cannot perceive that there is any considerable difference between his bulk and their own. They can't get a perspective on him and it is only by a perspective that the difference between him and the rest of their limited circle can be perceived.

St. Peter's cannot be impressive for size to a person who has always seen it close at hand and has never been outside of Rome; it is only the stranger, approaching from far away in the Campagna, who sees Rome as an indistinct and characterless blur, with the mighty cathedral standing up out of it all lonely and unfellowed in its majesty. Thousands of geniuses live and die undiscovered—either by themselves or by others. But for the Civil War, Lincoln and Grant and Sherman and Sheridan would not have been discovered, nor have risen into notice. I have touched upon this matter in a small book which I wrote a generation ago and which I have not published as yet—*Captain Stormfield's Visit to Heaven*. When Stormfield

---

[3] In 1866, after leaving the *Morning Call*, Mark Twain spent three months in the "pocket" mines of Calaveras County at Jackass Gulch, but found no pockets.

arrived in heaven he was eager to get a sight of those un-
rivaled and incomparable military geniuses, Caesar, Alexander
and Napoleon, but was told by an old resident of heaven that
they didn't amount to much there as military geniuses,
that they ranked as obscure corporals only, by comparison
with a certain colossal military genius, a shoemaker by trade,
who had lived and died unknown in a New England village
and had never seen a battle in all his earthly life. He had
not been discovered while he was in the earth but heaven
knew him as soon as he arrived there and lavished upon
him the honors which he would have received in the earth if
the earth had known that he was the most prodigious military
genius the planet had ever produced.

I spent three months in the log-cabin home of Jim Gillis
and his "pard," Dick Stoker, in Jackass Gulch, that serene
and reposeful and dreamy and delicious sylvan paradise of
which I have already spoken. Every now and then Jim
would have an inspiration and he would stand up before the
great log fire, with his back to it and his hands crossed behind him, and deliver himself of an elaborate impromptu
lie—a fairy tale, an extravagant romance—with Dick Stoker
as the hero of it as a general thing. Jim always soberly pretended that what he was relating was strictly history,
veracious history, not romance. Dick Stoker, gray-headed and
good-natured, would sit smoking his pipe and listen with a
gentle serenity to these monstrous fabrications and never
utter a protest.

In one of my books—*Huckleberry Finn,* I think—I have
used one of Jim's impromptu tales, which he called "The
Tragedy of the Burning Shame." I had to modify it considerably to make it proper for print and this was a great
damage. As Jim told it, inventing it as he went along, I think
it was one of the most outrageously funny things I have ever
listened to. How mild it is in the book and how pale; how
extravagant and how gorgeous in its unprintable form! I
used another of Jim's impromptus in a book of mine called
A Tramp Abroad, a tale of how the poor innocent and
ignorant woodpeckers[4] tried to fill up a house with acorns.
It is a charming story, a delightful story, and full of happy
fancies. Jim stood before the fire and reeled it off with the
easiest facility, inventing its details as he went along and
claiming as usual that it was all straight fact, unassailable fact,

---

[4] Blue jays.

history pure and undefiled. I used another of Jim's inventions in one of my books, the story of Jim Baker's cat, the remarkable Tom Quartz.[5] Jim Baker was Dick Stoker, of course; Tom Quartz had never existed; there was no such cat, at least outside of Jim Gillis' imagination.

Once or twice Jim's energetic imagination got him into trouble. A squaw came along one day and tried to sell us some wild fruit that looked like large greengages. Dick Stoker had lived in that cabin eighteen years and knew that that product was worthless and inedible; but heedlessly and without purpose he remarked that he had never heard of it before. That was enough for Jim. He launched out with fervent praises of that devilish fruit, and the more he talked about it the warmer and stronger his admiration of it grew. He said that he had eaten it a thousand times; that all one needed to do was to boil it with a little sugar and there was nothing on the American continent that could compare with it for deliciousness. He was only talking to hear himself talk; and so he was brought up standing and for just one moment, or maybe two moments, smitten dumb when Dick interrupted him with the remark that if the fruit was so delicious why didn't he invest in it on the spot? Jim was caught but he wouldn't let on; he had gotten himself into a scrape but he was not the man to back down or confess; he pretended that he was only too happy to have this chance to enjoy once more this precious gift of God. Oh, he was a loyal man to his statements! I think he would have eaten that fruit if he had known it would kill him. He bought the lot and said airily and complacently that he was glad enough to have that benefaction, and that if Dick and I didn't want to enjoy it with him we could let it alone—he didn't care.

Then there followed a couple of the most delightful hours I have ever spent. Jim took an empty kerosene can of about a three-gallon capacity and put it on the fire and filled it half full of water and dumped into it a dozen of those devilish fruits; and as soon as the water came to a good boil he added a handful of brown sugar; as the boiling went on he tested the odious mess from time to time; the unholy vegetables grew softer and softer, pulpier and pulpier, and now he began to make tests with a tablespoon. He would dip out a spoonful and taste it, smack his lips with fictitious satisfaction,

[5] In *Roughing It*.

remark that perhaps it needed a little more sugar—so he would dump in a handful and let the boiling go on a while longer; handful after handful of sugar went in and still the tasting went on for two hours, Stoker and I laughing at him, ridiculing him, deriding him, blackguarding him all the while, and he retaining his serenity unruffled.

At last he said the manufacture had reached the right stage, the stage of perfection. He dipped his spoon, tasted, smacked his lips and broke into enthusiasms of grateful joy; then he gave us a taste apiece. From all that we could discover, those tons of sugar had not affected that fruit's malignant sharpness in the least degree. Acid? It was all acid, vindictive acid, uncompromising acid, with not a trace of the modifying sweetness which the sugar ought to have communicated to it and would have communicated to it if that fruit had been invented anywhere outside of perdition. We stopped with that one taste, but that great-hearted Jim, that dauntless martyr, went on sipping and sipping and sipping, and praising and praising and praising and praising, until his teeth and tongue were raw, and Stoker and I nearly dead with gratitude and delight. During the next two days neither food nor drink passed Jim's teeth; so sore were they that they could not endure the touch of anything; even his breath passing over them made him wince; nevertheless he went steadily on voicing his adulations of that brutal mess and praising God. It was an astonishing exhibition of grit, but Jim was like all the other Gillises, he was made of grit.

About once a year he would come down to San Francisco, discard his rough mining costume, buy a fifteen-dollar suit of ready-made slops and stride up and down Montgomery Street with his hat tipped over one ear and looking as satisfied as a king. The sarcastic stares which the drifting stream of elegant fashion cast upon him did not trouble him; he seemed quite unaware. On one of these occasions Joe Goodman and I and one or two other intimates took Jim up into the Bank Exchange billiard room. It was the resort of the rich and fashionable young swells of San Francisco. The time was ten at night and the twenty tables were all in service, all occupied. We strolled up and down the place to let Jim have a full opportunity to contemplate and enjoy this notable feature of the city.

Every now and then a fashionable young buck dropped a sarcastic remark about Jim and his clothes. We heard these remarks but hoped that Jim's large satisfaction with himself would prevent his discovering that he was the object of them; but that hope failed; Jim presently began to take notice; then he began to try to catch one of these men in the act of making his remark. He presently succeeded. A large and handsomely dressed young gentleman was the utterer. Jim stepped toward him and came to a standstill, with his chin lifted and his haughty pride exhibiting itself in his attitude and bearing, and said impressively, "That was for me. You must apologize or fight."

Half a dozen of the neighboring players heard him say it and they faced about and rested the butts of their cues on the floor and waited with amused interest for results. Jim's victim laughed ironically and said, "Oh, is that so? What would happen if I declined?"

"You will get a flogging that will mend your manners."

"Oh, indeed! I wonder if that's so."

Jim's manner remained grave and unruffled. He said, "I challenge you. You must fight me."

"Oh, really! Will you be so good as to name the time?"

"*Now.*"

"How prompt we are! Place?"

"*Here.*"

"This is charming! Weapons?"

"Double-barreled shotguns loaded with slugs; distance, thirty feet."

It was high time to interfere. Goodman took the young fool aside and said, "You don't know your man and you are doing a most dangerous thing. You seem to think he is joking but he is not joking, he is not that kind; he's in earnest; if you decline the duel he will kill you where you stand; you must accept his terms and you must do it right away, for you have no time to waste; take the duel or apologize. You will apologize, of course, for two reasons: you insulted him when he was not offending you; that is one reason; the other is that you naturally neither want to kill an unoffending man nor be killed yourself. You will apologize and you will have to let him word the apology; it will be more strong and more uncompromising than any apology that you, even with the most liberal intentions, would be likely to frame."

The man apologized, repeating the words as they fell from Jim's lips—the crowd massed around the pair and listen-

ing—and the character of the apology was in strict accordance
with Goodman's prediction concerning it.

I mourn for Jim. He was a good and steadfast friend, a
manly one, a generous one; an honest and honorable man
and endowed with a lovable nature. He instituted no quarrels
himself but whenever a quarrel was put upon him he was on
deck and ready.

◇◇◇◇◇◇◇◇◇◇◇◇◇◇◇◇◇◇◇

CHAPTER 28

I returned from the "pocket" mines to San Francisco and
wrote letters to the Virginia *Enterprise* for a while and was
then sent to the Sandwich Islands by the Sacramento *Union*
to write about the sugar interests. While I was in Honolulu
the survivors of the clipper *Hornet* (burned on the line)
arrived, mere skin and bone relics, after a passage of forty-
three days in an open boat on ten days' provisions, and I
worked all day and all night and produced a full and complete
account of the matter and flung it aboard a schooner which
had already cast off. It was the only full account that went
to California, and the *Union* paid me ten-fold the current
rates for it.

After about four or five months I returned to California to
find myself about the best-known honest man on the Pacific
coast. Thomas McGuire, proprietor of several theaters, said
that now was the time to make my fortune—strike while the
iron was hot—break into the lecture field! I did it. I announced
a lecture on the Sandwich Islands, closing the advertisement
with the remark: "Admission one dollar; doors open at half
past seven, the trouble begins at eight." A true prophecy. The
trouble certainly did begin at eight, when I found myself in
front of the only audience I had ever faced, for the fright
which pervaded me from head to foot was paralyzing. It
lasted two minutes and was as bitter as death; the memory of
it is indestructible but it had its compensations, for it made
me immune from timidity before audiences for all time to
come.

Repetition is a mighty power in the domain of humor. If

frequently used, nearly any precisely worded and unchanging formula will eventually compel laughter if it be gravely and earnestly repeated, at intervals, five or six times. I undertook to prove the truth of this forty years ago in San Francisco on the occasion of my second attempt at lecturing. My first lecture had succeeded to my satisfaction. Then I prepared another one but was afraid of it because the first fifteen minutes of it was not humorous. I felt the necessity of preceding it with something which would break up the house with a laugh and get me on pleasant and friendly terms with it at the start, instead of allowing it leisure to congeal into a critical mood, since that could be disastrous. With this idea in mind I prepared a scheme of so daring a nature that I wonder now that I ever had the courage to carry it through. San Francisco had been persecuted for five or six years with a silly and pointless and unkillable anecdote which everybody had long ago grown weary of—weary unto death. It was as much as a man's life was worth to tell that moldy anecdote to a citizen. I resolved to begin my lecture with it, and keep on repeating it until the mere repetition should conquer the house and make it laugh. That anecdote is in one of my books.

There were fifteen hundred people present, and as I had been a reporter on one of the papers for a good while I knew several hundred of them. They loved me, they couldn't help it; they admired me; and I knew it would grieve them, disappoint them and make them sick at heart to hear me fetch out that odious anecdote with the air of a person who thought it new and good. I began with a description of my first day in the overland coach; then I said,

"At a little 'dobie station out on the plains, next day, a man got in and after chatting along pleasantly for a while he said 'I can tell you a most laughable thing indeed, if you would like to listen to it. Horace Greeley went over this road once. When he was leaving Carson City he told the driver, Hank Monk, that he had an engagement to lecture at Placerville and was very anxious to go through quick. Hank Monk cracked his whip and started off at an awful pace. The coach bounced up and down in such a terrific way that it jolted the buttons all off of Horace's coat and finally shot his head clean through the roof of the stage, and then he yelled at Hank Monk and begged him to go easier—said he warn't in as much of a hurry as he was a while ago. But Hank Monk said, "Keep your seat,

Horace, I'll get you there on time!"—and you bet he did, too, what was left of him!' "

I told it in a level voice, in a colorless and monotonous way, without emphasizing any word in it, and succeeded in making it dreary and stupid to the limit. Then I paused and looked very much pleased with myself and as if I expected a burst of laughter. Of course there was no laughter, nor anything resembling it. There was a dead silence. As far as the eye could reach that sea of faces was a sorrow to look upon; some bore an insulted look; some exhibited resentment; my friends and acquaintances looked ashamed, and the house, as a body, looked as if it had taken an emetic.

I tried to look embarrassed and did it very well. For a while I said nothing, but stood fumbling with my hands in a sort of mute appeal to the audience for compassion. Many did pity me—I could see it. But I could also see that the rest were thirsting for blood. I presently began again and stammered awkwardly along with some more details of the overland trip. Then I began to work up toward my anecdote again with the air of a person who thinks he did not tell it well the first time and who feels that the house will like it the next time, if told with a better art. The house perceived that I was working up toward the anecdote again and its indignation was very apparent. Then I said,

"Just after we left Julesburg, on the Platte, I was sitting with the driver and he said, 'I can tell you a most laughable thing indeed if you would like to listen to it. Horace Greeley went over this road once. When he was leaving Carson City he told the driver, Hank Monk, that he had an engagement to lecture at Placerville and was very anxious to go through quick. Hank Monk cracked his whip and started off at an awful pace. The coach bounced up and down in such a terrific way that it jolted the buttons all off of Horace's coat and finally shot his head clean through the roof of the stage, and then he yelled at Hank Monk and begged him to go easier—said he warn't in as much of a hurry as he was a while ago. But Hank Monk said, "Keep your seat, Horace, I'll get you there on time!"—and you bet he did, too, what was left of him!' "

I stopped again and looked gratified and expectant, but there wasn't a sound. The house was as still as the tomb. I looked embarrassed again. I fumbled again. I tried to seem ready to cry, and once more, after a considerable silence, I took up the overland trip again, and once more I stumbled and hesitated along—then presently began again to work up toward the anecdote. The house exhibited distinct impatience, but I worked along up, trying all the while to look like a person who was sure that there was some mysterious reason why these people didn't see how funny the anecdote was, and that they must see it if I could ever manage to tell it right, therefore I must make another effort. I said,

"A day or two after that we picked up a Denver man at the crossroads and he chatted along very pleasantly for a while. Then he said, 'I can tell you a most laughable thing indeed, if you would like to listen to it. Horace Greeley went over this road once. When he was leaving Carson City he told the driver, Hank Monk, that he had an engagement to lecture at Placerville and was very anxious to go through quick. Hank Monk cracked his whip and started off at an awful pace. The coach bounced up and down in such a terrific way that it jolted the buttons all off of Horace's coat and finally shot his head clean through the roof of the stage, and then he yelled at Hank Monk and begged him to go easier—said he warn't in as much of a hurry as he was a while ago. But Hank Monk said, "Keep your seat, Horace, I'll get you there on time!"— and you bet he did, too, what was left of him!' "

All of a sudden the front ranks recognized the sell and broke into a laugh. It spread back, and back, and back, to the furthest verge of the place; then swept forward again, and then back again, and at the end of a minute the laughter was as universal and as thunderously noisy as a tempest.

It was a heavenly sound to me, for I was nearly exhausted with weakness and apprehension, and was becoming almost convinced that I should have to stand there and keep on telling that anecdote all night, before I could make those people understand that I was working a delicate piece of satire. I am sure I should have stood my ground and gone on favoring them with that tale until I broke them down, under the unconquerable conviction that the monotonous repetition of it would infallibly fetch them some time or other.

A good many years afterward there was to be an Authors' Reading at Chickering Hall, in New York, and I thought I would try that anecdote again and see if the repetition would be effective with an audience wholly unacquainted with it and who would be obliged to find the fun solely in the repetition, if they found it at all, since there would be not a shred of anything in the tale itself that could stir anybody's sense of humor but an idiot's. I sat by James Russell Lowell on the platform and he asked me what I was going to read. I said I was going to tell a brief and wholly pointless anecdote in a dreary and monotonous voice and that therein would consist my whole performance. He said, "That is a strange idea. What do you expect to accomplish by it?"

I said, "Only a laugh. I want the audience to laugh."

He said, "Of course you do—that is your trade. They will require it of you. But do you think they are going to laugh at a silly and pointless anecdote drearily and monotonously told?"

"Yes," I said, "they'll laugh."

Lowell said, "I think you are dangerous company. I am going to move to the other end of this platform and get out of the way of the bricks."

When my turn came up I got up and exactly repeated—and most gravely and drearily—that San Francisco performance of so many years before. It was as deadly an ordeal as ever I have been through in the course of my checkered life. I never got a response of any kind until I had told that juiceless anecdote in the same unvarying words *five times;* then the house saw the point and annihilated the heartbreaking silence with a most welcome crash. It revived me, and I needed it, for if I had had to tell it four more times I should have died—but I would have done it, if I had had to get somebody to hold me up. The house kept up that crash for a minute or two, and it was a soothing and blessed thing to hear.

Mr. Lowell shook me cordially by the hand and said,

"Mark, it was a triumph of art! It was a triumph of grit, too. I would rather lead a forlorn hope and take my chances of a soldier's bloody death than try to duplicate that performance."

He said that during the first four repetitions, with that mute and solemn and wondering house before him, he thought he was going to perish with anxiety for me. He said he had never been so sorry for a human being before and that he was cold all down his spine until the fifth repetition broke up the house and brought the blessed relief.

CHAPTER 29

I lectured in all the principal California towns and in Nevada, then lectured once or twice more in San Francisco, then retired from the field rich—for me—and laid out a plan to sail westward from San Francisco and go around the world. The proprietors of the *Daily Alta California* engaged me to write an account of the trip for that paper—fifty letters of a column and a half each, which would be about 2,000 words per letter, and the pay to be twenty dollars per letter.

I went east to St. Louis to say good-by to my mother and then I was bitten by the prospectus of Captain Duncan of the *Quaker City* excursion and I ended by joining it. During the trip I wrote and sent the fifty letters; six of them miscarried and I wrote six new ones to complete my contract. Then I put together a lecture on the trip and delivered it in San Francisco at great and satisfactory pecuniary profit; then I branched out into the country and was aghast at the result: I had been entirely forgotten, I never had people enough in my houses to sit as a jury of inquest on my lost reputation! I inquired into this curious condition of things and found that the thrifty owners of that prodigiously rich *Alta* newspaper had *copyrighted* all those poor little twenty-dollar letters and had threatened with prosecution any journal which should venture to copy a paragraph from them!

And there I was! I had contracted to furnish a large book concerning the excursion to the American Publishing Co. of Hartford, and I supposed I should need all those letters to fill it out with. I was in an uncomfortable situation—that is, if the proprietors of this stealthily acquired copyright should refuse to let me use the letters. That is just what they did; Mr. Mac —something—I have forgotten the rest of his name[1]—said his firm were going to make a book out of the letters in order to get back the thousand dollars which they had paid for them. I said that if they had acted fairly and honorably and had al-

[1] May 20, 1906. I recall it now—MacCrellish.—M. T.

161

lowed the country press to use the letters or portions of them, my lecture skirmish on the coast would have paid me ten thousand dollars, whereas the *Alta* had lost me that amount. Then he offered a compromise: he would publish the book and allow me ten percent royalty on it. The compromise did not appeal to me and I said so. The book sale would be confined to San Francisco, and my royalty would not pay me enough to board me three months, whereas my eastern contract, if carried out, could be profitable to me, for I had a sort of reputation on the Atlantic seaboard, acquired through the publication of six excursion letters in the New York *Tribune* and one or two in the *Herald.*

In the end Mr. Mac agreed to suppress his book, on certain conditions: in my preface I must thank the *Alta* for waiving its "rights" and granting me permission. I objected to the thanks. I could not with any large degree of sincerity thank the *Alta* for bankrupting my lecture raid. After considerable debate my point was conceded and the thanks left out.

Noah Brooks was editor of the *Alta* at the time, a man of sterling character and equipped with a right heart, also a good historian where facts were not essential. In biographical sketches of me written many years afterward (1902) he was quite eloquent in praises of the generosity of the *Alta* people in giving to me without compensation a book which, as history had afterward shown, was worth a fortune. After all the fuss, I did not levy heavily upon the *Alta* letters. I found that they were newspaper matter, not book matter. They had been written here and there and yonder, as opportunity had given me a chance working moment or two during our feverish flight around about Europe or in the furnace heat of my stateroom on board the *Quaker City,* therefore they were loosely constructed and needed to have some of the wind and water squeezed out of them. I used several of them—ten or twelve, perhaps. I wrote the rest of *The Innocents Abroad* in sixty days and I could have added a fortnight's labor with the pen and gotten along without the letters altogether. I was very young in those days, exceedingly young, marvelously young, younger than I am now, younger than I shall ever be again, by hundreds of years. I worked every night from eleven or twelve until broad day in the morning, and as I did 200,000 words in the sixty days, the average was more than 3,000 words a day—nothing for Sir Walter Scott, nothing for Louis Stevenson, nothing for plenty of other people, but quite handsome for me. In 1897, when we were living in Tedworth Square, London, and I was writing the book called *Following the Equator*, my average was 1,800 words a day; here in Florence (1904) my average seems to be 1,400 words per sitting of four or five hours.

I was deducing from the above that I have been slowing down steadily in these thirty-six years, but I perceive that my statistics have a defect: 3,000 words in the spring of 1868, when I was working seven or eight or nine hours at a sitting, has little or no advantage over the sitting of to-day, covering half the time and producing half the output. Figures often beguile me, particularly when I have the arranging of them myself; in which case the remark attributed to Disraeli would often apply with justice and force:

"There are three kinds of lies: lies, damned lies and statistics."

I wrote *The Innocents Abroad* in the months of March and April, 1868, in San Francisco. It was published in August, 1869. Three years afterward Mr. Goodman of Virginia City, on whose newspaper I had served ten years before and of whom I have had much to say in the book called *Roughing It* —I seem to be overloading the sentence and I apologize— came East and we were walking down Broadway one day when he said:

"How did you come to steal Oliver Wendell Holmes's dedication and put it in your book?"

I made a careless and inconsequential answer, for I supposed he was joking. But he assured me that he was in earnest. He said:

"I'm not discussing the question of whether you stole it or didn't—for that is a question that can be settled in the first bookstore we come to. I am only asking you *how* you came to steal it, for that is where my curiosity is focalized."

I couldn't accommodate him with this information, as I hadn't it in stock. I could have made oath that I had not stolen anything, therefore my vanity was not hurt nor my spirit troubled. At bottom I supposed that he had mistaken another book for mine and was now getting himself into an untenable place and preparing sorrow for himself and triumph for me. We entered a bookstore and he asked for *The Innocents Abroad* and for the dainty little blue-and-gold edition of Dr. Oliver Wendell Holmes's poems. He opened the books, exposed their dedications, and said:

"Read them. It is plain that the author of the second one stole the first one, isn't it?"

I was very much ashamed and unspeakably astonished. We continued our walk but I was not able to throw any gleam of light upon that original question of his. I could not remember ever having seen Doctor Holmes's dedication. I knew the poems but the dedication was new to me.

I did not get hold of the key to that secret until months afterward; then it came in a curious way and yet it was a natural way; for the natural way provided by nature and the construction of the human mind for the discovery of a forgotten event is to employ another forgotten event for its resurrection.

I received a letter from the Reverend Doctor Rising, who had been rector of the Episcopal church in Virginia City in my time, in which letter Doctor Rising made reference to certain things which had happened to us in the Sandwich Islands six years before; among other things he made casual mention of the Honolulu Hotel's poverty in the matter of literature. At first I did not see the bearing of the remark; it called nothing to my mind. But presently it did—with a flash! There was but one book in Mr. Kirchhof's hotel and that was the first volume of Doctor Holmes's blue-and-gold series. I had had a fortnight's chance to get well acquainted with its contents, for I had ridden around the big island (Hawaii) on horseback and had brought back so many saddle boils that if there had been a duty on them it would have bankrupted me to pay it. They kept me in my room, unclothed and in persistent pain, for two weeks, with no company but cigars and the little volume of poems. Of course I read them almost constantly; I read them from beginning to end, then began in the middle and read them both ways. In a word, I read the book to rags and was infinitely grateful to the hand that wrote it.

Here we have an exhibition of what repetition can do when persisted in daily and hourly over a considerable stretch of time, where one is merely reading for entertainment, without thought or intention of preserving in the memory that which is read. It is a process which in the course of years dries all the juice out of a familiar verse of Scripture, leaving nothing but a sapless husk behind. In that case you at least know the origin of the husk, but in the case in point I apparently preserved the husk but presently forgot whence it came. It lay lost in some dim corner of my memory a year or two, then came forward when I needed a dedication and was promptly mistaken by me as a child of my own happy fancy.

I was new, I was ignorant, the mysteries of the human mind were a sealed book to me as yet, and I stupidly looked upon myself as a tough and unforgivable criminal. I wrote to Doctor Holmes and told him the whole disgraceful affair, implored him in impassioned language to believe that I never intended to commit this crime, and was unaware that I had committed it until I was confronted with the awful evidence. I have lost his answer. I could better have afforded to lose an uncle. Of these I had a surplus, many of them of no real value to me, but that letter was beyond price, beyond uncledom and unsparable. In it Doctor Holmes laughed the kindest and healingest laugh over the whole matter and at considerable length and in happy phrase assured me that there was no crime in unconscious plagiarism; that I committed it every day, that he committed it every day, that every man alive on the earth who writes or speaks commits it every day and not merely once or twice but every time he opens his mouth; that all our phrasings are spiritualized shadows cast multitudinously from our readings; that no happy phrase of ours is ever quite original with us; there is nothing of our own in it except some slight change born of our temperament, character, environment, teachings and associations; that this slight change differentiates it from another man's manner of saying it, stamps it with our special style and makes it our own for the time being; all the rest of it being old, moldy, antique and smelling of the breath of a thousand generations of them that have passed it over their teeth before!

In the thirty-odd years which have come and gone since then I have satisfied myself that what Doctor Holmes said was true.

◇◇◇◇◇◇◇◇◇◇◇◇◇◇◇◇◇◇◇◇

CHAPTER 30

To go back a bit: my experiences as an author began early in 1867. I came to New York from San Francisco in the first month of that year and presently Charles H. Webb, whom I had known in San Francisco as a reporter on *The Bulletin* and afterward editor of *The Californian,* suggested that I publish a volume of sketches. I had but a slender reputation to publish it on but I was charmed and excited by the suggestion and quite willing to venture it if some industrious person would save me the trouble of gathering the sketches together. I was loath to do it myself, for from the beginning of my sojourn in this world there was a persistent vacancy in me where the industry ought to be. ("Ought to was" is better, perhaps, though the most of the authorities differ as to this.)

Webb said I had some reputation in the Atlantic states but I knew quite well that it must be of a very attenuated sort. What there was of it rested upon the story of "The Jumping Frog." When Artemus Ward passed through California on a lecturing tour in 1865 or '66, I told him the "Jumping Frog" story in San Francisco and he asked me to write it out and send it to his publisher, Carleton, in New York, to be used in padding out a small book which Artemus had prepared for the press and which needed some more stuffing to make it big enough for the price which was to be charged for it.

It reached Carleton in time but he didn't think much of it and was not willing to go to the typesetting expense of adding it to the book. He did not put it in the wastebasket but made Henry Clapp a present of it and Clapp used it to help out the funeral of his dying literary journal, *The Saturday Press.* "The Jumping Frog" appeared in the last number of that paper, was the most joyous feature of the obsequies, and was at once copied in the newspapers of America and England. It certainly had a wide celebrity and it still had it at the time that I am speaking of—but I was aware that it was only the frog that was celebrated. It wasn't I. I was still an obscurity.

Webb undertook to collate the sketches. He performed this office, then handed the result to me and I went to Carleton's establishment with it. I approached a clerk and he bent eagerly over the counter to inquire into my needs; but when he found that I had come to sell a book and not to buy one, his temperature fell sixty degrees and the old-gold intrenchments in the roof of my mouth contracted three-quarters of an inch and my teeth fell out. I meekly asked the privilege of a word with Mr. Carleton and was coldly informed that he was in his private office. Discouragements and difficulties followed, but after a while I got by the frontier and entered the holy of holies. Ah, now I remember how I managed it! Webb had made an appointment for me with Carleton; otherwise I never should have gotten over that frontier. Carleton rose and said brusquely and aggressively,

"Well, what can I do for you?"

I reminded him that I was there by appointment to offer him my book for publication. He began to swell and went on swelling and swelling and swelling until he had reached the dimensions of a god of about the second or third degree. Then the fountains of his great deep were broken up and for two or three minutes I couldn't see him for the rain. It was words, only words, but they fell so densely that they darkened the atmosphere. Finally he made an imposing sweep with his right hand which comprehended the whole room and said,

"Books—look at those shelves! Every one of them is loaded with books that are waiting for publication. Do I want any more? Excuse me, I don't. Good morning."

Twenty-one years elapsed before I saw Carleton again. I was then sojourning with my family at the Schweizerhof, in Lucerne. He called on me, shook hands cordially and said at once without any preliminaries,

"I am substantially an obscure person but I have a couple of such colossal distinctions to my credit that I am entitled to immortality—to wit: I refused a book of yours and for this I stand without competitor as the prize ass of the nineteenth century."

It was a most handsome apology and I told him so and said it was a long delayed revenge but was sweeter to me than any other that could be devised, that during the lapsed twenty-one years I had in fancy taken his life several times every year and always in new and increasingly cruel and inhuman ways, but that now I was pacified, appeased, happy, even jubilant, and that thenceforth I should hold him my true and valued friend and never kill him again.

I reported my adventure to Webb and he bravely said that not all the Carletons in the universe should defeat that book, he would publish it himself on a ten per cent royalty. And so he did. He brought it out in blue and gold and made a very pretty little book of it. I think he named it *The Celebrated Jumping Frog of Calaveras County, and Other Sketches,* price $1.25. He made the plates and printed and bound the book through a job-printing house and published it through the American News Company.

In June I sailed in the *Quaker City* Excursion. I returned in

November and in Washington found a letter from Elisha Bliss of the American Publishing Company of Hartford, offering me five per cent royalty on a book which should recount the adventures of the Excursion. In lieu of the royalty I was offered the alternative of ten thousand dollars cash upon delivery of the manuscript. I consulted A. D. Richardson and he said, "Take the royalty." I followed his advice and closed with Bliss.

I was out of money and I went down to Washington to see if I could earn enough there to keep me in bread and butter while I should write the book. I came across William Swinton, brother of the historian, and together we invented a scheme for our mutual sustenance; we became the fathers and originators of what is a common feature in the newspaper world now, the syndicate. We became the old original first Newspaper Syndicate on the planet; it was on a small scale but that is usual with untried new enterprises. We had twelve journals on our list; they were all weeklies, all obscure and poor and all scattered far away among the back settlements. It was a proud thing for those little newspapers to have a Washington correspondent and a fortunate thing for us that they felt in that way about it. Each of the twelve took two letters a week from us, at a dollar per letter; each of us wrote one letter per week and sent off six duplicates of it to these benefactors, thus acquiring twenty-four dollars a week to live on, which was all we needed in our cheap and humble quarters.

Swinton was one of the dearest and loveliest human beings I have ever known, and we led a charmed existence together, in a contentment which knew no bounds. Swinton was refined by nature and breeding; he was a gentleman by nature and breeding; he was highly educated; he was of a beautiful spirit; he was pure in heart and speech. He was a Scotchman and a Presbyterian; a Presbyterian of the old and genuine school, being honest and sincere in his religion and loving it and finding serenity and peace in it. He hadn't a vice, unless a large and grateful sympathy with Scotch whisky may be called by that name. I didn't regard it as a vice, because he was a Scotchman, and Scotch whisky to a Scotchman is an innocent as milk is to the rest of the human race. In Swinton's case it was a virtue and not an economical one. Twenty-four dollars a week would really have been riches to us if we hadn't had to support that jug; because of the jug we were always sailing pretty close to the wind, and any tardiness in the arrival of any part of our income was sure to cause some inconvenience.

I remember a time when a shortage occurred; we had to have three dollars and we had to have it before the close of the day. I don't know now how we happened to want all that money at one time; I only know we had to have it. Swinton told me to go out and find it and he said he would also go out and see what he could do. He didn't seem to have any doubt that we would succeed but I knew that that was his religion working in him; I hadn't the same confidence; I hadn't any idea where to turn to raise all that bullion and I said so. I think he was ashamed of me, privately, because of my weak faith. He told me to give myself no uneasiness, no concern; and said in a simple, confident and unquestioning way, "The Lord will provide." I saw that he fully believed the Lord would provide but it seemed to me that if he had had my experience— But never mind that; before he was done with me his strong faith had had its influence and I went forth from the place almost convinced that the Lord really would provide.

I wandered around the streets for an hour, trying to think up some way to get that money, but nothing suggested itself. At last I lounged into the big lobby of the Ebbitt House, which was then a new hotel, and sat down. Presently a dog came loafing along. He paused, glanced up at me and said with his eyes, "Are you friendly?" I answered with my eyes that I was. He gave his tail a grateful wag and came forward and rested his jaw on my knee and lifted his brown eyes to my face in a winningly affectionate way. He was a lovely creature, as beautiful as a girl, and he was made all of silk and velvet. I stroked his smooth brown head and fondled his drooping ears and we were a pair of lovers right away. Pretty soon Brig.-Gen. Miles, the hero of the land, came strolling by in his blue and gold splendors, with everybody's admiring gaze upon him. He saw the dog and stopped, and there was a light in his eye which showed that he had a warm place in his heart for dogs like this gracious creature; then he came forward and patted the dog and said,

"He is very fine—he is a wonder; would you sell him?"

I was greatly moved; it seemed a marvelous thing to me, the way Swinton's prediction had come true.

I said, "Yes."

The General said, "What do you ask for him?"

"Three dollars."

The General was manifestly surprised. He said, "Three dollars? Only three dollars? Why that dog is a most uncommon dog; he can't possibly be worth less than fifty. If he were mine, I wouldn't take a hundred for him. I'm afraid you are not aware of his value. Reconsider your price if you like, I don't wish to wrong you."

But if he had known me he would have known that I was no more capable of wronging him than he was of wronging me. I responded with the same quiet decision as before.

"No, three dollars. That is his price."

"Very well, since you insist upon it," said the General, and he gave me three dollars and led the dog away and disappeared upstairs.

In about ten minutes a gentle-faced, middle-aged gentleman came along and began to look around here and there and under tables and everywhere, and I said to him, "Is it a dog you are looking for?"

His face had been sad before and troubled; but it lit up gladly now and he answered, "Yes—have you seen him?"

"Yes," I said, "he was here a minute ago and I saw him follow a gentleman away. I think I could find him for you if you would like me to try."

I have seldom seen a person look so grateful, and there was gratitude in his voice too when he conceded that he would like me to try. I said I would do it with great pleasure but that as it might take a little time I hoped he would not mind paying me something for my trouble. He said he would do it most gladly—repeating that phrase "most gladly"—and asked me how much.

I said, "Three dollars."

He looked surprised, and said, "Dear me, it is nothing! I will pay you ten, quite willingly."

But I said, "No, three is the price," and I started for the stairs without waiting for any further argument, for Swinton had said that that was the amount that the Lord would provide and it seemed to me that it would be sacrilegious to take a penny more than was promised.

I got the number of the General's room from the office clerk as I passed by his wicket, and when I reached the room I found the General there caressing his dog and quite happy. I said, "I am sorry, but I have to take the dog again."

He seemed very much surprised and said, "Take him again? Why, he is my dog; you sold him to me and at your own price."

"Yes," I said, "it is true—but I have to have him, because the man wants him again."

"What man?"

"The man that owns him; he wasn't my dog."

The General looked even more surprised than before, and for a moment he couldn't seem to find his voice; then he said, "Do you mean to tell me that you were selling another man's dog—and knew it?"

"Yes, I knew it wasn't my dog."

"Then why did you sell him?"

I said, "Well, that is a curious question to ask. I sold him because you wanted him. You offered to buy the dog; you can't deny that. I was not anxious to sell him—I had not even thought of selling him—but it seemed to me that if it could be any accommodation to you—"

He broke me off in the middle, and said, "*Accommodation* to me? It is the most extraordinary spirit of accommodation I have ever heard of—the idea of your selling a dog that didn't belong to you—"

I broke him off there and said, "There is no relevancy about this kind of argument; you said yourself that the dog was probably worth a hundred dollars. I only asked you three; was there anything unfair about that? You offered to pay more, you know you did. I only asked you three; you can't deny it."

"Oh, what in the world has that to do with it! The crux of the matter is that you didn't own the dog—can't you see that? You seem to think that there is no impropriety in selling property that isn't yours provided you sell it cheap. Now then—"

I said, "Please don't argue about it any more. You can't get around the fact that the price was perfectly fair, perfectly reasonable—considering that I didn't own the dog—and so arguing about it is only a waste of words. I have to have him back again because the man wants him; don't you see that I haven't any choice in the matter? Put yourself in my place. Suppose you had sold a dog that didn't belong to you; suppose you—"

"Oh," he said, "don't muddle my brains any more with your idiotic reasonings! Take him along and give me a rest."

So I paid back the three dollars and led the dog downstairs and passed him over to his owner and collected three for my trouble.

I went away then with a good conscience, because I had acted honorably; I never could have used the three that I sold the dog for, because it was not rightly my own, but the three

I got for restoring him to his rightful owner was righteously and properly mine, because I had earned it. That man might never have gotten that dog back at all, if it hadn't been for me. My principles have remained to this day what they were then. I was always honest; I know I can never be otherwise. It is as I said in the beginning—I was never able to persuade myself to use money which I had acquired in questionable ways.

Now then, that is the tale. Some of it is true.

◇◇◇◇◇◇◇◇◇◇◇◇◇◇◇◇◇◇◇

CHAPTER 31

By my contract I was to deliver the manuscript of *The Innocents Abroad* in July of 1868. I wrote the book in San Francisco, as I have said, and delivered the manuscript within contract time. Bliss provided a multitude of illustrations for the book and then stopped work on it. The contract date for the issue went by and there was no explanation of this. Time drifted along and still there was no explanation. I was lecturing all over the country; and about thirty times a day, on an average, I was trying to answer this conundrum: "When is your book coming out?"

I got tired of inventing new answers to that question and by and by I got horribly tired of the question itself. Whoever asked it became my enemy at once and I was usually almost eager to make that appear.

As soon as I was free of the lecture field I hastened to Hartford to make inquiries. Bliss said that the fault was not his; that he wanted to publish the book but the directors of his company were staid old fossils and were afraid of it. They had examined the book and the majority of them were of the opinion that there were places in it of a humorous character. Bliss said the house had never published a book that had a suspicion like that attaching to it and that the directors were afraid that a departure of this kind could seriously injure the house's reputation, that he was tied hand and foot and was not permitted to carry out his contract.

One of the directors, a Mr. Drake—at least he was the remains of what had once been a Mr. Drake—invited me to take a ride with him in his buggy and I went along. He was a pa-

thetic old relic and his ways and his talk were also pathetic.
He had a delicate purpose in view and it took him some time
to hearten himself sufficiently to carry it out, but at last he accomplished it. He explained the house's difficulty and distress,
as Bliss had already explained it. Then he frankly threw himself and the house upon my mercy and begged me to take
away *The Innocents Abroad* and release the concern from the
contract. I said I wouldn't—and so ended the interview and
the buggy excursion.

Then I warned Bliss that he must get to work or I should
make trouble. He acted upon the warning and set up the book
and I read the proofs. Then there was another long wait and
no explanation. At last toward the end of July (1869, I think)
I lost patience and telegraphed Bliss that if the book was not
on sale in twenty-four hours I should bring suit for damages.

That ended the trouble. Half a dozen copies were bound
and placed on sale within the required time. Then the canvassing began and went briskly forward. In nine months the
book took the publishing house out of debt, advanced its stock
from twenty-five to two hundred and left seventy thousand
dollars profit to the good. It was Bliss that told me this—but if
it was true it was the first time that he had told the truth in
sixty-five years. He was born in 1804.

But I must go back to Webb. When I got back from the
Quaker City Excursion in November, 1867, Webb told me
that *The Jumping Frog* book had been favorably received by
the press and that he believed it had sold fairly well, but that
he had found it impossible to get a statement of account from
the American News Company. He said the book had been
something of a disaster to him, since he had manufactured it
with his own private funds and was now not able to get any of
the money back because of the dishonest and dodging ways of
the News Company.

I was very sincerely sorry for Webb, sorry that he had lost
money by befriending me, also in some degree sorry that he
was not able to pay me my royalties.

I made my contract for *The Innocents Abroad* with the
American Publishing Company. Then after two or three
months had gone by it occurred to me that perhaps I was violating that contract, there being a clause in it forbidding me
to publish books with any other firm during a term of a year
or so. Of course that clause could not cover a book which had
been published before the contract was made; anybody else

would have known that. But I didn't know it, for I was not in
the habit of knowing anything that was valuable and I was
also not in the habit of asking other people for information.

It was my ignorant opinion that I was violating the Bliss
contract and that I was in honor bound to suppress *The Jumping Frog* book and take it permanently out of print. So I went
to Webb with the matter. He was willing to accommodate me
upon these terms: that I should surrender to him such royalties as might be due me; that I should also surrender to him,
free of royalty, all bound and unbound copies which might be
in the News Company's hands; also that I should hand him
eight hundred dollars cash; also that he should superintend
the breaking up of the plates of the book, and for that service
should receive such bounty as the type founders should pay
for the broken plates as old type metal. Type metal was worth
nine cents a pound and the weight of the plates was about
forty pounds. One may perceive by these details that Webb
had some talent as a trader.

After this Webb passed out of the field of my vision for a
long time. But meantime chance threw me in the way of the
manager of the American News Company, and I asked him
about Webb's difficulties with the concern and how they had
come about. He said he didn't know of any difficulties. I then
explained to him that Webb had never been able to collect
anything from the company. In turn, he explained to me that
my explanation was not sound. He said the company had always furnished statements to Webb at the usual intervals and
had accompanied them with the company's check to date. By
his invitation I went with him to his office and by his books
and accounts he proved to me that what he had said was true.
Webb had collected his dues and mine regularly from the beginning and had pocketed the money. At the time that Webb
and I had settled, he was owing me six hundred dollars on
royalties. The bound and unbound *Jumping Frogs* which he
had inherited from me at that time had since been sold and
the result had gone into his pocket—part of it being six hundred more that should have come to me on royalties.

To sum up, I was now an author, I was an author with
some little trifle of reputation, I was an author who had published a book, I was an author who had not become rich
through that publication, I was an author whose first book had
cost him twelve hundred dollars in unreceived royalties, eight
hundred dollars in blood money, and three dollars and sixty

cents smouched from old type metal. I was resolved from that
moment that I would not publish with Webb any more—unless
I could borrow money enough to support the luxury.

By and by when I became notorious through the publication
of *The Innocents Abroad*, Webb was able to satisfy the public
first that he had discovered me, later that he had created me.
It was quite generally conceded that I was a valuable asset to
the American nation and to the great ranks of literature, also
that for the acquisition of this asset a deep debt of gratitude
was due from the nation and the ranks—to Webb.

By and by Webb and his high service were forgotten. Then
Bliss and the American Publishing Company came forward
and established the fact that they had discovered me, later
that they had created me, therefore that some more gratitude
was due. In the course of time there were still other claimants
for these great services. They sprang up in California, Nevada
and around generally, and I came at last to believe that I had
been more multitudinously discovered and created than any
other animal that had ever issued from the Deity's hands.

Webb believed that he was a literary person. He might
have gotten this superstition accepted by the world if he had
not extinguished it by publishing his things. They gave him
away. His prose was enchantingly puerile, his poetry was not
any better, yet he kept on grinding out his commonplaces at
intervals until he died two years ago of over-cerebration. He
was a poor sort of a creature and by nature and training a
fraud. As a liar he was well enough and had some success but
no distinction, because he was a contemporary of Elisha Bliss
and when it came to lying Bliss could overshadow and blot out
a whole continent of Webbs like a total eclipse.

◇◇◇◇◇◇◇◇◇◇◇◇◇◇◇◇◇◇◇◇◇

CHAPTER 32

I began as a lecturer in 1866 in California and Nevada; in
1867 lectured in New York once and in the Mississippi Valley
a few times; in 1868 made the whole Western circuit; and in
the two or three following seasons added the Eastern circuit
to my route.

The "lyceum system" was in full flower in those days and

James Redpath's Bureau in School Street, Boston, had the management of it throughout the Northern States and Canada. Redpath farmed out the lectures in groups of six or eight to the lyceums all over the country at an average of about $100 a night for each lecture. His commission was ten per cent; each lecture appeared about 110 nights in the season. There were a number of good drawing names in his list: Henry Ward Beecher; Anna Dickinson; John B. Gough; Horace Greeley; Wendell Phillips; Petroleum V. Nasby; Josh Billings; Hayes, the Arctic Explorer; Vincent, the English astronomer; Parsons, Irish orator; Agassiz; *et al.* He had in his list twenty or thirty men and women of light consequence and limited reputation who wrought for fees ranging from twenty-five dollars to fifty dollars. Their names have perished long ago. Nothing but art could find them a chance on the platform. Redpath furnished that art. All the lyceums wanted the big guns and wanted them yearningly, longingly, strenuously. Redpath granted their prayers—on this condition: for each house-filler allotted them they must hire several of his house-emptiers. This arrangement permitted the lyceums to get through alive for a few years, but in the end it killed them all and abolished the lecture business.

The chief ingredients of Redpath's make-up were honesty, sincerity, kindliness and pluck. He wasn't afraid. He was one of Ossawatomie Brown's right-hand men in the bleeding Kansas days; he was all through that struggle. He carried his life in his hands and from one day to another it wasn't worth the price of a night's lodging. He had a small body of daring men under him and they were constantly being hunted by the "jayhawkers," who were pro-slavery Missourians, guerillas, modern free lances. I can't think of the name of that daredevil guerilla who led the jayhawkers and chased Redpath up and down the country and, in turn, was chased by Redpath. By grace of the chances of war, the two men never met in the field, though they several times came within an ace of it.

Ten or twelve years later, Redpath was earning his living in Boston as chief of the lecture business in the United States. Fifteen or sixteen years after his Kansas adventures I became a public lecturer and he was my agent. Along there somewhere was a press dinner one November night at the Tremont Hotel in Boston and I attended it. I sat near the head of the table, with Redpath between me and the chairman; a stranger sat on my other side. I tried several times to talk with the stranger but he seemed to be out of words and I presently ceased from troubling him. He was manifestly a very shy man and moreover he might have been losing sleep the night before.

The first man called up was Redpath. At the mention of the name the stranger started and showed interest. He fixed a fascinated eye on Redpath and lost not a word of his speech. Redpath told some stirring incidents of his career in Kansas and said, among other things:

"Three times I came near capturing the gallant jayhawker chief and once he actually captured *me*, but didn't know me and let me go, because he said he was hot on Redpath's trail and couldn't afford to waste time and rope on inconsequential small fry."

My stranger was called up next, and when Redpath heard his name he, in turn, showed a startled interest. The stranger said, bending a caressing glance upon Redpath and speaking gently—I may even say sweetly:

"You realize that I was that jayhawker chief. I am glad to know you now and take you to my heart and call you friend" —then he added, in a voice that was pathetic with regret, "but if I had only known you then, what tumultuous happiness I should have had in your society!—while it lasted."

Beecher, Gough, Nasby and Anna Dickinson were the only lecturers who knew their own value and exacted it. In towns their fee was $200 and $250; in cities $400. The lyceum always got a profit out of these four (weather permitting), but generally lost it again on the house-emptiers.

There were two women who should have been house-emptiers—Olive Logan and Kate Field—but during a season or two they were not. They charged $100 and were recognized house-fillers for certainly two years. After that they were capable emptiers and were presently shelved. Kate Field had made a wide, spasmodic notoriety in 1867 by some letters which she sent from Boston—by telegraph—to the *Tribune* about Dickens's readings there in the beginning of his triumphant American tour. The letters were a frenzy of praise—praise which approached idolatry—and this was the right and welcome key to strike, for the country was itself in a frenzy of enthusiasm about Dickens. Then the idea of *telegraphing* a newspaper letter was new and astonishing and the wonder of it was in everyone's mouth. Kate Field became a celebrity at once. By and by she went on the platform; but two or three

years had elapsed and her subject—Dickens—had now lost its
freshness and its interest. For a while people went to see *her*,
because of her name; but her lecture was poor and her delivery repellently artificial; consequently, when the country's desire to look at her had been appeased the platform forsook
her.

She was a good creature, and the acquisition of a perishable
and fleeting notoriety was the disaster of her life. To her it
was infinitely precious and she tried hard in various ways during more than a quarter of a century to keep a semblance of
life in it, but her efforts were but moderately successful. She
died in the Sandwich Islands, regretted by her friends and
forgotten of the world.

Olive Logan's notoriety grew out of—only the initiated knew
what. Apparently it was a manufactured notoriety, not an
earned one. She *did* write and publish little things in newspapers and obscure periodicals but there was no talent in
them, and nothing resembling it. In a century they would not
have made her known. Her name was really built up out of
newspaper paragraphs set afloat by her husband, who was a
small-salaried minor journalist. During a year or two this kind
of paragraphing was persistent; one could seldom pick up a
newspaper without encountering it.

It is said that Olive Logan has taken a cottage at
Nahant and will spend the summer there.

Olive Logan has set her face decidedly against the
adoption of the short skirt for afternoon wear.

The report that Olive Logan will spend the coming
winter in Paris is premature. She has not yet made up
her mind.

Olive Logan was present at Wallack's on Saturday evening and was outspoken in her approval of the new
piece.

Olive Logan has so far recovered from her alarming illness that if she continues to improve her physicians will
cease from issuing bulletins to-morrow.

The result of this daily advertising was very curious. Olive
Logan's name was as familiar to the simple public as was
that of any celebrity of the time, and people talked with interest about her doings and movements and gravely discussed
her opinions. Now and then an ignorant person from the back-

woods would proceed to inform himself and then there were
surprises in store for all concerned:

"Who *is* Olive Logan?"

The listeners were astonished to find that they couldn't answer the question. It had never occurred to them to inquire
into the matter.

"What has she *done?*"

The listeners were dumb again. They didn't know. They
hadn't inquired.

"Well, then, how does she come to be celebrated?"

"Oh, it's about *something,* I don't know what. I never inquired, but I supposed everybody knew."

For entertainment I often asked these questions myself, of
people who were glibly talking about that celebrity and her
doings and sayings. The questioned were surprised to find
that they had been taking this fame wholly on trust and had
no idea who Olive Logan was or what she had done—if anything.

On the strength of this oddly created notoriety Olive Logan
went on the platform and for at least two seasons the United
States flocked to the lecture halls to look at her. She was merely a name and some rich and costly clothes and neither of
these properties had any lasting quality, though for a while
they were able to command a fee of $100 a night. She dropped
out of the memories of men a quarter of a century ago.

I had pleasant company on my lecture flights out of Boston
and plenty of good talks and smokes after the committee had
escorted me to the inn and made their good-night. There was
always a committee and they wore a silk badge of office; they
received me at the station and drove me to the lecture
hall; they sat in a row of chairs behind me on the stage, minstrel fashion, and in the earliest days their chief used to introduce me to the audience; but these introductions were so
grossly flattering that they made me ashamed and so I began
my talk at a heavy disadvantage. It was a stupid custom.
There was no occasion for the introduction; the introducer
was almost always an ass and his prepared speech a jumble of
vulgar compliments and dreary effort to be funny; therefore
after the first season I always introduced myself—using, of
course, a burlesque of the timeworn introduction. This change
was not popular with committee chairmen. To stand up grand-
ly before a great audience of his townsmen and make his little

devilish speech was the joy of his life and to have that joy taken from him was almost more than he could bear.

My introduction of myself was a most efficient "starter" for a while, then it failed. It had to be carefully and painstakingly worded and very earnestly spoken, in order that all strangers present might be deceived into the supposition that I was only the introducer and not the lecturer; also that the flow of over-done compliments might sicken those strangers; then, when the end was reached and the remark casually dropped that I was the lecturer and had been talking about myself, the effect was very satisfactory. But it was a good card for only a little while, as I have said; for the newspapers printed it and after that I could not make it go, since the house knew what was coming and retained its emotions.

Next I tried an introduction taken from my Californian experiences. It was gravely made by a slouching and awkward big miner in the village of Red Dog. The house, very much against his will, forced him to ascend the platform and introduce me. He stood thinking a moment, then said:

"I don't know anything about this man. At least I know only two things; one is, he hasn't been in the penitentiary, and the other is [after a pause, and almost sadly], *I don't know why.*"

That worked well for a while, then the newspapers printed it and took the juice out of it, and after that I gave up introductions altogether.

Now and then I had a mild little adventure but none which couldn't be forgotten without much of a strain. Once I arrived late at a town and found no committee in waiting and no sleighs on the stand. I struck up a street in the gay moonlight, found a tide of people flowing along, judged it was on its way to the lecture hall—a correct guess—and joined it. At the hall I tried to press in, but was stopped by the ticket-taker.

"Ticket, please."

I bent over and whispered: "It's all right. I am the lecturer."

He closed one eye impressively and said, loud enough for all the crowd to hear: "No you don't. Three of you have got in, up to now, but the next lecturer that goes in here tonight *pays.*"

Of course I paid; it was the least embarrassing way out of the trouble.

◇◇◇◇◇◇◇◇◇◇◇◇◇◇◇◇◇◇

CHAPTER 33

We had to bring out a new lecture every season (Nasby with the rest), and expose it in the "Star Course," Boston, for a first verdict, before an audience of 2,500 in the old Music Hall; for it was by that verdict that all the lyceums in the country determined the lecture's commercial value. The campaign did not really *begin* in Boston but in the towns around. We did not appear in Boston until we had rehearsed about a month in those towns and made all the necessary corrections and revisings.

This system gathered the whole tribe together in the city early in October and we had a lazy and sociable time there for several weeks. We lived at Young's Hotel; we spent the days in Redpath's Bureau, smoking and talking shop; and early in the evenings we scattered out among the towns and made them indicate the good and poor things in the new lectures. The country audience is the difficult audience; a passage which it will approve with a ripple will bring a crash in the city. A fair success in the country means a triumph in the city. And so, when we finally stepped on to the great stage at the Music Hall we already had the verdict in our pocket.

But sometimes lecturers who were "new to the business" did not know the value of "trying it on the dog," and these were apt to come to the Music Hall with an untried product. There was one case of this kind which made some of us very anxious when we saw the advertisement. De Cordova—humorist—he was the man we were troubled about. I think he had another name but I have forgotten what it was. He had been printing some dismally humorous things in the magazines; they had met with a deal of favor and given him a pretty wide name; and now he suddenly came poaching upon our preserve and took us by surprise. Several of us felt pretty unwell—too unwell to lecture. We got outlying engagements postponed and remained in town. We took front seats in one of the great galleries—Nasby, Billings and I—and waited. The

house was full. When De Cordova came on he was received
with what we regarded as a quite overdone and almost inde-
cent volume of welcome. I think we were not jealous, nor even
envious, but it made us sick anyway. When I found he was
going to read a humorous *story*—from manuscript—I felt better and hopeful but still anxious. He had a Dickens arrangement of tall gallows frame adorned with upholsteries and he
stood behind it under its overhead row of hidden lights. The
whole thing had a quite stylish look and was rather impressive.
The audience was so sure that he was going to be funny that
they took a dozen of his first utterances on trust and laughed
cordially—so cordially, indeed, that it was very hard for us to
bear—and we felt very much disheartened. Still, I tried to believe he would fail, for I saw that he didn't know how to read.

Presently the laughter began to relax; then it began to
shrink in area; and next to lose spontaneity; and next to show
gaps between; the gaps widened; they widened more; more
yet; still more. It was getting to be almost all gaps and silence,
with that untrained and unlively voice droning through them.
Then the house sat dead and emotionless for a whole ten minutes. We drew a deep sigh; it ought to have been a sigh of
pity for a defeated fellow craftsman, but it was not—for we
were mean and selfish, like all the human race, and it was a
sigh of satisfaction to see our unoffending brother fail. He was
laboring now and distressed; he constantly mopped his face
with his handkerchief, and his voice and his manner became
a humble appeal for compassion, for help, for charity, and it
was a pathetic thing to see. But the house remained cold and
still and gazed at him curiously and wonderingly.

There was a great clock on the wall, high up; presently the
general gaze forsook the reader and fixed itself upon the clock
face. We knew by dismal experience what that meant; we
knew what was going to happen but it was plain that the
reader had not been warned and was ignorant. It was approaching nine now—half the house watching the clock, the
reader laboring on. At five minutes to nine, twelve hundred
people rose with one impulse and swept like a wave down the
aisles toward the doors! The reader was like a person stricken
with a paralysis; he stood choking and gasping for a few minutes, gazing in a white horror at that retreat, then he turned
drearily away and wandered from the stage with the groping
and uncertain step of one who walks in his sleep.

The management were to blame. They should have told him

that the last suburban cars left at nine and that half the house would rise and go then, no matter who might be speaking from the platform. I think De Cordova did not appear again in public.

I remember Petroleum Vesuvius Nasby (Locke) very well. When the Civil War began he was on the staff of the Toledo *Blade*, an old and prosperous and popular weekly newspaper. He let fly a Nasby letter and it made a fine strike. He was famous at once. He followed up his new lead and gave the Copperheads and the Democratic party a most admirable hammering every week, and his letters were copied everywhere, from the Atlantic to the Pacific, and read and laughed over by everybody—at least everybody except particularly dull and prejudiced Democrats and Copperheads. For suddenness, Nasby's fame was an explosion; for universality it was atmospheric. He was soon offered a company; he accepted and was straightway ready to leave for the front; but the Governor of the state was a wiser man than were the political masters of Körner and Petöfi, for he refused to sign Nasby's commission and ordered him to stay at home. He said that in the field Nasby would be only one soldier, handling one sword, but at home with his pen he was an army—with artillery! Nasby obeyed and went on writing his electric letters.

I saw him first when I was on a visit to Hartford; I think it was three or four years after the war. The Opera House was packed and jammed with people to hear him deliver his lecture on "Cussed be Canaan." He had been on the platform with that same lecture—and no other—during two or three years, and it had passed his lips several hundred times, yet even now he could not deliver any sentence of it without his manuscript —except the opening one. His appearance on the stage was welcomed with a prodigious burst of applause but he did not stop to bow or in any other way acknowledge the greeting, but strode straight to the reading desk, spread his portfolio open upon it, and immediately petrified himself into an attitude which he never changed during the hour and a half occupied by his performance, except to turn his leaves—his body bent over the desk, rigidly supported by his left arm, as by a stake, the right arm lying across his back. About once in two minutes his right arm swung forward, turned a leaf, then swung to its resting place on his back again—just the action of a machine, and suggestive of one; regular, recurrent, prompt, exact. You might imagine you heard it *clash*. He was a great, burly figure, uncouthly and provincially clothed, and he looked like a simple old farmer.

I was all curiosity to hear him begin. He did not keep me waiting. The moment he had crutched himself upon his left arm, lodged his right upon his back, and bent himself over his manuscript, he raised his face slightly, flashed a glance upon the audience, and bellowed this remark in a thundering bull-voice.

"We are all descended from grandfathers!"

Then he went right on roaring to the end, tearing his ruthless way through the continuous applause and laughter and taking no sort of account of it. His lecture was a volleying and sustained discharge of bull's-eye hits, with the slave power and its Northern apologists for target, and his success was due to his matter, not his manner; for his delivery was destitute of art, unless a tremendous and inspiring earnestness and energy may be called by that name. The moment he had finished his piece he turned his back and marched off the stage with the seeming of being not personally concerned with the applause that was booming behind him.

He had the constitution of an ox and the strength and endurance of a prize-fighter. Express trains were not very plentiful in those days. He missed a connection, and in order to meet this Hartford engagement he had traveled two-thirds of a night and a whole day in a *cattle car*—it was midwinter. He went from the cattle car to his reading desk without dining; yet on the platform his voice was powerful and he showed no signs of drowsiness or fatigue. He sat up talking and supping with me until after midnight and then it was I that had to give up, not he. He told me that in his first season he read his "Cussed be Canaan" twenty-five nights a month for nine successive months. No other lecturer ever matched that record, I imagine.

He said that as one result of repeating his lecture 225 nights straight along he was able to say its opening sentence without glancing at his manuscript; and sometimes even *did* it, when in a daring mood. And there was another result: he reached home the day after his long campaign and was sitting by the fire in the evening, musing, when the clock broke into his revery by striking eight. Habit is habit, and before he realized where he was he had thundered out, *"We are all descended from grandfathers!"*

CHAPTER 34

When Orion and I crossed the continent in the overland stage-coach in the summer of 1861 we stopped two or three days in Great Salt Lake City. I do not remember who the Governor of Utah Territory was at that time but I remember that he was absent—which is a common habit of territorial Governors, who are nothing but politicians who go out to the outskirts of countries and suffer the privations there in order to build up States and come back as United States Senators. But the man who was acting in the Governor's place was the Secretary of the Territory, Frank Fuller—called Governor, of course, just as Orion was in the great days when he got that accident-title through Governor Nye's absences. Titles of honor and dignity once acquired in a democracy, even by accident and properly usable for only forty-eight hours, are as permanent here as eternity is in heaven. You can never take away those titles. Once a justice of the peace for a week, always "judge" afterward. Once a major of militia for a campaign on the Fourth of July, always a major. To be called colonel, purely by mistake and without intention, confers that dignity on a man for the rest of his life. We adore titles and heredities in our hearts and ridicule them with our mouths. This is our democratic privilege.

Well, Fuller was acting Governor and he gave us a very good time during those two or three days that we rested in Great Salt Lake City. He was an alert and energetic man; a pushing man; a man who was able to take an interest in anything that was going—and not only that but take five times as much interest in it as it was worth and ten times as much as anybody else could take in it—a very live man.

I was on the Pacific coast thereafter five or six years and returned to the States by the way of the Isthmus in January, '67. When I arrived in New York I found Fuller there in some kind of business. He was very hearty, very glad to see me, and wanted to show me his wife. I had not heard of a wife

before; had not been aware that he had one. Well, he showed
me his wife, a sweet and gentle woman with most hospitable
and kindly and winning ways. Then he astonished me by
showing me his daughters. Upon my word, they were large
and matronly of aspect and married—he didn't say how long.
Oh, Fuller was full of surprises. If he had shown me some
little children, that would have been well enough and reasonable. But he was too young looking a man to have grown
children. Well, I couldn't fathom the mystery and I let it go.
Apparently it was a case where a man was well along in life
but had a handsome gift of not showing his age on the outside.

Governor Fuller—it is what all his New York friends called
him now, of course—was in the full storm of one of his enthusiasms. He had one enthusiasm per day and it was always
a storm. He said I must take the biggest hall in New York and
deliver that lecture of mine on the Sandwich Islands—said that
people would be wild to hear me. There was something
catching about that man's prodigious energy. For a moment
he almost convinced me that New York was wild to hear me.
I knew better. I was well aware that New York had never
heard of me, was not expecting to hear of me and didn't want
to hear of me—yet that man almost persuaded me. I protested, as soon as the fire which he had kindled in me had
cooled a little, and went on protesting. It did no good. Fuller
was sure that I should make fame and fortune right away
without any trouble. He said leave it to him—just leave everything to him—go to the hotel and sit down and be comfortable
—he would lay fame and fortune at my feet in ten days.

I was helpless. I was persuaded but I didn't lose *all* of my
mind, and I begged him to take a very small hall and reduce
the rates to side-show prices. No, he would not hear of that—
said he would have the biggest hall in New York City. He
would have the basement hall in Cooper Institute, which
seated three thousand people and there was room for half as
many more to stand up; and he said he would fill that place
so full, at a dollar a head, that those people would smother
and he could charge two dollars apiece to let them out. Oh,
he was all on fire with his project. He went ahead with it.
He said it shouldn't cost me anything. I said there would be
no profit. He said: "Leave that alone. If there is no profit that
is my affair. If there is profit it is yours. If it is loss, I stand
the loss myself and you will never hear of it."

He hired Cooper Institute and he began to advertise this lecture in the usual way—a small paragraph in the advertising columns of the newspapers. When this had continued about three days I had not yet heard anybody or any newspaper say anything about that lecture, and I got nervous. "Oh," he said, "it's working around underneath. You don't see it on the surface." He said, "Let it alone; now, let it work."

Very well, I allowed it to work—until about the sixth or seventh day. The lecture would be due in three or four days more—still I was not able to get down underneath, where it was working, and so I was filled with doubt and distress. I went to Fuller and said he must advertise more energetically.

He said he would. So he got a barrel of little things printed that you hang on a string—fifty in a bunch. They were for the omnibuses. You could see them swinging and dangling around in every omnibus. My anxiety forced me to haunt those omnibuses. I did nothing for one or two days but sit in buses and travel from one end of New York to the other and watch those things dangle and wait to catch somebody pulling one loose to read it. It never happened—at least it happened only once. A man reached up and pulled one of those things loose, said to his friend, "Lecture on the Sandwich Islands by Mark Twain. Who can that be, I wonder"—and he threw it away and changed the subject.

I couldn't travel in the omnibuses any more. I was sick. I went to Fuller and said: "Fuller, there is not going to be anybody in Cooper Institute that night but you and me. It will be a dead loss, for we shall both have free tickets. Something must be done. I am on the verge of suicide. I would commit suicide if I had the pluck and the outfit." I said, "You must paper the house, Fuller. You must issue thousands of complimentary tickets. You *must* do this. I shall die if I have to go before an empty house that is not acquainted with me and that has never heard of me and that has never traveled in the bus and seen those things dangle."

"Well," he said, with his customary enthusiasm, "I'll attend to it. It shall be done. I will paper that house, and when you step on the platform you shall find yourself in the presence of the choicest audience, the most intelligent audience, that ever a man stood before in the world."

And he was as good as his word. He sent whole basketsful of complimentary tickets to every public-school teacher within a radius of thirty miles of New York—he deluged those peo-

ple with complimentary tickets—and on the appointed night
they all came. There wasn't room in Cooper Institute for a
third of them. The lecture was to begin at half past seven. I
was so anxious that I had to go to that place at seven. I
couldn't keep away. I wanted to see that vast vacant Mammoth Cave and die. But when I got near the building I found
that all the streets for a quarter of a mile around were blocked
with people, and traffic was stopped. I couldn't believe that
those people were trying to get into Cooper Institute and yet
that was just what was happening. I found my way around
to the back of the building and got in there by the stage door.
And sure enough the seats, the aisles, the great stage itself
was packed with bright-looking human beings raked in from
the centers of intelligence—the schools. I had a deal of difficulty to shoulder my way through the mass of people on the
stage and when I had managed it and stood before the audience, that stage was full. There wasn't room enough left for a
child.

I was happy and I was excited beyond expression. I poured
the Sandwich Islands out on to those people with a free hand
and they laughed and shouted to my entire content. For an
hour and fifteen minutes I was in Paradise. From every pore
I exuded a divine delight—and when we came to count up
we had thirty-five dollars in the house.

Fuller was just as jubilant over it as if it had furnished the
fame and the fortune of his prophecy. He was perfectly delighted, perfectly enchanted. He couldn't keep his mouth shut
for several days. "Oh," he said, "the fortune didn't come in—
that didn't come in—that's all right. That's coming in later.
The fame is already here, Mark. Why, in a week you'll be the
best-known man in the United States. This is no failure. This
is a prodigious success."

That episode must have cost him four or five hundred dollars but he never said a word about that. He was as happy,
as satisfied, as proud, as delighted, as if he had laid the
fabled golden egg and hatched it.

He was right about the fame. I certainly did get a working
quantity of fame out of that lecture. The New York newspapers praised it. The country newspapers copied those
praises. The lyceums of the country—it was right in the heyday of the old lyceum lecture system—began to call for me. I
put myself in Redpath's hands and I caught the tail end of the
lecture season. I went West and lectured every night for six

or eight weeks at a hundred dollars a night—and I now considered that the whole of the prophecy was fulfilled. I had acquired fame and also fortune. I don't believe these details are right but I don't care a rap. They will do just as well as the facts. What I mean to say is that I don't know whether I made that lecturing excursion in that year or whether it was the following year. But the main thing is that I made it and that the opportunity to make it was created by that wild Frank Fuller and his insane and immortal project.

All this was thirty-eight or thirty-nine years ago.[1] Two or three times since then, at intervals of years, I have run across Frank Fuller for a moment—only a moment and no more. But he was always young. Never a gray hair; never a suggestion of age about him; always enthusiastic; always happy and glad to be alive. Last fall his wife's brother was murdered in a horrible way. Apparently a robber had concealed himself in Mr. Thompson's room and in the night had beaten him to death with a club. A couple of months ago I ran across Fuller on the street and he was looking so very, very old, so withered, so moldy, that I could hardly recognize him. He said his wife was dying of the shock caused by the murder of her brother; that nervous prostration was carrying her off and she could not live more than a few days—so I went with him to see her.

She was sitting upright on a sofa and was supported all about with pillows. Now and then she leaned her head for a little while on a support. Breathing was difficult for her. It touched me, for I had seen that picture so many, many times. During two or three months Mrs. Clemens sat up like that, night and day, struggling for breath. When she was made drowsy by opiates and exhaustion she rested her head a little while on a support, just as Mrs. Fuller was doing, and got naps of two minutes or three minutes duration.

I did not see Mrs. Fuller alive again. She passed to her rest about three days later.

[1] Written April 11, 1906.

CHAPTER 35

What is called a "reading," as a public platform entertainment, was first essayed by Charles Dickens, I think. He brought the idea with him from England in 1867. He had made it very popular at home and he made it so acceptable and so popular in America that his houses were crowded everywhere, and in a single season he earned two hundred thousand dollars. I heard him once during that season; it was in Steinway Hall, in December, and it made the fortune of my life—not in dollars, I am not thinking of dollars; it made the real fortune of my life in that it made the happiness of my life; on that day I called at the St. Nicholas Hotel to see my *Quaker City* Excursion shipmate, Charley Langdon, and was introduced to a sweet and timid and lovely young girl, his sister. The family went to the Dickens reading and I accompanied them. It was forty years ago; from that day to this the sister has never been out of my mind nor heart.

Mr. Dickens read scenes from his printed books. From my distance he was a small and slender figure, rather fancifully dressed, and striking and picturesque in appearance. He wore a black velvet coat with a large and glaring red flower in the buttonhole. He stood under a red upholstered shed behind whose slant was a row of strong lights—just such an arrangement as artists use to concentrate a strong light upon a great picture. Dickens's audience sat in a pleasant twilight, while he performed in the powerful light cast upon him from the concealed lamps. He read with great force and animation, in the lively passages, and with stirring effect. It will be understood that he did not merely read but also acted. His reading of the storm scene in which Steerforth lost his life was so vivid and so full of energetic action that his house was carried off its feet, so to speak.

Dickens had set a fashion which others tried to follow, but I do not remember that anyone was any more than temporarily successful in it. The public reading was discarded after a time and was not resumed until something more than twenty years after Dickens had introduced it; then it rose and struggled along for a while in that curious and artless industry called Authors' Readings. When Providence had had enough of that kind of crime the Authors' Readings ceased from troubling and left the world at peace.

Lecturing and reading were quite different things; the lecturer didn't use notes or manuscript or book, but got his lecture by heart and delivered it night after night in the same words during the whole lecture season of four winter months. The lecture field had been a popular one all over the country for many years when I entered it in 1868[1]; it was then at the top of its popularity; in every town there was an organization of citizens who occupied themselves in the off season, every year, in arranging for a course of lectures for the coming winter; they chose their platform people from the Boston Lecture Agency list and they chose according to the town's size and ability to pay the prices. The course usually consisted of eight or ten lectures. All that was wanted was that it should pay expenses; that it should come out with a money balance at the end of the season was not required. Very small towns had to put up with fifty-dollar men and women, with one or two second-class stars at a hundred dollars each as an attraction; big towns employed hundred-dollar men and women altogether and added John B. Gough or Henry Ward Beecher or Anna Dickinson or Wendell Phillips as a compelling attraction; large cities employed this whole battery of stars. Anna Dickinson's price was four hundred dollars a night; so was Henry Ward Beecher's; so was Gough's, when he didn't charge five or six hundred. I don't remember Wendell Phillips's price but it was high.

I remained in the lecture field three seasons—long enough to learn the trade; then domesticated myself in my new married estate after a weary life of wandering and remained under shelter at home for fourteen or fifteen years. Meantime, speculators and money-makers had taken up the business of hiring lecturers, with the idea of getting rich at it. In about five years they killed that industry dead and when I returned to the platform for a season, in 1884, there had been a happy and holy silence for ten years and a generation had come to the front who knew nothing about lectures and readings and didn't know how to take them nor what to make of them. They were

[1] In an earlier chapter he gives the date as 1866.

difficult audiences, those untrained squads, and Cable[2] and I had a hard time with them sometimes.

Cable had been scouting the country alone for three years with readings from his novels and he had been a good reader in the beginning, for he had been born with a natural talent for it, but unhappily he prepared himself for his public work by taking lessons from a teacher of elocution, and so by the time he was ready to begin his platform work he was so well and thoroughly educated that he was merely theatrical and artificial and not half as pleasing and entertaining to a house as he had been in the splendid days of his ignorance. I had never tried reading as a trade and I wanted to try it. I hired Major Pond on a percentage to conduct me over the country and I hired Cable as a helper at six hundred dollars a week and expenses, and we started out on our venture.

It was ghastly! At least in the beginning. I had selected my readings well enough but had not studied them. I supposed it would only be necessary to do like Dickens—get out on the platform and read from the book. I did that and made a botch of it. Written things are not for speech; their form is literary; they are stiff, inflexible and will not lend themselves to happy and effective delivery with the tongue—where their purpose is to merely entertain, not instruct; they have to be limbered up, broken up, colloquialized and turned into the common forms of unpremeditated talk—otherwise they will bore the house, not entertain it. After a week's experience with the book I laid it aside and never carried it to the platform again; but meantime I had memorized those pieces, and in delivering them from the platform they soon transformed themselves into flexible talk, with all their obstructing precisenesses and formalities gone out of them for good.

One of the readings which I used was a part of an extravagant chapter in dialect from *Roughing It* which I entitled "His Grandfather's Old Ram." After I had memorized it, it began to undergo changes on the platform and it continued to edit and revise itself night after night until, by and by, from dreading to begin on it before an audience I came to like it and enjoy it. I never knew how considerable the changes had been when I finished the season's work; I never knew until ten or eleven years later, when I took up that book in a parlor in New York one night to read that chapter to a dozen friends of the two sexes who had asked for it. It *wouldn't read*

[2] George Washington Cable, referred to previously.

—that is, it wouldn't read aloud. I struggled along with it for five minutes and then gave it up and said I should have to tell the tale as best I might from memory. It turned out that my memory was equal to the emergency; it reproduced the platform form of the story pretty faithfully after that interval of years. I still remember that form of it, I think, and I wish to recite it here, so that the reader may compare it with the story as told in *Roughing It*, if he pleases, and note how different the spoken version is from the written and printed version.

The idea of the tale is to exhibit certain bad effects of a good memory: the sort of memory which is too good, which remembers everything and forgets nothing, which has no sense of proportion and can't tell an important event from an unimportant one but preserves them all, states them all, and thus retards the progress of a narrative, at the same time making a tangled, inextricable confusion of it and intolerably wearisome to the listener. The historian of "His Grandfather's Old Ram" had that kind of a memory. He often tried to communicate that history to his comrades, the other surface miners, but he could never complete it because his memory defeated his every attempt to march a straight course; it persistently threw remembered details in his way that had nothing to do with the tale; these unrelated details would interest him and sidetrack him; if he came across a name or a family or any other thing that had nothing to do with his tale he would diverge from his course to tell about the person who owned that name or explain all about that family—with the result that as he plodded on he always got further and further from his grandfather's memorable adventure with the ram, and finally went to sleep before he got to the end of the story, and so did his comrades. Once he did manage to approach so nearly to the end, apparently, that the boys were filled with an eager hope; they believed that at last they were going to find out all about the grandfather's adventure and what it was that had happened. After the usual preliminaries, the historian said:

"Well, as I was a-sayin', he bought that old ram from a feller up in Siskiyou County and fetched him home and turned him loose in the medder, and next morning he went down to have a look at him, and accident'ly dropped a ten-cent piece in the grass and stooped down—so—and was a-fumblin' around in the grass to git it, and the ram he was a-standin' up the slope taking notice; but my grandfather wasn't taking notice, because he had his back to the ram and was int'rested about the dime. Well, there he was, as I was a-sayin', down at the foot of the slope a-bendin' over—so—fumblin' in the grass, and the ram he was up there at the top of the slope, and Smith—Smith was a'standin' there—no, not jest there, a little further away—fifteen foot perhaps—well, my grandfather was a-stoopin' way down—so—and the ram was up there observing, you know, and Smith he . . . (musing) . . . the ram he bent his head down, so . . . Smith of Calaveras . . . no, no it couldn't ben Smith of Calaveras—I remember now that he—b'George it was Smith of Tulare County—course it was, I remember it now perfectly plain.

"Well, Smith he stood just there, and my grandfather he stood just here, you know, and he was a-bendin' down just so, fumblin' in the grass, and when the old ram see him in that attitude he took it fur an invitation—and here he come! down the slope thirty mile an hour and his eye full of business. You see my grandfather's back being to him, and him stooping down like that, of course he—why sho! it *warn't* Smith of Tulare at all, it was Smith of Sacramento—my goodness, how did I ever come to get them Smiths mixed like that—why, Smith of Tulare was jest a nobody, but Smith of Sacramento—why the Smiths of Sacramento come of the best Southern blood in the United States; there warn't ever any better blood south of the line than the Sacramento Smiths. Why look here, one of them married a Whitaker! I reckon that gives you an idea of the kind of society the Sacramento Smiths could 'sociate around in; there ain't no better blood than that Whitaker blood; I reckon anybody'll tell you that.

"Look at Mariar Whitaker—there was a girl for you! Little? Why yes, she was little, but what of that? Look at the heart of her—had a heart like a bullock—just as good and sweet and lovely and generous as the day is long; if she had a thing and you wanted it, you could have it—have it and welcome; why Mariar Whitaker couldn't have a thing and another person need it and not get it—get it and welcome. She had a glass eye, and she used to lend it to Flora Ann Baxter that hadn't any, to receive company with; well, she was pretty large, and it didn't fit; it was a number seven, and she was excavated for a fourteen, and so that eye wouldn't lay still; every time she winked it would turn over. It was a beautiful eye and set her off admirable, because it was a lovely pale blue on the front side—the side you look out of—and it was gilded on the back side; didn't match the other eye, which was one of them browny-yellery eyes and tranquil and quiet, you know, the way that kind of eyes are; but that warn't any matter—they worked together all right and plenty picturesque. When Flora Ann winked, that blue and gilt eye would whirl over, and the other one stand still, and as soon as she begun to get excited that hand-made eye would give a whirl and then go on a-whirlin' and a-whirlin' faster and faster, and aflashin' first blue and then yaller and then blue and then yaller, and when it got to whizzing and flashing like that, the oldest man in the world couldn't keep up with the expression on that side of her face. Flora Ann Baxter married a Hogadorn. I reckon that lets you understand what kind of blood she was—old Maryland Eastern Shore blood; not a better family in the United States than the Hogadorns.

"Sally—that's Sally Hogadorn—Sally married a missionary, and they went off carrying the good news to the cannibals out in one of them way-off islands around the world in the middle of the ocean somers, and they et her; et him too, which was irregular; it warn't the custom to eat the missionary, but only the family, and when they see what they had done they was dreadful sorry about it, and when the relations sent down there to fetch away the things they said so—said so right out—said they was sorry, and 'pologized, and said it shouldn't happen again; said 'twas an accident.

"Accident! now that's foolishness; there ain't no such thing as an accident; there ain't nothing happens in the world but what's ordered just so by a wiser Power than us, and it's always fur a good purpose; we don't know what the good purpose was, sometimes—and it was the same with the families that was short a missionary and his wife. But that ain't no matter, and it ain't any of our business; all that concerns us is that it was a special providence and it had a good intention. No, sir, there ain't no such thing as an accident. Whenever a thing happens that you think is an accident you make up your mind it ain't no accident at all—it's a special providence.

"You look at my Uncle Lem—what do you say to that? That's all I ask you—you just look at my Uncle Lem and talk to me about accidents! It was like this: one day my Uncle Lem and his dog was downtown, and he was a-leanin' up against a scaffolding—sick, or drunk, or somethin'—and there was an Irishman with a hod of bricks up the ladder along about the third story, and his foot slipped and down he come, bricks and all, and hit a stranger fair and square and knocked the everlasting aspirations out of him; he was ready for the coroner in two minutes. Now then people said it was an accident.

"Accident! there warn't no accident about it; 'twas a special providence, and had a mysterious, noble intention back of it. The idea was to save that Irishman. If the stranger hadn't been there that Irishman would have been killed. The people said 'special providence—sho! the dog was there—why didn't the Irishman fall on the dog? Why warn't the dog app'inted?' Fer a mighty good reason—the dog would'a' seen him a-coming; you can't depend on no dog to carry out a special providence. You couldn't hit a dog with an Irishman because—lemme see, what was that dog's name . . . (musing) . . . oh, yes, Jasper—and a mighty good dog too; he wa'n't no common dog, he wa'n't no mongrel; he was a composite. A composite dog is a dog that's made up of all the valuable qualities that's in the dog breed—kind of a syndicate; and a mongrel is made up of the riffraff that's left over. That Jasper was one of the most wonderful dogs you ever see. Uncle Lem got him of the Wheelers. I reckon you've heard of the Wheelers; ain't no better blood south of the line than the Wheelers.

"Well, one day Wheeler was a-meditating and dreaming around in the carpet factory and the machinery made a snatch at him and first you know he was a-meandering all over that factory, from the garret to the cellar, and everywhere, at such another gait as—why, you couldn't even see him; you could only hear him whiz when he went by. Well, you know a person can't go through an experience like that and arrive back home the way he was when he went. No, Wheeler got wove up into thirty-nine yards of best three-ply carpeting. The widder was sorry, she was uncommon sorry, and loved him and done the best she could fur him in the circumstances, which was unusual. She took the whole piece—thirty-nine yards—and she wanted to give him proper and honorable burial, but she couldn't bear to roll him up; she took and spread him out full length, and said she wouldn't have it any other way. She wanted to buy a tunnel for him but there wasn't any tunnel for sale, so she boxed him in a beautiful box and stood it on the hill on a pedestal twenty-one foot high, and so it was monument and grave together, and economical—sixty foot high—you could see it from everywhere—

and she painted on it 'To the loving memory of thirty-nine yards best three-ply carpeting containing the mortal remainders of Millington G. Wheeler go thou and do likewise.' "

At this point the historian's voice began to wobble and his eyelids to droop with weariness and he fell asleep; and so from that day to this we are still in ignorance; we don't know whether the old grandfather ever got the ten-cent piece out of the grass; we haven't any idea what it was that happened or whether anything happened at all.

Upon comparing the above with the original in *Roughing It*, I find myself unable to clearly and definitely explain why the one can be effectively *recited* before an audience and the other can't; there is a reason but it is too subtle for adequate conveyance by the lumbering vehicle of words; I sense it but cannot express it; it is as elusive as an odor, pungent, pervasive, but defying analysis. I give it up. I merely know that the one version will recite and the other won't.

By reciting I mean, of course, delivery from memory; neither version can be read effectively from the book. There are plenty of good reasons why this should be so but there is one reason which is sufficient by itself, perhaps; in reading from the book you are telling another person's tale at second-hand; you are a mimic and not the person involved; you are an artificiality, not a reality; whereas in telling the tale without the book you absorb the character and presently become the man himself, just as is the case with the actor.

The greatest actor would not be able to carry his audience by storm with a book in his hand; reading from the book renders the nicest shadings of delivery impossible. I mean those studied fictions which seem to be the impulse of the moment and which are so effective: such as, for instance, fictitious hesitancies for the right word, fictitious unconscious pauses, fictitious unconscious side remarks, fictitious unconscious embarrassments, fictitious unconscious emphases placed upon the wrong word with a deep intention back of it—these and all the other artful fictive shades which give to a recited tale the captivating naturalness of an impromptu narration can be attempted by a book reader and are attempted, but they are easily detectable as artifice, and although the audience may admire their cleverness and their ingenuity as artifice, they only get at the intellect of the house, they don't get at its heart; and so the reader's success lacks a good deal of being complete.

When a man is reading from a book on the platform, he soon realizes that there is one powerful gun in his battery of artifice that he can't work with an effect proportionate to its caliber: that is the *pause*—that impressive silence, that eloquent silence, that geometrically progressive silence which often achieves a desired effect where no combination of words howsoever felicitous could accomplish it. The pause is not of much use to the man who is reading from a book because he cannot know what the exact length of it ought to be; he is not the one to determine the measurement—the audience must do that for him. He must perceive by their faces when the pause has reached the proper length, but his eyes are not on the faces, they are on the book; therefore he must determine the proper length of the pause by guess; he cannot guess with exactness and nothing but exactness, absolute exactness, will answer.

The man who recites without the book has all the advantage; when he comes to an old familiar remark in his tale which he has uttered nightly for a hundred nights—a remark preceded or followed by a pause—the faces of the audience tell him when to end the pause. For one audience the pause will be short, for another a little longer, for another a shade longer still; the performer must vary the length of the pause to suit the shades of difference between audiences. These variations of measurement are so slight, so delicate, that they may almost be compared with the shadings achieved by Pratt and Whitney's ingenious machine which measures the five-millionth part of an inch. An audience is that machine's twin; it can measure a pause down to that vanishing fraction.

I used to play with the pause as other children play with a toy. In my recitals, when I went reading around the world for the benefit of Mr. Webster's creditors, I had three or four pieces in which the pauses performed an important part, and I used to lengthen them or shorten them according to the requirements of the case, and I got much pleasure out of the pause when it was accurately measured and a certain discomfort when it wasn't. In the Negro ghost story of "The Golden Arm" one of these pauses occurs just in front of the closing remark. Whenever I got the pause the right length, the remark that followed it was sure of a satisfactorily startling effect, but if the length of the pause was wrong by the five-millionth of an inch the audience had had

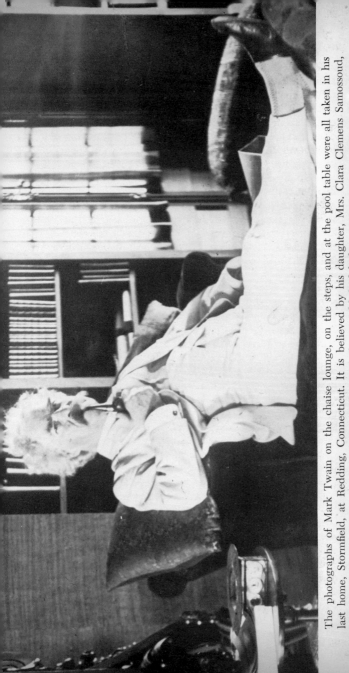

The photographs of Mark Twain on the chaise lounge, on the steps, and at the pool table were all taken in his last home, Stormfield, at Redding, Connecticut. It is believed by his daughter, Mrs. Clara Clemens Samossoud, that they have not been published before.

Mark Twain

Mark Twain at pool table in Stormfield library.

ends for the wife and ~~the~~ children. They all have

families--burglars have-- and they are always thoughtful

of them, always take a few necessaries of life for them-

selves, and ~~these~~ ^fill ^up ^with tokens of remembrance for the

family. In taking them they do not forget us: ~~T~~hose

+ also ^of ^our ^remembrance ^of ^him. very things represent tokens of his remembrance of us,

~~We~~ We never get them again. ~~T~~he memory of the at-

tention remains embalmed in our hearts."

~~She said~~ "Are you going down to see what it is

he wants now?"

"No," I said, I am no more interested than I was before. They ~~are~~ are experienced people, +burglars; _they_ know what they want. I should be no help to him. I _think_ he is, after ceramics and bric-à-brac and such things. If he knows the house he knows that that is all that he can find on the dining-room floor."

She said, with a strong interest perceptible in her tone, "Suppose he comes up here!"

I said, "It is all right. He will give us notice."

She said "What shall we do then?"

I said "Climb out of the window."

A page of Mark Twain's manuscript, showing corrections in his own hand.

In her portable Hoo Days & my barefoot Days

She was *Helen Kercheval*, a school-mate of mine.

children. I saw John's tomb when I made that Missouri visit.

Her Father,

Mr. Kercheval, had an apprentice in the early days

when I was nine years old, and he had also a slave woman

who had many merits. But I can't feel *always* very

kindly or forgivingly toward either that good apprentice

boy or that good slave woman, for they saved my life.

One day when I was playing on a loose log which I sup-

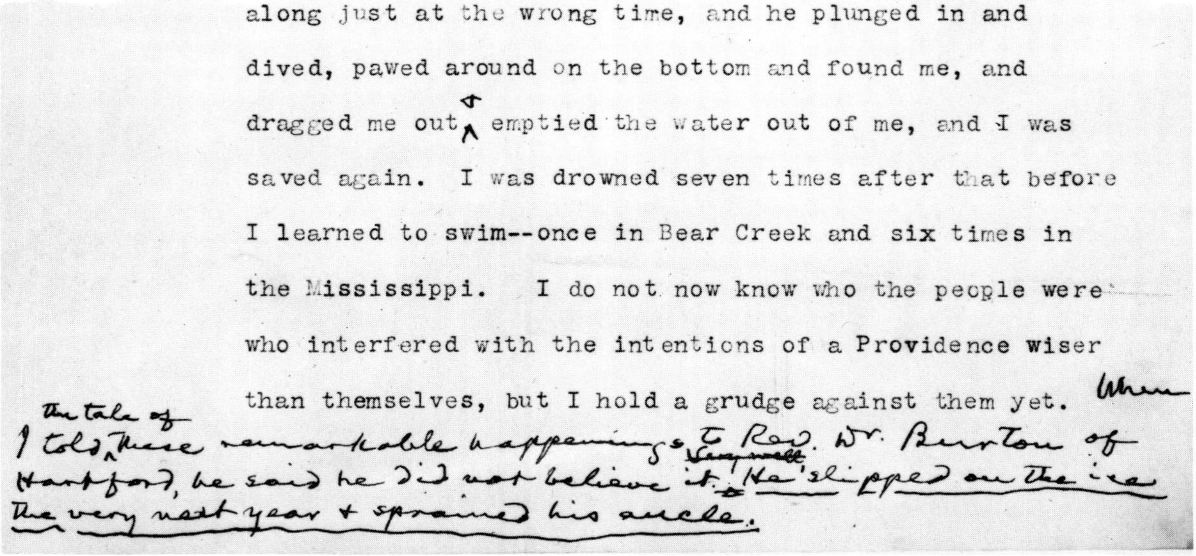

along just at the wrong time, and he plunged in and dived, pawed around on the bottom and found me, and dragged me out & emptied the water out of me, and I was saved again. I was drowned seven times after that before I learned to swim--once in Bear Creek and six times in the Mississippi. I do not now know who the people were who interfered with the intentions of a Providence wiser than themselves, but I hold a grudge against them yet. When I told the tale of these remarkable happenings to Rev. Dr. Burton of Hartford, he said he did not believe it. He slipped on the ice the very next year & sprained his ancle.

Another page of the corrected manuscript. Such corrections are now published for the first time.

No. 1

Shall
I learn to
be good?
. . . . . .
I will sit
here and
think it
over.

Truly Yours
Mark Twain
Sept 5

No. 2

There do seem
to be so many
diffi....

No. 5

.... But then I couldn't
break the Sab....

No. 6.

.... and there's so
many other privileges
that .... perhaps....

3

...and yet if I should really try...

No. 4

...and just put my whole heart in it...

7

Oh, never mind—I reckon I'm good enough just as I am.

"The pictures which Mr. Paine made on the portico here several weeks ago have been developed and are good. For the sake of the moral lesson which they teach I wish to insert a set of them here for future generations to study, with the result, I hope, that they will reform, if they need it—and I expect they will. I am sending half a dozen of these sets to friends of mine who need reforming, and I have introduced the pictures to them with this formula:

This series of photographs registers with scientific precision, stage by stage, the progress of a moral purpose through the mind of the human race's Oldest Friend."

—From a hitherto unpublished section of The Autobiography of Mark Twain, dictated August 31, 1906, at Dublin, New Hampshire, where the photographs were taken by Albert Bigelow Paine.

Susy Clemens at Bryn Mawr in 1890-91

Susy Clemens
(About the time she wrote the "Biography")

Clara Clemens Samossoud

Jean Clemens, 1909

Mark Twain as a pilot about 1859-60

Samuel L. Clemens at eighteen

THE RELATIVES OF SAMUEL L. CLEMENS

Henry Clemens
(About 1858)

Orion Clemens
(About 1861)

Pamela Clemens
(About 1850)

Mrs. Jane Clemens
(About 1870)

THE "ENTERPRISE" GROUP

Joseph T. Goodman
1863

Mark Twain
1864-65

Steve Gillis
1907

William Wright
(Dan De Quille) 1864-65

W. D. Howells, Mark Twain, George Harvey, H. M. Alden, David A. Munro and
M. W. Hazeltine at Lakewood.

A photographic oddity. The photographer, T. B. Hyde, explained: "This photograph of Mark Twain I spoiled in the developer. But when he saw a print he was extravagant in his praise and had a great number of post cards printed from it. The background is all mottled, as I forgot to add the metol to the developer. When no picture appeared I suddenly remembered it had been omitted. When I did add it the crystals settled on the plate, causing the mottled appearance. M. T. thought it 'tapestry-like.'"

time in that infinitesimal fraction of a moment to wake up
from its deep concentration in the grisly tale and foresee the
climax and be prepared for it before it burst upon them—
and so it fell flat.

In "His Grandfather's Old Ram" a pause has place; it
follows a certain remark, and Mrs. Clemens and Clara,[3] when
we were on our way around the world, would afflict themselves with my whole performance every night when there
was no sort of necessity for it in order that they might watch
the house when that pause came; they believed that by the
effect they could accurately measure the high or low intelligence of the audience. I knew better but it was not in my
interest to say so. When the pause was right the effect was
sure; when the pause was wrong in length, by the five-
millionth of an inch, the laughter was only mild, never a
crash. That passage occurs in "His Grandfather's Old Ram"
where the question under discussion is whether the falling
of the Irishman on the stranger was an accident or was a
special providence. If it was a special providence and if the
sole purpose of it was to save the Irishman, why was it
necessary to sacrifice the stranger? "The dog was there.
Why didn't he fall on the dog? Why wa'n't the dog app'inted?
Becuz *the dog would 'a' seen him a-comin'."* That last
remark was the one the family waited for. A pause *after*
the remark was absolutely necessary with any and all audiences because no man, howsoever intelligent he may be, can
instantly adjust his mind to a new and unfamiliar, and yet
for a moment or two apparently plausible, logic which recognizes in a dog an instrument too indifferent to pious restraints and too alert in looking out for his own personal
interest to be safely depended upon in an emergency requiring self-sacrifice for the benefit of another, even when
the command comes from on high.

---

[3] One of Mark Twain's daughters. The present volume is dedicated to her.

CHAPTER 36

In the beginning of February 1870 I was married to Miss Olivia L. Langdon, and I took up my residence in Buffalo, New York. Tomorrow[1] will be the thirty-sixth anniversary of our marriage. My wife passed from this life one year and eight months ago in Florence, Italy, after an unbroken illness of twenty-two months' duration.

I saw her first in the form of an ivory miniature in her brother Charley's stateroom in the steamer *Quaker City* in the Bay of Smyrna, in the summer of 1867, when she was in her twenty-second year. I saw her in the flesh for the first time in New York in the following December. She was slender and beautiful and girlish—and she was both girl and woman. She remained both girl and woman to the last day of her life. Under a grave and gentle exterior burned inextinguishable fires of sympathy, energy, devotion, enthusiasm and absolutely limitless affection. She was *always* frail in body and she lived upon her spirit, whose hopefulness and courage were indestructible.

She became an invalid at sixteen through a partial paralysis caused by falling on the ice and she was never strong again while her life lasted. After that fall she was not able to leave her bed during two years, nor was she able to lie in any position except upon her back. All the great physicians were brought to Elmira one after another during that time, but there was no helpful result. In those days both worlds were well acquainted with the name of Doctor Newton, a man who was regarded in both worlds as a quack. He moved through the land in state; in magnificence, like a potentate; like a circus. Notice of his coming was spread upon the dead walls in vast colored posters, along with his formidable portrait, several weeks beforehand.

One day Andrew Langdon, a relative of the Langdon

---

[1] Written February 1, 1906.

family, came to the house and said: "You have tried everybody else; now try Doctor Newton, the quack. He is downtown at the Rathbun House, practicing upon the well-to-do at war prices and upon the poor for nothing. *I saw him* wave his hands over Jake Brown's head and take his crutches away from him and send him about his business as good as new. *I saw him* do the like with some other cripples. *They* may have been 'temporaries' instituted for advertising purposes, and not genuine. But Jake is genuine. Send for Newton."

Newton came. He found the young girl upon her back. Over her was suspended a tackle from the ceiling. It had been there a long time but unused. It was put there in the hope that by its steady motion she might be lifted to a sitting posture, at intervals, for rest. But it proved a failure. Any attempt to raise her brought nausea and exhaustion and had to be relinquished. Newton opened the windows—long darkened—and delivered a short fervent prayer; then he put an arm behind her shoulders and said, "Now we will sit up, my child."

The family were alarmed and tried to stop him, but he was not disturbed, and raised her up. She sat several minutes without nausea or discomfort. Then Newton said, "Now we will walk a few steps, my child." He took her out of bed and supported her while she walked several steps; then he said: "I have reached the limit of my art. She is not cured. It is not likely that she will *ever* be cured. She will never be able to walk far, but after a little daily practice she will be able to walk one or two hundred yards, and she can depend on being able to do *that* for the rest of her life."

His charge was fifteen hundred dollars and it was easily worth a hundred thousand. For from the day that she was eighteen until she was fifty-six she was always able to walk a couple of hundred yards without stopping to rest; and more than once I saw her walk a quarter of a mile without serious fatigue.

Newton was mobbed in Dublin, in London and in other places. He was rather frequently mobbed in Europe and in America but never by the grateful Langdons and Clemenses. I met Newton once, in after years, and asked him what his secret was. He said he didn't know but thought perhaps some subtle form of electricity proceeded from his body and wrought the cures.

Perfect truth, perfect honesty, perfect candor, were qualities of my wife's character which were born with her. Her judgments of people and things were sure and accurate. Her intuitions almost never deceived her. In her judgments of the characters and acts of both friends and strangers there was always room for charity, and this charity never failed. I have compared and contrasted her with hundreds of persons and my conviction remains that hers was the most perfect character I have ever met. And I may add that she was the most winningly dignified person I have ever known. Her character and disposition were of the sort that not only invite worship but command it. No servant ever left her service who deserved to remain in it. And as she could choose with a glance of her eye, the servants she selected did in almost all cases deserve to remain and they *did* remain.

She was always cheerful; and she was always able to communicate her cheerfulness to others. During the nine years that we spent in poverty and debt she was always able to reason me out of my despairs and find a bright side to the clouds and make me see it. In all that time I never knew her to utter a word of regret concerning our altered circumstances, nor did I ever know her children to do the like. For she had taught them and they drew their fortitude from her. The love which she bestowed upon those whom she loved took the form of worship, and in that form it was returned—returned by relatives, friends and the servants of her household.

It was a strange combination which wrought into one individual, so to speak, by marriage—her disposition and character and mine. She poured out her prodigal affections in kisses and caresses and in a vocabulary of endearments whose profusion was always an astonishment to me. I was born *reserved* as to endearments of speech, and caresses, and hers broke upon me as the summer waves break upon Gibraltar. I was reared in that atmosphere of reserve. As I have already said, I never knew a member of my father's family to kiss another member of it except once, and that at a deathbed. And our village was not a kissing community. The kissing and caressing ended with courtship—along with the deadly piano-playing of that day.

She had the heart-free laugh of a girl. It came seldom, but when it broke upon the ear it was as inspiring as music. I heard it for the last time when she had been occupying her sick bed for more than a year and I made a written note of it at the time—a note not to be repeated.

Tomorrow will be the thirty-sixth anniversary. We were married in her father's house in Elmira, New York and went next day by special train to Buffalo, along with the whole Langdon family and with the Beechers and the Twichells, who had solemnized the marriage. We were to live in Buffalo, where I was to be one of the editors of the Buffalo *Express* and a part owner of the paper. I knew nothing about Buffalo but I had made my household arrangements there through a friend, by letter. I had instructed him to find a boarding-house of as respectable a character as my light salary as editor would command. We were received at about nine o'clock at the station in Buffalo and were put into several sleighs and driven all over America, as it seemed to me—for apparently we turned all the corners in the town and followed all the streets there were—I scolding freely and characterizing that friend of mine in very uncomplimentary ways for securing a boardinghouse that apparently had no definite locality. But there was a conspiracy—and my bride knew of it, but I was in ignorance. Her father, Jervis Langdon, had bought and furnished a new house for us in the fashionable street, Delaware Avenue, and had laid in a cook and house-maids and a brisk and electric young coachman, an Irish-man, Patrick McAleer—and we were being driven all over that city in order that one sleighful of these people could have time to go to the house and see that the gas was lighted all over it and a hot supper prepared for the crowd. We arrived at last, and when I entered that fairy place my in-dignation reached high-water mark, and without any reserve I delivered my opinion to that friend of mine for being so stupid as to put us into a boardinghouse whose terms would be far out of my reach. Then Mr. Langdon brought forward a very pretty box and opened it and took from it a deed of the house. So the comedy ended very pleasantly and we sat down to supper.

The company departed about midnight and left us alone in our new quarters. Then Ellen, the cook, came in to get orders for the morning's marketing—and neither of us knew whether beefsteak was sold by the barrel or by the yard. We exposed our ignorance and Ellen was full of Irish delight over it. Patrick McAleer, that brisk young Irishman, came in to get his orders for next day—and that was our first glimpse of him.

It sounds easy and swift and unobstructed but that was not the way of it. It did not happen in that smooth and comfortable way. There was a deal of courtship. There were three or four proposals of marriage and just as many declinations. I was roving far and wide on the lecture beat but I managed to arrive in Elmira every now and then and renew the siege. Once I dug an invitation out of Charley Langdon to come and stay a week. It was a pleasant week but it had to come to an end. I was not able to invent any way to get the invitation enlarged. No schemes that I could contrive seemed likely to deceive. They did not even deceive *me*, and when a person cannot deceive himself the chances are against his being able to deceive other people. But at last help and good fortune came and from a most unexpected quarter. It was one of those cases so frequent in the past centuries, so infrequent in our day—a case where the hand of Providence is in it.

I was ready to leave for New York. A democrat wagon stood outside the main gate with my trunk in it, and Barney, the coachman, in the front seat with the reins in his hand. It was eight or nine in the evening and dark. I bade good-by to the grouped family on the front porch, and Charley and I went out and climbed into the wagon. We took our places back of the coachman on the remaining seat, which was aft toward the end of the wagon and was only a temporary arrangement for our accommodation and was not fastened in its place; a fact which—most fortunately for me—we were not aware of. Charley was smoking. Barney touched up the horse with the whip. He made a sudden spring forward. Charley and I went over the stern of the wagon backward. In the darkness the red bud of fire on the end of his cigar described a curve through the air which I can see yet. This was the only visible thing in all that gloomy scenery. I struck exactly on the top of my head and stood up that way for a moment, then crumpled down to the earth unconscious. It was a very good unconsciousness for a person who had not rehearsed the part. It was a cobblestone gutter and they had been repairing it. My head struck in a dish formed by the conjunction of four cobblestones. That depression was half full of fresh new sand and this made a competent cushion. My head did not touch any of those cobble-

stones. I got not a bruise. I was not even jolted. Nothing
was the matter with me at all.

Charley was considerably battered, but in his solicitude
for me he was substantially unaware of it. The whole family
swarmed out, Theodore Crane in the van with a flask of
brandy. He poured enough of it between my lips to strangle
me and make me bark but it did not abate my unconsciousness. I was taking care of that myself. It was very pleasant
to hear the pitying remarks trickling around over me. That
was one of the happiest half dozen moments of my life. There
was nothing to mar it—except that I had escaped damage.
I was afraid that this would be discovered sooner or later
and would shorten my visit. I was such a dead weight that
it required the combined strength of Barney and Mr. Langdon, Theodore and Charley to lug me into the house, but it
was accomplished. I was there. I recognized that this was
victory. I was there. I was safe to be an incumbrance for an
indefinite length of time—but for a length of time, at any rate,
and a Providence was in it.

They set me up in an armchair in the parlor and sent for
the family physician. Poor old creature, it was wrong to rout
him out but it was business, and I was too unconscious to
protest. Mrs. Crane—dear soul, she was in this house three
days ago, gray and beautiful and as sympathetic as ever—
Mrs. Crane brought a bottle of some kind of liquid fire whose
function was to reduce contusions. But I knew that mine
would deride it and scoff at it. She poured this on my head
and pawed it around with her hand, stroking and massaging,
the fierce stuff dribbling down my backbone and marking its
way, inch by inch, with the sensation of a forest fire. But I
was satisfied. When she was getting worn out, her husband,
Theodore, suggested that she take a rest and let Livy carry
on the assuaging for a while. That was very pleasant. I should
have been obliged to recover presently if it hadn't been
for that. But under Livy's manipulations—if they had continued—I should probably be unconscious to this day. It was
very delightful, those manipulations. So delightful, so comforting, so enchanting, that they even soothed the fire out of
that fiendish successor to Perry Davis' "Pain-Killer."

Then that old family doctor arrived and went at the
matter in an educated and practical way—that is to say, he
started a search expedition for contusions and humps and
bumps and announced that there were none. He said that if

I would go to bed and forget my adventure I would be all right in the morning—which was not so. I was *not* all right in the morning. I didn't intend to be all right and I was far from being all right. But I said I only needed rest and I didn't need that doctor any more.

I got a good three days' extension out of that adventure and it helped a good deal. It pushed my suit forward several steps. A subsequent visit completed the matter and we became engaged conditionally; the condition being that the parents should consent.

In a private talk Mr. Langdon called my attention to something I had already noticed—which was that I was an almost entirely unknown person; that no one around about knew me except Charley, and he was too young to be a reliable judge of men; that I was from the other side of the continent and that only those people out there would be able to furnish me a character, in case I had one—so he asked me for references. I furnished them, and he said we would now suspend our industries and I could go away and wait until he could write to those people and get answers.

In due course answers came. I was sent for and we had another private conference. I had referred him to six prominent men, among them two clergymen (these were all San Franciscans), and he himself had written to a bank cashier who had in earlier years been a Sunday-school superintendent in Elmira and well known to Mr. Langdon. The results were not promising. All those men were frank to a fault. They not only spoke in disapproval of me but they were quite unnecessarily and exaggeratedly enthusiastic about it. One clergyman (Stebbins) and that ex-Sunday-school superintendent (I wish I could recall his name) added to their black testimony the conviction that I would fill a drunkard's grave. It was just one of those usual long-distance prophecies. There being no time limit, there is no telling how long you may have to wait. I have waited until now and the fulfillment seems as far away as ever.

The reading of the letters being finished, there was a good deal of a pause and it consisted largely of sadness and solemnity. I couldn't think of anything to say. Mr. Langdon was apparently in the same condition. Finally he raised his handsome head, fixed his clear and candid eye upon me and said: "What kind of people are these? Haven't you a friend in the world?"

I said, "Apparently not."

Then he said: "I'll be your friend myself. Take the girl. I know you better than they do."

Thus dramatically and happily was my fate settled. Afterward, hearing me talking lovingly, admiringly and fervently of Joe Goodman, he asked me where Goodman lived. I told him out on the Pacific coast. He said: "Why, he seems to be a friend of yours! Is he?"

I said, "Indeed he is; the best one I ever had."

"Why, then," he said, "what could you have been thinking of? Why didn't you refer me to him?"

I said: "Because he would have lied just as straightforwardly on the other side. The others gave me all the vices; Goodman would have given me all the virtues. You wanted unprejudiced testimony, of course. I knew you wouldn't get it from Goodman. I did believe you would get it from those others and possibly you did. But it was certainly less complimentary than I was expecting."

The date of our engagement was February 4, 1869. The engagement ring was plain and of heavy gold. That date was engraved inside of it. A year later I took it from her finger and prepared it to do service as a wedding ring by having the wedding date added and engraved inside of it— February 2, 1870. It was never again removed from her finger for even a moment.

In Italy when death had restored her vanished youth to her sweet face and she lay fair and beautiful and looking as she had looked when she was girl and bride, they were going to take that ring from her finger to keep for the children. But I prevented that sacrilege. It is buried with her.

In the beginning of our engagement the proofs of my first book, *The Innocents Abroad*, began to arrive and she read them with me. She also edited them. She was my faithful, judicious and painstaking editor from that day forth until within three or four months of her death—a stretch of more than a third of a century.

CHAPTER 37

Our first child, Langdon Clemens, was born the 7th of
November, 1870, and lived twenty-two months. I was the
cause of the child's illness. His mother trusted him to my care
and I took him for a long drive in an open barouche for an
airing. It was a raw, cold morning but he was well wrapped
about with furs and, in the hands of a careful person, no
harm would have come to him. But I soon dropped into a
reverie and forgot all about my charge. The furs fell away
and exposed his bare legs. By and by the coachman noticed
this and I arranged the wraps again, but it was too late. The
child was almost frozen. I hurried home with him. I was
aghast at what I had done and I feared the consequences. I
have always felt shame for that treacherous morning's work
and have not allowed myself to think of it when I could help
it. I doubt if I had the courage to make confession at that
time. I think it most likely that I have never confessed until
now.

Susy was born the 19th of March, 1872. The summer
seasons of her childhood were spent at Quarry Farm on the
hills east of Elmira, New York; the other seasons of the year
at the home in Hartford. (We removed to Hartford in October 1871 and presently built a house.) Like other children,
she was blithe and happy, fond of play; unlike the average
of children, she was at times much given to retiring within
herself and trying to search out the hidden meanings of the
deep things that make the puzzle and pathos of human
existence and in all the ages have baffled the inquirer and
mocked him. As a little child aged seven she was oppressed
and perplexed by the maddening repetition of the stock
incidents of our race's fleeting sojourn here, just as the same
thing has oppressed and perplexed maturer minds from the
beginning of time. A myriad of men are born; they labor
and sweat and struggle for bread; they squabble and scold
and fight; they scramble for little mean advantages over

each other. Age creeps upon them; infirmities follow; shames and humiliations bring down their prides and their vanities. Those they love are taken from them and the joy of life is turned to aching grief. The burden of pain, care, misery, grows heavier year by year. At length ambition is dead; pride is dead; vanity is dead; longing for release is in their place. It comes at last—the only unpoisoned gift earth ever had for them—and they vanish from a world where they were of no consequence; where they achieved nothing; where they were a mistake and a failure and a foolishness; where they have left no sign that they have existed—a world which will lament them a day and forget them forever. Then another myriad takes their place and copies all they did and goes along the same profitless road and vanishes as they vanished—to make room for another and another and a million other myriads to follow the same arid path through the same desert and accomplish what the first myriad and all the myriads that came after it accomplished—nothing!

"Mamma, what is it all for?" asked Susy, preliminarily stating the above details in her own halting language, after long brooding over them alone in the privacy of the nursery.

A year later she was groping her way alone through another sunless bog, but this time she reached a rest for her feet. For a week, her mother had not been able to go to the nursery, evenings, at the child's prayer hour. She spoke of it—was sorry for it and said she would come tonight and hoped she could continue to come every night and hear Susy pray, as before. Noticing that the child wished to respond but was evidently troubled as to how to word her answer, she asked what the difficulty was. Susy explained that Miss Foote (the governess) had been teaching her about the Indians and their religious beliefs, whereby it appeared that they had not only a god, but several. This had set Susy to thinking. As a result of this thinking she had stopped praying. She qualified this statement—that is, she modified it—saying she did not now pray "in the same way" as she had formerly done. Her mother said, "Tell me about it, dear."

"Well, mamma, the Indians believed they knew, but now we know they were wrong. By and by it can turn out that we are wrong. So now I only pray that there may be a God and a heaven—or something better."

I wrote down this pathetic prayer in its precise wording at the time in a record which we kept of the children's sayings and my reverence for it has grown with the years that have passed over my head since then. Its untaught grace and simplicity are a child's, but the wisdom and the pathos of it are of all the ages that have come and gone since the race of man has lived and longed and hoped and feared and doubted.

To go back a year—Susy aged seven. Several times her mother said to her, "There, there, Susy, you mustn't cry over little things."

This furnished Susy a text for thought. She had been breaking her heart over what had seemed vast disasters—a broken toy; a picnic canceled by thunder and lightning and rain; the mouse that was growing tame and friendly in the nursery caught and killed by the cat—and now came this strange revelation. For some unaccountable reason these were not vast calamities. Why? How is the size of calamities measured? What is the rule? There must be some way to tell the great ones from the small ones; what is the law of these proportions? She examined the problem earnestly and long. She gave it her best thought from time to time for two or three days—but it baffled her—defeated her. And at last she gave up and went to her mother for help.

"Mamma, what is 'little things'?"

It seemed a simple question—at first. And yet before the answer could be put into words, unsuspected and unforeseen difficulties began to appear. They increased; they multiplied; they brought about another defeat. The effort to explain came to a standstill. Then Susy tried to help her mother out—with an instance, an example, an illustration. The mother was getting ready to go downtown, and one of her errands was to buy a long-promised toy watch for Susy.

"If you forgot the watch, mamma, would that be a little thing?"

She was not concerned about the watch, for she knew it would not be forgotten. What she was hoping for was that the answer would unriddle the riddle and bring rest and peace to her perplexed little mind.

The hope was disappointed, of course—for the reason that the size of a misfortune is not determinable by an outsider's measurement of it but only by the measurements applied to it by the person specially affected by it. The king's lost crown is a vast matter to the king but of no consequence to the child. The lost toy is a great matter to the child but in the king's eyes it is not a thing to break the heart about. A verdict was

reached but it was based upon the above model and Susy was
granted leave to measure her disasters thereafter with her own
tapeline.

I will throw in a note or two here touching the time when
Susy was seventeen. She had written a play modeled upon
Greek lines, and she and Clara and Margaret Warner and
other young comrades had played it to a charmed houseful of
friends in our house in Hartford. Charles Dudley Warner and
his brother, George, were present. They were near neighbors
and warm friends of ours. They were full of praises of the
workmanship of the play, and George Warner came over the
next morning and had a long talk with Susy. The result of it
was this verdict:

"She is the most interesting person I have ever known, of
either sex."

Remark of a lady—Mrs. Cheney, I think, author of the biography of her father, Rev. Dr. Bushnell:

"I made this note after one of my talks with Susy: 'She
knows all there is of life and its meanings. She could not know
it better if she had lived it out to its limit. Her intuitions and
ponderings and analyzings seem to have taught her all that my
sixty years have taught me.'"

Remark of another lady; she is speaking of Susy's last days:[1]

"In those last days she walked as if on air, and her walk answered to the buoyancy of her spirits and the passion of intellectual energy and activity that possessed her."

I return now to the point where I made this diversion. From
her earliest days, as I have already indicated, Susy was given
to examining things and thinking them out by herself. She was
not trained to this; it was the make of her mind. In matters involving questions of fair or unfair dealing she reviewed the
details patiently and surely arrived at a right and logical conclusion. In Munich, when she was six years old, she was
harassed by a recurrent dream, in which a ferocious bear fig-
ured. She came out of the dream each time sorely frightened
and crying. She set herself the task of analyzing this dream.
The reasons of it? The purpose of it? The origin of it? No—the
moral aspect of it. Her verdict, arrived at after candid and
searching investigation, exposed it to the charge of being one-
sided and unfair in its construction: for (as she worded it) *she*
was "never the one that ate, but always the one that was
eaten."

[1] Susy died in 1896.

Susy backed her good judgment in matters of morals with conduct to match—even upon occasions when it caused her sacrifice to do it. When she was six and her sister Clara four, the pair were troublesomely quarrelsome. Punishments were tried as a means of breaking up this custom—these failed. Then rewards were tried. A day without a quarrel brought candy. The children were their own witnesses—each for or against her own self. Once Susy took the candy, hesitated, then returned it with a suggestion that she was not fairly entitled to it. Clara kept hers, so here was a conflict of evidence —one witness *for* a quarrel and one against it. But the better witness of the two was on the affirmative side and the quarrel stood proved and no candy due to either side. There seemed to be no defense for Clara—yet there was and Susy furnished it; and Clara went free. Susy said, "I don't know whether she felt wrong in *her* heart but I didn't feel right in *my* heart."

It was a fair and honorable view of the case and a specially acute analysis of it for a child of six to make. There was no way to convict Clara now, except to put her on the stand again and review her evidence. There was a doubt as to the fairness of this procedure, since her former evidence had been accepted and not challenged at the time. The doubt was examined and canvassed—then she was given the benefit of it and acquitted; which was just as well, for in the meantime she had eaten the candy anyway.

◇◇◇◇◇◇◇◇◇◇◇◇◇◇◇◇◇◇◇◇◇

CHAPTER 38

Whenever I think of Susy I think of Marjorie Fleming. There was but one Marjorie Fleming. There can never be another. No doubt I think of Marjorie when I think of Susy mainly because Dr. John Brown, that noble and beautiful soul—rescuer of marvelous Marjorie from oblivion—was Susy's great friend in her babyhood—her worshiper and willing slave.

In 1873, when Susy was fourteen months old, we arrived in Edinburgh from London, fleeing thither for rest and refuge after experiencing what had been to us an entirely new kind of life—six weeks of daily lunches, teas and dinners away from home. We carried no letters of introduction; we hid ourselves away in Veitch's family hotel in George Street and prepared to have a comfortable season all to ourselves. But by good fortune this did not happen. Straightway Mrs. Clemens needed a physician and I stepped around to 23 Rutland Street to see if the author of *Rab and His Friends* was still a practicing physician. He was. He came, and for six weeks thereafter we were together every day, either in his house or in our hotel.

His was a sweet and winning face—as beautiful a face as I have ever known. Reposeful, gentle, benignant—the face of a saint at peace with all the world and placidly beaming upon it the sunshine of love that filled his heart. Doctor John was beloved by everybody in Scotland; and I think that on its downward sweep southward it found no frontier. I think so because when, a few years later, infirmities compelled Doctor John to give up his practice, and Mr. Douglas, the publisher, and other friends set themselves the task of raising a fund of a few thousand dollars, whose income was to be devoted to the support of himself and his maiden sister (who was in age), the fund was not only promptly made up but so *very* promptly that the books were closed before friends a hundred miles south of the line had had an opportunity to contribute. No public appeal was made. The matter was never mentioned in print. Mr. Douglas and the other friends applied for contributions by private letter only. Many complaints came from London and everywhere between from people who had not been allowed an opportunity to contribute. This sort of complaint is so new to the world—so strikingly unusual—that I think it worth while to mention it.

Doctor John was very fond of animals, and particularly of dogs. No one needs to be told this who has read that pathetic and beautiful masterpiece, *Rab and His Friends*. After his death his son, Jock, published a brief memorial of him which he distributed privately among the friends; and in it occurs a little episode which illustrates the relationship that existed between Doctor John and the other animals. It is furnished by an Edinburgh lady whom Doctor John used to pick up and carry to school or back in his carriage frequently at a time when she was twelve years old. She said that they were chatting together tranquilly one day, when he suddenly broke off in the midst of a sentence and thrust his head out of the carriage window eagerly—then resumed his place with a disappointed look on his face. The girl said: "Who is it? Some one you know?" He said, "No, a dog I don't know."

He had two names for Susy—"Wee wifie" and "Megalopis." This formidable Greek title was conferred in honor of her big, big dark eyes. Susy and the Doctor had a good deal of romping together. Daily he unbent his dignity and played "bear" with the child. I do not now remember which of them was the bear but I think it was the child. There was a sofa across a corner of the parlor with a door behind it opening into Susy's quarters and she used to lie in wait for the Doctor behind the sofa—not lie in wait but stand in wait; for you could only get just a glimpse of the top of her yellow head when she stood upright. According to the rules of the game she was invisible and this glimpse did not count. I think she must have been the bear, for I can remember two or three occasions when she sprang out from behind the sofa and surprised the Doctor into frenzies of fright, which were not in the least modified by the fact that he knew that the "bear" was there and was coming.

It seems incredible that Doctor John should ever have wanted to tell a grotesque and rollicking anecdote. Such a thing seems so out of character with that gentle and tranquil nature that—but no matter. I tried to teach him the anecdote and he tried his best for two or three days to perfect himself in it—and he never succeeded. It was the most impressive exhibition that ever was. There was no human being nor dog of his acquaintance in all Edinburgh that would not have been paralyzed with astonishment to step in there and see Doctor John trying to do that anecdote. It was one which I have told some hundreds of times on the platform and which I was always very fond of because it worked the audience so hard. It was a stammering man's account of how he got cured of his infirmity—which was accomplished by introducing a whistle into the midst of every word which he found himself unable to finish on account of the obstruction of the stammering. And so his whole account was an absurd mixture of stammering and whistling—which was irresistible to an audience properly keyed up for laughter. Doctor John learned to do the mechanical details of the anecdote but he was never able to inform these details with expression. He was preternaturally grave and earnest all through, and so when he fetched up with the climaxing triumphant sentence at the end—but I must quote that sentence, or the reader will not understand. It was this:

"The doctor told me that whenever I wanted to sta- (whistle) sta- (whistle) sta- (whistle) *ammer*, I must whistle; and I did, and it k- (whistle) k- (whistle) k- (whistle) k- ured me *entirely!*"

The Doctor could not master that triumphant note. He always gravely stammered and whistled and whistled and stammered it through, and it came out at the end with the solemnity and the gravity of the judge delivering sentence to a man with the black cap on.

He was the loveliest creature in the world—except his aged sister, who was just like him. We made the round of his professional visits with him in his carriage every day for six weeks. He always brought a basket of grapes and we brought books. The scheme which we began with on the first round of visits was the one which was maintained until the end—and was based upon this remark, which he made when he was disembarking from the carriage at his first stopping place to visit a patient, "Entertain yourselves while I go in here and reduce the population."

◇◇◇◇◇◇◇◇◇◇◇◇◇◇◇◇◇◇◇

CHAPTER 39

As a child Susy had a passionate temper; and it cost her much remorse and many tears before she learned to govern it, but after that it was a wholesome salt and her character was the stronger and healthier for its presence. It enabled her to be good with dignity; it preserved her not only from being good for vanity's sake but from even the appearance of it. In looking back over the long-vanished years it seems but natural and excusable that I should dwell with longing affection and preference upon incidents of her young life which made it beautiful to us and that I should let its few and small offenses go unsummoned and unreproached.

In the summer of 1880, when Susy was just eight years of age, the family were at Quarry Farm, on top of a high hill, three miles from Elmira, New York, where we always spent our summers in those days. Hay-cutting time was approaching and Susy and Clara were counting the hours, for the time was big with a great event for them; they had been promised that they might mount the wagon and ride home from the fields on the summit of the hay mountain. This perilous privilege, so dear to their age and species, had never been granted them before. Their excitement had no bounds. They could talk of nothing but this epoch-making adventure now. But misfortune overtook Susy on the very morning of the important day. In a sudden outbreak of passion she corrected Clara—with a shovel or stick or something of the sort. At any rate, the offense committed was of a gravity clearly beyond the limit allowed in the nursery. In accordance with the rule and custom of the house, Susy went to her mother to confess and to help decide upon the size and character of the punishment due. It was quite understood that as a punishment could have but one rational object and function—to act as a reminder and warn the transgressor against transgressing in the same way again—the children would know about as well as any how to choose a penalty which would be rememberable and effective. Susy and her mother discussed various punishments but none of them seemed adequate. This fault was an unusually serious one and required the setting up of a danger signal in the memory that would not blow out nor burn out but remain a fixture there and furnish its saving warning indefinitely. Among the punishments mentioned was deprivation of the hay-wagon ride. It was noticeable that this one hit Susy hard. Finally, in the summing up, the mother named over the list and asked, "Which one do you think it ought to be, Susy?"

Susy studied, shrank from her duty, and asked, "Which do you think, mamma?"

"Well, Susy, I would rather leave it to you. *You* make the choice yourself."

It cost Susy a struggle and much and deep thinking and weighing—but she came out where anyone who knew her could have foretold she would:

"Well, mamma, I'll make it the hay wagon, because, you know, the other things might not make me remember not to do it again, but if I don't get to ride on the hay wagon I can remember it easily."

In this world the real penalty, the sharp one, the lasting one, never falls otherwise than on the wrong person. It was not *I* that corrected Clara but the remembrance of poor Susy's lost hay ride still brings *me* a pang—after twenty-six years.

Apparently Susy was born with humane feelings for the animals and compassion for their troubles. This enabled her to see a new point in an old story, once, when she was only six years old—a point which had been overlooked by older and

perhaps duller people for many ages. Her mother told her the
moving story of the sale of Joseph by his brethren, the stain-
ing of his coat with the blood of the slaughtered kid, and the
rest of it. She dwelt upon the inhumanity of the brothers, their
cruelty toward their helpless young brother, and the un-
brotherly treachery which they practiced upon him; for she
hoped to teach the child a lesson in gentle pity and merciful-
ness which she would remember. Apparently her desire was
accomplished, for the tears came into Susy's eyes and she was
deeply moved. Then she said, "Poor little kid!"

A child's frank envy of the privileges and distinctions of its
elders is often a delicately flattering attention and the reverse
of unwelcome, but sometimes the envy is not placed where the
beneficiary is expecting it to be placed. Once when Susy was
seven she sat breathlessly absorbed in watching a guest of
ours adorn herself for a ball. The lady was charmed by this
homage, this mute and gentle admiration, and was happy in
it. And when her pretty labors were finished and she stood
at last perfect, unimprovable, clothed like Solomon in his
glory, she paused, confident and expectant, to receive from
Susy's tongue the tribute that was burning in her eyes. Susy
drew an envious little sigh and said, "I wish *I* could have
crooked teeth and spectacles!"

Once, when Susy was six months along in her eighth year,
she did something one day in the presence of company which
subjected her to criticism and reproof. Afterward, when she
was alone with her mother, as was her custom she reflected a
little while over the matter. Then she set up what I think—
and what the shade of Burns would think—was a quite good
philosophical defense: "Well, mamma, you know I didn't see
myself and so I couldn't know how it looked."

In homes where the near friends and visitors are mainly literary people—lawyers, judges, professors and clergymen—the
children's ears become early familiarized with wide vocabu-
laries. It is natural for them to pick up any words that fall in
their way; it is natural for them to pick up big and little ones
indiscriminately; it is natural for them to use without fear any
word that comes to their net, no matter how formidable it
may be as to size. As a result, their talk is a curious and funny
musketry-clatter of little words, interrupted at intervals by the
heavy-artillery crash of a word of such imposing sound and
size that it seems to shake the ground and rattle the windows.
Sometimes the child gets a wrong idea of a word which it has

picked up by chance, and attaches to it a meaning which impairs its usefulness—but this does not happen as often as one might expect it would. Indeed, it happens with an infrequency which may be regarded as remarkable. As a child, Susy had good fortune with her large words and she employed many of them. She made no more than her fair share of mistakes. Once when she thought something very funny was going to happen (but it didn't) she was racked and torn with laughter, by anticipation. But apparently she still felt sure of her position, for she said, "If it had happened I should have been transformed [transported] with glee."

And earlier, when she was a little maid of five years, she informed a visitor that she had been in a church only once, and that was the time when Clara was "crucified" (christened).

In Heidelberg, when Susy was six, she noticed that the Schloss gardens were populous with snails creeping all about everywhere. One day she found a new dish on her table and inquired concerning it and learned that it was made of snails. She was awed and impressed and said, "Wild ones, mamma?"

She was thoughtful and considerate of others—an acquired quality, no doubt. No one seems to be born with it. One hot day, at home in Hartford, when she was a little child, her mother borrowed her fan several times (a Japanese one, value five cents), refreshed herself with it a moment or two, then handed it back with a word of thanks. Susy knew her mother would use the fan all the time if she could do it without putting a deprivation upon its owner. She also knew that her mother could not be persuaded to do that. A relief must be devised somehow; Susy devised it. She got five cents out of her money box and carried it to Patrick and asked him to take it downtown (a mile and a half) and buy a Japanese fan and bring it home. He did it—and thus thoughtfully and delicately was the exigency met and the mother's comfort secured. It is to the child's credit that she did not save herself expense by bringing down another and most costly kind of fan from upstairs but was content to act upon the impression that her mother desired the Japanese kind—content to accomplish the desire and stop with that, without troubling about the wisdom or unwisdom of it.

Sometimes while she was still a child her speech fell into quaint and strikingly expressive forms. Once—aged nine or ten—she came to her mother's room when her sister Jean was a baby and said Jean was crying in the nursery and asked if she might ring for the nurse. Her mother asked, "Is she crying hard?"—meaning cross, ugly.

"Well, no, mamma. It is a weary, lonesome cry."

It is a pleasure to me to recall various incidents which reveal the delicacies of feeling which were so considerable a part of her budding character. Such a revelation came once in a way which, while creditable to her heart, was defective in another direction. She was in her eleventh year then. Her mother had been making the Christmas purchases and she allowed Susy to see the presents which were for Patrick's children. Among these was a handsome sled for Jimmy, on which a stag was painted; also in gilt capitals the word "DEER." Susy was excited and joyous over everything until she came to this sled. Then she became sober and silent—yet the sled was the choicest of all the gifts. Her mother was surprised and also disappointed, and said:

"Why, Susy, doesn't it please you? Isn't it fine?"

Susy hesitated and it was plain that she did not want to say the thing that was in her mind. However, being urged, she brought it haltingly out:

"Well, mamma, it *is* fine and of course it *did* cost a good deal—but—but—why should that be mentioned?"

Seeing that she was not understood, she reluctantly pointed to the word "DEER." It was her orthography that was at fault, not her heart. She had inherited both from her mother.

CHAPTER 40

When Susy was thirteen and was a slender little maid with plaited tails of copper-tinged brown hair down her back and was perhaps the busiest bee in the household hive, by reason of the manifold studies, health exercises and recreations she had to attend to, she secretly and of her own motion and out of love added another task to her labors—the writing of a biography of me. She did this work in her bedroom at night and kept her record hidden. After a little the mother discovered it and filched it and let me see it; then told Susy what she had done and how pleased I was and how proud. I remember that time with a deep pleasure. I had had compliments before but none that touched me like this; none that could approach it for value in my eyes. It has kept that place always since. I have had no compliment, no praise, no tribute from any source that was so precious to me as this one was and still is. As I read it *now*, after all these many years, it is still a king's message to me and brings me the same dear surprise it brought me then—with the pathos added of the thought that the eager and hasty hand that sketched it and scrawled it will not touch mine again—and I feel as the humble and unexpectant must feel when their eyes fall upon the edict that raises them to the ranks of the noble.

It is quite evident that several times, at breakfast and dinner, in those long-past days, I was posing for the biography. In fact, I clearly remember that I *was* doing that—and I also remember that Susy detected it. I remember saying a very smart thing, with a good deal of an air, at the breakfast table one morning and that Susy observed to her mother privately a little later that papa was doing that for the biography.

I cannot bring myself to change any line or word in Susy's sketch of me but will introduce passages from it now and then just as they came in—their quaint simplicity out of her honest heart, which was the beautiful heart of a child. What comes from that source has a charm and grace of its own which may transgress all the recognized laws of literature, if it choose, and yet be literature still and worthy of hospitality.

The spelling is frequently desperate but it was Susy's and it shall stand. I love it and cannot profane it. To me it is gold. To correct it would alloy it, not refine it. It would spoil it. It would take from it its freedom and flexibility and make it stiff and formal. Even when it is most extravagant I am not shocked. It is Susy's spelling and she was doing the best she could—and nothing could better it for me.

She learned languages easily; she learned history easily; she learned music easily; she learned all things easily, quickly and thoroughly except spelling. She even learned that after a while. But it would have grieved me but little if she had failed in it—for although good spelling was my one accomplishment I was never able to greatly respect it. When I was a schoolboy sixty years ago[1] we had two prizes in our school. One was for good spelling, the other for amiability. These things were thin, smooth, silver disks, about the size of a dollar. Upon the one was engraved in flowing Italian script the words "Good Spell-

[1] Written in 1906.

ing," on the other was engraved the word "Amiability." The holders of these prizes hung them about the neck with a string —and those holders were the envy of the whole school. There wasn't a pupil that wouldn't have given a leg for the privilege of wearing one of them a week, but no pupil ever got a chance except John RoBards and me. John RoBards was eternally and indestructibly amiable. I may even say devilishly amiable; fiendishly amiable; exasperatingly amiable. That was the sort of feeling that we had about that quality of his. So he always wore the amiability medal. I always wore the other medal. That word "always" is a trifle too strong. We lost the medals several times. It was because they became so monotonous. We needed a change—therefore several times we traded medals. It was a satisfaction to John RoBards to *seem* to be a good speller —which he wasn't. And it was a satisfaction to me to seem to be amiable, for a change. But of course these changes could not long endure—for some schoolmate or other would presently notice what had been happening and that schoolmate would not have been human if he had lost any time in reporting this treason. The teacher took the medals away from us at once, of course—and we always had them back again before Friday night. If we lost the medals Monday morning, John's amiability was at the top of the list Friday afternoon when the teacher came to square up the week's account. The Friday-afternoon session always closed with "spelling down." Being in disgrace, I necessarily started at the foot of my division of spellers, but I always slaughtered both divisions and stood alone with the medal around my neck when the campaign was finished. I *did* miss on a word once, just at the end of one of these conflicts, and so lost the medal. I left the first *r* out of February—but that was to accommodate a sweetheart. My passion was so strong just at that time that I would have left out the whole alphabet if the word had contained it.

As I have said before, I never had any large respect for good spelling. That is my feeling yet. Before the spelling book came with its arbitrary forms, men unconsciously revealed shades of their characters and also added enlightening shades of expression to what they wrote by their spelling, and so it is possible that the spelling book has been a doubtful benevolence to us.

Susy began the biography in 1885, when I was in the fiftieth year of my age, and she in the fourteenth of hers. She begins in this way:

We are a very happy family. We consist of Papa, Mamma, Jean, Clara and me. It is papa I am writing about, and I shall have no trouble in not knowing what to say about him, as he is a *very* striking character.

Papa's appearance has been described many times, but very incorrectly. He has beautiful gray hair, not any too thick or any too long, but just right; a Roman nose, which greatly improves the beauty of his features; kind blue eyes and a small mustache. He has a wonderfully shaped head and profile. He has a very good figure—in short, he is an extrodinarily fine looking man. All his features are perfect, exept that he hasn't extraordinary teeth. His complexion is very fair, and he doesn't ware a beard. He is a very good man and a very funny one. He *has* got a temper, but we all of us have in this family. He is the loveliest man I ever saw or ever hope to see—and oh, so absent-minded. He does tell perfectly delightful stories. Clara and I used to sit on each arm of his chair and listen while he told us stories about the pictures on the wall.

I remember the storytelling days vividly. They were a difficult and exacting audience—those little creatures.

Along one side of the library, in the Hartford home, the bookshelves joined the mantelpiece—in fact, there were shelves on both sides of the mantelpiece. On these shelves and on the mantelpiece stood various ornaments. At one end of the procession was a framed oil painting of a cat's head; at the other end was a head of a beautiful young girl, life size—called Emmeline, because she looked just about like that—an impressionist water color. Between the one picture and the other there were twelve or fifteen of the bric-à-brac things already mentioned, also an oil painting by Elihu Vedder, "The Young Medusa." Every now and then the children required me to construct a romance—always impromptu—not a moment's preparation permitted—and into that romance I had to get all that bric-à-brac and the three pictures. I had to start always with the cat and finish with Emmeline. I was never allowed the refreshment of a change, end for end. It was not permissible to introduce a bric-à-brac ornament into the story out of its place in the procession.

These bric-à-bracs were never allowed a peaceful day, a reposeful day, a restful Sabbath. In their lives there was no Sabbath; in their lives there was no peace; they knew no existence but a monotonous career of violence and bloodshed. In the course of time the bric-à-brac and the pictures showed wear. It was because they had had so many and such tumultuous adventures in their romantic careers.

As romancer to the children I had a hard time, even from the beginning. If they brought me a picture in a magazine and required me to build a story to it, they would cover the rest of the page with their pudgy hands to keep me from stealing an idea from it. The stories had to be absolutely original and fresh. Sometimes the children furnished me simply a character or two, or a dozen, and required me to start out at once on that slim basis and deliver those characters up to a vigorous and entertaining life of crime. If they heard of a new trade or an unfamiliar animal or anything like that, I was pretty sure to have to deal with those things in the next romance. Once Clara required me to build a sudden tale out of a plumber and a "bawgun strictor," and I had to do it. She didn't know what a boa constrictor was until he developed in the tale—then she was better satisfied with it than ever.

Papa's favorite game is billiards, and when he is tired and wishes to rest himself he stays up all night and plays billiards, it seems to rest his head. He smokes a great deal almost incessantly. He has the mind of an author exactly, some of the simplest things he can't understand. Our burglar alarm is often out of order, and papa had been obliged to take the mahogany room off from the alarm altogether for a time, because the burglar alarm had been in the habit of ringing even when the mahogany-room window was closed. At length he thought that perhaps the burglar alarm might be in order, and he decided to try and see; accordingly he put it on and then went down and opened the window; consequently the alarm bell rang, it would even if the alarm had been in order. Papa went despairingly upstairs and said to mamma, "Livy the mahogany room won't go on. I have just opened the window to see."

"Why, Youth," mamma replied. "If you've opened the window, why of course the alarm will ring!"

"That's what I've opened it for, why I just went down to see if it would ring!"

Mamma tried to explain to papa that when he wanted

to go and see whether the alarm would ring while the window was closed he *mustn't* go and open the window —but in vain, papa couldn't understand, and got very impatient with mamma for trying to make him believe an impossible thing true.

This is a frank biographer and an honest one; she uses no sandpaper on me. I have to this day the same dull head in the matter of conundrums and perplexities which Susy had discovered in those long-gone days. Complexities annoy me; they irritate me; then this progressive feeling presently warms into anger. I cannot get far in the reading of the commonest and simplest contract—with its "parties of the first part" and "parties of the second part" and "parties of the third part"—before my temper is all gone. Ashcroft[3] comes up here every day and pathetically tries to make me understand the points of the lawsuit which we are conducting against Henry Butters, Harold Wheeler and the rest of those Plasmon buccaneers, but daily he has to give it up. It is pitiful to see, when he bends his earnest and appealing eyes upon me and says after one of his efforts, "Now you *do* understand *that*, don't you?"

I am always obliged to say, "I *don't*, Ashcroft. I wish I could understand it but I don't. Send for the cat."

In the days which Susy is talking about, a perplexity fell to my lot one day. F. G. Whitmore was my business agent and he brought me out from town in his buggy. We drove by the porte-cochère and toward the stable. Now this was a *single* road and was like a spoon whose handle stretched from the gate to a great round flower bed in the neighborhood of the stable. At the approach to the flower bed the road divided and circumnavigated it, making a loop, which I have likened to the bowl of the spoon. I was sitting on the starboard side. As we neared the loop, I sitting as I say on the starboard side (and that was the side on which the house was), I saw that Whitmore was laying his course to port and was going to start around that spoon bowl on that left-hand side. I said: "Don't do that, Whitmore; take the right-hand side. Then I shall be next to the house when we get to the door."

He said: "*That* will happen in *any* case. It doesn't make any difference which way I go around this flower bed."

I explained to him that he was an ass but he stuck to his proposition, and I said, "Go on and try it and see."

MARK TWAIN225

He went on and tried it and sure enough he fetched me up at the door on the very side that he had said I would be. I was not able to believe it then and I don't believe it yet.

I said: "Whitmore, that is merely an accident. You can't do it again." He said he could—and he drove down into the street, fetched around, came back, and actually did it again. I was stupefied, paralyzed, petrified with these strange results but they did not convince me. I didn't believe he could do it another time but he did. He said he could do it all day and fetch up the same way every time. By that time my temper was gone and I asked him to go home and apply to the asylum and I would pay the expenses. I didn't want to see him any more for a week.

I went upstairs in a rage and started to tell Livy about it, expecting to get her sympathy for me and to breed aversion in her for Whitmore; but she merely burst into peal after peal of laughter as the tale of my adventure went on, for her head was like Susy's. Riddles and complexities had no terrors for it. Her mind and Susy's were analytical. I have tried to make it appear that mine was different. Many and many a time I have told that buggy experiment, hoping against hope that I would some time or other find somebody who would be on my side—but it has never happened. And I am never able to go glibly forward and state the circumstances of that buggy's progress without having to halt and consider and call up in my mind the spoon handle, the bowl of the spoon, the buggy and the horse, and my position in the buggy—and the minute I have got that far and try to turn it to the left, it goes to ruin. I can't see how it is ever going to fetch me out right when we get to the door. Susy is right in her estimate. I can't understand things.

That burglar alarm which Susy mentions led a gay and careless life and had no principles. It was generally out of order at one point or another and there was plenty of opportunity, because all the windows and doors in the house, from the cellar up to the top floor, were connected with it. However, in its seasons of being out of order it could trouble us for only a very little while: we quickly found out that it was fooling us and that it was buzzing its blood-curdling alarm merely for its own amusement. Then we would shut it off and send to New York for the electrician—there not being one in all Hartford in those days. When the repairs were finished we would set the alarm again and reestablish our confidence in it. It never did any real business except upon one single occasion. All the rest of its expensive career was frivolous and without purpose. Just that one time it performed its duty, and its whole duty—gravely, seriously, admirably. It let fly about two o'clock one black and dreary March morning and I turned out promptly, because I knew that it was not fooling this time. The bathroom door was on my side of the bed. I stepped in there, turned up the gas, looked at the annunciator, turned off the alarm—so far as the door indicated was concerned—thus stopping the racket. Then I came back to bed. Mrs. Clemens opened the debate:

"What was it?"

"It was the cellar door."

"Was it a burglar, do you think?"

"Yes," I said, "of course it was. Did you suppose it was a Sunday-school superintendent?"

"No. What do you suppose he wants?"

"I suppose he wants jewelry, but he is not acquainted with the house and he thinks it is in the cellar. I don't like to disappoint a burglar whom I am not acquainted with and who has done me no harm, but if he had had common sagacity enough to inquire, I could have told him we kept nothing down there but coal and vegetables. Still, it may be that he *is* acquainted with this place and that what he really wants is coal and vegetables. On the whole, I think it is vegetables he is after."

"Are you going down to see?"

"No. I could not be of any assistance. Let him select for himself; I don't know where the things are."

Then she said, "But suppose he comes up to the ground floor!"

"That's all right. We shall know it the minute he opens a door on that floor. It will set off the alarm."

Just then the terrific buzzing broke out again. I said: "He has arrived. I told you he would. I know all about burglars and their ways. They are systematic people."

I went into the bathroom to see if I was right, and I was. I shut off the dining room and stopped the buzzing and came back to bed. My wife said:

"What do you suppose he is after now?"

I said, "I think he has got all the vegetables he wants and is coming up for napkin rings and odds and ends for the wife and children. They all have families—burglars have—and they are always thoughtful of them, always take a few necessaries of life for themselves, and fill out with tokens of remembrance for the family. In taking them they do not forget us: those very things represent tokens of his remembrance of us, and also of our remembrance of him. We never get them again; the memory of the attention remains embalmed in our hearts."

"Are you going down to see what it is he wants now?"

"No," I said; "I am no more interested than I was before. They are experienced people—burglars; *they* know what they want. I should be no help to him. I *think* he is after ceramics and bric-à-brac and such things. If he knows the house he knows that that is all that he can find on the dining-room floor."

She said, with a strong interest perceptible in her tone, "Suppose he comes up here!"

I said, "It is all right. He will give us notice."

"What shall we do then?"

"Climb out of the window."

She said, a little restively, "Well, what is the use of a burglar alarm for us?"

"You have seen, dear heart, that it has been useful up to the present moment, and I have explained to you how it will be continuously useful after he gets up here."

That was the end of it. He didn't ring any more alarms.

Presently I said, "He is disappointed, I think. He has gone off with the vegetables and the bric-à-brac and I think he is dissatisfied."

We went to sleep and at a quarter before eight in the morning I was out and hurrying, for I was to take the 8:29 train for New York. I found the gas burning brightly—full head—all over the first floor. My new overcoat was gone; my old umbrella was gone; my new patent-leather shoes, which I had never worn, were gone. The large window which opened into the ombra at the rear of the house was standing wide. I passed out through it and tracked the burglar down the hill through the trees; tracked him without difficulty, because he had blazed his progress with imitation-silver napkin rings and my umbrella, and various other things which he had disapproved of; and I went back in triumph and proved to my wife that he *was* a disappointed burglar. I had suspected he would be, from the start, and from his not coming up to our floor to get human beings.

CHAPTER 41

Papa has a peculiar gait we like, it seems just to sute him, but most people do not; he always walks up and down the room while thinking and between each coarse at meals.

A lady distantly related to us came to visit us once in those days. She came to stay a week but all our efforts to make her happy failed and we could not imagine why, and she got up her anchor and sailed the next morning. We did much guessing but could not solve the mystery. Later we found out what the trouble was. It was my tramping up and down between the courses. She conceived the idea that I could not stand her society.

That word "Youth," as the reader has perhaps already guessed, was my wife's pet name for me. It was gently satirical but also affectionate. I had certain mental and material peculiarities and customs proper to a much younger person than I was.

Papa is very fond of animals particularly of cats, we had a dear little gray kitten once that he named "Lazy" (papa always wears gray to match his hair and eyes) and he would carry him around on his shoulder, it was a mighty pretty sight! the gray cat sound asleep against papa's gray coat and hair. The names that he has given our different cats, are realy remarkably funny, they are namely Stray Kit, Abner, Motley, Fraeulein, Lazy, Bufalo Bill, Soapy Sall, Cleveland, Sour Mash, and Pestilence and Famine.

At one time when the children were small we had a very black mother cat named Satan, and Satan had a small black offspring named Sin. Pronouns were a difficulty for the children. Little Clara came in one day, her black eyes snapping with indignation, and said: "Papa, Satan ought to be punished. She is out there at the greenhouse and there she stays and stays, and his kitten is downstairs, crying."

Papa uses very strong language, but I have an idea not nearly so strong as when he first maried mamma. A lady acquaintance of his is rather apt to interupt what one is saying, and papa told mamma that he thought he should say to the lady's husband "I am glad your wife wasn't present when the Deity said Let there be light."

It is as I have said before. This is a frank historian. She doesn't cover up one's deficiences but gives them an equal showing with one's handsomer qualities. Of course I made the remark which she has quoted—and even at this distant day I am still as much as half persuaded that if that lady mentioned had been present when the Creator said "Let there be light" she would have interrupted him and we shouldn't ever have got it.

Papa said the other day, "I am a mugwump and a mugwump is pure from the marrow out." (Papa knows that I am writing this biography of him, and he said this for it.) He doesn't like to go to church at all, why I never understood, until just now, he told us the other day that he couldn't bear to hear any one talk but himself, but that he could listen to himself talk for hours without getting tired, of course he said this in joke, but I've no dought it was founded on truth.

Susy's remark about my strong language troubles me, and I must go back to it. All through the first ten years of my married life I kept a constant and discreet watch upon my tongue while in the house, and went outside and to a distance when circumstances were too much for me and I was obliged to seek relief. I prized my wife's respect and approval above all the rest of the human race's respect and approval. I dreaded the day when she should discover that I was but a whited sepulcher partly freighted with suppressed language. I was so careful, during ten years, that I had not a doubt that my suppressions had been successful. Therefore I was quite as happy in my guilt as I could have been if I had been innocent. But at last an accident exposed me. I went into the bathroom one morning to make my toilet and carelessly left the door two or three inches ajar. It was the first time that I had ever failed to take the precaution of closing it tightly. I knew the necessity of being particular about this, because shaving was always a trying ordeal for me, and I could seldom carry it through to a finish without verbal helps. Now this time I was unprotected and did not suspect it. I had no extraordinary trouble with my razor on this occasion and was able to worry through with mere mutterings and growlings of an improper sort but with nothing noisy or emphatic about them—no snapping and barking. Then I put on a shirt. My shirts are an invention of my own. They open in the back and are buttoned there—when there are buttons. This time the button was missing. My temper jumped up several degrees in a moment and my remarks rose accordingly, both in loudness and vigor of expression. But I was not troubled, for the bathroom door was a solid one and I supposed it was firmly closed. I flung up the window and threw the shirt out. It fell upon the shrubbery where the people on their way to church could admire it if they wanted to; there was merely fifty feet of grass between the shirt and the passer-by. Still rumbling and thundering distantly, I put on another shirt. Again the button was absent. I augmented my language to meet the emergency and threw that shirt out of the window. I was too angry—too insane—to examine the third shirt, but put it furiously on. Again the button was absent, and that shirt followed its comrades out of the window. Then I straightened up, gathered my reserves, and let myself go like a cavalry charge. In the midst of that great assault my eye fell upon that gaping door and I was paralyzed.

It took me a good while to finish my toilet. I extended the time unnecessarily in trying to make up my mind as to what I would best do in the circumstances. I tried to hope that Mrs. Clemens was asleep but I knew better. I could not escape by the window. It was narrow and suited only to shirts. At last I made up my mind to boldly loaf through the bedroom with the air of a person who had not been doing anything. I made half the journey successfully. I did not turn my eyes in her direction, because that would not be safe. It is very difficult to look as if you have not been doing anything when the facts are the other way, and my confidence in my performance oozed steadily out of me as I went along. I was aiming for the left-hand door because it was farthest from my wife. It had never been opened from the day that the house was built but it seemed a blessed refuge for me now. The bed was this one, wherein I am lying now and dictating these histories morning after morning with so much serenity.[1] It was this same old elaborately carved black Venetian bedstead—the most comfortable bedstead that ever was, with space enough in it for a family, and carved angels enough surmounting its twisting columns and its headboard and footboard to bring peace to the sleepers, and pleasant dreams. I had to stop in the middle of the room. I hadn't the strength to go on. I believed that I was under accusing eyes—that even the carved angels were inspecting me with an unfriendly gaze. You know how it is when you are convinced that somebody behind you is looking steadily at you. You *have* to turn your face—you can't help it. I turned mine. The bed was placed as it is now, with the foot where the head ought to be. If it had been placed as it should have been, the high headboard would have sheltered me. But the footboard was no sufficient protection and I could be seen over it. I was exposed. I was wholly without protection. I turned, because I couldn't help it—and my memory of what I saw is still vivid after all these years.

Against the white pillows I saw the black head—I saw that young and beautiful face; and I saw the gracious eyes with a something in them which I had never seen there before. They were snapping and flashing with indignation. I felt myself crumbling; I felt myself shrinking away to nothing under that accusing gaze. I stood silent under that desolating fire for as much as a minute, I should say—it seemed a very, very long time. Then my wife's lips parted and from them issued—*my latest bathroom remark*. The language perfect, but the expression velvety, unpractical, apprentice-like, ignorant, inexperienced, comically inadequate, absurdly weak and unsuited to the great language. In my lifetime I had never heard anything so out of tune, so inharmonious, so incongruous, so ill suited to each other as were those mighty words set to that feeble music. I tried to keep from laughing, for I was a guilty person in deep need of charity and mercy. I tried to keep from bursting, and I succeeded—until she gravely said, "There, now you know how it sounds."

Then I exploded; the air was filled with my fragments and you could hear them whiz. I said, "Oh, Livy, if it sounds like that, God forgive me, I will never do it again!"

[1] Written in 1906.

Then she had to laugh herself. Both of us broke into convulsions and went on laughing until we were physically exhausted and spiritually reconciled.

The children were present at breakfast—Clara, aged six, and Susy, eight—and the mother made a guarded remark about strong language; guarded because she did not wish the children to suspect anything—a guarded remark which censured strong language. Both children broke out in one voice with this comment: "Why, mamma, papa uses it!" I was astonished. I had supposed that that secret was safe in my own breast and that its presence had never been suspected. I asked, "How did you know, you little rascals?"

"Oh," they said, "we often listen over the balusters when you are in the hall explaining things to George."

One of papa's latest books is "The Prince and the Pauper" and it is unquestionably the best book he has ever written, some people want him to keep to his old style, some gentleman wrote him, "I enjoyed Huckleberry Finn immensely and am glad to see that you have returned to your old style." That enoyed me that enoyed me greatly, because it trobles me [Susy was troubled by that word, and uncertain; she wrote a *u* above it in the proper place, but reconsidered the matter and struck it out] to have so few people know papa, I mean realy know him, they think of Mark Twain as a humorist joking at everything; "And with a mop of reddish brown hair which sorely needs the barbars brush a roman nose, short stubby mustache, a sad care-worn face, with maney crow's feet," etc. That is the way people picture papa, I have wanted papa to write a book that would reveal something of his kind sympathetic nature, and "The Prince and the Pauper" partly does it. The book is full of lovely charming ideas, and oh the language! It is *perfect*. I think that one of the most touching scenes in it, is where the pauper is riding on horseback with his nobles in the "recognition procession" and he sees his mother oh and then what followed! How she runs to his side, when she sees him throw up his hand palm outward, and is rudely pushed off by one of the King's officers, and then how the little pauper's conscience troubles him when he remembers the shameful words that were falling from his lips, when she was turned from his side "I know you not woman" and how his grandeurs were stricken valueless, and his pride consumed to ashes. It is a wonderfully beautiful and touching little scene, and papa has described it so wonderfully. I never saw a man with so much variety of feeling as papa has; now the "Prince and the Pauper" is full of touching places, but there is most always a streak of humor in them somewhere. Now in the coronation—in the stirring coronation, just after the little king has got his crown back again papa brings that in about the Seal, where the pauper says he used the Seal "to crack nuts with." Oh it is so funny and nice! Papa very seldom writes a passage without some humor in it somewhere, and I don't think he ever will.

The children always helped their mother to edit my books in manuscript. She would sit on the porch at the farm and read aloud, with her pencil in her hand, and the children would keep an alert and suspicious eye upon her right along, for the belief was well grounded in them that whenever she came across a particularly satisfactory passage she would strike it out. Their suspicions were well founded. The passages which were so satisfactory to them always had an element of strength in them which sorely needed modification or expurgation, and was always sure to get it at their mother's hand. For my own entertainment and to enjoy the protests of the children, I often abused my editor's innocent confidence. I often interlarded remarks of a studied and felicitously atrocious character purposely to achieve the children's brief delight and then see the remorseless pencil do its fatal work. I often joined my supplications to the children's for mercy and strung the argument out and pretended to be in earnest. They were deceived and so was their mother. It was three against one and most unfair. But it was very delightful and I could not resist the temptation. Now and then we gained the victory and there was much rejoicing. Then I privately struck the passage out myself. It had served its purpose. It had furnished three of us with good entertainment, and in being removed from the book by me it was only suffering the fate originally intended for it.

Clara and I are sure that papa played the trick on Grandma, about the whipping, that is related in "The Adventures of Tom Sawyer": "Hand me that switch."

The switch hovered in the air, the peril was desperate—
"My, look behind you Aunt!" The old lady whirled
around and snatched her skirts out of danger. The lad
fled on the instant, scrambling up the high board fence
and disappeared over it.

Susy and Clara were quite right about that.
Then Susy says:

And we know papa played "Hookey" all the time.
And how readily would papa pretend to be dying so as
not to have to go to school!

These revelations and exposures are searching but they are
just. If I am as transparent to other people as I was to Susy
I have wasted much effort in this life.

Grandma couldn't make papa go to school, so she let
him go into a printing-office to learn the trade. He did
so, and gradually picked up enough education to enable
him to do about as well as those who were more studious
in early life.

It is noticeable that Susy does not get overheated when
she is complimenting me but maintains a proper judicial and
biographical calm. It is noticeable also and it is to her credit
as a biographer that she distributes compliment and criticism
with a fair and even hand.

◇◇◇◇◇◇◇◇◇◇◇◇◇◇◇◇◇◇◇

CHAPTER 42

The world loses a good deal by the laws of decorum; gains a
good deal, of course, but certainly loses a good deal. I remember a case in point. I started to walk to Boston once with
my pastor[1]—pastor and old familiar friend in one. At nine
that night, twelve hours out, we had tramped nearly thirty
miles and I was nearly dead with fatigue, cold, pain and
lameness; skin mostly gone from my heels, tendons of my
legs shortened by a couple of inches, each and every limp

[1] Joseph Twichell. The walk occurred in 1874.

a sharp agony. But the Reverend was as fresh as ever; and light-hearted and happy to a degree that was not easy to bear. There were small farmhouses at intervals but the occupants all fled down cellar whenever we hailed or knocked, for the roads were alive with murderous tramps in those days.

By ten at night I had dragged myself another half mile and this, to my unutterable gratitude, brought us to a village —call it Duffield, any name will do. We were soon in the bar of the inn and I dropped at once into a chair behind the big hot stove, full of content, happy to the marrow and desiring only to be left unmolested. But the Reverend did not care to sit down; he was brimming with unexpended vigors, his jaw was not tired with twelve hours' wagging, he must stir about, he must ask some questions.

The room was about twelve by sixteen, a snug little place —unpainted counter at one end, four or five feet long, three unpainted white-pine shelves behind it with ten or twelve bottles scattered along them, containing liquor and flies; no carpet, no decorations except a lithograph on the wall—horse race in a hailstorm, apparently; hail turns out to be flyspecks. Two men present: No. 1, the old village bummer, seated and hovering over the stove, opposite side from me—expectorating on it occasionally, where he could find a red-hot spot; No. 2 was a young and vigorous man, in a chair tilted back against the white-pine partitions; chin buried in his breast; coonskin cap on, its natural tail sticking down past left ear; heels propped on round of chair; breeches rolled to boot tops. Now and then *he* shot at the stove, five feet away, and hit it without breaking up his attitude.

These men had not moved since we entered, nor made utterance except to answer our greeting, in the beginning, with a grunt, courteously meant. The Reverend browsed around, now here, now there, plying me with remarks which I did not disturb my bliss to respond to; so, at last he was obliged to apply elsewhere. He is an observer. He had observed signs and smelt smells which suggested that although these men seemed so dumb and dead, the one tilted against the wall might possibly be coaxed into a state of semi-interest by some reference to horses:—an ostler, the Reverend guessed, and was right, as transpired later. So he said, "Well, ostler, I suppose you raise some pretty fine breeds of horses around here?"

The young fellow unbent right away; and his face, which was a good face, lighted pleasantly, eagerly in fact. He untilted, planted his feet on the floor, shoved his coon tail around to the rear, spread his broad hands upon his knees, beamed up at the tall Reverend, and turned himself loose:

"Well, now, I tell *you!—pretty* fine ain't the word!—and it don't *begin!*"

Evidently he was as goodhearted a young fellow as ever was, and as guiltless of wish or intent to offend; yet into the chance chinks of that single little short sentence he managed to wattle as much as two yards and a half of the most varied and wonderful profanity! And that sentence did not end his speech—no, it was the mere introduction; straight after it followed the speech—a speech five minutes long, full of enthusiastic horse statistics; poured out with the most fluent facility, as from an inexhaustible crater, and all ablaze from beginning to end with crimson lava jets of desolating and utterly unconscious profanity! It was his native tongue; he had no idea that there was any harm in it.

When the speech ended there was a mighty silence; the Reverend was in a state of stupefaction—dumb, he was, for once. The situation was unique, delicious. The bliss which I had been feeling before was tame to what I was feeling now. Skinned heels were nothing; I could have enjoyed this thing if I had been skinned all over. I did not laugh exteriorly, for that would be indecorous. I made no motion, gave no sign; simply sat still and slowly died with joy. The Reverend looked at me appealingly, as much as to say, "Don't desert a friend in heavy trouble—help me out of this." I did nothing —was too near dissolution to be useful—and the ostler turned himself loose once more—once more he oozed eloquent profanity and incredible smut from every pore; and all so naturally and sweetly and innocently that it would have been flattery to call it a sin.

In desperation the Reverend broke in with a question about some other matter—mild, commonplace, less exciting than horse affairs: something about the roads and distances thence to Boston; hoped and believed that this cold topic would furnish no chances for lurid language. A mistake; the ostler sailed into that subject, rained, hailed, blew great guns and thundered and lightened over it, under it, around it and through it, with all the profane splendor which had distinguished his horse talk.

The Reverend rushed to the front again, pulled the ostler loose from the roads and got him to tackle the crops. Another failure. He went into the crops with as fresh a zeal as ever and drove his dialectic night cart through it at as rattling a gait and with as fragrant effect as in the beginning. In a sort of pathetic despair the Reverend fled, as a refuge, to the ancient bummer at the stove and uncorked him with a most innocuous remark, a colorless and unincendiary remark, about my lame and sore condition; whereupon the bummer, a pitying and kindly creature, turned *him*self loose with a perfectly Vesuvian eruption of charitable dirt and blasphemy concerning the healing properties of "Karosine" externally applied; appealed to the ostler to confirm the almost miraculous excellence of Karosine for bruises and abrasions; the ostler responded with mephitic enthusiasm; and for five minutes the Reverend stood speechless there while the unutterable tides from these two sewers swept over him.

At last a saving thought slipped into his brain. He sauntered to the counter, got a letter out of his pocket, glanced through it, returned it to its envelope, laid it on the counter, ciphered aimlessly upon it with a pencil; then presently sauntered away and left it there with a sinful pretense of having forgotten it. There was a pale joy in his jaded eye when he saw the bait take; saw the ostler loaf toward the counter; saw him take up the envelope and drop his eye on it. There was a pause, and silence! then the ostler broke out with glad surprise:

"What!—you are a preacher?"

(Prodigious and long-continued thunderpeal of improprieties and profanities), "Why didn't you *tell* a body so! I didn't know you was anybody!"

And straightway he flew around with loving alacrity, routed the cook out of bed, chambermaid likewise, and in two minutes these people were hard at work in our behalf. Then the delightful and delighted orator seated the Reverend in the place of honor and told him all about the state of church matters in Duffield: a flowing, masterly, goodhearted, rightpurposed narrative which was fifteen minutes passing a given point, and was torch-lighted with indelicacies from end to end, which flickered lambent through a misty red hell of profanity rent and torn at four-foot intervals all down the line by sky-cleaving rocket explosions of gorgeous blasphemy! Admirable artist!—all his previous efforts were but lightning-bug-and-glowworm displays compared to this final and supreme conflagration!

As we turned in, in a double-bedded room, the Reverend remarked, with subdued gratefulness:

"Well, as to this thing, there is one comfort, anyway—such as it is: You can't *print* it, Mark."

He was right about that, of course. It was extravagantly funny. But only because those men were innocent of harmful intent. Otherwise it would have been barren of fun and merely disgusting. Next morning the warm-blooded ostler bounded into the breakfast room, perishing with laughter, and told the grave and respectable landlady and her little daughter how he had found the geese frozen fast in the pond; and his language was just as terrific as it had been the night before. These persons showed great interest in the geese but none at all in the language—they were used to that and found no offense in it.

◇◇◇◇◇◇◇◇◇◇◇◇◇◇◇◇◇◇◇

CHAPTER 43

To get back to Orion. One day, back in the Sixties when I was living in San Francisco, I got a tip from Mr. Camp, a bold man who was always making big fortunes in ingenious speculations and losing them again in the course of six months by other speculative ingenuities. Camp told me to buy some shares in the Hale and Norcross. I bought fifty shares at three hundred dollars a share. I bought on a margin and put up twenty per cent. It exhausted my funds. I wrote Orion and offered him half and asked him to send his share of the money. I waited and waited. He wrote and said he was going to attend to it. The stock went along up pretty briskly. It went higher and higher. It reached a thousand dollars a share. It climbed to two thousand, then to three thousand; then to twice that figure. The money did not come but I was not disturbed. By and by that stock took a turn and began to gallop down. Then I wrote urgently. Orion answered that he had sent the money long ago—said he had sent it to the Occidental Hotel. I inquired for it. They said it was not there. To cut a long story short, that stock went on down until it fell below the price I had paid for it. Then it began to eat up the margin, and when at last I got out I was very badly crippled.

When it was too late I found out what had become of Orion's money. Any other human being would have sent a check but he sent gold. The hotel clerk put it in the safe and never thought of it again, and there it reposed all this time, enjoying its fatal work, no doubt. Another man might have thought to tell me that the money was not in a letter but was in an express package, but it never occurred to Orion to do that.

Later, Mr. Camp gave me another chance. He agreed to buy our Tennessee land for two hundred thousand dollars, pay a part of the amount in cash and give long notes for the rest. His scheme was to import foreigners from grape-growing and winemaking districts in Europe, settle them on the land and turn it into a winegrowing country. He knew what Mr. Longworth thought of those Tennessee grapes and was satisfied. I sent the contracts and things to Orion for his signature, he being one of the three heirs. But they arrived at a bad time—in a doubly bad time, in fact. The temperance virtue was temporarily upon him in strong force and he wrote and said that he would not be a party to debauching the country with wine. Also he said how could he know whether Mr. Camp was going to deal fairly and honestly with those poor people from Europe or not?—and so, without waiting to find out, he quashed the whole trade and there it fell, never to be brought to life again. The land, from being suddenly worth two hundred thousand dollars, became as suddenly worth what it was before—nothing, and taxes to pay. I had paid the taxes and the other expenses for some years but I dropped the Tennessee land there and have never taken any interest in it since, pecuniarily or otherwise, until yesterday.

I had supposed, until yesterday,[1] that Orion had frittered away the last acre, and indeed that was his impression. But a gentleman arrived yesterday from Tennessee and brought a map showing that by a correction of the ancient surveys we still own a thousand acres, in a coal district, out of the hundred thousand acres which my father left us when he died in 1847. The gentleman brought a proposition; also he brought a reputable and well-to-do citizen of New York. The proposition was that the Tennessean gentleman should sell that land; that the New York gentleman should pay all the

[1] Written April 5, 1906.

expenses and fight all the lawsuits, in case any should turn up, and that of such profit as might eventuate the Tennessean gentleman should take a third, the New Yorker a third, and Sam Moffett and his sister (Mrs. Charles L. Webster) and I—who are the surviving heirs—the remaining third.

This time I hope we shall get rid of the Tennessee land for good and all and never hear of it again. It was created under a misapprehension; my father loaded himself up with it under a misapprehension; he unloaded it on to us under a misapprehension and I should like to get rid of the accumulated misapprehensions and what is left of the land as soon as possible.

I came East in January, 1867. Orion remained in Carson City perhaps a year longer. Then he sold his twelve-thousand-dollar house and its furniture for thirty-five hundred in greenbacks at about thirty per cent discount. He and his wife took first-class passage in the steamer for New York. In New York they stopped at an expensive hotel; explored the city in an expensive way; then fled to Keokuk and arrived there about as nearly penniless as they were when they had migrated thence in July, '61. About 1871 or '72 they came to New York. They were obliged to go somewhere. Orion had been trying to make a living in the law ever since he had arrived from the Pacific coast but he had secured only two cases. Those he was to try free of charge—but the possible result will never be known because the parties settled the case out of court without his help.

I had bought my mother a house in Keokuk. I was giving her a stated sum monthly, and Orion another stated sum. They all lived together in the house. Orion could have had all the work he wanted, at good wages, in the composing room of the *Gate City* (a daily paper), but his wife had been a Governor's wife and she was not able to permit that degradation. It was better in her eyes that they live upon charity.

But, as I say, they came East and Orion got a job as proofreader on the New York *Evening Post* at ten dollars a week. They took a single small room, and in it they cooked, and lived on that money. By and by Orion came to Hartford and wanted me to get him a place as reporter on a Hartford paper. Here was a chance to try my scheme again and I did it. I made him go to the Hartford *Evening Post* without any letter of introduction and propose to scrub and sweep and do all sorts of things for nothing, on the plea that he didn't need money but only needed work and that was what he was pining for. Within six weeks he was on the editorial staff of that paper at twenty dollars a week and he was worth the money. He was presently called for by some other paper at better wages but I made him go to the *Post* people and tell them about it. They stood the raise and kept him. It was the pleasantest berth he had ever had in his life. It was an easy berth. He was in every way comfortable. But ill luck came. It was bound to come.

A new Republican daily was to be started in Rutland, Vermont by a stock company of well-to-do politicians and they offered Orion the chief editorship at three thousand a year. He was eager to accept. His wife was equally eager—no, twice as eager, three times as eager. My beseechings and reasonings went for nothing. I said:

"You are as weak as water. Those people will find it out right away. They will easily see that you have no backbone; that they can deal with you as they would deal with a slave. You may last six months but not longer. Then they will not dismiss you as they would dismiss a gentleman: they will fling you out as they would fling out an intruding tramp."

It happened just so. Then Orion and his wife migrated to that persecuted and unoffending Keokuk once more. Orion wrote from there that he was not resuming the law; that he thought that what his health needed was the open air, in some sort of outdoor occupation; that his old father-in-law had a strip of ground on the river border a mile above Keokuk with some sort of a house on it, and his idea was to buy that place and start a chicken farm and provide Keokuk with chickens and eggs and perhaps butter—but I don't know whether you can raise butter on a chicken farm or not. He said the place could be had for three thousand dollars cash and I sent the money. Orion began to raise chickens and he made a detailed monthly report to me, whereby it appeared that he was able to work off his chickens on the Keokuk people at a dollar and a quarter a pair. But it also appeared that it cost a dollar and sixty cents to raise the pair. This did not seem to discourage Orion and so I let it go. Meantime he was borrowing a hundred dollars per month of me regularly, month by month. Now to show Orion's stern and rigid business ways—and he really prided himself on his large business capacities—the moment he received the advance of a hundred dollars at the beginning of each month he sent me his note for the amount and with it he sent, out of that money, *three months' interest* on the hundred dollars at 6 per cent per annum, these notes being always for three months. I did not keep them, of course. They were of no value to anybody.

As I say, he always sent a detailed statement of the month's profit and loss on the chickens—at least the month's loss on the chickens—and this detailed statement included the various items of expense—corn for the chickens, a bonnet for the wife, boots for himself and so on; even car fares and the weekly contribution of ten cents to help out the missionaries who were trying to damn the Chinese after a plan not satisfactory to those people. But at last when among those details I found twenty-five dollars for pew rent I struck. I told him to change his religion and sell the pew.

I think the poultry experiment lasted only a year, possibly two years. It had then cost me six thousand dollars. It is my impression that Orion was not able to give the farm away and that his father-in-law took it back as a kindly act of self-sacrifice.

Orion returned to the law business and I suppose he remained in that harness off and on for the succeeding quarter of a century, but so far as my knowledge goes he was only a lawyer in name and had no clients.

My mother died in the summer of 1890. She had saved some money and she left it to me, because it had come from me. I gave it to Orion and he said, with thanks, that I had supported him long enough and now he was going to relieve me of that burden and would also hope to pay back some of that expense and maybe the whole of it. Accordingly, he proceeded to use up that money in building a considerable addition to the house, with the idea of taking boarders and getting rich. We need not dwell upon this venture. It was another of his failures. His wife tried hard to make the scheme succeed and if anybody could have made it succeed she would have done it. She was a good woman and was greatly liked. Her vanity was pretty large and inconvenient but she had a practical side too and she would have made that boardinghouse lucrative if circumstances had not been against her.

Orion had other projects for recouping me but as they always required capital I stayed out of them, but they did not materialize. Once he wanted to start a newspaper. It was a ghastly idea and I squelched it with a promptness that was almost rude. Then he invented a wood-sawing machine and patched it together himself and he really sawed wood with it. It was ingenious; it was capable; and it would have made a comfortable little fortune for him; but just at the wrong time Providence interfered again. Orion applied for a patent and found that the same machine had already been patented and had gone into business and was thriving.

Presently the State of New York offered a fifty-thousand-dollar prize for a practical method of navigating the Erie Canal with steam canal boats. Orion worked at that thing two or three years, invented and completed a method and was once more ready to reach out and seize upon imminent wealth, when somebody pointed out a defect. His steam canal boat could not be used in the wintertime; and in the summertime the commotion its wheels would make in the water would wash away the State of New York on both sides.

Innumerable were Orion's projects for acquiring the means to pay off his debt to me. These projects extended straight through the succeeding thirty years, but in every case they failed. During all those thirty years Orion's well-established honesty kept him in offices of trust where other people's money had to be taken care of but where no salary was paid. He was treasurer of all the benevolent institutions; he took care of the money and other property of widows and orphans; he never lost a cent for anybody and never made one for himself. Every time he changed his religion the church of his new faith was glad to get him; made him treasurer at once and at once he stopped the graft and the leaks in that church. He exhibited a facility in changing his political complexion that was a marvel to the whole community. Once this curious thing happened and he wrote me all about it himself.

One morning he was a Republican, and upon invitation he agreed to make a campaign speech at the Republican mass meeting that night. He prepared the speech. After luncheon he became a Democrat and agreed to write a score of exciting mottoes to be painted upon the transparencies which the Democrats would carry in their torchlight procession that night. He wrote these shouting Democratic mottoes during the afternoon and they occupied so much of his time that it was night before he had a chance to change his politics again; so he actually made a rousing Republican campaign speech in the open air while his Democratic tranparencies passed by in front of him, to the joy of every witness present.

He was a most strange creature—but in spite of his eccentricities he was beloved all his life in whatsoever community he lived. And he was also held in high esteem, for at bottom he was a sterling man.

Whenever he had a chance to get into a ridiculous position he was generally competent for that occasion. When he and his wife were living in Hartford at the time when he was on the staff of the *Evening Post* they were boarders and lodgers in a house that was pretty well stocked with nice men and women of moderate means. There was a bathroom that was common to the tribe, and one Sunday afternoon when the rest of the house was steeped in restful repose Orion thought he would take a bath and he carried that idea to a more or less successful issue. But he didn't lock the door. It was his custom, in summer weather, to fill the long bathtub nearly full of cold water and then get in it on his knees with his nose on the bottom and maintain this pleasant attitude a couple of minutes at a time. A chambermaid came in there and then rushed out and went shrieking through the house, "Mr. Clemens is drowned."

Everybody came flying out of the doors, and Mrs. Clemens rushed by, crying out in agony, "How do you know it is Mr. Clemens?"

And the chambermaid said, "I don't."

It reminds me of Billy Nye, poor fellow—that real humorist, that gentle good soul. Well, he is dead. Peace to his ashes. He was the baldest human being I ever saw. His whole skull was brilliantly shining. It was like a dome with the sun flashing upon it. He had hardly even a fringe of hair. Once somebody admitted astonishment at his extraordinary baldness.

"Oh," he said, "it is nothing. You ought to see my brother."

One day he fell overboard from a ferry boat and when he came up a woman's voice broke high over the tumult of frightened and anxious exclamations and said,

"You shameless thing! And ladies present! Go down and come up the other way."

About twenty-five years ago—along there somewhere—I wrote and suggested to Orion that he write an autobiography. I asked him to try to tell the straight truth in it; to refrain from exhibiting himself in creditable attitudes exclusively and to honorably set down all the incidents of his life which he had found interesting to him, including those which were burned into his memory because he was ashamed of them. I said that this had never been done and that if he could do it his autobiography would be a most valuable piece of literature. I said I was offering him a job which I could not duplicate in my own case but I would cherish the hope that he might succeed with it. I recognize now that I was trying to saddle upon him an impossibility. I have been dictating this autobiography of mine daily for three months[2]; I have thought of fifteen hundred or two thousand incidents in my life which I am ashamed of but I have not gotten one of them to consent to go on paper yet. I think that that stock will still be complete and unimpaired when I finish this autobiography, if I ever finish it. I believe that if I should put in all those incidents I would be sure to strike them out when I came to revise this book.

Orion wrote his autobiography and sent it to me. But great was my disappointment; and my vexation too. In it he was constantly making a hero of himself, exactly as I should have done and am doing now, and he was constantly forgetting to put in the episodes which placed him in an unheroic light. I knew several incidents of his life which were distinctly and painfully unheroic but when I came across them in his autobiography they had changed color. They had turned themselves inside-out and were things to be intemperately proud of.

While we were living in Vienna in 1898 a cablegram came from Keokuk announcing Orion's death. He was seventy-two years old. He had gone down to the kitchen in the early hours of a bitter December morning; he had built the fire and then sat down at a table to write something, and there he died, with the pencil in his hand and resting against the paper in the middle of an unfinished word—an indication that his release from the captivity of a long and troubled and pathetic and unprofitable life was swift and painless.

◇◇◇◇◇◇◇◇◇◇◇◇◇◇◇◇◇◇

CHAPTER 44

About 1872 I wrote another book, *Roughing It*. I had published *The Innocents Abroad* on a five per cent royalty, which would amount to about twenty-two cents per volume. Pro-

[2] Written April 6, 1906.

posals were coming in now from several other good houses. One offered fifteen per cent royalty; another offered to give me *all* of the profits and be content with the advertisement which the book would furnish the house. I sent for Bliss and he came to Elmira. If I had known as much about book publishing then as I know now, I would have required of Bliss seventy-five or eighty per cent of the profits above cost of manufacture, and this would have been fair and just. But I knew nothing about the business and had been too indolent to try to learn anything about it. I told Bliss I did not wish to leave his corporation and that I did not want extravagant terms. I said I thought I ought to have half the profit above cost of manufacture and he said with enthusiasm that that was exactly right, exactly right.

He went to his hotel and drew the contract and brought it to the house in the afternoon. I found a difficulty in it. It did not name "half profits," but named a seven-and-a-half per cent royalty instead. I asked him to explain that. I said that that was not the understanding. He said "No, it wasn't," but that he had put in a royalty to simplify the matter—that seven-and-a-half per cent royalty represented fully half the profit and a little more, up to a sale of a hundred thousand copies, that after that the publishing company's half would be a shade superior to mine.

I was a little doubtful, a little suspicious, and asked him if he could swear to that. He promptly put up his hand and made oath to it, exactly repeating the words which he had just used.

It took me nine or ten years to find out that that was a false oath and that seven-and-a-half per cent did not represent one-fourth of the profits. But in the meantime I had published several books with Bliss on seven-and-a-half and ten per cent royalties and of course had been handsomely swindled on all of them.

In 1879 I came home from Europe with a book ready for the press, *A Tramp Abroad*. I sent for Bliss and he came out to the house to discuss the book. I said that I was not satisfied about those royalties and that I did not believe in their "half-profit" pretenses, that this time he must put the "half-profit" in the contract and make no mention of royalties—otherwise I would take the book elsewhere. He said he was perfectly willing to put it in, for it was right and just, and that if his directors opposed it and found fault with it he would withdraw from the concern and publish the book himself—fine talk, but I knew that he was master in that concern and that it would have to accept any contract that had been signed by him. This contract lay there on the billiard table with his signature attached to it. He had ridden his directors roughshod ever since the days of *The Innocents Abroad* and more than once he had told me that he had made his directors do things which they hadn't wanted to do, with the threat that if they did not comply he would leave the company's service and take me along with him.

I don't know how a grown person could ever be so simple and innocent as I was in those days. It ought to have occurred to me that a man who could talk like that must either be a fool or convinced that I was one. However, I was the one. And so even very simple and rudimentary wisdoms were not likely to find their way into my head.

I reminded him that his company would not be likely to make any trouble about a contract which had been signed by him. Then, with one of his toothless smiles, he pointed out a detail which I had overlooked, to wit: the contract was with Elisha Bliss, a private individual, and the American Publishing Company was not mentioned in it.

He told me afterward that he took the contract to the directors and said that he would turn it over to the company for one-fourth of the profits of the book together with an increase of salary for himself and for Frank, his son, and that if these terms were not satisfactory he would leave the company and publish the book himself, whereupon the directors granted his demands and took the contract. The fact that Bliss told me these things with his own mouth is unassailable evidence that they were not true. Six weeks before the book issued from the press Bliss told the truth once, to see how it would taste, but it overstrained him and he died.

When the book had been out three months there was an annual meeting of the stockholders of the company and I was present, as a half-partner in the book. The meeting was held in the house of a neighbor of mine, Newton Case, a director in the company from the beginning. A statement of the company's business was read and to me it was a revelation. Sixty-four thousand copies of the book had been sold and my half of the profit was thirty-two thousand dollars. In 1872 Bliss had made out to me that seven-and-a-half per cent royalty, some trifle over twenty cents a copy, represented one-half of the profits, whereas at that earlier day it hardly represented a sixth of the profits. Times were not so good now, yet it took all of fifty cents a copy to represent half.

Well, Bliss was dead and I couldn't settle with him for his ten years of swindlings. He has been dead a quarter of a century now. My bitterness against him has faded away and disappeared. I feel only compassion for him and if I could send him a fan I would.

When the balance sheets exposed to me the rascalities which I had been suffering at the hands of the American Publishing Company I stood up and delivered a lecture to Newton Case and the rest of the conspirators—meaning the rest of the directors.

My opportunity was now come to right myself and level up matters with the publishing company but I didn't see it, of course. I was seldom able to see an opportunity until it had ceased to be one. I knew all about that house now and I ought to have remained with it. I ought to have put a tax upon its profits for my personal benefit, the tax to continue until the difference between royalties and half profits should in time return from the company's pocket to mine and the company's robbery of me be thus wiped off the slate. But of course I couldn't think of anything so sane as that and I didn't. I only thought of ways and means to remove my respectability from that tainted atmosphere. I wanted to get my books out of the company's hands and carry them elsewhere. After a time I went to Newton Case—in his house as before—and proposed that the company cancel the contracts and restore my books to me free and unencumbered, the company retaining as a consideration the money it had swindled me out of on *Roughing It, The Gilded Age, Sketches New and Old* and *Tom Sawyer.*

Mr. Case demurred at my language but I told him I was not able to modify it, that I was perfectly satisfied that he and the rest of the Bible Class were aware of the fraud practiced on me in 1872 by Bliss—aware of it when it happened and consenting to it by silence. He objected to my calling the Board of Directors a Bible Class. And I said then it ought to stop opening its meetings with prayer—particularly when it was getting ready to swindle an author. I was expecting that Mr. Case would deny the charge of guilty knowledge and resent it but he didn't do it. That convinced me that my charge was well founded, therefore I repeated it and pro-

ceeded to say unkind things about his theological seminary.
I said, "You have put seventy-five thousand dollars into that
factory and are getting a great deal of praise for it, whereas
my share in that benefaction goes unmentioned—yet I *have* a
share in it, for of every dollar that you put into it a portion was
stolen out of my pocket." He returned no thanks for these
compliments. He was a dull man and unappreciative.

Finally I tried to buy my contracts but he said it would be
impossible for the Board to entertain a proposition to sell,
for the reason that nine-tenths of the company's livelihood
was drawn from my books and therefore its business would
be worth nothing if they were taken away. At a later time
Judge What's-his-name, a director, told me I was right, that
the Board did know all about the swindle which Bliss had
practiced upon me at the time that the fraud was committed.

As I have remarked, I ought to have remained with the
company and leveled up the account. But I didn't. I removed
my purity from that mephitic atmosphere and carried my next
book to James R. Osgood of Boston, formerly of the firm
of Field, Osgood and Company. That book was *Old Times
on the Mississippi*.[1] Osgood was to manufacture the book at
my expense, publish it by subscription and charge me a
royalty for his services.

Osgood was one of the dearest and sweetest and loveliest human beings to be found on the planet anywhere, but
he knew nothing about subscription publishing and he made
a mighty botch of it. He was a sociable creature and we
played much billiards and daily and nightly had a good
time. And in the meantime his clerks ran our business for
us and I think that neither of us inquired into their methods
or knew what they were doing. That book was a long
time getting built; and when at last the final draft was made
upon my purse I realized that I had paid out fifty-six
thousand dollars upon that structure. Bliss could have built
a library for that money. It took a year to get the fifty-six
thousand back into my pocket, and not many dollars followed
it. So this first effort of mine to transact that kind of business
on my own hook was a failure.

Osgood tried again. He published *The Prince and the
Pauper*. He made a beautiful book of it but all the profit I
got out of it was seventeen thousand dollars.

---

[1] An early title of *Life on the Mississippi*, used in the *Atlantic*, in which the
first part of the book appeared in 1875.

Next, Osgood thought he could make a success with a book in the *trade*. He had been trained to trade publishing. He was a little sore over his subscription attempts and wanted to try. I gave him *The Stolen White Elephant*, which was a collection of rubbishy sketches, mainly. I offered to bet he couldn't sell ten thousand copies in six months and he took me up, stakes five dollars. He won the money but it was something of a squeeze. However, I think I am wrong in putting that book last. I think that that was Osgood's first effort, not his third. I should have continued with Osgood after his failure with *The Prince and the Pauper* because I liked him so well, but he failed and I had to go elsewhere.

◇◇◇◇◇◇◇◇◇◇◇◇◇◇◇◇◇◇◇

CHAPTER 45

Meantime I had been having an adventure on the outside. An old and particular friend of mine unloaded a patent on me, price fifteen thousand dollars. It was worthless and he had been losing money on it a year or two, but I did not know those particulars because he neglected to mention them. He said that if I would buy the patent he would do the manufacturing and selling for me. So I took him up. Then began a cash outgo of five hundred dollars a month. That raven flew out of the Ark regularly every thirty days but it never got back with anything and the dove didn't report for duty. After a time and half a time and another time, I relieved my friend and put the patent into the hands of Charles L. Webster, who had married a niece of mine and seemed a capable and energetic young fellow. At a salary of fifteen hundred a year he continued to send the raven out monthly, with the same old result to a penny.

At last, when I had lost forty-two thousand dollars on that patent I gave it away to a man whom I had long detested and whose family I desired to ruin. Then I looked around for other adventures. That same friend was ready with another patent. I spent ten thousand dollars on it in eight months. Then I tried to give that patent to the man whose family I was after. He was very grateful but he was also

experienced by this time and was getting suspicious of benefactors. He wouldn't take it and I had to let it lapse.

Meantime, another old friend arrived with a wonderful invention. It was an engine or a furnace or something of the
kind which would get out ninety-nine per cent of all the
steam that was in a pound of coal. I went to Mr. Richards
of the Colt Arms Factory and told him about it. He was a
specialist and knew all about coal and steam. He seemed to
be doubtful about this machine and I asked him why. He
said, because the amount of steam concealed in a pound of
coal was known to a fraction and that my inventor was
mistaken about his ninety-nine per cent. He showed me a
printed book of solid pages of figures, figures that made me
drunk and dizzy. He showed me that my man's machine
couldn't come within ninety per cent of doing what it proposed to do. I went away a little discouraged. But I thought
that maybe the book was mistaken and so I hired the inventor
to build the machine on a salary of thirty-five dollars a week,
I to pay all expenses. It took him a good many weeks to build
the thing. He visited me every few days to report progress
and I early noticed by his breath and gait that he was spending thirty-six dollars a week on whisky, and I couldn't ever
find out where he got the other dollar.

Finally, when I had spent five thousand on this enterprise
the machine was finished, but it wouldn't go. It did save
one per cent of the steam that was in a pound of coal
but that was nothing. You could do it with a teakettle. I
offered the machine to the man whose family I was after, but
without success. So I threw the thing away and looked around
for something fresh. But I had become an enthusiast on steam
and I took some stock in a Hartford company which proposed
to make and sell and revolutionize everything with a new
kind of steam pulley. The steam pulley pulled thirty-two
thousand dollars out of my pocket in sixteen months, then
went to pieces and I was alone in the world again, without
an occupation.

But I found one. I invented a scrapbook—and if I do say
it myself, it was the only rational scrapbook the world has
ever seen. I patented it and put it in the hands of that old
particular friend of mine who had originally interested me in
patents and he made a good deal of money out of it. But by
and by, just when I was about to begin to receive a share of
the money myself, his firm failed. I didn't know his firm

was going to fail—he didn't say anything about it. One day he asked me to lend the firm five thousand dollars and said he was willing to pay seven per cent. As security he offered the firm's note. I asked for an endorser. He was much surprised and said that if endorsers were handy and easy to get at he wouldn't have to come to me for the money, he could get it anywhere. That seemed reasonable and so I gave him the five thousand dollars. They failed inside of three days—and at the end of two or three years I got back two thousand dollars of the money.

That five thousand dollars had a history. Early in 1872 Joe Goodman wrote me from California that his friend and mine, Senator John P. Jones, was going to start a rival in Hartford to the Traveler's Accident Insurance Company, and that Jones wanted Joe to take twelve thousand of the stock and had said he would see that Joe did not lose the money. Joe now proposed to transfer this opportunity to me and said that if I would make the venture Jones would protect me from loss. So I took the stock and became a director. Jones's brother-in-law, Lester, had been for a long time actuary in the Traveler's Company. He was now transferred to our company and we began business. There were five directors. Three of us attended every Board meeting for a year and a half.

At the end of eighteen months the company went to pieces and I was out of pocket twenty-three thousand dollars. Jones was in New York, tarrying for a while at a hotel which he had bought, the St. James, and I sent Lester down there to get the twenty-three thousand dollars. But he came back and reported that Jones had been putting money into so many things that he was a good deal straitened and would be glad if I would wait a while. I did not suspect that Lester was drawing upon his fancy but it was so. He hadn't said anything to Jones about it. But his tale seemed reasonable, because I knew that Jones had built a line of artificial ice factories clear across the Southern states—nothing like it this side of the Great Wall of China. I knew that the factories had cost him a million dollars or so and that the people down there hadn't been trained to admire ice and didn't want any and wouldn't buy any—that therefore the Chinese Wall was an entire loss and failure.

I also knew that Jones's St. James Hotel had ceased to be a profitable house because Jones, who was a big-hearted man with ninety-nine parts of him pure generosity—and that is the case to this day—had filled his hotel from roof to cellar with poor relations gathered from the four corners of the earth—plumbers, bricklayers, unsuccessful clergymen and in fact all the different kinds of people that knew nothing about the hotel business. I was also aware that there was no room in the hotel for the public, because all its rooms were occupied by a multitude of other poor relations gathered from the four corners of the earth at Jones's invitation and waiting for Jones to find lucrative occupations for them. I was also aware that Jones had bought a piece of the state of California with some spacious city sites on it, with room for railroads and a very fine and spacious and valuable harbor on its city front, and that Jones was in debt for these properties. Therefore I was content to wait a while.

As the months drifted by, Lester now and then volunteered to go and see Jones on his own hook. His visits produced nothing. The fact is, Lester was afraid of Jones and felt a delicacy about troubling him with my matter while he had so many burdens on his shoulders. He preferred to pretend to me that he had seen Jones and had mentioned my matter to him, whereas in truth he had never mentioned it to Jones at all. At the end of two or three years Mr. Slee of our Elmira coal firm proposed to speak to Jones about it and I consented. Slee visited Jones and began in his tactful and diplomatic way to lead up to my matter, but before he had got well started Jones glanced up and said, "Do you mean to say that that money has never been paid to Clemens?" He drew his check for twenty-three thousand at once, said it ought to have been paid long ago and that it would have been paid the moment it was due if he had known the circumstances.

This was in the spring of 1877. With that check in my pocket I was prepared to seek sudden fortune again. The reader, deceived by what I have been saying about my adventures, will jump to the conclusion that I sought an opportunity at once. I did nothing of the kind. I was the burnt child. I wanted nothing further to do with speculations. General Hawley sent for me to come to the *Courant* office. I went there with my check in my pocket. There was a young fellow there who said that he had been a reporter on a Providence newspaper but that he was in another business now. He was with Graham Bell and was agent for a new invention called the telephone. He believed there was great fortune in

store for it and wanted me to take some stock. I declined.
I said I didn't want anything more to do with wildcat speculation. Then he offered the stock to me at twenty-five. I said
I didn't want it at any price. He became eager—insisted that
I take five hundred dollars' worth. He said he would sell me
as much as I wanted for five hundred dollars—offered to let
me gather it up in my hands and measure it in a plug hat—
said I could have a whole hatful for five hundred dollars.
But I was the burnt child and I resisted all these temptations,
resisted them easily, went off with my check intact, and next
day lent five thousand of it on an unendorsed note to my
friend who was going to go bankrupt three days later.

About the end of the year (or possibly in the beginning
of 1878) I put up a telephone wire from my house down to
the *Courant* office, the only telephone wire in town, and the
first one that was ever used in a private house in the world.

That young man couldn't sell *me* any stock but he sold a
few hatfuls of it to an old dry-goods clerk in Hartford for
five thousand dollars. That was that clerk's whole fortune.
He had been half a lifetime saving it. It is strange how foolish
people can be and what ruinous risks they can take when
they want to get rich in a hurry. I was sorry for that man
when I heard about it. I thought I might have saved him if
I had had an opportunity to tell him about my experiences.

We sailed for Europe on the 10th of April, 1878. We were
gone fourteen months and when we got back one of the first
things we saw was that clerk driving around in a sumptuous
barouche with liveried servants all over it—and his telephone
stock was emptying greenbacks into his premises at such a rate
that he had to handle them with a shovel. It is strange the
way the ignorant and inexperienced so often and so un-
deservedly succeed when the informed and the experienced
fail.

◇◇◇◇◇◇◇◇◇◇◇◇◇◇◇◇◇◇

CHAPTER 46

As I have already remarked, I had imported my nephew-in-
law, Webster, from the village of Dunkirk, New York, to
conduct that original first patent-right business for me, at a

salary of fifteen hundred dollars. That enterprise had lost forty-two thousand dollars for me, so I thought this a favorable time to close it up. I proposed to be my own publisher now and let young Webster do the work. He thought he ought to have twenty-five hundred dollars a year while he was learning the trade. I took a day or two to consider the matter and study it out searchingly. So far as I could see, this was a new idea. I remembered that printers' apprentices got *no* salary. Upon inquiry I found that this was the case with stone masons, brick masons, tinners and the rest. I found that not even lawyers or apprenticed doctors got any salary for learning the trade. I remembered that on the river an apprentice pilot not only got nothing in the way of salary but he also had to pay some pilot a sum in cash which he didn't have—a large sum. It was what I had done myself. I had paid Bixby a hundred dollars and it was borrowed money. I was told by a person who said he was studying for the ministry that even Noah got no salary for the first six months—partly on account of the weather and partly because he was learning navigation.

The upshot of these thinkings and searchings of mine was that I believed I had secured something entirely new to history in Webster. And also I believed that a young backwoodsman who was starting life in New York without equipment of any kind, without proved value of any kind, without prospective value of any kind, yet able without blinking an eye to propose to learn a trade at another man's expense and charge for this benefaction an annual sum greater than any president of the United States had ever been able to save out of his pay for running the most difficult country on the planet, after Ireland, must surely be worth securing—and instantly—lest he get away. I believed that if some of his gigantic interest in No. 1 could be diverted to the protection of No. 2, the result would be fortune enough for me.

I erected Webster into a firm—a firm entitled Webster and Company, Publishers—and installed him in a couple of offices at a modest rental on the second floor of a building somewhere below Union Square, I don't remember where. For assistants he had a girl and perhaps a masculine clerk of about eight-hundred-dollar size. For a while Webster had another helper. This was a man who had long been in the subscription-book business, knew all about it and was able to teach it to Webster—which he did—I paying the cost of tuition.

I am talking about the early part of 1884 now. I handed
Webster a competent capital and along with it I handed him
the manuscript of *Huckleberry Finn*. Webster's function was
general agent. It was his business to appoint sub-agents
throughout the country. At that time there were sixteen of
these sub-agencies. They had canvassers under them who
did the canvassing. In New York City Webster was his own
sub-agent.

Before ever any of these minor details that I am talking
about had entered into being, the careful Webster had suggested that a contract be drawn and signed and sealed before
we made any real move. That seemed sane, though I should
not have thought of it myself—I mean it *was* sane *because* I
had not thought of it myself. So Webster got his own lawyer
to draw the contract. I was coming to admire Webster very
much and at this point in the proceedings I had one of those
gushing generosities surge up in my system, and before I had
thought I had tried to confer upon Webster a tenth interest
in the business in addition to his salary, free of charge.
Webster declined promptly—with thanks, of course, the usual
kind. That raised him another step in my admiration. I knew
perfectly well that I was offering him a partnership interest
which would pay him two or three times his salary within
the next nine months, but he didn't know that. He was coldly
and wisely discounting all my prophecies about *Huckleberry
Finn's* high commercial value. And here was this new
evidence that in Webster I had found a jewel, a man who
would not get excited; a man who would not lose his head;
a cautious man; a man who would not take a risk of any kind
in fields unknown to him. Except at somebody else's expense, I mean.

The contract was drawn, as I say, by a young lawyer from
Dunkirk, New York, which produced him as well as Webster
and has not yet gotten over the strain. Whitford was
privileged to sign himself "of the firm of Alexander and
Green." Alexander and Green had a great and lucrative
business and not enough conscience to damage it—a fact
which came out rather prominently last month when the
earthquake came which shook the entrails out of the three
great life insurance companies.[1] Alexander and Green had
their offices in the Mutual Building. They kept a job lot of
twenty-five lawyers on salary and he was one of these. He was

[1] Written May 26, 1906.

good-natured, obliging and immensely ignorant, and was endowed with a stupidity which by the least little stretch would go around the globe four times and tie.

That first contract was all right. There was nothing the matter with it. It placed all obligations, all expenses, all liability, all responsibilities upon *me*, where they belonged.

It was a happy combination, Webster and his lawyer. The amount that the two together didn't know about anything was to me a much more awful and paralyzing spectacle than it would be to see the Milky Way get wrecked and drift off in rags and patches through the sky. When it came to courage, moral or physical, they hadn't any. Webster was afraid to venture anything in the way of business without first getting a lawyer's assurance that there was nothing jailable about it. Lawyer was consulted so nearly constantly that he was about as much a member of the staff as were the girl and the subscription expert. But as neither Webster nor he had had any personal experience of money, his lawyer was not an expensive incumbent, though he probably thought he was.

At the break of the autumn I went off with George W. Cable on a four months' reading campaign in the East and West—the last platform work which I was ever to do in this life in my own country. I resolved at the time that I would never rob the public from the platform again unless driven to it by pecuniary compulsions. After eleven years the pecuniary compulsions came and I lectured all around the globe.

Ten years have since elapsed, during which time I have only lectured for public charities and without pay. On the 19th of last month, I took a public and formal leave of the platform—a thing which I had not done before—in a lecture on Robert Fulton for the benefit of the Robert Fulton Monument Fund.

I seem to be getting pretty far away from Webster and Whitford but it's no matter. It is one of those cases where distance lends enchantment to the view. Webster was successful with *Huckleberry Finn* and a year later handed me the firm's check for fifty-four thousand five hundred dollars, which included the fifteen thousand dollars capital which I had originally handed to him.

Once more I experienced a new birth. I have been born more times than anybody except Krishna, I suppose.

Webster conceived the idea that he had discovered me to

the world but he was reasonably modest about it. He did much less cackling over his egg than Webb and Bliss had done.

CHAPTER 47

It had never been my intention to publish anybody's books but my own. An accident diverted me from this wise purpose. That was General Grant's memorable book. One night in the first week of November, 1884 I had been lecturing in Chickering Hall and was walking homeward. It was a rainy night and but few people were about. In the midst of a black gulf between lamps, two dim figures stepped out of a doorway and moved along in front of me. I heard one of them say, "Do you know General Grant has actually determined to write his memoirs and publish them? He has said so today, in so many words."

That was all I heard—just those words—and I thought it great good luck that I was permitted to overhear them.

In the morning I went out and called on General Grant. I found him in his library with Col. Fred Grant, his son. The General said in substance this: "Sit down and keep quiet until I sign a contract"—and added that it was for a book which he was going to write.

Fred Grant was apparently conducting a final reading and examination of the contract himself. He found it satisfactory and said so and his father stepped to the table and took up the pen. It might have been better for me, possibly, if I had let him alone but I didn't. I said, "Don't sign it. Let Col. Fred read it to me first."

Col. Fred read it and I said I was glad I had come in time to interfere. The Century Company was the party of the second part. It proposed to pay the General ten per cent royalty. Of course this was nonsense—but the proposal had its source in ignorance, not dishonesty. The great Century Company knew all about magazine publishing. No one could teach them anything about that industry. But at that time they had had no experience of subscription publishing and they probably had nothing in their minds except trade publishing. They could not even have had any valuable experience in trade publishing or they would not have asked General Grant to furnish a book on the royalty commonly granted to authors of no name or repute.

I explained that these terms would never do; that they were all wrong, unfair, unjust. I said, "Strike out the ten per cent and put twenty per cent in its place. Better still, put seventy-five per cent of the net returns in its place."

The General demurred, and quite decidedly. He said they would never pay those terms.

I said that that was a matter of no consequence, since there was not a reputable publisher in America who would not be very glad to pay them.

The General still shook his head. He was still desirous of signing the contract as it stood.

I pointed out that the contract as it stood had an offensive detail in it which I had never heard of in the ten per cent contract of even the most obscure author—that this contract not only proposed a ten per cent royalty for such a colossus as General Grant, but it also had in it a requirement that out of that ten per cent must come some trivial tax for the book's share of clerk hire, house rent, sweeping out the offices, or some such nonsense as that. I said he ought to have three-fourths of the profits and let the publisher pay running expenses out of his remaining fourth.

The idea distressed General Grant. He thought it placed him in the attitude of a robber—robber of a publisher. I said that if he regarded that as a crime it was because his education was limited. I said it was not a crime and was always rewarded in heaven with two halos. Would be, if it ever happened.

The General was immovable and challenged me to name the publisher that would be willing to have this noble deed perpetrated upon him. I named the American Publishing Company of Hartford. He asked if I could prove my position. I said I could furnish the proof by telegraph in six hours—three hours for my despatch to go to Hartford, three hours for Bliss's jubilant acceptance to return by the same electric gravel train—that if he needed this answer quicker I would walk up to Hartford and fetch it.

The General still stood out. But Fred Grant was beginning to be persuaded. He proposed that the Century contract be laid on the table for twenty-four hours and that meantime the situation be examined and discussed. He said that this thing was not a matter of sentiment; it was a matter of pure business and should be examined from that point of view alone. His remark about sentiment had a bearing. The reason was this. The broking firm of Grant and Ward—consisting of General Grant, Mr. Ward (called for a time the "Little Napoleon of Finance") and Ward's confederate, Fish—had swindled General Grant out of every penny he had in the world. And at a time when he did not know where to turn for bread, Roswell Smith, head of the Century Company, offered him five hundred dollars per article for four magazine articles about certain great battles of the Civil War. The offer came to the despairing old hero like the fabled straw to the drowning man. He accepted it with gratitude and wrote the articles and delivered them. They were easily worth ten thousand dollars apiece but he didn't know it. Five hundred dollars apiece seemed to him fabulous pay for a trifle of pleasant and unlaborious scribbling.

He was now most loath to desert these benefactors of his. To his military mind and training it seemed disloyalty. If I remember rightly, his first article lifted the Century's subscription list from a hundred thousand copies to two hundred and twenty thousand. This made the Century's advertisement pages, for that month, worth more than double the money they had ever commanded in any previous month. As a guess, I should say that this increase of patronage was worth, that month, eight thousand dollars. This is a safe estimate, a conservative estimate.

The doubled subscription list established in that month was destined to continue for years. It was destined to increase the magazine's advertisement income about eight or ten thousand dollars a month during six years. I have said that each of General Grant's articles was worth ten thousand dollars instead of five hundred. I could say that each of the four articles was worth twenty-five thousand dollars and still be within bounds.

I began to tout for the American Publishing Company. I argued that the company had been first in the field as applicants for a volume of Grant memoirs and that perhaps they ought to have a chance at a bid before the Century Company. This seemed to be news to General Grant. But I reminded him that once during the apparently wonderfully prosperous days of the firm of Grant and Ward I called upon him in his private office one day, helped him to consume his luncheon and begged him to write his memoirs and give them to the American Publishing Company. He had declined at the time, and most decidedly, saying he was not in need of money and that he was not a literary person and could not write the memoirs.

I think we left the contract matter to stew for that time and took it up again the next morning. I did a good deal of thinking during the interval. I knew quite well that the American Publishing Company would be glad to get General Grant's memoirs on a basis of three-quarters profit for him, to one-quarter for themselves. Indeed I knew quite well that there was not a publisher in the country—I mean a publisher experienced in the subscription publishing business—who would not be glad to get the book on those terms. I was fully expecting to presently hand that book to Frank Bliss and the American Publishing Company and enrich that den of reptiles—but the sober second thought came then. I reflected that the company had been robbing me for years and building theological factories out of the proceeds and that now was my chance to feed fat the ancient grudge I bore them.

At the second conference with the General and Fred, the General exhibited some of the modesty which was so large a feature of his nature. General Sherman had published his *Memoirs* in two large volumes with Scribner's, and that publication had been a notable event. General Grant said:

"Sherman told me that his profits on that book were twenty-five thousand dollars. Do you believe I could get as much out of my book?"

I said I not only believed but I *knew* that he would achieve a vastly greater profit than that—that Sherman's book was published in the trade; that it was a suitable book for subscription distribution and ought to have been published in that way; that not many books were suitable to that method of publishing, but that the memoirs of such illustrious persons as Sherman and Grant were peculiarly adapted to that method; that a book which contained the right material for that method would harvest from eight to ten times as much profit by subscription as it could be made to produce by trade sale.

The General had his doubts that he could gather twenty-five thousand dollars profit for his memoirs. I inquired why. He said he had already applied the test and had secured the evidence and the verdict. I wondered where he could have gotten such evidence and such a verdict, and he explained. He said he had offered to sell his memoirs out and out to Roswell Smith for twenty-five thousand dollars and that the proposition had so frightened Smith that he hardly had breath enough left in his clothes to decline with.

Then I had an idea. It suddenly occurred to me that I was a publisher myself. I had not thought of it before. I said, "Sell *me* the memoirs, General. I am a publisher. I will pay double price. I have a checkbook in my pocket; take my check for fifty thousand dollars now and let's draw the contract."

General Grant was as prompt in declining this as Roswell Smith had been in declining the other offer. He said he wouldn't hear of such a thing. He said we were friends and if I should fail to get the money back out of his book— He stopped there and said there was no occasion to go into particulars, he simply would not consent to help a friend run any such risk.

Then I said, "Give me the book on the terms which I have already suggested that you make with the Century people— twenty per cent royalty or in lieu of that seventy-five per cent of the profits on the publication to go to you, I to pay all running expenses such as salaries, etc., out of my fourth."

He laughed at that and asked me what my profit out of that remnant would be. I said, a hundred thousand dollars in six months.

He was dealing with a literary person. He was aware, by authority of all the traditions, that literary persons are flighty, romantic, unpractical, and in business matters do not know enough to come in when it rains or at any other time. He did not say that he attached no value to these flights of my imagination, for he was too kindly to say hurtful things, but he might better have said it because he looked it with tenfold emphasis and the look covered the whole ground. To make conversation, I suppose, he asked me what I based this dream upon—if it had a basis.

I said, "I base it upon the difference between your literary commercial value and mine. My first two books sold a hundred and fifty thousand copies each—three dollars and a half per volume in cloth, costlier volumes at a higher price according to binding—average price of the hundred and fifty thousand, four dollars apiece. I know that your commercial value is easily four times as great as mine; therefore I know it to be a perfectly safe guess that your book will sell six hundred thousand single volumes and that the clear profit to you will be half a million dollars and the clear profit to me a hundred thousand."

We had a long discussion over the matter. Finally General Grant telegraphed for his particular friend, George W. Childs of the Philadelphia *Ledger*, to come up to New York and furnish an opinion. Childs came. I convinced him that Webster's publishing machinery was ample and in good order. Then Childs delivered the verdict, "Give the book to Clemens." Col. Fred Grant endorsed and repeated the verdict, "Give the book to Clemens." So the contract was drawn and signed and Webster took hold of his new job at once.

◇◇◇◇◇◇◇◇◇◇◇◇◇◇◇◇◇◇◇

CHAPTER 48 .

The first time I ever saw General Grant was in the fall or winter of 1866 at one of the receptions at Washington, when he was general of the army. I merely saw and shook hands with him along with the crowd but had no conversation. It was there also that I first saw General Sheridan.

I next saw General Grant during his first term as President. Senator Bill Stewart of Nevada proposed to take me in and see the President. We found him in his working costume, with an old, short, linen duster on and it was well spattered with ink. I had acquired some trifle of notoriety through some letters which I had written in the New York *Tribune* during my trip round about the world in the *Quaker City* expedition. I shook hands and then there was a pause and silence. I couldn't think of anything to say. So I merely looked into the General's grim, immovable countenance a moment or two in silence and then I said: "Mr. President, I am embarrassed. Are you?" He smiled a smile which would have done no discredit to a cast-iron image and I got away under the smoke of my volley.

I did not see him again for some ten years. In the meantime I had become very thoroughly notorious.

Then, in 1879, the General had just returned from his journey through the European and Asiatic world, and his progress from San Francisco eastward had been one continuous ovation; and now he was to be feasted in Chicago by the veterans of the Army of the Tennessee—the first army over which he had had command. The preparations for this occasion were in keeping with the importance of it. The toast committee telegraphed me and asked me if I would be present and respond at the grand banquet to the toast to the ladies. I telegraphed back that the toast was worn out. Everything had been said about the ladies that could be said at a banquet, but there was one class of the community that had always been overlooked upon such occasions and if they would allow me I would take that class for my toast—*The Babies*. They were willing, so I prepared my toast and went out to Chicago.

There was to be a prodigious procession. General Grant was to review it from a rostrum which had been built out for the purpose from the second-story window of the Palmer House. The rostrum was carpeted and otherwise glorified with flags and so on.

The best place of all to see the procession was, of course, from this rostrum, so I sauntered upon that rostrum while as yet it was empty, in the hope that I might be permitted to sit there. It was rather a conspicuous place, since upon it the public gaze was fixed and there was a countless multitude below. Presently two gentlemen came upon that platform from the window of the hotel and stepped forward to the front. A prodigious shout went up from the vast multitude below and I recognized in one of these two gentlemen General Grant; the other was Carter Harrison, the Mayor of Chicago, with whom I was acquainted. He saw me, stepped over to me, and said wouldn't I like to be introduced to the General? I said I should. So he walked over with me and said, "General, let me introduce Mr. Clemens." We shook hands. There was the usual momentary pause and then the General said: "I am not embarrassed. Are you?"

It showed that he had a good memory for trifles as well as for serious things.

That banquet was by all odds the most notable one I was ever present at. There were six hundred persons present, mainly veterans of the Army of the Tennessee, and that in itself would have made it a most notable occasion of the kind in my experience, but there were other things which contributed. General Sherman, and in fact nearly all of the surviving great generals of the war, sat in a body on a dais round about General Grant.

The speakers were of a rare celebrity and ability.

That night I heard for the first time a slang expression which had already come into considerable vogue, but I had not myself heard it before.

When the speaking began about ten o'clock I left my place at the table and went away over to the front side of the great dining room, where I could take in the whole spectacle at one glance. Among others, Colonel Vilas was to respond to a toast, and also Colonel Ingersoll, the silver-tongued infidel, who had begun life in Illinois and was exceedingly popular there. Vilas was from Wisconsin and was very famous as an orator. He had prepared himself superbly for this occasion.

He was about the first speaker on the list of fifteen toasts and Bob Ingersoll was the ninth.

I had taken a position upon the steps in front of the brass band, which lifted me up and gave me a good general view. Presently I noticed, leaning against the wall near me, a simple-looking young man wearing the uniform of a private and the badge of the Army of the Tennessee. He seemed to be nervous and ill at ease about something; presently, while the second speaker was talking, this young man said, "Do you know Colonel Vilas?" I said I had been introduced to him. He sat silent awhile and then said, "They say he is hell when he gets started!"

I said: "In what way? What do you mean?"

"Speaking! Speaking! They say he is lightning!"

"Yes," I said, "I have heard that he is a great speaker."

The young man shifted about uneasily for a while and then he said, "Do you reckon he can get away with Bob Ingersoll?"

I said, "I don't know."

Another pause. Occasionally he and I would join in the applause when a speaker was on his legs but this young man seemed to applaud unconsciously.

Presently he said, "Here, in Illinois, we think there can't nobody get away with Bob Ingersoll."

I said, "Is that so?"

He said, "Yes; we don't think anybody can lay over Bob Ingersoll." Then he added sadly, "But they do say that Vilas is pretty nearly hell."

At last Vilas rose to speak, and this young man pulled himself together and put on all his anxiety. Vilas began to warm up and the people began to applaud. He delivered himself of one especially fine passage and there was a general shout: "Get up on the table! Get up on the table! Stand up on the table! We can't see you!" So a lot of men standing there picked Vilas up and stood him on the table in full view of the whole great audience and he went on with his speech. The young man applauded with the rest and I could hear the young fellow mutter without being able to make out what he said. But presently, when Vilas thundered out something especially fine, there was a tremendous outburst from the whole house, and then this young man said, in a sort of despairing way:

"It ain't no use. Bob can't climb up to that!"

During the next hour he held his position against the wall in a sort of dazed abstraction, apparently unconscious of place or anything else, and at last, when Ingersoll mounted the supper table, his worshiper merely straightened up to an attitude of attention, but without manifesting any hope.

Ingersoll, with his fair and fresh complexion, handsome figure and graceful carriage, was beautiful to look at.

He was to respond to the toast of "The Volunteers," and his first sentence or two showed his quality. As his third sentence fell from his lips the house let go with a crash and my private looked pleased and for the first time hopeful, but he had been too much frightened to join in the applause. Presently, when Ingersoll came to the passage in which he said that these volunteers had shed their blood and periled their lives in order that a mother might own her own child, the language was so fine, whatever it was (for I have forgotten), and the delivery was so superb that the vast multitude rose as one man and stood on their feet, shouting, stamping, and filling all the place with such a waving of napkins that it was like a snowstorm. This prodigious outburst continued for a minute or two, Ingersoll standing and waiting. And now I happened to notice my private. He was stamping, clapping, shouting, gesticulating like a man who had gone truly mad. At last, when quiet was restored once more, he glanced up at me with the tears in his eyes and said:

"Egod! He *didn't* get left!"

My own speech was granted the perilous distinction of the place of honor. It was the last speech on the list, an honor which no person, probably, has ever sought. It was not reached until two o'clock in the morning. But when I got on my feet I knew that there was at any rate one point in my favor: the text was bound to have the sympathy of nine-tenths of the men present and of every woman, married or single, of the crowds of the sex who stood huddled in the various doorways.

I expected the speech to go off well—and it did.

In it I had a drive at General Sheridan's comparatively new twins and various other things calculated to make it go. There was only one thing in it that I had fears about and that one thing stood where it could not be removed in case of disaster. It was the last sentence in the speech.

I had been picturing the America of fifty years hence, with a population of two hundred million souls, and was saying that the future President, admiral, and so forth, of that great coming time were now lying in their various cradles, scattered abroad over the vast expanse of this country, and then said "and now in his cradle somewhere under the flag the future illustrious commander-in-chief of the American armies is so little burdened with his approaching grandeur and responsi-bilities as to be giving his whole strategic mind at this moment to trying to find some way to get his big toe into his mouth—something, meaning no disrespect to the illustrious guest of this evening, which he turned his entire attention to some fifty-six years ago—"

And here, as I had expected, the laughter ceased and a sort of shuddering silence took its place—for this was apparently carrying the matter too far.

I waited a moment or two to let this silence sink well home, then, turning toward the general, I added:

"And if the child is but the father of the man there are mighty few who will doubt that he succeeded."

Which relieved the house, for when they saw the General break up in good-sized pieces they followed suit with great enthusiasm.

CHAPTER 49

By my existing contract with Webster he merely had a salary of twenty-five hundred dollars a year. He had declined to accept, gratis, an interest in the business, for he was a cautious person and averse from running risks. I now offered him, gratis, a tenth share in the business—the contract as to other details to remain as before. Then, as a counter proposition, he modestly offered this: that his salary be increased to thirty-five hundred dollars a year; that he have ten per cent of the profits accruing from the Grant book, and that I furnish all the capital required at seven per cent.

I said I should be satisfied with this arrangement.

Then he called in his pal, Whitford, who drew the contract. I couldn't understand the contract—I never could understand any contract—and I asked my brother-in-law, General Langdon, a trained business man, to understand it for me. He read it and said it was all right. So we signed it and sealed it. I was to find out later that the contract gave Webster ten per cent of the profits on the Grant book *and* ten per cent interest in the profits of the whole business—but not any interest in such losses as might occur.

The news went forth that General Grant was going to write his memoirs and that the firm of Charles L. Webster & Co. would publish them. The announcement produced a vast sensation throughout the country. The nation was glad and this feeling poured itself heartily out in all the newspapers. On the one day, young Webster was as unknown as the unborn babe. The next day he was a notoriety. His name was in every paper in the United States. He was young, he was human, he naturally mistook this transient notoriety for fame, and by consequence he had to get his hat enlarged. His juvenile joy in his new grandeur was a pretty and pleasant spectacle to see. The first thing he did was to move out of his modest quarters and secure quarters better suited to his new importance as the most distinguished publisher in the country.

His new quarters were on the second or third floor of a tall building which fronted on Union Square, a commercially aristocratic locality. His previous quarters had consisted of two good-sized rooms. His new ones occupied the whole floor. What Webster really needed was a cubbyhole up a back street somewhere, with room to swing a cat in—a long cat; this cubbyhole for office work. He needed no storage rooms, no cellars. The printers and binders of the great memoir took care of the sheets and the bound volumes for us and charged storage and insurance. Conspicuous quarters were not needed for that mighty book. You couldn't have hidden General Grant's publisher where the agent and the canvasser could not find him. The cubbyhole would have been sufficient for all our needs. Almost all the business would be transacted by correspondence. That correspondence would be with the sixteen general agents, none of it with their ten thousand canvassers.

However, it was a very nice spread that we made as far as spaciousness and perspective went. These were impressive —that is, as impressive as nakedness long drawn out and plenty of it could be. It seemed to me that the look of the place was going to deceive country people and drive them away and I suggested that we put up a protecting sign just inside the door: "Come in. It is not a rope walk."

It was a mistake to deal in sarcasms with Webster. They cut deep into his vanity. He hadn't a single intellectual weapon in his armory and could not fight back. It was unchivalrous in me to attack with mental weapons this mentally weaponless man and I tried to refrain from it but couldn't. I ought to have been large enough to endure his vanities but I wasn't. I am not always large enough to endure my own. He had one defect which particularly exasperated me, because I didn't have it myself. When a matter was mentioned of which he was ignorant, he not only would not protect himself by remarking that he was not acquainted with the matter, but he had not even discretion enough to keep his tongue still. He would say something intended to deceive the hearers into the notion that he knew something about that subject himself—a most unlikely condition, since his ignorance covered the whole earth like a blanket and there was hardly a hole in it anywhere. Once in a drawing-room company some talk sprang up about George Eliot and her literature. I saw Webster getting ready to contribute. There was no way to hit him with a brick or a Bible or something and reduce him to unconsciousness and save him, because it would have attracted attention—and therefore I waited for his mountain to bring forth its mouse, which it did as soon as there was a vacancy between speeches. He filled that vacancy with this remark, uttered with tranquil complacency: "I've never read any of his books, on account of prejudice."

Before we had become fairly settled in the new quarters, Webster had suggested that we abolish the existing contract and make a new one. Very well, it was done. I probably never read it nor asked anybody else to read it. I probably merely signed it and saved myself further bother in that way. Under the preceding contracts Webster had been my paid servant; under the new one I was his slave, his absolute slave, and without salary. I owned nine-tenths of the business, I furnished all the capital. I shouldered all the losses, I was responsible for everything, but Webster was sole master. This new condition and my sarcasms changed the atmosphere. I could no longer give orders as before. I could not even make a suggestion with any considerable likelihood of its acceptance.

General Grant was a sick man but he wrought upon his memoirs like a well one and made steady and sure progress.

Webster throned himself in the rope walk and issued a summons to the sixteen general agents to come from the sixteen quarters of the United States and sign contracts. They came. They assembled. Webster delivered the law to them as from Mt. Sinai. They kept their temper wonderfully, marvelously. They furnished the bonds required. They signed the contracts and departed. Ordinarily they would have resented the young man's arrogance but this was not an ordinary case. The contracts were worth to each general agent a good many thousands of dollars. They knew this and the knowledge helped them to keep down their animosities.

Whitford was on hand. He was always at Webster's elbow. Webster was afraid to do anything without legal advice. He could have all the legal advice he wanted, because he had now hired Whitford by the year. He was paying him ten thousand dollars a year out of my pocket. And indeed Whitford was worth part of it—the two-hundred part of it. It was the first time he had ever earned anything worth speaking of and he was content. The phrase "worth speaking of" is surplusage. Whitford had never earned anything. Whitford was never destined to earn anything. He did not earn the ten thousand dollars nor any part of it. In two instances his services proved a pecuniary damage to the firm. His other services were inconsequential and unnecessary. The bookkeeper could have performed them.

This is not a time nor a place to damn Webster, yet it must be done. It is a duty. Let us proceed. It is not my purpose in this history to be more malicious toward any person than I am. I am not alive. I am dead. I wish to keep that fact plainly before the reader. If I were alive I should be writing an autobiography on the usual plan. I should be feeling just as malicious toward Webster as I am feeling this moment—dead as I am—but instead of expressing it freely and honestly I should be trying to conceal it: trying to swindle the reader and not succeeding. He would read the malice between the lines and would not admire me. Nothing worse will happen if I let my malice have frank and free expression. The very reason that I speak from the grave is that I want the satisfaction of sometimes saying everything that is in me instead of bottling the pleasantest of it up for home consumption. I can speak more frankly from the grave than most historians would be able to do, for the reason that whereas they would not be able to *feel* dead, howsoever hard they might try, I myself am able to do that. They would be making believe to be dead. With me, it is not make-believe. They would all the time be feeling, in a tolerably definite way, that that thing in the grave which represents them is a conscious entity; conscious of what it is saying about people; an entity capable of feeling shame; an entity capable of shrinking from full and frank expression, for they believe in immortality. They believe that death is only a sleep, followed by an immediate waking, and that their spirits are conscious of what is going on here below and take a deep and continuous interest in the joys and sorrows of the survivors whom they love and don't.

But I have long ago lost my belief in immortality—also my interest in it. I can say now what I could not say while alive—things which it would shock people to hear; things which I could not say when alive because I should be aware of that shock and would certainly spare myself the personal pain of inflicting it. When we believe in immortality we have a reason for it. Not a reason founded upon information, or even plausibilities, for we haven't any. Our reason for choosing to believe in this dream is that we desire immortality, for some reason or other, I don't know what. But I have no such desire. I have sampled this life and it is sufficient. Another one would be another experiment. It would proceed from the same source as this one. I should have no large expectations concerning it, and if I may be excused from assisting in the experiment I shall be properly grateful. Annihilation has no terrors for me, because I have already tried it before I was born—a hundred million years—and I have suffered more in an hour, in this life, than I remember to have suffered in the whole hundred million years put together. There was a peace, a serenity, an absence of all sense of responsibility, an absence of worry, an absence of care, grief, perplexity; and the presence of a deep content and unbroken satisfaction in that hundred million years of holiday which I look back upon with a tender longing and with a grateful desire to resume, when the opportunity comes.

It is understandable that when I speak from the grave it is not a spirit that is speaking; it is a nothing; it is an emptiness; it is a vacancy; it is a something that has neither feeling nor consciousness. It does not know what it is saying. It is not aware that it is saying anything at all, therefore it can speak frankly and freely, since it cannot know that it is inflicting pain, discomfort, or offense of any kind.

I am talking freely about Webster because I am expecting my future editors to have judgment enough and charity enough to suppress all such chapters in the early editions of this book, and keep them suppressed, edition after edition, until all whom they could pain shall be at rest in their graves. But after that, let them be published. It is my desire, and at that distant date they can do no harm.

◇◇◇◇◇◇◇◇◇◇◇◇◇◇◇◇◇◇

CHAPTER 50

In the history of the United States there had been one officer bearing that supreme and stately and simple one-word title, "General." Possibly there had been two. As to that I do not remember. In the long stretch of years lying between the American Revolution and our Civil War, that title had had no existence. It was an office which was special in its nature. It did not belong among our military ranks. It was only conferrable by Act of Congress and upon a person specially named in the Act. No one could inherit it. No one could succeed to it by promotion.

It had been conferred upon General Grant but he had surrendered it to become President. He was now in the grip of death, with the compassionate and lamenting eyes of all the nation upon him—a nation eager to testify its gratitude to him by granting any wish that he might express. It was known to his friends that it was the dearest ambition of his heart to die a General. On the last day of Mr. Arthur's term and of the Congress then sitting, a bill to confer the title was taken up at the last moment. There was no time to lose. Messengers were sent flying to the White House. Mr. Arthur came in all haste to the Capitol. There was great anxiety and excitement. And, after all, these strenuous efforts were instituted too late! In the midst of the taking of the vote upon the bill the life of the Congress expired. No, would have expired—but some thoughtful person turned the clock back half an hour and the bill went through! Mr. Arthur signed it at once and the day was saved.

The news was despatched to General Grant by telegram, and I was present, with several others, when it was put into his hands. Every face there betrayed strong excitement and emotion—except one, General Grant's. He read the telegram, but not a shade or suggestion of a change exhibited itself in his iron countenance. The volume of his emotion was greater than all the other emotions there present combined, but he was able to suppress all expression of it and make no sign.

I had seen an exhibition of General Grant's ability to conceal his emotions once before, on a less memorable occasion. This was in Chicago, in 1879, when he arrived there from his triumphal progress around the globe and was fêted during three days by Chicago and by the first army he commanded— the Army of the Tennessee. I sat near him on the stage of a theatre which was packed to the ceiling with surviving heroes of that army and their wives. When General Grant, attended by other illustrious generals of the war, came forward and took his seat the house rose and a deafening storm of welcome burst forth which continued during two or three minutes. There wasn't a soldier on that stage who wasn't visibly affected, except the man who was being welcomed, Grant. No change of expression crossed his face.

Then the eulogies began. Sherman was present, Sheridan was present, Schofield, Logan and half a dozen other bearers of famous military names were there. The orators always began by emptying Niagaras of glory upon Grant. They always came and stood near him and over him and emptied the Niagara down on him at short range, but it had no more effect upon him than if he had been a bronze image. In turn, each orator passed from Grant to Sherman, then to Sheridan and to the rest and emptied barrels of inflamed praise upon each. And in every case it was as if the orator was emptying fire upon the man, the victim so writhed and fidgeted and squirmed and suffered. With a spyglass you could have picked out the man that was being martyrized, at a distance of three miles. Not one of them was able to sit still under the fiery deluge of praise except that one man, Grant. He got his Niagara every quarter of an hour for two hours and a half, and yet when the ordeal was over he was still sitting in precisely the same attitude which he had assumed when he first took that chair. He had never moved a hand or foot, head, or anything. It would have been a sufficiently amazing thing to see a man sit without change of position during such a stretch of time without anything whatever on his mind, nothing to move him, nothing to excite him; but to see this one sit like that for two hours and a half under such awful persecution was an achievement which I should not have believed if I had not seen it with my own eyes.

Whenever galley proofs or revises went to General Grant a set came also to me. General Grant was aware of this. Sometimes I referred to the proofs casually but entered into no particulars concerning them. By and by I learned through a member of the household that he was disturbed and disappointed because I had never expressed an opinion as to the literary quality of the memoirs. It was also suggested that a word of encouragement from me would be a help to him. I was as much surprised as Columbus's cook would have been to learn that Columbus wanted his opinion as to how Columbus was doing his navigating. It could not have occurred to me that General Grant could have any use for anybody's assistance or encouragement in any work which he might undertake to do. He was the most modest of men and this was another instance of it.

He was venturing upon a new trade, an uncharted sea, and stood in need of the encouraging word, just like any creature of common clay. It was a great compliment that he should care for my opinion and should desire it and I took the earliest opportunity to diplomatically turn the conversation in that direction and furnish it without seeming to lug it in by the ears.

By chance, I had been comparing the memoirs with Caesar's "Commentaries" and was qualified to deliver judgment. I was able to say in all sincerity that the same high merits distinguished both books—clarity of statement, directness, simplicity, unpretentiousness, manifest truthfulness, fairness and justice toward friend and foe alike, soldierly candor and frankness and soldierly avoidance of flowery speech. I placed the two books side by side upon the same high level and I still think that they belonged there. I learned afterward that General Grant was pleased with this verdict. It shows that he was just a man, just a human being, just an author. An author values a compliment even when it comes from a source of doubtful competency.

General Grant wrought heroically with his pen while his disease made its steady inroads upon his life, and at last his work stood completed. He was moved to Mount McGregor and there his strength passed gradually away. Toward the last he was not able to speak, but used a pencil and small slips of paper when he needed to say anything.

I went there to see him once toward the end, and he asked me with his pencil, and evidently with anxious solicitude, if there was a prospect that his book would make something for his family.

I said that the canvass for it was progressing vigorously, that the subscriptions and the money were coming in fast, that the campaign was not more than half completed yet—but that if it should stop where it was there would be two hundred thousand dollars coming to his family. He expressed his gratification, with his pencil.

When I was entering the house, the Confederate general, Buckner, was leaving it. Buckner and Grant had been fellow cadets at West Point, about 1840. I think they had served together in the Mexican War, a little later. After that war Grant (then a captain in the regular army) was ordered to a military post in Oregon. By and by he resigned and came East and found himself in New York penniless. On the street he met Buckner and borrowed fifty dollars of him. In February, 1862,

Buckner was in command of the Confederate garrison of Fort Donelson. General Grant captured the fortress by assault and took fifteen thousand prisoners. After that, the two soldiers did not meet again until that day at Mount McGregor twenty-three years later.

Several visitors were present and there was a good deal of chaffing and joking, some of it at Buckner's expense.

Finally General Buckner said, "I have my full share of admiration and esteem for Grant. It dates back to our cadet days. He has as many merits and virtues as any man I am acquainted with but he has one deadly defect. He is an incurable borrower and when he wants to borrow he knows of only one limit—he wants what you've got. When I was poor he borrowed fifty dollars of me; when I was rich he borrowed fifteen thousand men."

General Grant died at Mount McGregor on the 23rd of July. In September or October the memoirs went to press. Several sets of plates were made; the printing was distributed among several great printing establishments; a great number of steam presses were kept running night and day on the book; several large binderies were kept at work binding it. The book was in sets of two volumes—large octavo. Its price was nine dollars in cloth. For costlier bindings the price was proportionately higher. Two thousand sets in tree-calf were issued at twenty-five dollars per set.

The book was issued on the 10th of December and I turned out to be a competent prophet. In the beginning I had told General Grant that his book would sell six hundred thousand single volumes and that is what happened. It sold three hundred thousand sets. The first check that went to Mrs. Grant was for two hundred thousand dollars; the next one, a few months later, was for a hundred and fifty thousand. I do not remember about the subsequent checks but I think that in the aggregate the book paid Mrs. Grant something like half a million dollars.

Webster was in his glory. In his obscure days his hat was number six and a quarter; in these latter days he was not able to get his head into a barrel. He loved to descant upon the wonders of the book. He liked to go into the statistics. He liked to tell that it took thirteen miles of gold leaf to print the gilt titles on the book backs; he liked to tell how many thousand tons the three hundred thousand sets weighed. Of course that same old natural thing happened: Webster thought it was *he* that sold the book. He thought that General Grant's great name helped but he regarded himself as the main reason of the book's prodigious success. This shows that Webster was merely human and merely a publisher. All publishers are Columbuses. The successful author is their America. The reflection that they—like Columbus—didn't discover what they expected to discover, and didn't discover what they started out to discover, doesn't trouble them. All they remember is that they discovered America; they forgot that they started out to discover some patch or corner of India.

In the early days, when the general agents were being chosen, Webster conferred one of the best Western general agencies upon an ex-preacher, a professional revivalist whom God had deposited in Iowa for improprieties of one kind and another which had been committed by that State. All the other candidates for agencies warned Webster to keep out of that man's hands, assuring him that no sagacities of Whitford or anybody else would be able to defeat that revivalist's inborn proclivity to steal. Their persuasions went for nothing. Webster gave him the agency. We furnished him the books. He did a thriving trade. He collected a gross sum of thirty-six thousand dollars and Webster never got a cent of it.

It is no great marvel to me that Mrs. Grant got a matter of half a million dollars out of that book. The miracle is that it didn't run her into debt. It was fortunate for her that we had only one Webster. It was an unnatural oversight in me that I didn't hunt for another one.

◇◇◇◇◇◇◇◇◇◇◇◇◇◇◇◇◇◇◇◇

CHAPTER 51

Let me try to bring this painful business to a close. One of the things which poisoned Webster's days and nights was the aggravating circumstances that whereas he, Charles L. Webster, was the great publisher—the greatest of publishers—and my name did not appear anywhere as a member of the firm, the public persisted in regarding me as the substance of that firm and Webster the shadow. Everybody who had a book to publish offered it to me, not to Webster. I accepted several excellent books but Webster declined them every time, and he was

master. But if anybody offered *him* a book, he was so charmed
with the compliment that he took the book without examining
it. He was not able to get hold of one that could make its living.

Joe Jefferson wrote me and said he had written his autobiography and he would like me to be the publisher. Of course
I wanted the book. I sent his letter to Webster and asked him
to arrange the matter. Webster did not decline the book. He
simply ignored it and brushed the matter out of his mind. He
accepted and published two or three war books that furnished
no profit. He accepted still another one: distributed the
agency contracts for it, named its price (three dollars and a
half in cloth) and also agreed to have the book ready by a
certain date, two or three months ahead. One day I went
down to New York and visited the office and asked for a sight
of that book. I asked Webster how many thousand words it
contained. He said he didn't know. I asked him to count the
words, by rough estimate. He did it. I said, "It doesn't contain
words enough for the price and dimensions, by four-fifths.
You will have to pad it with a brick. We must start a brick-
yard, and right away, because it is much cheaper to make
bricks than it is to buy them in the market."

It set him in a fury. Any little thing like that would have
that effect. He was one of the most sensitive creatures I ever
saw, for the quality of the material that he was made of.

He had several books on hand—worthless books which he
had accepted because they had been offered to him instead of
to me—and I found that he had never counted the words in
any of them. He had taken them without examination. Webster was a good general agent but he knew nothing about
publishing and he was incapable of learning anything about
it. By and by I found that he had agreed to resurrect Henry
Ward Beecher's *Life of Christ*. I suggested that he ought to
have tried for Lazarus, because that had been tried once and
we knew it could be done. He was exasperated again. He certainly was the most sensitive creature that ever was, for his
make. He had also advanced to Mr. Beecher, who was not in
prosperous circumstances at the time, five thousand dollars on
the future royalties. Mr. Beecher was to revamp the book—or
rather I think he was to finish the book. I think he had just
issued the first of the two volumes of which it was to consist
when that ruinous scandal broke out and suffocated the enterprise. I think the second volume had not been written and

that Mr. Beecher was now undertaking to write it. If he failed to accomplish this within a given time he was to return the money. He did not succeed and the money was eventually returned.

Webster kept back a book of mine, *A Connecticut Yankee in King Arthur's Court,* as long as he could and finally published it so surreptitiously that it took two or three years to find out that there was any such book. He suppressed a compilation made by Howells and me, *The Library of Humor,* so long and finally issued it so clandestinely that I doubt if anybody in America ever did find out that there was such a book.

William M. Laffan told me that Mr. Walters, of Baltimore, was going to have a sumptuous book made which should illustrate in detail his princely art collection; that he was going to bring the best artists from Paris to make the illustrations; that he was going to make the book himself and see to it that it was made exactly to his taste; that he was going to spend a quarter of a million dollars on it; that he wanted it issued at a great price—a price consonant with its sumptuous character, and that he wanted no penny of the proceeds. The publisher would have nothing to do but distribute the book and take the whole of the profit.

Laffan said, "There, Mark, you can make a fortune out of that without any trouble at all, and without risk or expense."

I said I would send Webster down to Baltimore at once. I tried to do it but I never succeeded. Webster never touched the matter in any way whatever. If it had been a secondhand dog that Mr. Walters wanted published, he would have only needed to apply to Webster. Webster would have broken his neck getting down to Baltimore to annex that dog. But Mr. Walters had applied to the wrong man. Webster's pride was hurt and he would not look at Mr. Walters' book. Webster had immense pride but he was short of other talents.

Webster was the victim of a cruel neuralgia in the head. He eased his pain with the new German drug, phenacetine. The physicians limited his use of it but he found a way to get it in quantity: under our free institutions anybody can poison himself that wants to and will pay the price. He took this drug with increasing frequency and in increasing quantity. It stupefied him and he went about as one in a dream. He ceased from coming to the office except at intervals, and when he came he was pretty sure to exercise his authority in ways perilous for the business. In his condition, he was not responsible for his acts.

Something had to be done. Whitford explained that there was no way to get rid of this dangerous element except by buying Webster out. But what was there to buy? Webster had always promptly collected any money that was due him. He had squandered, long ago, my share of the book's profit—a hundred thousand dollars. The business was gasping, dying. The whole of it was not worth a dollar and a half. Then what would be a fair price for me to pay for a tenth interest in it? After much consultation and much correspondence, it transpired that Webster would be willing to put up with twelve thousand dollars and step out. I furnished the check.

Webster's understudy and business manager had now been for some time a young fellow named Frederick J. Hall, another Dunkirk importation. We got all our talents from that stud farm at Dunkirk. Poor Hall meant well but he was wholly incompetent for the place. He carried it along for a time with the heroic hopefulness of youth, but there was an obstruction which was bound to defeat him sooner or later. It was this:

Stedman, the poet, had made a compilation, several years earlier, called *The Library of American Literature*—nine or ten octavo volumes. A publisher in Cincinnati had tried to make it succeed. It swallowed up that publisher, family and all. If Stedman had offered me the book I should have said "Sold by subscription and on the installment plan, there is nothing in this book for us at a royalty above four per cent, but in fact it would swamp us at any kind of royalty, because such a book would require a cash capital of several hundred thousand dollars and we haven't a hundred thousand."

But Stedman didn't bring the book to me. He took it to Webster. Webster was delighted and flattered. He accepted the book on an eight per cent royalty and thereby secured the lingering suicide of Charles L. Webster and Company. We struggled along two or three years under that deadly load. After Webster's time, poor little Hall struggled along with it and got to borrowing money of a bank in which Whitford was a director—borrowing on notes endorsed by me and renewed from time to time. These notes used to come to me in Italy for renewals. I endorsed them without examining them and sent them back. At last I found that additions had been made to the borrowings, without my knowledge or consent. I began to feel troubled. I wrote Mr. Hall about it and said I would like to have an exhaustive report of the condition of the business. The next mail brought that exhaustive report, whereby it appeared that the concern's assets exceeded its liabilities by ninety-two thousand dollars. Then I felt better. But there was no occasion to feel better, for the report ought to have read the other way. Poor Hall soon wrote to say that we needed more money and must have it right away or the concern would fail.

I sailed for New York. I emptied into the till twenty-four thousand dollars which I had earned with the pen. I looked around to see where we could borrow money. There wasn't any place. This was in the midst of the fearful panic of '93. I went up to Hartford to borrow—couldn't borrow a penny. I offered to mortgage our house and grounds and furniture for any small loan. The property had cost a hundred and sixty-seven thousand dollars, and seemed good for a small loan. Henry Robinson said, "Clemens, I give you my word, you can't borrow three thousand dollars on that property." Very well, I knew that if that was so, I couldn't borrow it on a basketful of government bonds.

Webster and Company failed. The firm owed me about sixty thousand dollars, borrowed money. It owed Mrs. Clemens sixty-five thousand dollars, borrowed money. Also it owed ninety-six creditors an average of a thousand dollars or so apiece. The panic had stopped Mrs. Clemens's income. It had stopped my income from my books. We had but nine thousand dollars in the bank. We hadn't a penny wherewith to pay the Webster creditors. Henry Robinson said, "Hand over everything belonging to Webster and Company to the creditors and ask them to accept that in liquidation of the debts. They'll do it. You'll see that they'll do it. They are aware that you are not individually responsible for those debts, that the responsibility rests upon the firm as a firm."

I didn't think much of that way out of the difficulty and when I made my report to Mrs. Clemens she wouldn't hear of it at all. She said, "This is my house. The creditors shall have it. Your books are your property—turn them over to the creditors. Reduce the indebtedness in every way you can think of— then get to work and earn the rest of the indebtedness, if your life is spared. And don't be afraid. We shall pay a hundred cents on the dollar yet."

It was sound prophecy. Mr. Rogers[1] stepped in about this

[1] Henry H. Rogers.

time and preached to the creditors. He said they could not
have Mrs. Clemens's house—that she must be a preferred credi-
tor and would give up the Webster notes for sixty-five thousand dollars, money borrowed of her. He said they could not
have my books, that they were not an asset of Webster and
Company, that the creditors could have everything that belonged to Webster and Company, that I would wipe from the
slate the sixty thousand dollars I had lent to the Company,
and that I would now make it my task to earn the rest of the
Webster indebtedness, if I could, and pay a hundred cents on
the dollar—but that this must not be regarded as a promise.

◇◇◇◇◇◇◇◇◇◇◇◇◇◇◇◇◇◇◇◇◇◇

CHAPTER 52

Since Mr. Rogers passed from life many months have gone by[1]
and still I have not found myself competent to put into words
my feelings for him and my estimate of him. For he is as yet
too near, the restraint of his spirit too effective.

All through my life I have been the easy prey of the cheap
adventurer. He came, he lied, he robbed and went his way,
and the next one arrived by the next train and began to scrape
up what was left. I was in the toils of one of these creatures
sixteen years ago and it was Mr. Rogers who got me out. We
were strangers when we met and friends when we parted, half
an hour afterward. The meeting was accidental and unforeseen but it had memorable and fortunate consequences for
me. He dragged me out of that difficulty and also out of the
next one—a year or two later—which was still more formidable
than its predecessor. He did these saving things at no cost to
my self-love, no hurt to my pride; indeed, he did them with so
delicate an art that I almost seemed to have done them myself. By no sign, no hint, no word did he ever betray any consciousness that I was under obligations to him. I have never
been so great as that and I have not known another who was.
I have never approached it; it belongs among the loftiest of
human attributes. This is a world where you get nothing for
nothing; where you pay value for everything you get and 50
per cent over; and when it is gratitude you owe, you have to

[1] Written in 1909.

pay a thousand. In fact, gratitude is a debt which usually goes on accumulating, like blackmail; the more you pay, the more is exacted. In time you are made to realize that the kindness done you is become a curse and you wish it had not happened. You find yourself situated as was Mr. W., a friend of friends of mine, years ago. He was rich and goodhearted and appreciative. His wife's life was saved by a grocer's young man, who stopped her runaway horses. Her husband was grateful beyond words. For he supposed gratitude was a sentiment; he did not know it had a price and that *he* was not the one to determine the rate. But by and by he was educated. Then he said to the grocer's young man, "Take this five hundred dollars and vanish; I have had you and your tribe on my back three years, and if ever another man saves my wife's life, let him buy a coffin, for he will need it."

Mr. Rogers was a great man. No one denies him that praise. He was great in more ways than one—ways in which other men are great, ways in which he had not a monopoly; but in that fine trait which I have mentioned he was uniquely great; he held that high place almost alone, almost without a sharer. If nobilities of character were accorded decorations symbolizing degrees of merit and distinction, I think this one could claim rank, unchallenged, with the Garter and the Golden Fleece.

But what I am trying to place before unfamiliar eyes is the heart of him.

When the publishing house of Webster & Company failed, in the early '90's, its liabilities exceeded its assets by sixty-six per cent. I was morally bound for the debts, though not legally. The panic was on, business houses were falling to ruin everywhere, creditors were taking the assets—when there were any—and letting the rest go. Old business friends of mine said: "Business is business, sentiment is sentiment—and this is business. Turn the assets over to the creditors and compromise on that; other creditors are not getting thirty-three per cent." Mr. Rogers was certainly a business man—no one doubts that. People who know him only by printed report will think they know what his attitude would be in the matter. And they will be mistaken. He sided with my wife. He was the only man who had a clear eye for the situation and could see that it differed from other apparently parallel situations. In substance he said this: "Business has its laws and customs and they are justified; but a literary man's reputation is his life; he can afford to be money poor but he cannot afford to be character poor; you must earn the cent per cent and pay it." My nephew, the late Samuel E. Moffett—himself a literary man—felt in the same way, naturally enough; but I only mention him to recall and revivify a happy remark which he made and which traveled around the globe: "Honor knows no statute of limitations."

So it was decided. I must cease from idling and take up work again. I must write a book; also I must return to the lecture platform. My wife said I could clear off the load of debt in four years. Mr. Rogers was more cautious, more conservative, more liberal. He said I could have as many years as I wanted—seven to start with. That was his joke. When he was not in the humor for pleasantry it was because he was asleep. Privately I was afraid his seven might be nearer the mark than Mrs. Clemens's four.

One day I got a shock—a shock which disturbed me a good deal. I overheard a brief conversation between Mr. Rogers and a couple of seasoned men of affairs.

First Man of Affairs: "How old is Clemens?"

Mr. Rogers: "Fifty-eight."

First Man of Affairs: "Ninety-five per cent of the men who fail at fifty-eight never get up again."

Second Man of Affairs: "You can make it ninety-eight per cent and be nearer right."

Those sayings haunted me for several days, troubling me with melancholy forebodings, and would not be reasoned away by me. There wasn't any room for reasoning, anyway, so far as I could see. If, at fifty-eight, ninety-eight men in a hundred who fail never get up again, what chance had I to draw No. 99 or No. 100? However, the depression did not last; it soon passed away, because Mrs. Clemens took her always-ready pencil and paper, when she learned my trouble, and clearly and convincingly ciphered out the intake of the four years and the resultant success. I could see that she was right. Indeed, she was always right. In foresight, wisdom, accurate calculation, good judgment and the ability to see all sides of a problem, she had no match among people I have known, except Mr. Rogers.

Necessarily it took a good while to arrange the details and make the engagements for a lecture trip around the globe, but this labor was completed at last and we made our start in the middle of July, 1895, booked ahead for twelve months.

Meantime he was in command, in the matter of the creditors—and had been from the beginning. There were ninety-six creditors. He had meetings with them, discussions, arguments, persuasions, but no quarrels. Mrs. Clemens wanted to turn over to the creditors the house she had built in Hartford and which stood in her name, but he would not allow it. Neither would he allow my copyrights to go to them. Mrs. Clemens had lent the Webster firm $65,000 upon its notes in its perishing days, in the hope of saving its life, and Mr. Rogers insisted upon making her a preferred creditor and letting her have the copyrights in liquidation of the notes. He would not budge from this position and the creditors finally yielded the point.

Mr. Rogers insisted upon just two things besides the relinquishment of the copyrights: the creditors must be content with the Webster assets for the present and give me time to earn the rest of the firm's debt. He won them over. There were a clarity about his reasonings and a charm about his manner, his voice and the kindness and sincerity that looked out of his eyes that could win anybody that had brains in his head and a heart in his body. Of the ninety-six creditors only three or four stood out for rigorous and uncompromising measures against me and refused to relent. The others said I could go free and take my own time. They said they would obstruct me in no way and would bring no actions; and they kept their word. As to the three or four, I have never resented their animosity, except in my Autobiography. And even here not in spite, not in malice, but only frankly. It can never wound them, for I have every confidence that they will be in hell before it is printed.

The long, long head that Mr. Rogers carried on his shoulders! When he was so strenuous about my copyrights and so determined to keep them in the family I was not able to understand why he should think the matter so important. He insisted that they were a great asset. I said they were not an asset at all; I couldn't even *give* them away. He said, wait—let the panic subside and business revive, and I would see; they would be worth more than they had ever been worth before.

That was his idea—the idea of a financier, familiar with finance; of a capitalist, deep in railroads, oil, banks, iron, copper, telegraphs and so on, and familiar with those things, but what could he know about books? What was his opinion about copyright values worth if it clashed with the opinion of experienced old publishers? Which it did. The Webster failure threw seven of my books on my hands. I had offered them to three first-class publishers; they didn't want them. If Mr. Rogers had let Mrs. Clemens and me have our way the copyrights would have been handed over to the publishers.

I am grateful to his memory for many a kindness and many a good service he did me but gratefulest of all for the saving of my copyrights—a service which saved me and my family from want and assured us permanent comfort and prosperity.

How could he look into the future and see all that, when the men whose trade and training it was to exercise that technical vision were forecast blind and saw no vestige of it? This is only one example of the wonders of his mind; his intimates could cite many others, products of that rich treasury.

I was never able to teach him anything about finance, though I tried hard and did the best I could. I was not able to move him. Once I had hopes for a little while. The Standard Oil declared one of its customary fury-breeding 40- or 50-percent dividends on its $100,000,000 capital, and the storm broke out as usual. To the unposted public a 40- or 50-per-cent dividend could mean only one thing—the giant Trust was squeezing an utterly and wickedly unfair profit out of the helpless people; whereas in truth the giant Trust was not doing anything of the kind but was getting only five or six per cent on the money actually invested in its business, which was eight or ten times a hundred millions. In my quality of uneducated financial expert I urged that the nominal capital be raised to $1,000,000,000; then next year's dividend would drop to four or five per cent, the year's profit would be the same as usual but the usual storm would not happen. If I remember rightly, I think he offered the objection that the tenfold increase of taxes would be too heavy and I rejoined that by the ill-veiled exultation in his eye I knew he regarded my suggestion as of vast value and was trying to invent some plausible way of getting out of paying a commission on it. I often gave him fresh financial ideas, quite uninvited; and in return—uninvited—he told me how to write my literature better; but nothing came of it, both of us remained as poor as ever.

Unconsciously we all have a standard by which we measure other men, and if we examine closely we find that this standard is a very simple one and is this: we admire them, we envy them, for great qualities which we ourselves lack. Hero worship consists in just that. Our heroes are the men who do things which we recognize with regret and sometimes with a secret shame that we cannot do. We find not much in ourselves to admire, we are always privately wanting to be like somebody else. If everybody was satisfied with himself there would be no heroes.

Mr. Rogers was endowed with many great qualities; but the one which I most admired and which was to me a constant reproach because I lacked it was his unselfishness where a friend or a cause that was near his heart was concerned, and his native readiness to come forward and take vigorous hold of the difficulty involved and abolish it. I was born to indolence, idleness, procrastination, indifference—the qualities that constitute a shirk; and so he was always a wonder to me and a delight—he who never shirked anything, but kept his master brain and his master hands going all day long and every day and was happiest when he was busiest and apparently lightest of heart when his burden of labor and duty was heaviest.

He could take trouble; I could not take trouble, either for myself or for anyone else. I dreaded anything that might disturb my ease and comfort, and would put that thing from me even when it cost me shame to do it; and so to see him take trouble, no end of trouble, days and days of trouble, and take it so patiently, so placidly, so interestedly—and so affectionately, too, if it was for somebody else—was to me a strange and marvelous thing, and beautiful. It probably never occurred to him to admire it; no, he would be occupied in admiring some quality in some one else which was lacking in his own composition.

Mrs. Clemens and Clara and I started, on the 15th of July, 1895, on our lecturing raid around the world. We lectured and robbed and raided for thirteen months. I wrote a book and published it.[2] I sent the book money and lecture money to Mr. Rogers as fast as we captured it. He banked it and saved it up for the creditors. We implored him to pay off the smaller creditors straightway, for they needed the money, but he wouldn't do it. He said that when I had milked the world dry we would take the result and distribute it *pro rata* among the Webster people.

At the end of '98 or the beginning of '99 Mr. Rogers cabled me, at Vienna, "The creditors have all been paid a hundred

[2] *Following the Equator,* 1897.

cents on the dollar. There is eighteen thousand five hundred dollars left. What shall I do with it?"

I answered, "Put it in Federal Steel"—which he did, all except a thousand dollars, and took it out again in two months with a profit of a hundred and twenty-five per cent.

There— Thanks be! A hundred times I have tried to tell this intolerable story with a pen but I never could do it. It always made me sick before I got halfway to the middle of it. But this time I have held my grip and walked the floor and emptied it all out of my system, and I hope to never hear of it again.

◇◇◇◇◇◇◇◇◇◇◇◇◇◇◇◇◇◇◇◇

CHAPTER 53

There has never been a time in the past thirty-five years[1] when my literary shipyard hadn't two or more half-finished ships on the ways, neglected and baking in the sun; generally there have been three or four; at present there are five. This has an unbusiness-like look but it was not purposeless, it was intentional. As long as a book would write itself I was a faithful and interested amanuensis and my industry did not flag, but the minute that the book tried to shift to *my* head the labor of contriving its situations, inventing its adventures and conducting its conversations, I put it away and dropped it out of my mind. Then I examined my unfinished properties to see if among them there might not be one whose interest in itself had revived through a couple of years' restful idleness and was ready to take me on again as amanuensis.

It was by accident that I found out that a book is pretty sure to get tired along about the middle and refuse to go on with its work until its powers and its interest should have been refreshed by a rest and its depleted stock of raw materials reinforced by lapse of time. It was when I had reached the middle of *Tom Sawyer* that I made this invaluable find. At page 400 of my manuscript the story made a sudden and determined halt and refused to proceed another step. Day after day it still refused. I was disappointed, distressed and immeasurably as-

---
[1] Written August 30, 1906.

tonished, for I knew quite well that the tale was not finished and I could not understand why I was not able to go on with it. The reason was very simple—my tank had run dry; it was empty; the stock of materials in it was exhausted; the story could not go on without materials; it could not be wrought out of nothing.

When the manuscript had lain in a pigeonhole two years I took it out one day and read the last chapter that I had written. It was then that I made the great discovery that when the tank runs dry you've only to leave it alone and it will fill up again in time, while you are asleep—also while you are at work at other things and are quite unaware that this unconscious and profitable cerebration is going on. There was plenty of material now and the book went on and finished itself without any trouble.

Ever since then, when I have been writing a book I have pigeonholed it without misgivings when its tank ran dry, well knowing that it would fill up again without any of my help within the next two or three years, and that then the work of completing it would be simple and easy. *The Prince and the Pauper* struck work in the middle because the tank was dry, and I did not touch it again for two years. A dry interval of two years occurred in *A Connecticut Yankee in King Arthur's Court*. A like interval had occurred in the middle of other books of mine. Two similar intervals have occurred in a story of mine called "Which Was It?" In fact, the second interval has gone considerably over time, for it is now four years since that second one intruded itself. I am sure that the tank is full again now and that I could take up that book and write the other half of it without a break or any lapse of interest—but I shan't do it. The pen is irksome to me. I was born lazy, and dictating has spoiled me. I am quite sure I shall never touch a pen again; therefore that book will remain unfinished—a pity, too, for the idea of it is (actually) new and would spring a handsome surprise upon the reader at the end.

There is another unfinished book, which I should probably entitle "The Refuge of the Derelicts." It is half finished and will remain so. There is still another one, entitled "The Adventures of a Microbe During Three Thousand Years—by a Microbe." It is half finished and will remain so. There is yet another—*The Mysterious Stranger*. It is more than half finished. I would dearly like to finish it and it causes me a real pang to reflect that it is not to be.[2] These several tanks are full now and those books would go gaily along and complete themselves if I would hold the pen, but I am tired of the pen.

There was another of these half-finished stories. I carried it as far as thirty-eight thousand words four years ago, then destroyed it for fear I might some day finish it. Huck Finn was the teller of the story and of course Tom Sawyer and Jim were the heroes of it. But I believed that that trio had done work enough in this world and were entitled to a permanent rest.

In Rouen in '93 I destroyed $15,000 worth of manuscript, and in Paris in the beginning of '94 I destroyed $10,000 worth —I mean, estimated as magazine stuff. I was afraid to keep those piles of manuscript on hand lest I be tempted to sell them, for I was fairly well persuaded that they were not up to standard. Ordinarily there would have been no temptation present and I would not think of publishing doubtful stuff— but I was heavily in debt then and the temptation to mend my condition was so strong that I burnt the manuscript to get rid of it. My wife not only made no objection but encouraged me to do it, for she cared more for my reputation than for any other concern of ours.

About that time she helped me put another temptation behind me. This was an offer of $16,000 a year, for five years, to let my name be used as editor of a humorous periodical. I praise her for furnishing her help in resisting that temptation, for it is her due. There was no temptation about it, in fact, but she would have offered her help just the same if there had been one. I can conceive of many wild and extravagant things when my imagination is in good repair but I can conceive of nothing quite so wild and extravagant as the idea of my accepting the editorship of a humorous periodical. I should regard that as the saddest (for me) of all occupations. If I should undertake it I should have to add to it the occupation of undertaker, to relieve it in some degree of its cheerlessness. I could edit a serious periodical with relish and a strong interest but I have never cared enough about humor to qualify me to edit it or sit in judgment upon it.

There are some books that refuse to be written. They stand their ground year after year and will not be persuaded. It isn't because the book is not there and worth being written—it is only because the right form for the story does not present itself. There is only one right form for a story and if you fail to

<hr>

2 Although he was unaware of the fact he had already finished this work.

find that form the story will not tell itself. You may try a dozen wrong forms but in each case you will not get very far before you discover that you have not found the right one—then that story will always stop and decline to go any further. In the story of *Joan of Arc* I made six wrong starts and each time that I offered the result to Mrs. Clemens she responded with the same deadly criticism—silence. She didn't say a word but her silence spoke with the voice of thunder. When at last I found the right form I recognized at once that it was the right one and I knew what she would say. She said it, without doubt or hesitation.

In the course of twelve years I made six attempts to tell a simple little story which I knew would tell itself in four hours if I could ever find the right starting point. I scored six failures; then one day in London I offered the text of the story to Robert McClure and proposed that he publish that text in the magazine and offer a prize to the person who should tell it best. I became greatly interested and went on talking upon the text for half an hour; then he said, "You have told the story yourself. You have nothing to do but put it on paper just as you have told it."

I recognized that this was true. At the end of four hours it was finished, and quite to my satisfaction. So it took twelve years and four hours to produce that little bit of a story, which I have called "The Death Wafer."

To start right is certainly an essential. I have proved this too many times to doubt it. Twenty-five or thirty years ago I began a story which was to turn upon the marvels of mental telegraphy. A man was to invent a scheme whereby he could synchronize two minds, thousands of miles apart, and enable them to freely converse together through the air without the aid of a wire. Four times I started it in the wrong way and it wouldn't go. Three times I discovered my mistake after writing about a hundred pages. I discovered it the fourth time when I had written four hundred pages—then I gave it up and put the whole thing in the fire.

CHAPTER 54

1601 was a letter which I wrote to Twichell, about 1876, from my study at Quarry Farm one summer day when I ought to have been better employed. I remember the incident very well. I had been diligently reading up for a story which I was minded to write, *The Prince and the Pauper.* I was reading ancient English books with the purpose of saturating myself with archaic English to a degree which would enable me to do plausible imitations of it in a fairly easy and unlabored way. In one of these old books I came across a brief conversation which powerfully impressed me, as I had never been impressed before, with the frank indelicacies of speech permissible among ladies and gentlemen in that ancient time. I was thus powerfully impressed because this conversation seemed real, whereas that kind of talk had not seemed real to me before. It had merely seemed Rabelaisian—exaggerated, artificial, made up by the author for his passing needs. It had not seemed to me that the blushful passages in Shakespeare were of a sort which Shakespeare had actually heard people use but were inventions of his own, liberties which he had taken with the facts under the protection of a poet's license.

But here at last was one of those dreadful conversations which commended itself to me as being absolutely real, and as being the kind of talk which ladies and gentlemen did actually indulge in in those pleasant and lamented ancient days now gone from us forever. I was immediately full of a desire to practice my archaics and contrive one of those stirring conversations out of my own head. I thought I would practice on Twichell. I have always practiced doubtful things on Twichell from the beginning, thirty-nine years ago.

So I contrived that meeting of the illustrious personages in Queen Elizabeth's private parlor and started a most picturesque and lurid and scandalous conversation between them. The Queen's cupbearer, a dried-up old nobleman, was present to take down the talk—not that he wanted to do it but because it was the Queen's desire and he had to. He loathed all those people because they were of offensively low birth and because they hadn't a thing to recommend them except their incomparable brains. He dutifully set down everything they said, and commented upon their words and their manners with bitter scorn and indignation. I put into the Queen's mouth, and into the mouths of those other people, grossnesses not to be found outside of Rabelais, perhaps. I made their stateliest remarks reek with them, and all this was charming to me—delightful, delicious—but their charm was as nothing to that which was afforded me by that outraged old cupbearer's comments upon them.

It is years since I have seen a copy of *1601*. I wonder if it would be as funny to me now as it was in those comparatively youthful days when I wrote it. It made a fat letter. I bundled it up and mailed it to Twichell in Hartford. And in the fall, when we returned to our home in Hartford and Twichell and I resumed the Saturday ten-mile walk to Talcott Tower and back, every Saturday, as had been our custom for years, we used to carry that letter along. There was a grove of hickory trees by the roadside, six miles out, and close by it was the only place in that whole region where the fringed gentian grew. On our return from the Tower we used to gather the gentians, then lie down on the grass upon the golden carpet of fallen hickory leaves and get out that letter and read it by the help of these poetical surroundings. We used to laugh ourselves lame and sore over the cupbearer's troubles. I wonder if we could laugh over them now? We were so young then!— and maybe there was not so much to laugh at in the letter as we thought there was.

However, in the winter Dean Sage came to Twichell's on a visit, and Twichell, who was never able to keep a secret when he knew it ought to be revealed, showed him the letter. Sage carried it off. He was greatly tickled with it himself and he wanted to know how it might affect other people. He was under the seal of confidence and could not show the letter to anyone—still he wanted to try it on a dog, as the stage phrase is, and he dropped it in the aisle of the smoking car accidentally and sat down near by to wait for results. The letter traveled from group to group around the car and when he finally went and claimed it he was convinced that it possessed literary merit. So he got a dozen copies privately printed in Brooklyn. He sent one to David Gray in Buffalo, one to a friend in Japan, one to Lord Houghton in England, and one to a Jewish Rabbi in Albany, a very learned man and an able critic and lover of old-time literatures.

1601 was privately printed in Japan and in England and by and by we began to hear from it. The learned Rabbi said it was a masterpiece in its verities and in its imitation of the obsolete English of Elizabeth's day. And the praises delivered to me by the poet, David Gray, were very precious. He said, "Put your name to it. Don't be ashamed of it. It is a great and fine piece of literature and deserves to live, and will live. Your *Innocents Abroad* will presently be forgotten, but this will survive. Don't be ashamed; don't be afraid. Leave the command in your will that your heirs shall put on your tombstone these words, and these alone: '*He wrote the immortal 1601.*'"

When we sailed for Europe in 1891 I left those sumptuous West Point copies hidden away in a drawer of my study, where I thought they would be safe. We were gone nearly ten years, and whenever anybody wanted a copy I promised it— the promise to be made good when we should return to America. In Berlin I promised one to Rudolph Lindau, of the Foreign Office. He still lives, but I have not been able to make that promise good. I promised one to Mommsen and one to William Walter Phelps, who was our Minister at the Berlin court. These are dead but maybe they don't miss *1601* where they are. When I went lecturing around the globe I promised *1601* pretty liberally, these promises all to be made good when I should return home.

In 1890 I had published in *Harper's Monthly* a sketch called "Luck," the particulars of which had been furnished to Twichell by a visiting English army chaplain. The next year, in Rome, an English gentleman introduced himself to me on the street and said, "Do you know who the chief figure in that 'Luck' sketch is?" "No," I said, "I don't." "Well," he said, "it is Lord Wolseley—and don't you go to England if you value your scalp." In Venice another English gentleman said the same to me. These gentlemen said, "Of course Wolseley is not to blame for the stupendous luck that has chased him up ever since he came shining out of Sandhurst in that most unexpected and victorious way, but he will recognize himself in that sketch, and so will everybody else, and if you venture into England he will destroy you."

In 1900, in London, I went to the Fourth of July banquet, arriving after eleven o'clock at night at a time when the place

was emptying itself. Choate was presiding. An English admiral
was speaking and some two or three hundred men were still
present. I was to speak and I moved along down behind the
chairs, which had been occupied by guests, toward Choate.
These chairs were now empty. When I had reached within
three chairs of Choate, a handsome man put out his hand
and said, "Stop. Sit down here. I want to get acquainted with
you. I am Lord Wolseley." I was falling but he caught me and
I explained that I was often taken that way. We sat and chatted together and had a very good time—and he asked me for
a copy of *1601* and I was very glad to get off so easy. I said
he should have it as soon as I reached home.

We reached home the next year and not a sign of those
precious masterpieces could be found on the premises anywhere. And so all those promises remain unfulfilled to this
day. Two or three days ago I found out that they have reap-
peared and are safe in our house in New York. But I shall not
make any of those promises good until I shall have had an opportunity to examine that masterpiece and see whether it really is a masterpiece or not. I have my doubts, though I had
none a quarter of a century ago. In that day I believed *1601*
was inspired.

A Connecticut Yankee in King Arthur's Court was an attempt to imagine, and after a fashion set forth, the hard conditions of life for the laboring and defenseless poor in bygone
times in England, and incidentally contrast these conditions
with those under which the civil and ecclesiastical pets of
privilege and high fortune lived in those times. I think I was
purposing to contrast that English life, not just the English
life of Arthur's day but the English life of the whole of the
Middle Ages, with the life of modern Christendom and modern civilization—to the advantage of the latter, of course. That
advantage is still claimable and does creditably and handsomely exist everywhere in Christendom—if we leave out Russia
and the royal palace of Belgium.

The royal palace of Belgium is still what it has been for
fourteen years, the den of a wild beast, King Leopold II, who
for money's sake mutilates, murders and starves half a million
of friendless and helpless poor natives in the Congo State
every year, and does it by the silent consent of all the Christian powers except England, none of them lifting a hand or a
voice to stop these atrocities, although thirteen of them are by

solemn treaty pledged to the protecting and uplifting of those wretched natives. In fourteen years Leopold has deliberately destroyed more lives than have suffered death on all the battle-fields of this planet for the past thousand years. In this vast statement I am well within the mark, several millions of lives within the mark. It is curious that the most advanced and most enlightened century of all the centuries the sun has looked upon should have the ghastly distinction of having pro-duced this moldy and piety-mouthing hypocrite, this bloody monster whose mate is not findable in human history any-where, and whose personality will surely shame hell itself when he arrives there—which will be soon, let us hope and trust.

The conditions under which the poor lived in the Middle Ages were hard enough, but those conditions were heaven itself as compared with those which have obtained in the Congo State for these past fourteen years. I have mentioned Russia. Cruel and pitiful as was life throughout Christendom in the Middle Ages, it was not as cruel, not as pitiful, as is life in Russia today. In Russia for three centuries the vast popula-tion has been ground under the heels, and for the sole and sordid advantage of a procession of crowned assassins and robbers who have all deserved the gallows. Russia's hundred and thirty millions of miserable subjects are much worse off today than were the poor of the Middle Ages whom we so pity. We are accustomed now to speak of Russia as medieval and as standing still in the Middle Ages, but that is flattery. Russia is way back of the Middle Ages; the Middle Ages are a long way in front of her and she is not likely to catch up with them so long as the Czardom continues to exist.

◇◇◇◇◇◇◇◇◇◇◇◇◇◇◇◇◇◇

CHAPTER 55

The western pirate of whom Duneka[1] had heard rumor has really published his book and my copyright lawyer has sent

[1] "F. A. Duneka was vice-president of Harper & Brothers, Mark Twain's pub-lishers. The allusion is to a spurious reprint of *Mark Twain's Library of Humor*, an anthology edited by Howells and Charles H. Clark under Mark's supervision and first published by Mark's own firm." (DeVoto.)

me a copy of it—a great fat, coarse, offensive volume, not with
my name on it as perpetrator but with its back inflamed with
a big picture of me in lurid colors, placed there, of course, to
indicate that I am the author of the crime. This book is a very
interesting curiosity, in one way. It reveals the surprising fact
that within the compass of these forty years wherein I have
been playing professional humorist before the public, I have
had for company seventy-eight other American humorists.
Each and every one of the seventy-eight rose in my time, became conspicuous and popular, and by and by vanished. A
number of these names were as familiar in their day as are the
names of George Ade and Dooley today—yet they have all so
completely passed from sight now that there is probably not a
youth of fifteen years of age in the country whose eye would
light with recognition at the mention of any one of the seventy-eight names.

This book is a cemetery; and as I glance through it I am reminded of my visit to the cemetery in Hannibal, Missouri,
four years ago,[2] where almost every tombstone recorded a forgotten name that had been familiar and pleasant to my ear
when I was a boy there fifty years before. In this mortuary
volume I find Nasby, Artemus Ward, Yawcob Strauss, Derby,
Burdette, Eli Perkins, the "Danbury News Man," Orpheus C.
Kerr, Smith O'Brien, Josh Billings and a score of others, maybe two score, whose writings and sayings were once in everybody's mouth but are now heard of no more and are no longer
mentioned. Seventy-eight seems an incredible crop of well-
known humorists for one forty-year period to have produced,
and yet this book has not harvested the entire crop—far from
it. It has no mention of Ike Partington, once so welcome and
so well known; it has no mention of Doesticks, nor of the Pfaff
crowd, nor of Artemus Ward's numerous and perishable imi-
tators, nor of three very popular Southern humorists whose
names I am not able to recall, nor of a dozen other sparkling
transients whose light shone for a time but has now, years ago,
gone out.

Why have they perished? Because they were merely humorists. Humorists of the "mere" sort cannot survive. Humor is
only a fragrance, a decoration. Often it is merely an odd trick
of speech and of spelling, as in the case of Ward and Billings
and Nasby and the "Disbanded Volunteer," and presently the

[2] Written July 31, 1906.

fashion passes and the fame along with it. There are those
who say a novel should be a work of art solely and you must
not preach in it, you must not teach in it. That may be true as
regards novels but it is not true as regards humor. Humor
must not professedly teach and it must not professedly preach,
but it must do both if it would live forever. By forever, I
mean thirty years. With all its preaching it is not likely to outlive so long a term as that. The very things it preaches about
and which are novelties when it preaches about them can
cease to be novelties and become commonplaces in thirty
years. Then that sermon can thenceforth interest no one.

I have always preached. That is the reason that I have
lasted thirty years. If the humor came of its own accord and
uninvited I have allowed it a place in my sermon, but I was
not writing the sermon for the sake of the humor. I should
have written the sermon just the same, whether any humor
applied for admission or not. I am saying these vain things in
this frank way because I am a dead person speaking from the
grave. Even I would be too modest to say them in life. I think
we never become really and genuinely our entire and honest
selves until we are dead—and not then until we have been
dead years and years. People ought to start dead and then
they would be honest so much earlier.

I believe that the trade of critic in literature, music and the
drama is the most degraded of all trades and that it has no
real value—certainly no large value. When Charles Dudley
Warner and I were about to bring out *The Gilded Age* the
editor of the *Daily Graphic* persuaded me to let him have an
advance copy, he giving me his word of honor that no notice
of it should appear in his paper until after the *Atlantic Monthly* notice should have appeared. This reptile published a review of the book within three days afterward. I could not
really complain, because he had only given me his word of
honor as security. I ought to have required of him something
substantial. I believe his notice did not deal mainly with the
merit of the book or the lack of it but with my moral attitude
toward the public. It was charged that I had used my reputation to play a swindle upon the public—that Mr. Warner had
written as much as half of the book and that I had used my
name to float it and give it currency—a currency which it
could not have acquired without my name—and that this con-

duct of mine was a grave fraud upon the people. The *Graphic* was not an authority upon any subject whatever. It had a sort of distinction in that it was the first and only illustrated daily newspaper that the world had seen; but it was without character, it was poorly and cheaply edited, its opinion of a book or of any other work of art was of no consequence. Everybody knew this, yet all the critics in America, one after the other, copied the *Graphic's* criticism, merely changing the phraseology, and left me under that charge of dishonest conduct. Even the great Chicago *Tribune,* the most important journal in the Middle West, was not able to invent anything fresh but adopted the view of the humble *Daily Graphic,* dishonesty charge and all. However, let it go. It is the will of God that we must have critics and missionaries and congressmen and humorists, and we must bear the burden.

What I have been traveling toward all this time is this: The first critic that ever had occasion to describe my personal appearance littered his description with foolish and inexcusable errors whose aggregate furnished the result that I was distinctly and distressingly unhandsome. That description floated around the country in the papers and was in constant use and wear for a quarter of a century. It seems strange to me that apparently no critic in the country could be found who could look at me and have the courage to take up his pen and destroy that lie. That lie began its course on the Pacific coast in 1864 and it likened me in personal appearance to Petroleum V. Nasby, who had been out there lecturing. For twenty-five years afterward, no critic could furnish a description of me without fetching in Nasby to help out my portrait. I knew Nasby well and he was a good fellow, but in my life I have not felt malignantly enough about any more than three persons to charge those persons with resembling Nasby. It hurts me to the heart, these things. To this day it hurts me to the heart and it had long been a distress to my family—including Susy—that the critics should go on making this wearisome mistake year after year, when there was no foundation for it. Even when a critic wanted to be particularly friendly and complimentary to me, he didn't dare to go beyond my clothes. He did not venture beyond that frontier. When he had finished with my clothes he had said all the kind things, the pleasant things, the complimentary things he could risk. Then he dropped back on Nasby.

Yesterday[2] I found this clipping in the pocket of one of those ancient memorandum-books of mine. It is of the date of thirty-nine years ago, and both the paper and the ink are yellow with the bitterness that I felt in that old day when I clipped it out to preserve it and brood over it and grieve about it. I will copy it here, to wit:

A correspondent of the Philadelphia *Press*, writing of one of Schuyler Colfax's receptions, says of our Washington correspondent: "Mark Twain, the delicate humorist, was present; quite a lion, as he deserves to be. Mark is a bachelor, faultless in taste, whose snowy vest is suggestive of endless quarrels with Washington washerwomen; but the heroism of Mark is settled for all time, for such purity and smoothness were never seen before. His lavender gloves might have been stolen from some Turkish harem, so delicate were they in size; but more likely—anything else were more likely than that. In form and feature he bears some resemblance to the immortal Nasby; but whilst Petroleum is brunette to the core, Twain is golden, amber-hued, melting, blonde."

<><><><><><><><><><><><><>

CHAPTER 56

I first knew Capt. Wakeman thirty-nine years ago. I made two voyages with him and we became fast friends. He was a great burly, handsome, weather-beaten, symmetrically built and powerful creature, with coal-black hair and whiskers and the kind of eye which men obey without talking back. He was full of human nature, and the best kind of human nature. He was as hearty and sympathetic and loyal and loving a soul as I have found anywhere and when his temper was up he performed all the functions of an earthquake, without the noise.

He was all sailor from head to heel; and this was proper enough, for he was born at sea; and in the course of his sixty-five years he had visited the edges of all the continents and archipelagoes, but had never been on land except incidentally

[2] Written February 7, 1906.

and spasmodically, as you may say. He had never had a day's schooling in his life but had picked up worlds and worlds of knowledge at secondhand and none of it correct. He was a liberal talker and inexhaustibly interesting. In the matter of a wide and catholic profanity he had not his peer on the planet while he lived. It was a deep pleasure to me to hear him do his stunts in this line. He knew the Bible by heart and was profoundly and sincerely religious. He was always studying the Bible when it was his watch below and always finding new things, fresh things and unexpected delights and surprises in it—and he loved to talk about his discoveries and expound them to the ignorant. He believed that he was the only man on the globe that really knew the secret of the Biblical miracles. He had what he believed was a sane and rational explanation of every one of them and he loved to teach his learning to the less fortunate.

I have said a good deal about him in my books. In one of them I have told how he brought the murderer of his colored mate to trial in the Chincha Islands before the assembled captains of the ships in port, and how when sentence had been passed he drew the line there. He had intended to capture and execute the murderer all by himself but had been persuaded by the captains to let them try him with the due formalities and under the forms of law. He had yielded that much, though most reluctantly, but when the captains proposed to do the executing also, that was too much for Wakeman and he struck. He hanged the man. himself. He put the noose around the murderer's neck, threw the bight of the line over the limb of a tree, and made his last moments a misery to him by reading him nearly into premature death with random and irrelevant chapters from the Bible.

He was a most winning and delightful creature. When he was fifty-three years old he started from a New England port, master of a great clipper ship bound around the Horn for San Francisco, and he was not aware that he had a passenger but he was mistaken as to that. He had never had a love passage but he was to have one now. When he was out from port a few weeks he was prowling about some remote corner of his ship, by way of inspection, when he came across a beautiful girl, twenty-four or twenty-five years old, prettily clothed and lying asleep with one plump arm under her neck. He stopped in his tracks and stood and gazed, enchanted. Then he said, "It's an angel—that's what it is. It's an angel. When it opens its eyes if they are blue I'll marry it."

The eyes turned out to be blue and the pair were married when they reached San Francisco. The girl was to have taught school there. She had her appointment in her pocket—but the Captain saw to it that that arrangement did not materialize. He built a little house in Oakland—ostensibly a house, but really it was a ship, and had all a ship's appointments, binnacle, scuppers and everything else—and there he and his little wife lived an ideal life during the intervals that intervened between his voyages. They were a devoted pair and worshiped each other. By and by there were two little girls and then the nautical paradise was complete.

Captain Wakeman had a fine large imagination and he once told me of a visit which he had made to heaven. I kept it in my mind and a month or two later I put it on paper—this was in the first quarter of 1868, I think. It made a small book of about forty thousand words and I called it *Captain Stormfield's Visit to Heaven.* Five or six years afterward I showed the manuscript to Howells and he said, "Publish it."

But I didn't. I had turned it into a burlesque of *The Gates Ajar*, a book which had imagined a mean little ten-cent heaven about the size of Rhode Island—a heaven large enough to accommodate about a tenth of one per cent of the Christian billions who had died in the past nineteen centuries. I raised the limit; I built a properly and rationally stupendous heaven and augmented its Christian population to ten per cent of the contents of the modern cemeteries; also, as a volunteer kindness I let in a tenth of one per cent of the pagans who had died during the preceding eons—a liberty which was not justifiable because those people had no business there, but as I had merely done it in pity and out of kindness I allowed them to stay. Toward the end of the book my heaven grew to such inconceivable dimensions on my hands that I ceased to apply poor little million-mile measurements to its mighty territories and measured them by light-years only! and not only that, but a million of them linked together in a stretch.[1]

In the thirty-eight years which have since elapsed I have taken out that rusty old manuscript several times and ex-

[1] Light-year. This is without doubt the most stupendous and impressive phrase that exists in any language. It is restricted to astronomy. It describes the distance which light, moving at the rate of 186,000 miles per second, travels in our year of 52 weeks. (M.T.)

amined it with the idea of printing it, but I always concluded to let it rest. However, I mean to put it into this autobiography now.[2] It is not likely to see the light for fifty years yet, and at that time I shall have been so long under the sod that I shan't care about the results.[3]

I used to talk to Twichell about Wakeman, there in Hartford thirty years ago and more, and by and by a curious thing happened: Twichell went off on a vacation and as usual he followed his vacation custom, that is to say he traveled under an alias so that he could associate with all kinds of disreputable characters and have a good time and nobody be embarrassed by his presence, since they wouldn't know that he was a clergyman. He took a Pacific mail ship and started south for the Isthmus. Passenger traffic in that line had ceased almost entirely. Twichell found but one other passenger on board. He noticed that that other passenger was not a saint, so he went to foregathering with him at once, of course. After that passenger had delivered himself of about six majestically and picturesquely profane remarks Twichell (alias Peters) said, "Could it be, by chance, that you are Captain Ned Wakeman of San Francisco?"

His guess was right and the two men were inseparable during the rest of the voyage. One day Wakeman asked Peters-Twichell if he had ever read the Bible. Twichell said a number of things in reply, things of a rambling and noncommittal character, but, taken in the sum, they left the impression that Twichell—well, never mind the impression; suffice it that Wakeman set himself the task of persuading Twichell to read that book. He also set himself the task of teaching Twichell how to understand the miracles. He expounded to him, among other miracles, the adventure of Isaac with the prophets of Baal. Twichell could have told him that it wasn't Isaac, but that wasn't Twichell's game and he didn't make the correction. It was a delicious story and it is delightful to hear Twichell tell it. I have printed it in full in one of my books—I don't remember which one.

---

[2] *Three hours later.* I have just burned the closing two-thirds of it. (M.T.) He did not burn any of it. (C.N.)

[3] He changed his mind a year later and published *An Extract from Captain Stormfield's Visit to Heaven* first in *Harper's* for December, 1907, and January, 1908, and then as a book. He did not publish all of it.

CHAPTER 57

I believe that our Heavenly Father invented man because he was disappointed in the monkey. I believe that whenever a human being, of even the highest intelligence and culture, delivers an opinion upon a matter apart from his particular and especial line of interest, training and experience, it will always be an opinion of so foolish and so valueless a sort that it can be depended upon to suggest to our Heavenly Father that the human being is another disappointment and that he is no considerable improvement upon the monkey. Congresses and Parliaments are not made up of authors and publishers but of lawyers, agriculturists, merchants, manufacturers, bankers and so on. When bills are proposed affecting these great industries they get prompt and intelligent attention, because there are so many members of the lawmaking bodies who are personally and profoundly interested in these things and ready to rise up and fight for or against them with their best strength and energy. These bills are discussed and explained by men who know all about the interests involved in them; men recognized as being competent to explain and discuss and furnish authoritative information to the ignorant.

As a result, perhaps no important American or English statutes are uncompromisingly and hopelessly idiotic except the copyright statutes of these two countries. The Congresses and the Parliaments are always, and must always remain, in the condition of the British Parliaments of seventy-five and eighty years ago, when they were called upon to legislate upon a matter which was absolutely new to the whole body of them and concerning which they were as strictly and comprehensively ignorant as the unborn child is of theology and copyright.

There were no railroad men in those Parliaments; the members had to inform themselves through the statements made to them by Stephenson, and they considered him a visionary, a half-lunatic, possibly even ass and poet. Through lack of previous knowledge and experience of railway matters, they were unable to understand Stephenson. His explanations, so simple to himself, were but a fog to those well-meaning legislators; so far as they were concerned, he was talking riddles, and riddles which seemed to be meaningless, riddles which seemed also to be dreams and insanities. Still, being gentlemen and kindly and humane, they listened to Stephenson patiently, benevolently, charitably, until at last, in a burst of irritation, he lost his prudence and proclaimed that he would yet prove to the world that he could drive a steam locomotive over iron rails at the impossible speed of twelve miles an hour! That finished him. After that the lawmakers imposed upon themselves no further polite reserves but called him, frankly, a dreamer, a crank, a lunatic.

Copyright has always had to face what Stephenson faced, bodies of lawmakers absolutely ignorant of the matter they were called upon to legislate about, also absolutely unteachable in the circumstances and bound to remain so—themselves and their successors—until a day when they shall be stockholders in publishing houses and personally interested in finding out something about authorship and the book trade—a day which is not at all likely to arrive during the term of the present geological epoch.

Authors sometimes understand their side of the question but this is rare; none of them understands the publisher's side of it. A man must be both author and publisher, and experienced in the scorching griefs and trials of both industries, before he is competent to go before a Copyright Committee of Parliament or Congress and afford it information of any considerable value. A thousand, possibly ten thousand, valuable speeches have been made in Congresses and Parliaments upon great corporation interests, for the men who made them had been competently equipped by personal suffering and experience to treat those great matters intelligently; but so far as I know, no publisher of great authority has ever sat in a lawmaking body and made a speech in his trade's interest that was worth remembering or that has been remembered. So far as I know, only one author has ever made a memorable speech before a lawmaking body in the interest of his trade—that was Macaulay. I think his speech is called great to this day by both authors and publishers; whereas the speech is so exhaustively ignorant of its subject and so trivial and jejune in its reasonings that to the person who has been both author and publisher it ranks as another and formidable evidence, and possibly even proof, that in discarding the monkey and substituting man, our Father in Heaven did the monkey an undeserved injustice.

Consider a simple example. If you could prove that only twenty idiots are born in a century and that each of them, by special genius, was able to make an article of commerce which no one else could make; and which was able to furnish the idiot and his descendants after him an income sufficient for the modest and economical support of half a dozen persons, there is no Congress and no Parliament in all Christendom that would dream of descending to the shabbiness of limiting that trifling income to a term of years, in order that it might be enjoyed thereafter by persons who had no sort of claim upon it. I know that this would happen because all Congresses and Parliaments have a kindly feeling for idiots and a compassion for them, on account of personal experience and heredity. Neither England nor America has been able to produce in a century any more than twenty authors whose books have been able to outlive the copyright limit of forty-two years,[1] yet the Congresses and the Parliaments stick to the forty-two-year limit greedily, intensely, pathetically, and do seem to believe by some kind of insane reasoning that somebody is in some way benefited by this trivial robbery inflicted upon the families of twenty authors in the course of a hundred years. The most uncompromising and unlimited stupidity can invent nothing stupider than this; not even the monkey can get down to its level.

In a century we have produced two hundred and twenty thousand books; not a bathtub-full of them are still alive and marketable. The case would have been the same if the copyright limit had been a thousand years. It would be entirely safe to make it a thousand years and it would also be properly respectable and courteous to do it.

When I was in London seven years ago[2] I was haled before the Copyright Committee of the House of Lords, who were considering a bill to add eight entire years to the copyright limit and make it fifty. One of the ablest men in the House of Lords did the most of the question asking—Lord Thring—but he seemed to me to be a most striking example of how

---

[1] At present (1959), fifty-six years.
[2] Written in 1906.

unintelligent a human being can be when he sets out to discuss a matter about which he has had no personal training and no personal experience.

There was a long talk, but I wish to confine myself to a single detail of it. Lord Thring asked me what I thought would be a fair and just copyright limit. I said a million years—that is to say, copyright in perpetuity. The answer seemed to outrage him; it quite plainly irritated him. He asked me if I was not aware of the fact that it had long ago been decided that there could be no property in ideas and that as a book consisted merely of ideas it was not entitled to rank as property or enjoy the protections extended to property. I said I was aware that somebody, at some time or other, had given birth to that astonishing superstition and that an ostensibly intelligent human race had accepted it with enthusiasm, without taking the trouble to examine it and find out that it was an empty inspiration and not entitled to respect. I added that in spite of its being regarded as a fact and also well charged with wisdom, it had not been respected by any Parliament or Congress since Queen Anne's time; that in her day, and the changing of perpetual copyright to a limited copyright of fourteen years, its claim as property was *recognized;* that the retaining of a limit of any kind—of even fourteen years, for instance—was a recognition of the fact that the ideas of which a book consisted were property.

Lord Thring was not affected by these reasonings—certainly he was not convinced. He said that the fact remained that a book, being merely a collocation of ideas, was not in any sense property and that no book was entitled to perpetual existence as property, or would ever receive that grace at the hands of a legislature entrusted with the interests and well-being of the nation.

I said I should be obliged to take issue with that statement, for the reason that perpetual copyright was already existent in England, and had been granted by a Parliament or Parliaments entrusted with the duty of protecting the interests and well-being of the nation. He asked for the evidence of this and I said that the New and Old Testaments had been granted perpetual copyright in England and that several other religious books had also been granted perpetual copyright in England, and that these perpetual copyrights were not enjoyed by the hungry widows and children of poor authors but were the property of the press of Oxford University, an institution quite well able to live without this charitable favoritism. I was vain of this unanswerable hit but I concealed it.

With the gentleness and modesty which were born in me, I then went on and pleaded against the assumption that a book is not properly property because it is founded upon ideas and is built of ideas from its cellar to its roof. I said it would not be possible for anybody to mention to me a piece of property of any kind which was not based in the same way and built from cellar to roof out of just that same material, ideas.

Lord Thring suggested real estate. I said there was not a foot of real estate on the globe whose value, if it had any, was not the result of ideas and of nothing except ideas. I could have given him a million instances. I could have said that if a man should take an ignorant and useless dog and train him to be a good setter, or a good shepherd dog, the dog would now be more or less valuable property and would be salable at a more or less profitable figure, and that this acquired value would be merely the result of an idea practically and intelligently applied—the idea of making valuable a dog that had previously possessed no value. I could have said that the smoothing iron, the washtub, the shingle or the slate for a roof, the invention of clothing and all the improvements that the ages have added, were all the results of men's thinkings and men's application of ideas; that but for these ideas these properties would not have existed; that in all cases they owe their existence to ideas and that in this way they become property and valuable.

I could have said that but for those inspirations called ideas there would be no railways, no telegraphs, no printing press, no phonographs, no telephones—no anything in the whole earth that is called property and has a value. I did say that that holy thing, real estate, that sacred thing which enjoys perpetual copyright everywhere, is like all other properties —its value is born of an idea, and every time that that value is increased it is because of the application of further ideas to it and for no other reason.

I said that if by chance there were a company of twenty white men camping in the middle of Africa, it could easily happen that while all of the twenty realized that there was not an acre of ground in the whole vast landscape in view at the time that possessed even the value of a discarded oyster can, it could also happen that there could be one man in that company equipped with ideas, a far-seeing man who could

perceive that at some distant day a railway would pass through
this region and that this camping ground would infallibly
become the site of a prosperous city, of flourishing industries.
It could easily happen that that man would be bright enough
to gather together the black chiefs of the tribes of that region
and buy that whole district for a dozen rifles and a barrel of
whisky, and go home and lay the deeds away for the eventual
vast profit of his children. It could easily come true that in
time that city would be built and that land made valuable
beyond imagination and the man's children rich beyond their
wildest dreams, and that this shining result would proceed
from that man's idea and from no other source; that if there
were any real justice in the world the idea in a book would
rank breast to breast with the ideas which created value
for real estate and all other properties in the earth, and then
it would be recognized that an author's children are fairly entitled to the results of his ideas, as are the children of any
brewer in England, or of any owner of houses and lands and
perpetual-copyright Bibles.

CHAPTER 58

There is one great trouble about dictating an autobiography
and that is the multiplicity of texts that offer themselves when
you sit down and let your mouth fall open and are ready to
begin. Sometimes the texts come flooding from twenty directions at once and for a time you are overwhelmed with this
Niagara and submerged and suffocated under it. You can use
only one text at a time and you don't know which one to
choose out of the twenty—still you must choose; there is no
help for it; and you choose with the understanding that the
nineteen left over are probably left over for good, and lost,
since they may never suggest themselves again. But this time
a text is forced upon me. This is mainly because it is the
latest one that has suggested itself in the last quarter of an
hour, and therefore the warmest one, because it has not had
a chance to cool off yet. It is a couple of amateur literary
offerings. From old experience I know that amateur produc-
tions, offered ostensibly for one's honest cold judgment, to

be followed by an uncompromisingly sincere verdict, are not really offered in that spirit at all. The thing really wanted and expected is compliment and encouragement. Also, my experience has taught me that in almost all amateur cases compliment and encouragement are impossible—if they are to be backed by sincerity.

I have this moment finished reading this morning's pair of offerings and am a little troubled. If they had come from strangers I should not have given myself the pain of reading them, but should have returned them unread, according to my custom, upon the plea that I lack an editor's training and therefore am not qualified to sit in judgment upon any one's literature but my own. But this morning's harvest came from friends and that alters the case. I have read them and the result is as usual: they are not literature. They do contain meat but the meat is only half cooked. The meat is certainly there and if it could pass through the hands of an expert cook the result would be a very satisfactory dish indeed. One of this morning's samples does really come near to being literature, but the amateur hand is exposed with a fatal frequency and the exposure spoils it. The author's idea is, in case I shall render a favorable verdict, to offer the manuscript to a magazine.

There is something about this naïve intrepidity that compels admiration. It is a lofty and reckless daring which I suppose is exhibited in no field but one—the field of literature. We see something approaching it in war, but approaching it only distantly. The untrained common soldier has often offered himself as one of a forlorn hope and stood cheerfully ready to encounter all its perils—but we draw the line there. Not even the most confident untrained soldier offers himself as a candidate for a brigadier-generalship, yet this is what the amateur author does. With his untrained pen he puts together his crudities and offers them to all the magazines, one after the other—that is to say, he proposes them for posts restricted to literary generals who have earned their rank and place by years and even decades of hard and honest training in the lower grades of the service.

I am sure that this affront is offered to no trade but ours. A person untrained to shoemaking does not offer his services as a shoemaker to the foreman of a shop—not even the crudest literary aspirant would be so unintelligent as to do that. He would see the humor of it; he would see the impertinence of it; he would recognize as the most commonplace of facts that an apprenticeship is necessary in order to qualify a person to be tinner, bricklayer, stonemason, printer, horse doctor, butcher, brakeman, car conductor, midwife—and any and every other occupation whereby a human being acquires bread and fame. But when it comes to doing literature, his wisdoms vanish all of a sudden and he thinks he finds himself now in the presence of a profession which requires no apprenticeship, no experience, no training—nothing whatever but conscious talent and a lion's courage.

We do not realize how strange and curious a thing this is until we look around for an object lesson whereby to realize it to us. We must imagine a kindred case—the aspirant to operatic distinction and cash, for instance. The aspirant applies to the management for a billet as second tenor. The management accepts him, arranges the terms and puts him on the payroll. Understand, this is an imaginary case; I am not pretending that it has happened. Let us proceed.

After the first act the manager calls the second tenor to account and wants to know. He says:

"Have you ever studied music?"

"A little—yes, by myself, at odd times, for amusement."

"You have never gone into regular and laborious training, then, for the opera, under the masters of the art?"

"No."

"Then what made you think you could do second tenor in Lohengrin?"

"I thought I could. I wanted to try. I seemed to have a voice."

"Yes, you have a voice, and with five years of diligent training under competent masters you could be successful, perhaps, but I assure you you are not ready for second tenor yet. You have a voice; you have presence; you have a noble and childlike confidence; you have a courage that is stupendous and even superhuman. These are all essentials and they are in your favor but there are other essentials in this great trade which you still lack. If you can't afford the time and labor necessary to acquire them leave opera alone and try something which does not require training and experience. Go away now and try for a job in surgery."

CHAPTER 59

This morning's[1] cables contain a verse or two from Kipling, voicing his protest against a liberalizing new policy of the British government which he fears will deliver the balance of power in South Africa into the hands of the conquered Boers. Kipling's name and Kipling's words always stir me now, stir me more than do any other living man's. But I remember a time, seventeen or eighteen years back, when the name did not suggest anything to me and only the words moved me. At that time Kipling's name was beginning to be known here and there in spots in India, but had not traveled outside of that empire. He came over and traveled about America, maintaining himself by correspondence with Indian journals. He wrote dashing, free-handed, brilliant letters but no one outside of India knew about it.

On his way through the State of New York he stopped off at Elmira and made a tedious and blistering journey up to Quarry Farm in quest of me. He ought to have telephoned the farm first; then he would have learned that I was at the Langdon homestead, hardly a quarter of a mile from his hotel. But he was only a lad of twenty-four and properly impulsive and he set out without inquiring on that dusty and roasting journey up the hill. He found Susy Crane and my little Susy there and they came as near making him comfortable as the weather and the circumstances would permit.

The group sat on the veranda and while Kipling rested and refreshed himself he refreshed the others with his talk, talk of a quality which was well above what they were accustomed to, talk which might be likened to footprints, so strong and definite was the impression which it left behind. They often spoke wonderingly of Kipling's talk afterward and they recognized that they had been in contact with an extraordinary man, but it is more than likely that they were the only persons who had perceived that he was extraordinary. It is not likely

[1] Written August 11, 1906.

that they perceived his full magnitude, it is most likely that they were Eric Ericsons who had discovered a continent but did not suspect the horizonless extent of it. His was an unknown name and was to remain unknown for a year yet, but Susy kept his card and treasured it as an interesting possession. Its address was Allahabad.

No doubt India had been to her an imaginary land up to this time, a fairyland, a dreamland, a land made out of poetry and moonlight for the Arabian Nights to do their gorgeous miracles in; and doubtless Kipling's flesh and blood and modern clothes realized it to her for the first time and solidified it. I think so because she more than once remarked upon its incredible remoteness from the world that we were living in, and computed that remoteness and pronounced the result with a sort of awe, fourteen thousand miles, or sixteen thousand, whichever it was. Kipling had written upon the card a compliment to me. This gave the card an additional value in Susy's eyes, since as a distinction it was the next thing to being recognized by a denizen of the moon.

Kipling came down that afternoon and spent a couple of hours with me, and at the end of that time I had surprised him as much as he had surprised me, and the honors were easy. I believed that he knew more than any person I had met before, and I knew that he knew I knew less than any person he had met before—though he did not say it and I was not expecting that he would. When he was gone, Mrs. Langdon wanted to know about my visitor. I said, "He is a stranger to me but he is a most remarkable man—and I am the other one. Between us, we cover all knowledge; he knows all that can be known and I know the rest."

He was a stranger to me and to all the world and remained so for twelve months, then he became suddenly known and universally known. From that day to this he has held this unique distinction: that of being the only living person, not head of a nation, whose voice is heard around the world the moment it drops a remark, the only such voice in existence that does not go by slow ship and rail but always travels first-class by cable.

About a year after Kipling's visit in Elmira, George Warner came into our library one morning in Hartford with a small book in his hand and asked me if I had ever heard of Rudyard Kipling. I said, "No."

He said I would hear of him very soon and that the noise he was going to make would be loud and continuous. The little book was the *Plain Tales* and he left it for me to read, saying it was charged with a new and inspiriting fragrance and would blow a refreshing breath around the world that would revive the nations. A day or two later he brought a copy of the London *World,* which had a sketch of Kipling in it and a mention of the fact that he had traveled in the United States. According to this sketch he had passed through Elmira. This remark, added to the additional fact that he hailed from India, attracted my attention—also Susy's. She went to her room and brought his card from its place in the frame of her mirror, and the Quarry Farm visitor stood identified.

I am not acquainted with my own books but I know Kipling's—at any rate I know them better than I know anybody else's books. They never grow pale to me; they keep their color; they are always fresh. Certain of the ballads have a peculiar and satisfying charm for me. To my mind, the incomparable Jungle Books must remain unfellowed permanently. I think it was worth the journey to India to qualify myself to read *Kim* understandingly and to realize how great a book it is. The deep and subtle and fascinating charm of India pervades no other book as it pervades *Kim; Kim* is pervaded by it as by an atmosphere. I read the book every year and in this way I go back to India without fatigue—the only foreign land I ever daydream about or deeply long to see again.

It was on a bench in Washington Square that I saw the most of Louis Stevenson. It was an outing that lasted an hour or more and was very pleasant and sociable. I had come with him from his house, where I had been paying my respects to his family. His business in the square was to absorb the sunshine. He was most scantily furnished with flesh, his clothes seemed to fall into hollows as if there might be nothing inside but the frame for a sculptor's statue. His long face and lank hair and dark complexion and musing and melancholy expression seemed to fit these details justly and harmoniously, and the altogether of it seemed especially planned to gather the rags of your observation and focalize them upon Stevenson's special distinction and commanding feature, his splendid eyes. They burned with a smoldering rich fire under the penthouse of his brows and they made him beautiful.

I said I thought he was right about the others, but mistaken as to Bret Harte; in substance I said that Harte was good company and a thin but pleasant talker; that he was always bright but never brilliant; that in this matter he must not be classed with Thomas Bailey Aldrich, nor must any other man, ancient or modern; that Aldrich was always witty, always brilliant, if there was anybody present capable of striking his flint at the right angle; that Aldrich was as sure and prompt and unfailing as the red-hot iron on the blacksmith's anvil—you had only to hit it competently to make it deliver an explosion of sparks. I added:

"Aldrich has never had his peer for prompt and pithy and witty and humorous sayings. None has equaled him, certainly none has surpassed him, in the felicity of phrasing with which he clothed these children of his fancy. Aldrich was always brilliant, he couldn't help it; he is a fire opal set round with rose diamonds; when he is not speaking, you know that his dainty fancies are twinkling and glimmering around in him; when he speaks the diamonds flash. Yes, he was always brilliant; he will always be brilliant; he will be brilliant in hell—you will see."

Stevenson, smiling a chuckly smile, "I hope not."

"Well, you will, and he will dim even those ruddy fires and look like a blond Venus backed against a pink sunset."

There on that bench we struck out a new phrase—one, or the other of us, I don't remember which—"submerged renown." Variations were discussed: submerged fame, submerged reputation and so on, and a choice was made; submerged renown was elected, I believe. This important matter rose out of an incident which had been happening to Stevenson in Albany. While in a bookshop or bookstall there he had noticed a long rank of small books cheaply but neatly gotten up and bearing such titles as *Davis's Selected Speeches*, *Davis's Selected Poetry*, Davis's this and Davis's that and Davis's the other thing; compilations every one of them, each with a brief, compact, intelligent and useful introductory chapter by this same Davis, whose first name I have forgotten. Stevenson had begun the matter with this question:

"Can you name the American author whose fame and acceptance stretch widest and furthest in the States?"

I thought I could but it did not seem to me that it would be modest to speak out, in the circumstances. So I diffidently said nothing. Stevenson noticed and said:

"Save your delicacy for another time—you are not the one.

For a shilling you can't name the American author of widest note and popularity in the States. But I can."

Then he went on and told about that Albany incident. He had inquired of the shopman, "Who is this Davis?"

The answer was, "An author whose books have to have freight trains to carry them, not baskets. Apparently you have not heard of him?"

Stevenson said no, this was the first time. The man said: "Nobody has heard of Davis; you may ask all round and you will see. You never see his name mentioned in print, not even in advertisements; these things are of no use to Davis, not any more than they are to the wind and the sea. You never see one of Davis's books floating on top of the United States, but put on your diving armor and get yourself lowered away down and down and down till you strike the dense region, the sunless region of eternal drudgery and starvation wages—there you will find them by the million. The man that gets that market, his fortune is made, his bread and butter are safe, for those people will never go back on him. An author may have a reputation which is confined to the surface and lose it and become pitied, then despised, then forgotten, entirely forgotten—the frequent steps in a surface reputation. A surface reputation, however great, is always mortal and always killable if you go at it right—with pins and needles and quiet slow poison, not with the club and the tomahawk. But it is a different matter with the submerged reputation—down in the deep water; once a favorite there, always a favorite; once beloved, always beloved; once respected, always respected, honored and believed in. For what the reviewer says never finds its way down into those placid deeps, nor the newspaper sneers, nor any breath of the winds of slander blowing above. Down there they never hear of these things. Their idol may be painted clay, up there at the surface, and fade and waste and crumble and blow away, there being much weather there; but down below he is gold and adamant and indestructible."

CHAPTER 60

Murat Halstead is dead.[1] He was a most likable man. He lived to be not far short of eighty and he devoted about sixty years to diligent, hard slaving at editorial work. His life and mine make a curious contrast. From the time that my father died, March 24, 1847, when I was past eleven years old, until the end of 1856, or the first days of 1857, I worked—not diligently, not willingly, but fretfully, lazily, repiningly, complainingly, disgustedly, and always shirking the work when I was not watched. The statistics show that I was a worker during about ten years. I am approaching seventy-three and I believe I have never done any work since—unless I may call two or three years of lazy effort as reporter on the Pacific Coast by that large and honorable name—and so I think I am substantially right in saying that when I escaped from the printing office fifty or fifty-one years ago I ceased to be a worker and ceased permanently.

Piloting on the Mississippi River was not work to me; it was play—delightful play, vigorous play, adventurous play—and I loved it; silver mining in the Humboldt Mountains was play, only play, because I did not do any of the work; my pleasant comrades did it and I sat by and admired; my silver mining in Esmeralda was not work, for Higbie and Robert Howland did it and again I sat by and admired. I accepted a job of shoveling tailings in a quartz mill there, and that was really work and I had to do it myself, but I retired from that industry at the end of two weeks, and not only with my own approval but with the approval of the people who paid the wages. These mining experiences occupied ten months and came to an end toward the close of September, 1862.

I then became a reporter in Virginia City, Nevada, and later in San Francisco, and after something more than two years of this salaried indolence I retired from my position on the *Morning Call*, by solicitation. Solicitation of the proprietor.

[1] Written July 7, 1908.

Then I acted as San Franciscan correspondent of the Virginia City *Enterprise* for two or three months; next I spent three months in pocket-mining at Jackass Gulch with the Gillis boys; then I went to the Sandwich Islands and corresponded thence for the Sacramento *Union* five or six months; in October, 1866, I broke out as a lecturer, and from that day to this I have always been able to gain my living without doing any work; for the writing of books and magazine matter was always play, not work. I enjoyed it; it was merely billiards to me.

I wonder why Murat Halstead was condemned to sixty years of editorial slavery and I let off with a lifetime of delightful idleness. There seems to be something most unfair about this—something not justifiable. But it seems to be a law of the human constitution that those that deserve shall not have and those that do not deserve shall get everything that is worth having. It is a sufficiently crazy arrangement, it seems to me.

On the 10th of April, a little more than thirty years ago, I sailed for Germany in the steamer *Holsatia* with my little family—at least we got ready to sail, but at the last moment concluded to remain at our anchorage in the Bay to see what the weather was going to be. A great many people came down in a tug to say good-by to the passengers, and at dark, when we had concluded to go to sea, they left us.

When the tug was gone it was found that Murat Halstead was still with us; he had come to say good-by to his wife and daughter; he had to remain with us, there was no alternative. We presently went to sea. Halstead had no clothing with him except what he had on, and there was a fourteen-day voyage in front of him. By happy fortune there was one man on board who was as big as Halstead, and only that one man; he could get into that man's clothes but not into any other man's in that company. That lucky accident was Bayard Taylor; he was an unusually large man and just the size of Halstead and he had an abundance of clothes and was glad to share them with Halstead, who was a close friend of his of long standing.

Toward midnight I was in the smoking cabin with them and then a curious fact came out; they had not met for ten years and each was surprised to see the other looking so bulky and hearty and so rich in health; each had for years been expecting to hear of the other's death; for when they had last parted both had received death sentences at the hands of the physician. Heart disease in both cases, with death certain within two years. Both were required to lead a quiet life, walk and not run, climb no stairs when not obliged to do it, and above all things avoid surprises and sudden excitements, if possible. They understood that a single sudden and violent excitement would be quite sufficient for their needs and would promptly end their days, and so for ten years these men had been creeping and never trotting nor running; they had climbed stairs at gravel-train speed only and they had avoided excitements diligently and constantly—and all that time they were as hearty as a pair of elephants and could not understand why they continued to live.

Then something happened. And it happened to both at about the same time. The thing that happened was a sudden and violent surprise followed immediately by another surprise—surprise that they didn't fall dead in their tracks. These surprises happened about a week before the *Holsatia* sailed. Halstead was editor and proprietor of the Cincinnati *Commercial* and was sitting at his editorial desk at midnight, high up in the building, when a mighty explosion occurred close by which rocked the building to its foundations and shivered all its glass, and before Halstead had time to reflect and not let the explosion excite him, he had sailed down six flights of stairs in thirty-five seconds and was standing panting in the street trying to say, "Thy will be done," and deadly afraid that that was what was going to happen. But nothing happened, and from that time forth he had been an emancipated man, and now for a whole week had been making up for ten years' lost time, hunting for excitements and devouring them like a famished person.

Bayard Taylor's experience had been of the like character. He turned a corner in the country and crossed a railway track just in time for an express train to nip a corner off the seat of his breeches and blow him into the next county by compulsion of the hurricane produced by the onrush of the train. He mourned and lamented, thinking that the fatal surprise had come at last; then he put his hand on his heart and got another surprise, for he found that it was still beating. He rose up and dusted himself off and became jubilant and gave praise and went off like Halstead to hunt up some more excitements and make up for ten years' lost time.

Bayard Taylor was on his way to Berlin as our new minister to Germany; he was a genial, lovable, simple-hearted soul, and as happy in his new dignity as ever a new plenipotentiary was since the world began. He was a poet and had written voluminously in verse and had also made the best of all English translations of Goethe's "Faust." But all his poetry is forgotten now except two very fine songs, one about the Scotch soldiers singing "Annie Laurie" in the trenches before Sebastopol, and the other the tremendously inspiriting love song of an Arab lover to his sweetheart. No one has gathered together his odds and ends and started a memorial museum with them, and if he is still able to think and reflect he is glad of it.

He had a prodigious memory and one night while we were walking the deck he undertook to call up out of the deeps of his mind a yard-long list of queer and quaint and unrelated words which he had learned, as a boy, by reading the list twice over, for a prize, and had easily won it for the reason that the other competitors after studying the list an hour were not able to recite it without making mistakes. Taylor said he had not thought of that list since that time, but was sure he could reproduce it after half an hour's digging in his mind. We walked the deck in silence during the half hour, then he began with the first word and sailed glibly through without a halt and also without a mistake, he said.

He had a Negro manservant with him who came on board dressed up in the latest agony of the fashion and looking as fine as a rainbow; then he disappeared and we never saw him again for ten or twelve days; then he came on deck drooping and meek, subdued, subjugated, the most completely wilted and disreputable looking flower that was ever seen outside of a conservatory, or inside of it either. The mystery was soon explained. The sea had gotten his works out of order the first day on board and he went to the ship's doctor to acquire a purge. The doctor gave him fourteen large pills and told him, in German, to take one every three hours till he found relief; but he didn't understand German, so he took the whole fourteen at one dose, with the result above recorded.

CHAPTER 61

In the early days I liked Bret Harte and so did the others, but by and by I got over it; so also did the others. He couldn't keep a friend permanently. He was bad, distinctly bad; he had no feeling and he had no conscience. His wife was all that a good woman, a good wife, a good mother and a good friend can be; but when he went to Europe as consul he left her and his little children behind and never came back again from that time until his death twenty-six years later.

He was an incorrigible borrower of money; he borrowed from all his friends; if he ever repaid a loan the incident failed to pass into history. He was always ready to give his note but the matter ended there. We sailed for Europe on the 10th of April, 1878, and on the preceding night there was a banquet to Bayard Taylor, who was going out in the same ship as our minister to Germany. At that dinner I met a gentleman whose society I found delightful, and we became very friendly and communicative. He fell to talking about Bret Harte and it soon appeared that he had a grievance against him. He had so admired Harte's writings that he had greatly desired to know Harte himself.

The acquaintanceship was achieved and the borrowing began. The man was rich and he lent gladly. Harte always gave his note, and of his own motion, for it was not required of him. Harte had then been in the East about eight years and these borrowings had been going on during several of those years; in the aggregate they amounted to about three thousand dollars. The man told me that Harte's notes were a distress to him, because he supposed that they were a distress to Harte.

Then he had what he thought was a happy idea: he compacted the notes into a bale and sent them to Harte on the 24th of December '77 as a Christmas present; and with them he sent a note begging Harte to allow him this privilege because of the warm and kind and brotherly feeling which

prompted it. Per next day's mail Harte fired the bale back
at him, accompanying it with a letter which was all afire
with insulted dignity and which formally and by irrevocable
edict permanently annulled the existing friendship. But there
was nothing in it about paying the notes sometime or other.

When Harte made his spectacular progress across the
continent in 1870 he took up his residence at Newport,
Rhode Island, that breeding place—that stud farm, so to
speak—of aristocracy; aristocracy of the American type; that
auction mart where the English nobilities come to trade
hereditary titles for American girls and cash. Within a
twelvemonth he had spent his ten thousand dollars and he
shortly thereafter left Newport, in debt to the butcher, the
baker and the rest, and took up his residence with his wife
and his little children in New York. I will remark that during
Harte's sojourns in Newport and Cohasset he constantly went
to dinners among the fashionables where he was the only
male guest whose wife had not been invited. There are some
harsh terms in our language but I am not acquainted with any
that is harsh enough to properly characterize a husband
who will act like that.

When Harte had been living in New York two or three
months he came to Hartford and stopped over night with us.
He said he was without money and without a prospect; that
he owed the New York butcher and baker two hundred and
fifty dollars and could get no further credit from them; also
he was in debt for his rent, and his landlord was threatening
to turn his little family into the street. He had come to me
to ask for a loan of two hundred and fifty dollars. I said that
that would relieve only the butcher and baker part of the
situation, with the landlord still hanging over him; he would
better accept five hundred, which he did. He employed the
rest of his visit in delivering himself of sparkling sarcasms
about our house, our furniture and the rest of our domestic
arrangements.

Howells was saying yesterday[1] that Harte was one of the
most delightful persons he had ever met and one of the wit-
tiest. He said that there was a charm about him that made a
person forget, for the time being, his meannesses, his shabbi-
nesses and his dishonesties, and almost forgive them. Howells
is right about Harte's bright wit but he had probably never

[1] Written February 4, 1907.

made a search into the character of it. The character of it spoiled it; it possessed no breadth and no variety; it consisted solely of sneers and sarcasms; when there was nothing to sneer at, Harte did not flash and sparkle and was not more entertaining than the rest of us.

Once he wrote a play with a perfectly delightful Chinese in it—a play which would have succeeded if anyone else had written it; but Harte had earned the enmity of the New York dramatic critics by freely and frequently charging them with being persons who never said a favorable thing about a new play except when the favorable thing was bought and paid for beforehand. The critics were waiting for him, and when his own play was put upon the stage they attacked it with joy, they abused it and derided it remorselessly. It failed, and Harte believed that the critics were answerable for the failure. By and by he proposed that he and I should collaborate in a play in which each of us should introduce several characters and handle them. He came to Hartford and remained with us two weeks. He was a man who could never persuade himself to do a stroke of work until his credit was gone, and all his money, and the wolf was at his door; then he could sit down and work harder—until temporary relief was secured—than any man I have ever seen.

To digress for a moment. He came to us once just upon the verge of Christmas, to stay a day and finish a short story for the New York *Sun* called "Faithful Blossom"[2]—if my memory serves me. He was to have a hundred and fifty dollars for the story in any case, but Mr. Dana had said he should have two hundred and fifty if he finished it in time for Christmas use. Harte had reached the middle of his story but his time limit was now so brief that he could afford no interruptions, wherefore he had come to us to get away from the persistent visits of his creditors.

He arrived about dinner time. He said his time was so short that he must get to work straightway after dinner; then he went on chatting in serenity and comfort all through dinner, and afterward by the fire in the library until ten o'clock; then Mrs. Clemens went to bed, and my hot whisky punch was brought; also a duplicate of it for Harte. The chatting continued. I generally consume only one hot whisky and allow

[2] "Thankful Blossom."

myself until eleven o'clock for this function; but Harte kept on pouring and pouring and consuming and consuming, until one o'clock; then I excused myself and said good-night. He asked if he could have a bottle of whisky in his room. We rang up George and he furnished it. It seemed to me that he had already swallowed whisky enough to incapacitate him for work but it was not so; moreover, there were no signs upon him that his whisky had had a dulling effect upon his brain.

He went to his room and worked the rest of the night, with his bottle of whisky and a big wood fire for comfort. At five or six in the morning he rang for George; his bottle was empty and he ordered another; between then and nine he drank the whole of the added quart and then came to breakfast not drunk, not even tipsy, but quite himself and alert and animated. His story was finished; finished within the time limit and the extra hundred dollars was secured. I wondered what a story would be like that had been completed in circumstances like these; an hour later I was to find out.

At ten o'clock the young girls' club—by name The Saturday Morning Club—arrived in our library. I was booked to talk to the lassies but I asked Harte to take my place and read his story. He began it but it was soon plain that he was like most other people—he didn't know how to read; therefore I took it from him and read it myself. The last half of that story was written under the unpromising conditions which I have described; it is a story which I have never seen mentioned in print and I think it is quite unknown, but it is my conviction that it belongs at the very top of Harte's literature.

To go back to that other visit. The next morning after his arrival we went to the billiard room and began work upon the play.[a] I named my characters and described them; Harte did the same by his. Then he began to sketch the scenario, act by act and scene by scene. He worked rapidly and seemed to be troubled by no hesitations or indecisions; what he accomplished in a hour or two would have cost me several weeks of painful and difficult labor and would have been valueless when I got through. But Harte's work was good and usable; to me it was a wonderful performance.

Then the filling in began. Harte set down the dialogue

[a] *Ah Sin.*

swiftly, and I had nothing to do except when one of my characters was to say something; then Harte told me the nature of the remark that was required, I furnished the language and he jotted it down. After this fashion we worked two or three or four hours every day for a couple of weeks and produced a comedy that was good and would act. His part of it was the best part of it but that did not disturb the critics; when the piece was staged they praised my share of the work with a quite suspicious prodigality of approval and gave Harte's share all the vitriol they had in stock. The piece perished.

All that fortnight at our house Harte made himself liberally entertaining at breakfast, at luncheon, at dinner and in the billiard room—which was our workshop—with smart and bright sarcasms leveled at everything on the place; and for Mrs. Clemens' sake I endured it all until the last day; then, in the billiard room, he contributed the last feather; it seemed to be a slight and vague and veiled satirical remark with Mrs. Clemens for a target; he denied that she was meant, and I might have accepted the denial if I had been in a friendly mood but I was not, and was too strongly moved to give his reasonings a fair hearing. I said in substance this:

"Harte, your wife is all that is fine and lovable and lovely, and I exhaust praise when I say she is Mrs. Clemens' peer—but in all ways you are a shabby husband to her and you often speak sarcastically, not to say sneeringly, of her, just as you are constantly doing in the case of other women; but your privilege ends there; you must spare Mrs. Clemens. It does not become you to sneer at all; you are not charged anything here for the bed you sleep in, yet you have been very smartly and wittily sarcastic about it, whereas you ought to have been more reserved in that matter, remembering that you have not owned a bed of your own for ten years; you have made sarcastic remarks about the furniture of the bedroom and about the tableware and about the servants and about the carriage and the sleigh and the coachman's livery—in fact about every detail of the house and half of its occupants; you have spoken of all these matters contemptuously, in your unwholesome desire to be witty, but this does not become you; you are barred from these criticisms by your situation and circumstances; you have a talent and a reputation which would enable you to support your family most respectably and independently if you were not a born bummer and tramp; you are a loafer and an idler and you go clothed in rags, with not a whole shred on you except your inflamed red tie, and *it* isn't paid for; nine-tenths of your income is borrowed money—money which, in fact, is stolen, since you never intended to repay any of it; you sponge upon your hardworking widowed sister for bread and shelter in the mechanics' boardinghouse which she keeps; latterly you have not ventured to show your face in her neighborhood because of the creditors who are on watch for you. Where have you lived? Nobody knows. Your own people do not know. But I know. You have lived in the Jersey woods and marshes and have supported yourself as do the other tramps; you have confessed it without a blush; you sneer at everything in this house but you ought to be more tender, remembering that everything in it was honestly come by and has been paid for."

Harte owed me fifteen hundred dollars at that time; later he owed me three thousand. He offered me his note but I was not keeping a museum and didn't take it.

Harte's indifference concerning contracts and engagements was phenomenal. He could be blithe and gay with a broken engagement hanging over him; he could even joke about the matter; if that kind of a situation ever troubled him, the fact was not discoverable by anybody. He entered into an engagement to write the novel, *Gabriel Conroy*, for my Hartford publisher, Bliss. It was to be published by subscription. With the execution of the contract, Bliss's sorrows began. The precious time wasted along; Bliss could get plenty of promises out of Harte but no manuscript—at least no manuscript while Harte had money or could borrow it. He wouldn't touch the pen until the wolf actually had him by the hind leg; then he would do two or three days' violent work and let Bliss have it for an advance of royalties.

About once a month Harte would get into desperate straits; then he would dash off enough manuscript to set him temporarily free and carry it to Bliss and get a royalty advance. These assaults upon his prospective profits were never very large, except in the eyes of Bliss; to Bliss's telescopic vision a couple of hundred dollars that weren't due, or hadn't been earned, were a prodigious matter. By and by Bliss became alarmed. In the beginning he had recognized that a contract for a full-grown novel from Bret Harte was a valuable prize and he had been indiscreet enough to let his good fortune be trumpeted about the country. The trumpeting could have been valuable for Bliss if he had been dealing with a man addicted to keeping his engagements; but he was not dealing with that kind of a man, therefore the influence of the trumpeting had died down and vanished away long before Harte had arrived at the middle of his book; that kind of an interest once dead is dead beyond resurrection.

Finally Bliss realized that *Gabriel Conroy* was a white elephant. The book was nearing a finish but as a subscription book its value had almost disappeared. He had advanced to Harte thus far—I think my figures are correct—thirty-six hundred dollars, and he knew that he should not be able to sleep much until he could find some way to make that loss good; so he sold the serial rights in *Gabriel Conroy* to one of the magazines for that trifling sum—and a good trade it was, for the serial rights were not really worth that money and the book rights were hardly worth the duplicate of it.

I think the sense of shame was left out of Harte's constitution. He told me once, apparently as an incident of no importance—a mere casual reminiscence—that in his early days in California when he was a blooming young chap with the world before him and bread and butter to seek, he kept a woman who was twice his age—no, the woman kept him. When he was consul in Great Britain, twenty-five or thirty years later, he was kept, at different times, by a couple of women—a connection which has gone into history, along with the names of those women. He lived in their houses, and in the house of one of them he died.

I call to mind an incident in my commerce with Harte which reminds me of one like it which happened during my sojourn on the Pacific Coast. When Orion's thoughtful carefulness enabled my Hale and Norcross stock speculation to ruin me, I had three hundred dollars left and nowhere in particular to lay my head. I went to Jackass Gulch and cabined for a while with some friends of mine, surface miners. They were lovely fellows; charming comrades in every way and honest and honorable men; their credit was good for bacon and beans and this was fortunate because their kind of mining was a peculiarly precarious one; it was called pocket-mining and so far as I have been able to discover, pocket-mining is confined and restricted on this planet to a very small region around about Jackass Gulch.

A "pocket" is a concentration of gold dust in one little spot on the mountainside; it is close to the surface; the rains wash its particles down the mountainside and they spread, fan-shape, wider and wider as they go. The pocket-miner washes a pan of dirt, finds a speck or two of gold in it, makes a step to the right or the left, washes another pan, finds another speck or two, and goes on washing to the right and to the left until he knows when he has reached both limits of the fan by the best of circumstantial evidence, to wit—that his pan-washings furnish no longer the speck of gold. The rest of his work is easy—he washes along up the mountainside, tracing the narrowing fan by his washings, and at last he reaches the gold deposit. It may contain only a few hundred dollars, which he can take out with a couple of dips of his shovel; also it may contain a concentrated treasure worth a fortune. It is the fortune he is after and he will seek it with a never-perishing hope as long as he lives.

These friends of mine had been seeking that fortune daily for eighteen years; they had never found it but they were not at all discouraged; they were quite sure they would find it some day. During the three months that I was with them they found nothing, but we had a fascinating and delightful good time trying. Not long after I left, a greaser (Mexican) came loafing along and found a pocket with a hundred and twenty-five thousand dollars in it on a slope which our boys had never happened to explore. Such is luck! And such the treatment which honest, good perseverance gets so often at the hands of unfair and malicious Nature!

Our clothes were pretty shabby but that was no matter; we were in the fashion; the rest of the slender population were dressed as we were. Our boys hadn't had a cent for several months and hadn't needed one, their credit being perfectly good for bacon, coffee, flour, beans and molasses. If there was any difference, Jim[4] was the worst dressed of the three of us; if there was any discoverable difference in the matter of age, Jim's shreds were the oldest; but he was a gallant creature and his style and bearing could make any costume regal. One day we were in the decayed and naked and rickety inn when a couple of musical tramps appeared; one of them played the banjo and the other one danced unscientific clog-dances and

---

[4] Jim Gillis.

sang comic songs that made a person sorry to be alive. They passed the hat and collected three or four dimes from the dozen bankrupt pocket-miners present. When the hat approached Jim he said to me, with his fine millionaire air, "Let me have a dollar."

I gave him a couple of halves. Instead of modestly dropping them into the hat, he pitched them into it at the distance of a yard, just as in the ancient novels milord the Duke doesn't hand the beggar a benefaction but "tosses" it to him or flings it at his feet—and it is always a "purse of gold." In the novel, the witnesses are always impressed; Jim's great spirit was the spirit of the novel; to him the half-dollars were a purse of gold; like the Duke he was playing to the gallery, but the parallel ends there. In the Duke's case, the witnesses knew he could afford the purse of gold, and the largest part of their admiration consisted in envy of the man who could throw around purses of gold in that fine and careless way. The miners admired Jim's handsome liberality but they knew he couldn't afford what he had done, and that fact modified their admiration. Jim was worth a hundred of Bret Harte, for he was a man, and a whole man. In his little exhibition of vanity and pretense he exposed a characteristic which made him resemble Harte, but the resemblance began and ended there.

I come to the Harte incident now. When our play was in a condition to be delivered to Parsloe, the lessee of it, I had occasion to go to New York and I stopped at the St. James Hotel, as usual. Harte had been procrastinating; the play should have been in Parsloe's hands a day or two earlier than this but Harte had not attended to it. About seven in the evening he came into the lobby of the hotel, dressed in an ancient gray suit so out of repair that the bottoms of his trousers were frazzled to a fringe; his shoes were similarly out of repair and were sodden with snow-slush and mud, and on his head and slightly tipped to starboard rested a crumpled little soft hat which was a size or two too small for him; his bright little red necktie was present, and rather more than usually cheery and contented and conspicuous. He had the play in his hand. Parsloe's theatre was not three minutes' walk distant; I supposed he would say, "Come along—let's take the play to Parsloe."

But he didn't; he stepped up to the counter, offered his parcel to the clerk, and said with the manner of an earl, "It is for Mr. Parsloe—send it to the theater."

The clerk looked him over austerely and said, with the air

of a person who is presenting a checkmating difficulty, "The messenger's fee will be ten cents."

Harte said, "Call him."

Which the clerk did. The boy answered the call, took the parcel and stood waiting for orders. There was a certain malicious curiosity visible in the clerk's face. Harte turned toward me and said, "Let me have a dollar."

I handed it to him. He handed it to the boy and said, "Run along."

The clerk said, "Wait, I'll give you the change."

Harte gave his hand a ducal wave and said, "Never mind it. Let the boy keep it."

◇◇◇◇◇◇◇◇◇◇◇◇◇◇◇◇◇◇◇◇◇

CHAPTER 62

Edward Everett Hale wrote a book which made a great and pathetic sensation when it issued from the press in the lurid days when the Civil War was about to break out and the North and South were crouched for a spring at each other's throats. It was called *The Man Without a Country*. Harte, in a mild and colorless way, was that kind of a man—that is to say, he was a man without a country; no, not man—man is too strong a term; he was an invertebrate without a country. He hadn't any more passion for his country than an oyster has for its bed; in fact not so much and I apologize to the oyster. The higher passions were left out of Harte; what he knew about them he got from books. When he put them into his own books they were imitations; often good ones, often as deceptive to people who did not know Harte as are the actor's simulation of passions on the stage when he is not feeling them but is only following certain faithfully studied rules for their artificial reproduction.

On the 7th of November, 1876—I think it was the 7th—he suddenly appeared at my house in Hartford and remained there during the following day, election day. As usual, he was tranquil; he was serene; doubtless the only serene and tranquil voter in the United States; the rest—as usual in our country—were excited away up to the election limit, for that vast political conflagration was blazing at white heat which was presently to end in one of the Republican party's most cold-blooded swindles of the American people, the stealing of the presidential chair from Mr. Tilden, who had been elected, and the conferring of it upon Mr. Hayes, who had been defeated.

I was an ardent Hayes man but that was natural, for I was pretty young at the time. I have since convinced myself that the political opinions of a nation are of next to no value, in any case, but that what little rag of value they possess is to be found among the old, rather than among the young. I was as excited and inflamed as was the rest of the voting world, and I was surprised when Harte said he was going to remain with us until the day after the election; but not much surprised, for he was such a careless creature that I thought it just possible that he had gotten his dates mixed. There was plenty of time for him to correct his mistake and I suggested that he go back to New York and not lose his vote. But he said he was not caring about his vote; that he had come away purposely, in order that he might avoid voting and yet have a good excuse to answer the critics with.

Then he told me why he did not wish to vote. He said that through influential friends he had secured the promise of a consulate from Mr. Tilden and the same promise from Mr. Hayes, that he was going to be taken care of no matter how the contest might go, and that his interest in the election began and ended there. He said he could not afford to vote for either of the candidates, because the other candidate might find it out and consider himself privileged to cancel his pledge. It was a curious satire upon our political system! Why should a president care how an impending consul had voted? Consulships are not political offices; naturally and properly a consul's qualifications should begin and end with fitness for the post; and in an entirely sane political system the question of a man's political complexion could have nothing to do with the matter. However, the man who was defeated by the nation was placed in the presidential chair and the man without a country got his consulship.

Harte had no feeling, for the reason that he had no machinery to feel with. John McCullough, the tragedian, was a man of high character; a generous man, a lovable man and a man whose truthfulness could not be challenged. He was a great admirer of Harte's literature, and in the early days in San Francisco he had had a warm fondness for Harte himself; as the years went by this fondness cooled to some extent, a circumstance for which Harte was responsible. However, in the days of Harte's consulship McCullough's affection for him had merely undergone a diminution; it had by no means disappeared; but by and by something happened which abolished what was left of it. John McCullough told me all about it.

One day a young man appeared in his quarters in New York and said he was Bret Harte's son and had just arrived from England with a letter of introduction and recommendation from his father—and he handed the letter to McCullough. McCullough greeted him cordially and said, "I was expecting you, my boy. I know your errand, through a letter which I have already received from your father; and by good luck I am in a position to satisfy your desire. I have just the place for you, and you can consider yourself on salary from today, and now."

Young Harte was eloquently grateful and said, "I knew you would be expecting me, for my father promised me that he would write you in advance."

McCullough had Harte's letter in his pocket but he did not read it to the lad. In substance it was this:

"My boy is stage-struck and wants to go to you for help, for he knows that you and I are old friends. To get rid of his importunities, I have been obliged to start him across the water equipped with a letter strongly recommending him to your kindness and protection, and begging you to do the best you can to forward his ambition, for my sake. I was obliged to write the letter, I couldn't get out of it, but the present letter is to warn you beforehand to pay no attention to the other one. My son is stage-struck but he isn't of any account and will never amount to anything; therefore don't bother yourself with him; it wouldn't pay you for your lost time and sympathy."

John McCullough stood by the boy and pushed his fortunes on the stage and was the best father the lad ever had.

I have said more than once in these pages that Harte had no heart and no conscience, and I have also said that he was mean and base. I have not said, perhaps, that he was treacherous, but if I have omitted that remark I wish to add it now.

All of us at one time or another blunder stupidly into indiscreet acts and speeches; I am not an exception; I have done it myself. About a dozen years ago I drifted into the Players Club one night and found half a dozen of the boys grouped cozily in a private corner sipping punches and talking. I joined them and assisted. Presently Bret Harte's name was mentioned and straightway that mention fired a young fellow who sat at my elbow, and for the next ten minutes he talked as only a person can talk whose subject lies near his heart. Nobody interrupted; everybody was interested. The young fellow's talk was made up of strong and genuine enthusiasms; its subject was praise—praise of Mrs. Harte and her daughters. He told how they were living in a little town in New Jersey and how hard they worked and how faithfully and how cheerfully and how contentedly, to earn their living—Mrs. Harte by teaching music, the daughters by exercising the arts of drawing, embroidery and such things—I meantime listening as eagerly as the rest, for I was aware that he was speaking the truth and not overstating it.

But presently he diverged into eulogies of the ostensible head of that deserted family, Bret Harte. He said that the family's happiness had one defect in it; the absence of Harte. He said that their love and their reverence for him was a beautiful thing to see and hear; also their pity of him on account of his enforced exile from home. He also said that Harte's own grief, because of this bitter exile, was beautiful to contemplate; that Harte's faithfulness in writing by every steamer was beautiful too; that he was always longing to come home in his vacations but his salary was so small that he could not afford it; nevertheless, in his letters he was always promising himself this happiness in the next steamer or the next one after that one; and that it was pitiful to see the family's disappointment when the named steamers kept on arriving without him; that his self-sacrifice was an ennobling spectacle; that he was man enough and fine enough to deny himself in order that he might send to the family every month, for their support, that portion of his salary which a more selfish person would devote to the Atlantic voyage.

Up to this time I had "stood the raise," as the poker players say, but now I broke out and called the young fellow's hand—as the poker players also say. I couldn't help it. I saw that he had been misinformed. It seemed to be my duty to set him right.

I said, "Oh, that be hanged! There's nothing in it. Bret Harte has deserted his family and that is the plain English of it. Possibly he writes to them, but I am not weak enough to believe it until I see the letters; possibly he is pining to come home to his deserted family, but no one that knows him will believe that. But there is one thing about which I think there can be no possibility of doubt—and that is, that he has never sent them a dollar and has never intended to send them a dollar. Bret Harte is the most contemptible, poor little soulless blatherskite that exists on the planet today—"

I had been dimly aware, very vaguely aware, by fitful glimpses of the countenances around me, that something was happening. It was I that was happening but I didn't know it.

But when I had reached the middle of that last sentence somebody seized me and whispered into my ear, with energy, "For goodness sake shut up! This young fellow is Steele. He's engaged to one of the daughters."

◇◇◇◇◇◇◇◇◇◇◇◇◇◇◇◇◇◇

CHAPTER 63

It is my conviction that a person's temperament is a law, an iron law, and has to be obeyed, no matter who disapproves; manifestly, as it seems to me, temperament is a law of God and is supreme and takes precedence of all human laws. It is my conviction that each and every human law that exists has one distinct purpose and intention and only one: to oppose itself to a law of God and defeat it, degrade it, deride it and trample upon it. We find no fault with the spider for ungenerously ambushing the fly and taking its life; we do not call it murder; we concede that it did not invent its own temperament, its own nature, and is therefore not blamable for the acts which the law of its nature requires and commands. We even concede this large point: that no art and no ingenuity can ever reform the spider and persuade her to cease from her assassinations. We do not blame the tiger for obeying the ferocious law of the temperament which God lodged in him and which the tiger must obey. We do not blame the wasp for her fearful cruelty in half paralyzing a spider with her sting and then stuffing the spider down a hole in the ground to suffer there many days, while the wasp's nursery gradually tortures the helpless creature through a long and miserable death by gnawing rations from its person daily; we concede that the wasp is strictly and blamelessly obeying the law of God as required by the temperament which He has put into her. We do not blame the fox, the blue jay and the many other creatures that live by theft; we concede that they are obeying the law of God promulgated by the temperament with which He provided for them. We do not say to the ram and the goat, "Thou shalt not commit adultery," for we know that ineradicably embedded in their temperament—that is to say in their born nature—God has said to them, "Thou *shalt* commit it."

If we should go on until we had singled out and mentioned the separate and distinct temperaments which have been distributed among the myriads of the animal world, we should find that the reputation of each species is determined by one special and prominent trait; and then we should find that all of these traits, and all the shadings of these many traits, have also been distributed among mankind; that in every man a dozen or more of these traits exist, and that in many men traces and shadings of the whole of them exist. In what we call the lower animals, temperaments are often built out of merely one or two or three of these traits; but man is a complex animal and it takes all of the traits to fit him out. In the rabbit we always find meekness and timidity, and in him we never find courage, insolence, aggressiveness; and so when the rabbit is mentioned we always remember that he is meek and timid; if he has any other traits or distinctions—except, perhaps, an extravagant and inordinate fecundity—they never occur to us. When we consider the housefly and the flea, we remember that in splendid courage the belted knight and the tiger cannot approach them and that in impudence and insolence they lead the whole animal world, including even man; if those creatures have other traits they are so overshadowed by those which I have mentioned that we never think of them at all. When the peacock is mentioned, vanity occurs to us and no other trait; when we think of the goat, unchastity occurs to us and no other trait; when certain kinds of dogs are mentioned, loyalty occurs to us and no other trait; when the cat is mentioned, her independence—a trait which she alone of all created creatures, including man, possesses—occurs to us and no other trait; except we be of the stupid and the ignorant —then we think of treachery, a trait which is common to many breeds of dogs but is not common to the cat. We can find one or two conspicuous traits in each family of what we impudently call the lower animals; in each case these one or two conspicuous traits distinguish that family of animals from the other families; also in each case those one or two traits are found in every one of the members of each family and are so prominent as to eternally and unchangeably establish the character of that branch of the animal world. In all these cases we concede that the several temperaments constitute a law of God, a command of God, and that whatsoever is done in obedience to that law is blameless.

Man was descended from those animals; from them he inherited every trait that is in him; from them he inherited the whole of their numerous traits in a body, and with each trait its share of the law of God. He widely differs from them in this: that he possesses not a single trait that is similarly and equally prominent in each and every member of his race. You can say the housefly is limitlessly brave, and in saying it you describe the whole housefly tribe; you can say the rabbit is limitlessly timid, and by that phrase you describe the whole rabbit tribe; you can say the spider is limitlessly murderous, and by that phrase you describe the whole spider tribe; you can say the lamb is limitlessly innocent and sweet and gentle, and by that phrase you describe all the lambs; you can say the goat is limitlessly unchaste and by that phrase you describe the whole tribe of goats. There is hardly a creature which you cannot definitely and satisfactorily describe by one single trait —but you cannot describe man by one single trait. Men are not all cowards, like the rabbit; nor all brave, like the housefly; nor all sweet and innocent and gentle, like the lamb; nor all murderous, like the spider and the wasp; nor all thieves, like the fox and the blue jay; nor all vain, like the peacock; nor all beautiful, like the angel-fish; nor all frisky, like the monkey; nor all unchaste, like the goat.

The human family cannot be described by any one phrase; each individual has to be described by himself. One is brave, another is a coward; one is gentle and kindly, another is ferocious; one is proud and vain, another is modest and humble. The multifarious traits that are scattered, one or two at a time, throughout the great animal world, are all concentrated, in varying and nicely shaded degrees of force and feebleness, in the form of instincts in each and every member of the human family. In some men the vicious traits are so slight as to be imperceptible, while the nobler traits stand out conspicuously. We describe that man by those fine traits and we give him praise and accord him high merit for their possession. It seems comical. He did not invent his traits; he did not stock himself with them; he inherited them at his birth; God conferred them

upon him; they are the law that God imposed upon him, and
he could not escape obedience if he should try. Sometimes a
man is a born murderer, or a born scoundrel—like Stanford
White—and upon him the world lavishes censure and dis-
praise; but he is only obeying the law of his nature, the law of
his temperament; he is not at all likely to try to disobey it, and
if he should try he would fail. It is a curious and humorous
fact that we excuse all the unpleasant things that the creatures
that crawl and fly and swim and go on four legs do, for the
recognizably sufficient reason that they are but obeying the
law of their nature, which is the law of God, and are therefore
innocent; then we turn about and with the fact plain before
us that we get all our unpleasant traits by inheritance from
those creatures, we blandly assert that we did not inherit the
immunities along with them, but that it is our duty to ignore,
abolish and break these laws of God. It seems to me that this
argument has not a leg to stand upon and that it is not merely
and mildly humorous but violently grotesque.

By ancient training and inherited habit, I have been heaping blame after blame, censure after censure, upon Bret
Harte, and have felt the things I have said, but when my temper is cool I have no censures for him. The law of his nature
was stronger than man's statutes and he had to obey it. It is
my conviction that the human race is no proper target for
harsh words and bitter criticisms, and that the only justifiable
feeling toward it is compassion; it did not invent itself, and it
had nothing to do with the planning of its weak and foolish
character.

CHAPTER 64

In 1890 we visited Mary Mapes Dodge in Onteora. It was a
bright and jolly company—Laurence Hutton, Charles Dudley
Warner and Carroll Beckwith and their wives. Some of those
choice people are still with us; the others have passed from
this life: Mrs. Clemens, Susy, Mr. Warner, Mary Mapes
Dodge, Laurence Hutton, Dean Sage—peace to their ashes!

We arrived at nightfall, dreary from a tiresome journey;
but the dreariness did not last. Mrs. Dodge had provided a

homemade banquet and the happy company sat down to it, twenty strong or more. Then the thing happened which always happens at large dinners and is always exasperating: everybody talked to his elbow-mates and all talked at once and gradually raised their voices higher and higher and higher in the desperate effort to be heard. It was like a riot, an insurrection; it was an intolerable volume of noise. Presently I said to the lady next to me—

"I will subdue this riot, I will silence this racket. There is only one way to do it but I know the art. You must tilt your head toward mine and seem to be deeply interested in what I am saying; I will talk in a low voice; then, just because our neighbors won't be able to hear me, they will *want* to hear me. If I mumble long enough—say two minutes—you will see that the dialogues will one after another come to a standstill and there will be silence, not a sound anywhere but my mumbling."

Then in a very low voice I began:

"When I went out to Chicago, eleven years ago, to witness the Grant festivities, there was a great banquet on the first night, with six hundred ex-soldiers present. The gentleman who sat next to me was Mr. X. X. He was very hard of hearing and he had a habit common to deaf people of shouting his remarks instead of delivering them in an ordinary voice. He would handle his knife and fork in reflective silence for five or six minutes at a time and then suddenly fetch out a shout that would make you jump out of the United States."

By this time the insurrection at Mrs. Dodge's table—at least that part of it in my immediate neighborhood—had died down and the silence was spreading, couple by couple, down the long table. I went on in a lower and still lower mumble, and most impressively—

"During one of Mr. X. X.'s mute intervals, a man opposite us approached the end of a story which he had been telling his elbow-neighbor. He was speaking in a low voice—there was much noise—I was deeply interested, and straining my ears to catch his words, stretching my neck, holding my breath, to hear, unconscious of everything but the fascinating tale. I heard him say, 'At this point he seized her by her long hair—she shrieking and begging—bent her neck across his knee, and with one awful sweep of the razor—'"

"HOW DO YOU LIKE CHICA-A-AGO?!!!"

That was X. X.'s interruption, hearable at thirty miles. By

the time I had reached that place in my mumblings, Mrs. Dodge's dining room was so silent, so breathlessly still, that if you had dropped a thought anywhere in it you could have heard it smack the floor.[1] When I delivered that yell the entire dinner company jumped as one person and punched their heads through the ceiling, damaging it, for it was only lath and plaster, and it all came down on us, and much of it went into the victuals and made them gritty, but no one was hurt. Then I explained why it was that I had played that game, and begged them to take the moral of it home to their hearts and be rational and merciful thenceforth, and cease from screaming in mass, and agree to let one person talk at a time and the rest listen in grateful and unvexed peace. They granted my prayer and we had a happy time all the rest of the evening; I do not think I have ever had a better time in my life. This was largely because the new terms enabled me to keep the floor—now that I had it—and do all the talking myself. I do like to hear myself talk.

Dean Sage was a delightful man, yet in one way a terror to his friends, for he loved them so well that he could not refrain from playing practical jokes on them. We have to be pretty deeply in love with a person before we can do him the honor of joking familiarly with him. Dean Sage was the best citizen I have known in America. It takes courage to be a good citizen and he had plenty of it. He allowed no individual and no corporation to infringe his smallest right and escape unpunished. He was very rich and very generous and benevolent, and he gave away his money with a prodigal hand; but if an individual or corporation infringed a right of his to the value of ten cents, he would spend thousands of dollars' worth of time and labor and money and persistence on the matter and would not lower his flag until he had won his battle or lost it.

He and Rev. Mr. Harris had been classmates in college, and to the day of Sage's death they were as fond of each other as an engaged pair. It follows, without saying, that whenever Sage found an opportunity to play a joke upon Harris, Harris was sure to suffer.

Along about 1873 Sage fell a victim to an illness which reduced him to a skeleton and defied all the efforts of the physicians to cure it. He went to the Adirondacks and took Harris with him. Sage had always been an active man and he couldn't idle any day wholly away in inanition, but walked every day

[1] This was tried. I well remember it.—M. T., *October, '06.*

to the limit of his strength. One day, toward nightfall, the pair came upon a humble log cabin which bore these words painted upon a shingle: "Entertainment for Man and Beast." They were obliged to stop there for the night, Sage's strength being exhausted. They entered the cabin and found its owner and sole occupant there, a rugged and sturdy and simple-hearted man of middle age. He cooked supper and placed it before the travellers—salt junk, boiled beans, corn bread and black coffee. Sage's stomach could abide nothing but the most delicate food, therefore this banquet revolted him, and he sat at the table unemployed while Harris fed ravenously, limit-lessly, gratefully; for he had been chaplain in a fighting regiment all through the war and had kept in perfection the grand and uncritical appetite and splendid physical vigor which those four years of tough fare and activity had fur-nished him. Sage went supperless to bed and tossed and writhed all night upon a shuck mattress that was full of atten-tive and interested corncobs. In the morning Harris was raven-ous again and devoured the odious breakfast as contentedly and as delightedly as he had devoured its twin the night be-fore. Sage sat upon the porch, empty, and contemplated the performance and meditated revenge. Presently he beckoned to the landlord and took him aside and had a confidential talk with him. He said,

"I am the paymaster. What is the bill?"

"Two suppers, fifty cents; two beds, thirty cents; two break-fasts, fifty cents—total, a dollar and thirty cents."

Sage said, "Go back and make out the bill and fetch it to me here on the porch. Make it thirteen dollars."

"Thirteen dollars! Why it's impossible! I am no robber. I am charging you what I charge everybody. It's a dollar and thirty cents and that's all it is."

"My man, I've got something to say about this as well as you. It's thirteen dollars. You'll make out your bill for that and you'll *take* it, too, or you'll not get a cent."

The man was troubled and said, "I don't understand this. I can't make it out."

"Well, I understand it. I know what I am about. It's thir-teen dollars and I want the bill made out for that. There's no other terms. Get it ready and bring it out here. I will examine it and be outraged. You understand? I will dispute the bill. You must stand to it. You must refuse to take less. I will begin to lose my temper; you must begin to lose yours. I will call you hard names; you must answer with harder ones. I will raise my voice; you must raise yours. You must go into a rage —foam at the mouth, if you can; insert some soap to help it along. Now go along and follow your instructions."

The man played his assigned part and played it well. He brought the bill and stood waiting for results. Sage's face began to cloud up, his eyes to snap and his nostrils to inflate like a horse's; then he broke out with—

"*Thirteen dollars!* You mean to say that you charge thirteen dollars for these damned inhuman hospitalities of yours? Are you a professional buccaneer? Is it your custom to—"

The man burst in with spirit: "Now, I don't want any more out of you—that's a plenty. The bill is thirteen dollars and you'll *pay* it—that's all; a couple of characterless adventurers bilking their way through this country and attempting to dictate terms to a gentleman! a gentleman who received you supposing you were gentlemen yourselves, whereas in my opinion hell's full of—"

Sage broke in—

"Not another word of that!—I won't have it. I regard you as the lowest-down thief that ever—"

"Don't you use that word again! By ——, I'll take you by the neck and—"

Harris came rushing out, and just as the two were about to grapple he pushed himself between them and began to implore—

"Oh, Dean, don't, *don't*—now, Mr. Smith, control yourself! Oh, think of your family, Dean!—think what a scandal—"

But they burst out with maledictions, imprecations and all the hard names they could dig out of the rich accumulations of their educated memories, and in the midst of it the man shouted—

"When *gentlemen* come to this house, I treat them *as* gentlemen. When people come to this house with the ordinary appetites of gentlemen, I charge them a dollar and thirty cents for what I furnished you; but when a man brings a hell-fired Famine here that gorges a barrel of pork and four barrels of beans at two sittings—"

Sage broke in, in a voice that was eloquent with remorse and self-reproach, "I never thought of that, and I ask your pardon; I am ashamed of myself and of my friend. Here's your thirteen dollars, and my apologies along with it."

CHAPTER 65

We have lived in a Florentine villa before.[1] This was twelve years ago. This was the Villa Viviani and was pleasantly and commandingly situated on a hill in the suburb of Settignano, overlooking Florence and the great valley. It was secured for us and put in comfortable order by a good friend, Mrs. Ross, whose stately castle was a twelve minutes' walk away. She still lives there, and has been a help to us more than once since we established relations with the titled owner of the Villa di Quarto. The year spent in the Villa Viviani was something of a contrast to the five months which we have now spent in this ducal barrack. Among my old manuscripts and random and spasmodic diaries I find some account of that pleasantly remembered year and will make some extracts from the same and introduce them here.

When we were passing through Florence in the spring of '92 on our way to Germany, the diseased-world's bathhouse, we began negotiations for a villa, and friends of ours completed them after we were gone. When we got back three or four months later everything was ready, even to the servants and the dinner. It takes but a sentence to state that but it makes an indolent person tired to think of the planning and work and trouble that lie concealed in it. For it is less trouble and more satisfaction to bury two families than to select and equip a home for one.

The situation of the villa was perfect. It was three miles from Florence, on the side of a hill. The flowery terrace on which it stood looked down upon sloping olive groves and vineyards; to the right, beyond some hill spurs, was Fiesole, perched upon its steep terraces; in the immediate foreground was the imposing mass of the Ross castle, its walls and turrets rich with the mellow weather stains of forgotten centuries; in the distant plain lay Florence, pink and gray and brown, with the rusty huge dome of the cathedral dominating its center

[1] Written at the Villa di Quarto in 1904.

like a captive balloon, and flanked on the right by the smaller bulb of the Medici chapel and on the left by the airy tower of the Palazzo Vecchio; all around the horizon was a billowy rim of lofty blue hills, snowed white with innumerable villas. After nine months of familiarity with this panorama I still think, as I thought in the beginning, that this is the fairest picture on our planet, the most enchanting to look upon, the most satisfying to the eye and the spirit. To see the sun sink down, drowned on his pink and purple and golden floods, and overwhelm Florence with tides of color that make all the sharp lines dim and faint and turn the solid city to a city of dreams, is a sight to stir the coldest nature and make a sympathetic one drunk with ecstasy.

Sept. 26, '92.—Arrived in Florence. Got my head shaved. This was a mistake. Moved to the villa in the afternoon. Some of the trunks brought up in the evening by the *contadino*—if that is his title. He is the man who lives on the farm and takes care of it for the owner, the marquis. The *contadino* is middle-aged and like the rest of the peasants—that is to say, brown, handsome, good-natured, courteous and entirely independent without making any offensive show of it. He charged too much for the trunks, I was told. My informant explained that this was customary.

Sept. 27.—The rest of the trunks brought up this morning. He charged too much again but I was told that this also was customary. It is all right, then. I do not wish to violate the customs. Hired landau, horses and coachman. Terms, four hundred and eighty francs a month and a *pourboire* to the coachman, I to furnish lodging for the man and the horses but nothing else. The landau has seen better days and weighs thirty tons. The horses are feeble and object to the landau; they stop and turn around every now and then and examine it with surprise and suspicion. This causes delay. But it entertains the people along the road. They came out and stood around with their hands in their pockets and discussed the matter with one another. I was told they said that a forty-ton landau was not the thing for horses like those—what they needed was a wheelbarrow.

I will insert in this place some notes made in October concerning the villa:

This is a two-story house. It is not an old house—from an Italian standpoint, I mean. No doubt there has always been a nice dwelling on this eligible spot since a thousand years

B.C., but this present one is said to be only two hundred years
old. Outside, it is a plain square building like a box and is
painted a light yellow and has green window shutters. It
stands in a commanding position on an artificial terrace of
liberal dimensions which is walled around with strong mason-
ry. From the walls the vineyards and olive orchards of the
estate slant away toward the valley; the garden about the
house is stocked with flowers and a convention of lemon
bushes in great crockery tubs; there are several tall trees—
stately stone pines—also fig trees and trees of breeds not
familiar to me; roses overflow the retaining walls and the battered and mossy stone urns on the gateposts in pink and yellow cataracts, exactly as they do on the drop curtains of
theaters; there are gravel walks shut in by tall laurel hedges.
A back corner of the terrace is occupied by a dense grove of
old ilex trees. There is a stone table in there, with stone
benches around it. No shaft of sunlight can penetrate that
grove. It is always deep twilight in there, even when all outside is flooded with the intense sun glare common to this region. The carriage road leads from the inner gate eight hundred feet to the public road through the vineyard, and there
one may take the horsecar for the city and will find it a swifter
and handier convenience than a sixty-ton landau. On the east
(or maybe it is the south) front of the house is the Viviani
coat of arms in plaster and near it a sun dial which keeps
very good time.

The house is a very fortress for strength. The main walls—of
brick covered with plaster—are about three feet thick; the
partitions of the rooms, also of brick, are nearly the same
thickness. The ceilings of the rooms on the ground floor are
more than twenty feet high; those of the upper floors are also
higher than necessary. I have several times tried to count the
rooms in the house but the irregularities baffle me. There seem
to be twenty-eight.

The ceilings are frescoed, the walls are papered. All the
floors are of red brick covered with a coating of polished and
shining cement which is as hard as stone and looks like it; for
the surfaces have been painted in patterns, first in solid colors
and then snowed over with varicolored freckles of paint to im-
itate granite and other stones. Sometimes the body of the floor
is an imitation of gray granite with a huge star or other orna-
mental pattern of imitation fancy marbles in the center; with
a two-foot band of imitation red granite all around the room,

whose outer edge is bordered with a six-inch stripe of imitation lapislazuli; sometimes the body of the floor is red granite,
then the gray is used as a bordering stripe. There are plenty
of windows and worlds of sun and light; these floors are slick
and shiny and full of reflections, for each is a mirror in its way,
softly imaging all objects after the subdued fashion of forest
lakes.

There is a tiny family chapel on the main floor, with benches
for ten or twelve persons, and over the little altar is an ancient
oil painting which seems to me to be as beautiful and as rich
in tone as any of those old-master performances down yonder
in the galleries of the Pitti and the Uffizi. Botticelli, for instance; I wish I had time to make a few remarks about Botticelli—whose real name was probably Smith.

The curious feature of the house is the *salon*. This is a spacious and lofty vacuum which occupies the center of the
house; all the rest of the house is built around it; it extends
up through both stories and its roof projects some feet above
the rest of the building. That vacuum is very impressive. The
sense of its vastness strikes you the moment you step into it
and cast your eyes around it and aloft. I tried many names
for it: the Skating Rink, the Mammoth Cave, the Great Sahara
and so on, but none exactly answered. There are five divans
distributed along its walls; they make little or no show, though
their aggregate length is fifty-seven feet. A piano in it is a lost
object. We have tried to reduce the sense of desert space and
emptiness with tables and things but they have a defeated
look and do not do any good. Whatever stands or moves
under that soaring painted vault is belittled.

Over the six doors are huge plaster medallions which are
supported by great naked and handsome plaster boys and in
these medallions are plaster portraits in high relief of some
grave and beautiful men in stately official costumes of a long-
past day—Florentine senators and judges, ancient dwellers
here and owners of this estate. The date of one of them is
1305—middle-aged, then, and a judge—he could have known,
as a youth, the very creators of Italian art; he could have
walked and talked with Dante and probably did. The date
of another is 1343—he could have known Boccaccio and spent
his afternoons yonder in Fiesole gazing down on plague-reek-
ing Florence and listening to that man's improper tales, and
he probably did. The date of another is 1463—he could have
met Columbus, and he knew the Magnificent Lorenzo, of

course. These are all Cerretanis—or Cerretani-Twains, as I may say, for I have adopted myself into their family on account of its antiquity, my origin having been heretofore too recent to suit me.

But I am forgetting to state what it is about that Rink that is so curious—which is, that it is not really vast but only seems so. It is an odd deception and unaccountable; but a deception it is. Measured by the eye it is sixty feet square and sixty feet high; but I have been applying the tapeline and find it to be but forty feet square and forty high. These are the correct figures; and what is interestingly strange is that the place continues to look as big now as it did before I measured it.

This is a good house but it cost very little and is simplicity itself and pretty primitive in most of its features. The water is pumped to the ground floor from a well by hand labor and then carried upstairs by hand. There is no drainage; the cesspools are right under the windows. This is the case with everybody's villa.

The doors in this house are like the doors of the majority of the houses and hotels of Italy—plain, thin, unpaneled boards painted white. This makes the flimsiest and most unattractive door known to history. The knob is not a knob but a thing like the handle of a gimlet—you can get hold of it only with your thumb and forefinger. Still, even that is less foolish than our American door knob, which is always getting loose and turning futilely round and round in your hand, accomplishing nothing.

The windows are all of the rational continental breed; they open apart, like doors; and when they are bolted for the night they don't rattle and a person can go to sleep.

There are cunning little fireplaces in the bedrooms and sitting rooms and lately a big, aggressive-looking German stove has been set up on the south frontier of the Great Sahara.

The stairs are made of granite blocks, the hallways of the second floor are of red brick. It is a safe house. Earthquakes cannot shake it down, fire cannot burn it. There is absolutely nothing burnable but the furniture, the curtains and the doors. There is not much furniture; it is merely summer furniture—or summer bareness, if you like. When a candle set fire to the curtains in a room over my head the other night where samples of the family slept, I was wakened out of my sleep by shouts and screams and was greatly terrified until an answer from the window told me what the matter was—that the window curtains and hangings were on fire. In America I should have been more frightened than ever then but this was not the case here. I advised the samples to let the fire alone and go to bed; which they did, and by the time they got to sleep there was nothing of the attacked fabrics left. We boast a good deal in America of our fire departments, the most efficient and wonderful in the world, but they have something better than that to boast of in Europe—a rational system of building which makes human life safe from fire and renders fire departments needless. We boast of a thing which we ought to be ashamed to require.

This villa has a roomy look, a spacious look; and when the sunshine is pouring in and lighting up the bright colors of the shiny floors and walls and ceilings there is a large and friendly suggestion of welcome about the aspects, but I do not know that I have ever seen a continental dwelling which quite met the American standard of a home in all the details. There is a trick about an American house that is like the deep-lying untranslatable idioms of a foreign language—a trick uncatchable by the stranger, a trick incommunicable and indescribable; and that elusive trick, that intangible something, whatever it is, is just the something that gives the home look and the home feeling to an American house and makes it the most satisfying refuge yet invented by men—and women, mainly women. The American house is opulent in soft and varied colors that please and rest the eye, and in surfaces that are smooth and pleasant to the touch, in forms that are shapely and graceful, in objects without number which compel interest and cover nakedness; and the night has even a higher charm than the day, there, for the artificial lights do really give light instead of merely trying and failing; and under their veiled and tinted glow all the snug coziness and comfort and charm of the place is at best and loveliest. But when night shuts down on the continental home there is no gas or electricity to fight it, but only dreary lamps of exaggerated ugliness and of incomparable poverty in the matter of effectiveness.

Sept. 29, '92.—I seem able to forget everything except that I have had my head shaved. No matter how closely I shut myself away from draughts it seems to be always breezy up there. But the main difficulty is the flies. They like it up there better than anywhere else; on account of the view, I suppose. It seems to me that I have never seen any flies before that were shod like these. These appear to have talons. Wherever they put their foot down they grab. They walk over my head all the time and cause me infinite torture. It is their park, their club, their summer resort. They have garden parties there and conventions and all sorts of dissipation. And they fear nothing. All flies are daring but these are more daring than those of other nationalities. These cannot be scared away by any device. They are more diligent, too, than the other kinds; they come before daylight and stay till after dark. But there are compensations. The mosquitoes are not a trouble. There are very few of them, they are not noisy, and not much interested in their calling. A single unkind word will send them away; if said in English, which impresses them because they do not understand it, they come no more that night. We often see them weep when they are spoken to harshly. I have got some of the eggs to take home. If this breed can be raised in our climate they will be a great advantage. There seem to be no fleas here. This is the first time we have struck this kind of an interregnum in fifteen months. Everywhere else the supply exceeds the demand.

Oct. 1.—Finding that the coachman was taking his meals in the kitchen, I reorganized the contract to include his board, at thirty francs a month. That is what it would cost him up above us in the village and I think I can feed him for two hundred and save thirty out of it. Saving thirty is better than not saving anything.

That passage from the diary reminds me that I did an injudicious thing along about that time which bore fruit later. As I was to give the coachman, Vittorio, a monthly *pourboire*, of course I wanted to know the amount. So I asked the coachman's *padrone* (master), instead of asking somebody else—anybody else. He said thirty francs a month would be about right. I was afterward informed that this was an overcharge but that it was customary, there being no customary charges except overcharges. However, at the end of that month the coachman demanded an extra *pourboire* of fifteen francs. When I asked why, he said his *padrone* had taken his other *pourboire* away from him. The *padrone* denied this in Vittorio's presence and Vittorio seemed to retract. The *padrone* said he did, and he certainly had that aspect, but I had to take the *padrone's* word for it as interpreter of the coachman's Italian. When the *padrone* was gone the coachman resumed the charge, and as we liked him—and also believed him—we made his aggregate *pourboire* forty-five francs a month after that and never doubted that the *padrone* took two-thirds of it. We were told by citizens that it was customary for the *padrone* to seize a considerable share of his dependent's *pourboire*, and also the custom for the *padrone* to deny it. That *padrone* is an accommodating man and a most capable and agreeable talker, speaking English like an archangel and making it next to impossible for a body to be dissatisfied with him; yet his seventy-ton landau has kept us supplied with lame horses for nine months, whereas we were entitled to a light carriage suited to hill-climbing, and fastidious people would have made him furnish it.

The Cerretani family, of old and high distinction in the great days of the Republic, lived on this place during many centuries. Along in October we began to notice a pungent and suspicious odor which we were not acquainted with and which gave us some little apprehension, but I laid it on the dog and explained to the family that that kind of dog always smelled that way when he was up to windward of the subject, but privately I knew it was not the dog at all. I believed it was our adopted ancestors, the Cerretanis. I believed they were preserved under the house somewhere and that it would be a good scheme to get them out and air them. But I was mistaken. I made a secret search and had to acquit the ancestors. It turned out that the odor was a harmless one. It came from the wine crop, which was stored in a part of the cellars to which we had no access. This discovery gave our imaginations a rest and it turned a disagreeable smell into a pleasant one. But not until we had so long and lavishly flooded the house with odious disinfectants that the dog left and the family had to camp in the yard most of the time. It took two months to disinfect the disinfectants and persuade our wealth of atrocious stenches to emigrate. When they were finally all gone and the wine fragrance resumed business at the old stand we welcomed it with effusion and have had no fault to find with it since.

Oct. 6.—I find myself at a disadvantage here. Four persons in the house speak Italian and nothing else, one person speaks German and nothing else, the rest of the talk is in the French, English and profane languages. I am equipped with but the merest smattering in these tongues, if I except one or two. Angelo speaks French—a French which he could get a patent on, because he invented it himself; a French which no one can understand, a French which resembles no other confusion of sounds heard since Babel, a French which curdles the milk. He prefers it to his native Italian. He loves to talk it; loves to listen to himself; to him it is music; he will not let it alone. The family would like to get their little Italian savings into circulation but he will not give change. It makes no difference what language he is addressed in, his reply is in French, his peculiar French, his grating, uncanny French, which sounds like shoveling anthracite down a coal chute. I know a few Italian words and several phrases, and along at first I used to keep them bright and fresh by whetting them on Angelo; but he partly couldn't understand them and partly didn't want to, so I have been obliged to withdraw them from the market for the present. But this is only temporary. I am practicing, I am preparing. Some day I shall be ready for him, and not in ineffectual French but in his native tongue. I will seethe this kid in its mother's milk.

Oct. 27.—The first month is finished. We are wonted now. It is agreed that life at a Florentine villa is an ideal existence. The weather is divine, the outside aspects lovely, the days and the nights tranquil and reposeful, the seclusion from the world and its worries as satisfactory as a dream. There is no housekeeping to do, no plans to make, no marketing to superintend —all these things do themselves, apparently. One is vaguely aware that somebody is attending to them, just as one is aware that the world is being turned over and the constellations worked and the sun shoved around according to the schedule, but that is all; one does not feel personally concerned or in any way responsible. Yet there is no head, no chief executive; each servant minds his or her own department, requiring no supervision and having none. They hand in elaborately itemized bills once a week; then the machinery goes silently on again, just as before. There is no noise or fussing or quarreling or confusion—upstairs. I don't know what goes on below. Late in the afternoons friends come out from the city and drink tea in the open air and tell what is happening in the world; and when the great sun sinks down upon Florence and the daily miracle begins, they hold their breaths and look. It is not a time for talk.

CHAPTER 66

Susy passed from life in the Hartford home the 18th of August, 1896. With her when the end came were Jean, and Katy Leary, and John and Ellen (the gardener and his wife). Clara and her mother and I arrived in England from around the world on the 31st of July and took a house in Guildford. A week later, when Susy, Katy and Jean should have been arriving from America, we got a letter instead.

It explained that Susy was slightly ill—nothing of consequence. But we were disquieted and began to cable for later news. This was Friday. All day no answer—and the ship to leave Southampton next day at noon. Clara and her mother began packing, to be ready in case the news should be bad. Finally came a cablegram saying, "Wait for cablegram in the morning." This was not satisfactory—not reassuring. I cabled again, asking that the answer be sent to Southampton, for the day was now closing. I waited in the post office that night till the doors were closed, toward midnight, in the hope that good news might still come, but there was no message. We sat silent at home till one in the morning, waiting—waiting for we knew not what. Then we took the earliest morning train and when we reached Southampton the message was there. It said the recovery would be long but certain. This was a great relief to me but not to my wife. She was frightened. She and Clara went aboard the steamer at once and sailed for America to nurse Susy. I remained behind to search for another and larger house in Guildford.

That was the 15th of August, 1896. Three days later, when my wife and Clara were about halfway across the ocean, I was standing in our dining room, thinking of nothing in particular, when a cablegram was put in my hand. It said, "Susy was peacefully released to-day."

It is one of the mysteries of our nature that a man, all unprepared, can receive a thunder-stroke like that and live. There is but one reasonable explanation of it. The intellect is

351

stunned by the shock and but gropingly gathers the meaning of the words. The power to realize their full import is mercifully wanting. The mind has a dumb sense of vast loss—that is all. It will take mind and memory months and possibly years to gather together the details and thus learn and know the whole extent of the loss. A man's house burns down. The smoking wreckage represents only a ruined home that was dear through years of use and pleasant associations. By and by, as the days and weeks go on, first he misses this, then that, then the other thing. And when he casts about for it he finds that it was in that house. Always it is an *essential*—there was but one of its kind. It cannot be replaced. It was in that house. It is irrevocably lost. He did not realize that it was an essential when he had it; he only discovers it now when he finds himself balked, hampered, by its absence. It will be years before the tale of lost essentials is complete, and not till then can he truly know the magnitude of his disaster.

The 18th of August brought me the awful tidings. The mother and the sister were out there in mid-Atlantic, ignorant of what was happening, flying to meet this incredible calamity. All that could be done to protect them from the full force of the shock was done by relatives and good friends. They went down the Bay and met the ship at night but did not show themselves until morning, and then only to Clara. When she returned to the stateroom she did not speak and did not need to. Her mother looked at her and said, "Susy is dead."

At half past ten o'clock that night Clara and her mother completed their circuit of the globe and drew up at Elmira by the same train and in the same car which had borne them and me westward from it one year, one month and one week before. And again Susy was there—not waving her welcome in the glare of the lights as she had waved her farewell to us thirteen months before, but lying white and fair in her coffin in the house where she was born.

The last thirteen days of Susy's life were spent in our own house in Hartford, the home of her childhood and always the dearest place in the earth to her. About her she had faithful old friends—her pastor, Mr. Twichell, who had known her from the cradle and who had come a long journey to be with her; her uncle and aunt, Mr. and Mrs. Theodore Crane; Patrick, the coachman; Katy, who had begun to serve us when Susy was a child of eight years; John and Ellen, who had been with us many years. Also Jean was there.

At the hour when my wife and Clara set sail for America, Susy was in no danger. Three hours later there came a sudden change for the worse. Meningitis set in and it was immediately apparent that she was death-struck. That was Saturday, the 15th of August.

"That evening she took food for the last time." (Jean's letter to me.) The next morning the brain fever was raging. She walked the floor a little in her pain and delirium, then succumbed to weakness and returned to her bed. Previously she had found hanging in a closet a gown which she had seen her mother wear. She thought it was her mother, dead, and she kissed it and cried. About noon she became blind (an effect of the disease) and bewailed it to her uncle.

From Jean's letter I take this sentence, which needs no comment:

"About one in the afternoon Susy spoke for the last time."

It was only one word that she said when she spoke that last time and it told of her longing. She groped with her hands and found Katy and caressed her face and said, "Mamma."

How gracious it was that in that forlorn hour of wreck and ruin, with the night of death closing around her, she should have been granted that beautiful illusion—that the latest vision which rested upon the clouded mirror of her mind should have been the vision of her mother, and the latest emotion she should know in life the joy and peace of that dear imagined presence.

About two o'clock she composed herself as if for sleep and never moved again. She fell into unconsciousness and so remained two days and five hours, until Tuesday evening at seven minutes past seven, when the release came. She was twenty-four years and five months old.

On the 23rd her mother and her sisters saw her laid to rest—she that had been our wonder and our worship.

◇◇◇◇◇◇◇◇◇◇◇◇◇◇◇◇◇◇

CHAPTER 67

Tomorrow will be the 5th of June,[1] a day which marks the disaster of my life—the death of my wife. It occurred two years

[1] Written in 1906.

ago, in Florence, Italy, whither we had taken her in the hope of restoring her broken health.

The dictating of this autobiography, which was begun in Florence in the beginning of 1904, was soon suspended because of the anxieties of the time, and I was never moved to resume the work until January 1906, for I did not see how I was ever going to bring myself to speak in detail of the mournful episodes and experiences of that desolate interval and of the twenty-two months of wearing distress which preceded it. I wish to bridge over that hiatus now with an outline sketch. I can venture nothing more as yet.

Mrs. Clemens had never been strong, and a thirteen months' journey around the world seemed a doubtful experiment for such a physique as hers, but it turned out to be a safe one. When we took the train westward-bound at Elmira on the 15th of July, 1895, we moved through blistering summer heats and, by and by, through summer heats with the heat of burning forests added. This for twenty-three days—I lecturing every night. Notwithstanding these trying conditions, Mrs. Clemens reached Vancouver in as good health as she was when she began the journey. From that day her health seemed improved, although the summer continued thereafter for five months without a break. It was summer at the Sandwich Islands. We reached Sydney, Australia, thirty-four degrees south of the equator, in October, just when the Australian summer was getting well under way. It was summer during our whole stay in Australia, New Zealand and Tasmania. It was still summer when we sailed from Melbourne on the 1st of January '96. It was blistering summer in Ceylon, of course, as it always is. It was supposed by the English residents of Bombay to be winter there, when we reached that city in January, but we couldn't recognize that our climate had ever changed since our departure from Elmira in mid-July. It was still summer to us all over India until the 17th of March, when an English physician in Jeypore told us to fly for Calcutta and get out of India immediately, because the warm weather could come at any time now and it would be perilous for us. So we sweltered along through the "cold weather," as they called it there, clear from Rawal Pindi to Calcutta, and took ship for South Africa—and still Mrs. Clemens's health had steadily improved. She and Clara went with me all over my lecture course in South Africa, except to Pretoria, and she never had a day's illness.

We finally finished our lecture raid on the 14th of July '96, sailed for England the next day and landed at Southampton on the 31st. A fortnight later Mrs. Clemens and Clara sailed for home to nurse Susy through a reported illness and found her in her coffin in her grandmother's house.

The diminished family presently joined me in England. We lived in London, in Switzerland, in Vienna, in Sweden, and again in London, until October 1900. And when at that time we took ship, homeward bound, Mrs. Clemens's health and strength were in better condition than they had ever been before since she was sixteen years old and met with the accident which I have before mentioned.

We took No. 14 West 10th Street, just out of Fifth Avenue, for a year, and there the over-taxing of Mrs. Clemens's strength began. The house was large; housekeeping was a heavy labor—as indeed it always is in New York—but she would not have a housekeeper. She had resisted, and successfully resisted, all my persuasions in that direction from the day that we were married. Social life was another heavy tax upon her strength. In the drive and rush and hurly-burly of the mid-winter New York season my correspondence grew beyond my secretary's strength and mine, and I found that Mrs. Clemens was trying to ease our burden for us. One day I wrote thirty-two brief letters with my own hand, and then found, to my dismay, that Mrs. Clemens had written the same number. She had added this labor to her other labors and they were already too heavy for her.

By the following June this kind of life, after her nine and a half years of tranquil and effortless life in Europe, began to exhibit effects. Three months' repose and seclusion in the Adirondacks did her manifest good. Then we took a house in Riverdale-on-the-Hudson. It was a large house, and again the housekeeping burden was heavy. Early in 1902 she was threatened with a nervous breakdown, but soon the danger seemed past.

At the end of June we secured a furnished house in the outskirts of York Harbor for the summer. Mr. Rogers brought his *Kanawha*, the fastest steam yacht in American waters, cast anchor and sent the launch ashore at our river front, and Mrs. Clemens and Jean and I went down to embark. I found, then, that Mrs. Clemens was not taking a servant along. This was because she was so afraid of being an inconvenience and an incumbrance to Mr. Rogers. It was too bad. She could have had the whole ship and welcome. Jean's health was bad, and she would need much attention. This service would fall upon Mrs. Clemens. My services would be of a stupid and ignorant sort and worthless. It was too late. She had arranged to ship the entire household and all the baggage by rail to York Harbor.

It was lovely weather and we sped over the sparkling seas like a bird, chasing all craft in sight, sending them all astern, one by one. But these delights were not for Mrs. Clemens. She had to stay below and take care of Jean. As night fell we took refuge from heavy weather in the harbor of New London. Mrs. Clemens did not get much rest or sleep, because of Jean. The next morning we sailed to Fairhaven. That was Mrs. Clemens's opportunity to lie at rest on board the yacht two or three hours, while the rest of us went ashore and visited Mr. Rogers's family at his country place. But she elected to go ashore. She fatigued herself in many ways. She continued to add to these fatigues by nursing Jean during the rest of the voyage to York Harbor.

Once again, here was opportunity to rest, but she would not rest. She could not rest. She never was intended to rest. She had the spirit of a steam engine in a frame of flesh. It was always racking that frame with its tireless energy; it was always exacting of it labors that were beyond its strength. Her heart soon began to alarm her. Twelve years before, two Hartford physicians of high repute had ordered her to the baths of Aix-les-Bains and had told her that with care she would live two years. Two physicians of Aix-les-Bains said that with care she would live longer than that. Physicians of repute in Rome, Florence and Berlin had given her the usual two years—and at Nauheim (Germany) the physician lowest in the published and authorized list of physicians chartered by that Bath examined Mrs. Clemens and told me that there was nothing very serious the matter with her; that she would probably live a good many years yet. I was affronted. I was indignant that this ignorant apprentice should be allowed to play with people's lives, and I paid his bill and discharged him on the spot, without a recommendation. Yet he was the only physician of the dozen whose prediction was worth anything. When we took up our residence in York Harbor Mrs. Clemens had outlived all the other predictions by eleven years.

But, as I have said, she became alarmed about her heart in York Harbor early in July. Her alarm increased rapidly. Within a fortnight she began to dread driving out. Anything approaching swift motion terrified her. She was afraid of descending grades, even such slight ones as to be indeterminable and imperceptible in the summer twilights. She would implore the coachman not only to walk his horses down those low and imperceptible hills, but she watched him with fear and distress, and if the horses stepped out of a walk for only a moment she would seize me on one side and the carriage on the other, in an ecstasy of fright. This was the condition of things all through July.

Now comes a curious thing. Howells[2] was living at Kittery Point, three-quarters of an hour away by trolley, and one day in July or early in August he made his second visit to us. It was afternoon, and Mrs. Clemens's resting time. She was upstairs in her room. Howells and I sat on the veranda overlooking the river and chatting, and presently he drifted into the history of a pathetic episode in the life of a friend of his, one or two of whose most moving features were soon to find strange duplication in Mrs. Clemens's case.

While he sat there that afternoon telling the curious story, neither of us suspected that it was prophetic, yet it was. I at once wrote it out in the form of a tale—using fictitious names, of course—and sent it to *Harper's Monthly*.

◇◇◇◇◇◇◇◇◇◇◇◇◇◇◇◇◇◇

CHAPTER 68

York Harbor consists of a widely scattered cluster of independent little villages called York, York Harbor, York Village, York Center, West York, East York, South York—I think those are the names but I am not certain and it is not important. The whole of them together are bunched under one simple, rational name, York. About the 6th of August a celebration broke out among these hives—a celebration in commemoration of the two hundred and fiftieth anniversary of the institution of municipal self-constituted government on the continent of America. For two or three days there were quaint back-settlement processions, mass meetings, orations and so on, by day, and fireworks by night.

[2] William Dean Howells.

Mrs. Clemens was always young and these things had a strong interest for her. She even took more interest in my speeches than I took in them myself. During three days she went about behind horses in the daytime and by boat at night, seeing and hearing and enjoying all that was going on. She was overexerting herself, overtaxing her strength, and she began to show it. With difficulty I persuaded her to forego the grand performances of the closing night, and we observed their firework effects from the piazza, across the intervening distance of two or three miles. But my interference had come too late. The overtaxing of her strength had already been over-sufficient.

The next afternoon was the last she ever spent in this life as a person personally and intimately connected with this world's affairs. It was the last time she was to receive and entertain a visitor. This visit promised to be commonplace and instantly and easily forgettable, but by grace of my native talent for making innocent and discomforting blunders it wasn't. The visitor was a lady. She had forwarded to us a letter of introduction and now she was come, upon our invitation, to spend the afternoon and dine with us. She was a beautiful creature. She said she was thirty years old and had been married fifteen years. Her manner, and her English, would have convicted her of being of foreign origin, and if any evidence were needed to clinch the conviction and justify the verdict it was present in her alien and unpronounceable name, which no inexperienced Christian might try to pronounce and live. Yet she was not a foreigner at all. She was American born, of native American parents. Her tongue had never known any language but the American language until she married the unpronounceable foreigner at fifteen in Paris. Her English was quaint and pretty, graceful and understandable, but it was not English.

The letter of introduction which she had forwarded to me was one of those formidable great missives which are the specialty of royalty and it was from the Queen of Rumania. It said that the bearer and her husband, who was a Rumanian nobleman, had resided at the Rumanian court for fifteen years, where the husband had held an important post under the Government. The letter spoke affectionately of the wife. It also said that she was a highly accomplished musician and competent to teach, and that she was returning to her own country in the hope of being able to earn a living there by teaching. Her Majesty thought that perhaps I could be useful in finding classes for this exiled friend of hers.

Carmen Sylva's letter was in English, a language of which she is a master, and the letter explained why these people, so comfortably nested in her court and in her affections for fifteen years, were suddenly become exiles, wanderers in the earth, friendless, forlorn and driven to earn their bread by the sweat of their accomplishments. But just as we were going to find out *what* it was that had caused this disaster—if it was a disaster—just as my wife and I had reached the summit of eagerness to get at the kernel of that interesting secret, the Queen delivered that kernel in *French*. It was a single phrase—two or three words—but they made a combination which we had never encountered before and which we were not able to cipher the meaning of. The Queen said in substance—I have forgotten the exact words—that the husband had been obliged to resign his post or posts and retire from the court on account of—then followed that fiendish French sentence. For a moment I was so exasperated that I wished I never had learned the French language—plainly a language likely to fail a person at the crucial moment.

At mid-afternoon Mrs. Clemens, the beautiful American foreigner and I sat grouped together and chatting on the piazza. I had in my hand the current *North American Review,* fresh, enticing, inviting, with the fragrance of the printer's ink still breathing from its pages and making me long to open it and see what was in it. That court-bred creature had her eyes about her. She was accustomed to reading people's concealed feelings and desires by help of treacherous exterior indications such as attitude, fidgets and so on. She saw what was the matter with me and she most winningly and beseechingly asked me to open the magazine and read aloud. I was most cordially grateful. I opened the magazine, and the first thing that attracted me was an article by an Austrian prince on Dueling in Court and Military Circles on the Continent of Europe. It profoundly interested me and I read along with vigor and emphasis. The Prince was hostile to the dueling system. He told of the measures which were being taken by generals and great nobles in Austria—particularly in Austria, I think—to abolish the system. In the course of his uncompromising indictment of the system he remarked upon the fact that no important official on the Continent of Europe could decline a challenge, from any motive whatever, and not by that act cover himself and his

family with shame and disgrace and be thenceforth spurned
and ignored by the society in which they moved, and even by
their friends.

I happened to lift my eyes—that poor woman's face was as
white as marble! The French phrase stood translated! I did
not read any more and we hurriedly changed to some other
topic.

As I have said, this was the last incident in Mrs. Clemens's
social life—a life in which she had been active and which she
had enjoyed with all her heart from the days of her young
girlhood. It was the last incident—it closed that volume. It
prefaced the next and final volume of her existence in this
earth. And I think I would remember it because of this distinction, even if it had been commonplace and colorless. But it
was not commonplace. It was not colorless. It stands out
sharply in my memory and will remain so, I think.

At seven the next morning (August the eleventh)[1] I was
wakened by a cry. I saw Mrs. Clemens standing on the opposite side of the room, leaning against the wall for support, and
panting. She said, "I am dying."

I helped her back to bed and sent for Dr. Leonard, a New
York physician. He said it was a nervous breakdown and that
nothing but absolute rest, seclusion and careful nursing could
help her. That was the beginning. During the twenty-two succeeding months she had for society physicians and trained
nurses only, broadly speaking.

The next sixty days were anxious ones for us. When we entered the month of October it was a question if we could get
her back to Riverdale. We could not venture transportation
by Mr. Rogers's yacht. She would not be able to endure the
sea effect. At last we resolved to try the rather poor contrivance called an invalid's car. I call it a poor contrivance because while it is spacious and has plenty of room in it for all
the friends and nurses and physicians you need, it has one
very great defect—the invalid's bed is stationary and immovable and responds to every jump and jerk and whirl of the
train, whereas if it were suspended from the roof by elastic
ropes, hammock fashion, the invalid would never feel a jolt or
a quiver. We secured a special train to take this car to Boston
and around Boston. Then we hitched it to a regular express
train which delivered us in the Grand Central Station in New

[1] 1902.

York on time. A locomotive stood ready and waiting, and in fifteen minutes it delivered us at our home—Riverdale.

The burly English butler carried Mrs. Clemens upstairs to her bed and left her there with the trained nurse. When he closed that bedroom door he shut the truth out from that bedchamber forevermore. The physician, Dr. Moffat, came once or twice a day and remained a few minutes. If any doctor-lies were needed he faithfully furnished them. When the trained nurse was on duty she furnished such lies as were needful. Clara stood a daily watch of three or four hours, and hers was a hard office indeed. Daily she sealed up in her heart a dozen dangerous truths and thus saved her mother's life and hope and happiness with holy lies. She had never told her mother a lie in her life before, and I may almost say that she never told her a truth afterward. It was fortunate for us all that Clara's reputation for truthfulness was so well established in her mother's mind. It was our daily protection from disaster. The mother never doubted Clara's word. Clara could tell her large improbabilities without exciting any suspicion, whereas if I had tried to market even a small and simple one the case would have been different. I was never able to get a reputation like Clara's. It would have been useful to me now, but it was too late to begin the labor of securing it, and I furnished no information in the bedchamber. But my protection lay in the fact that I was allowed in the bedchamber only once a day, then for only two minutes. The nurse stood at the door with her watch in her hand and turned me out when the time was up.

My room was next to Mrs. Clemens's, with a large bathroom between. I could not talk with her, but I could correspond by writing. Every night I slipped a letter under the bathroom door that opened near her bed—a letter which contained no information about current events and could do no harm. She responded, with pencil, once or twice a day—at first at some length, but as the months dragged along and her strength grew feebler, she put her daily message of love in trembling characters upon little scraps of paper, and this she continued until the day she died.

CHAPTER 69

I have mentioned that Clara's post was difficult, and indeed it was. Several times, in letters written to friends in those days, I furnished illustrations of the difficulties of Clara's position. One of these letters was written to Susy Crane at the end of 1902, two months and a half after we had come back from York Harbor.

Some days before Christmas, Jean came in from a long romp in the snow, in the way of coasting, skiing and so on, with the young Dodges, and she sat down, perspiring, with her furs on, and was presently struck with a violent chill. She fell into the doctor's hands at once and by Christmas Eve was become very ill. The disease was double pneumonia. From that time onward, to and beyond the date of this letter, her case was alarming. During all this time her mother never suspected that anything was wrong. She questioned Clara every day concerning Jean's health, spirits, clothes, employments and amusements, and how she was enjoying herself; and Clara furnished the information right along, in minute detail—every word of it false, of course. Every day she had to tell how Jean dressed; and in time she got so tired of using Jean's existing clothes over and over again and trying to get new effects out of them that finally, as a relief to her hard-worked invention, she got to adding imaginary clothes to Jean's wardrobe, and would probably have doubled it and trebled it if a warning note in her mother's comments had not admonished her that she was spending more money on these spectral gowns and things than the family income justified.

Of course Jean had to have a professional nurse, and a woman named Tobin was engaged for that office. Jean's room was at the other end of the house from her mother's quarters; and so, doctors and nurses could come and go without their presence being detected by Mrs. Clemens. During the middle, or the end, of January, Jean had become able to be about, and the Doctor ordered a change of scene for her. He said she must be taken South to Old Point Comfort, and this was done. Katy and Miss Tobin accompanied her and she remained at Old Point Comfort several weeks. The orders were to stay six weeks, but neither Jean nor Katy could endure that trained nurse and they returned to Riverdale before the term was up.

During the whole of Jean's absence Mrs. Clemens was happy in the thought that she was on the premises; that she was in blooming health; that she was having as joyous a time as any young girl in the region. Clara kept her mother posted every day concerning Jean's movements. On one day she would report Jean as being busy with her wood carving; the next day she would have Jean hard at work at her language-studies; the day after, she would report Jean as being busy typewriting literature for me. In the course of time she got as tired of these worn stage-properties as she had of Jean's clothes before.

I will here insert the Susy Crane letter.

CLARA'S DAY.

In bed, 9 P.M.
Riverdale, Dec. 29 '02.

Susy dear, two hours ago, Clara was recounting her day to me. Of course I can't get any of it right, there's so much detail; but with your York Harbor experience of the hardships attendant upon sickroom lying, you will get an idea, at any rate, of what a time that poor child has every day, picking her way through traps and pitfalls, and just barely escaping destruction two or three times in every hour.

[To-day. Jean's other lung attacked; a crisis expected to-night—Dr. Janeway to be summoned in the morning. Our doctor is to stay all night.]

Of course Clara does not go to her Monday lesson in New York to-day, on Jean's account—but judiciously forgets that fact, and enters her mother's room (where she has no business to be) toward train-time, *dressed in a wrapper*.

Livy. Why Clara, aren't you going to your lesson?

Clara. (almost caught) Yes.

Livy. In that costume?

Cl. Oh, no.

L. Well, you can't make your train, it's impossible.

Cl. I know, but I'm going to take the other one.

L. Indeed *that* won't do—you'll be ever so *much* too late for your lesson.

Cl. No, the lesson-time has been put an hour later. (sic)

L. (satisfied. Then suddenly) But Clara, that train and the late lesson together will make you late to Mrs. Hapgood's luncheon.

Cl. No, the train leaves 15 minutes earlier than it used to. (sic)

L. (satisfied) Tell Mrs. Hapgood etc., etc. (which Clara promised to do). Clara dear, after the luncheon—I hate to put this on you—but *could* you do two or three little shopping-errands for me?—it is a pity to send Miss Lyon[1] all the way to New York for so little.

Cl. Oh, it won't trouble me a bit—I can do it. (Takes a list of the things she is to buy—a list which she will presently hand to Miss Lyon and send her to New York to make the purchases.)

L. (reflectively) What is that name? Tobin—Toby—no, it's Tobin—Miss Tobin.

Cl. (turning cold to the marrow, but exhibiting nothing— Miss Tobin is Jean's trained nurse). What about Tobin—or Miss Tobin? Who is it?

L. A nurse—trained nurse. They say she is very good, and not talkative. Have you seen her?

Cl. (Desperately—not knowing anything to say in this mysterious emergency) Seen her? A Miss Tobin? No. Who is it?

L. (To Clara's vast relief) Oh, *I* don't know. The Doctor spoke of her—and praised her. I suppose it was a hint that we need another. But I didn't respond, and he dropped the matter. Miss Sherry is enough; we don't need another. If he approaches you about it, discourage him. I think it is time you were dressing, dear—remember and tell Mrs. Hapgood what I told you.

[Exit Clara—still alive—finds Miss Sherry waiting in the hall. They rehearse some lies together for mutual protection. Clara goes and hovers around in Jean's part of the house and pays her frequent visits of a couple of minutes but does not allow her to talk. At 3 or 4 P.M. takes the things Miss Lyon has brought from New York; studies over her part a little, then goes to her mother's room.]

Livy. It's very good of you, dear. Of course if I had known

---

[1] Mark Twain's secretary.

it was going to be so snowy and drizzly and sloppy I wouldn't have asked you to buy them. Did you get wet?

Cl. Oh, nothing to hurt.

L. You took a cab both ways?

Cl. Not from the station to the lesson—the weather was good enough till that was over.

L. Well, now, tell me everything Mrs. Hapgood said.

[Clara tells her a long yarn—avoiding novelties and surprises and anything likely to inspire questions difficult to answer; and of course detailing the menu, for if it had been the feeding of the 5,000, Livy would have insisted on knowing what kind of bread it was and how the fishes were served. By and by, while talking of something else—]

Livy. Clams!—in the end of December. Are you sure it was clams?

Cl. I didn't say cl— I meant blue-points.

L. (Tranquilized) It seemed odd. What is Jean doing?

Cl. She said she was going to do a little typewriting. [Lie, of course; Jean being barely alive.]

L. Has she been out to-day?

Cl. Only a moment, right after luncheon. She was determined to go out again, but—

L. How did you know she was out?

Cl. (saving herself in time) Katy told me. She was determined to go out again in the rain and snow, but I persuaded her to stay in.

L. (with moving and grateful admiration)—Clara, you *are* wonderful! The wise watch you keep over Jean, and the *influence* you have over her; it's so lovely of you, and I tied here and can't take care of her myself. (And she goes on with these undeserved praises till Clara is expiring with shame.) How did John Howells seem yesterday?

Cl. Oh, he was very well. Of course it seemed pretty desolate in that big dining room with only two at table.

L. Why only *two*?

Cl. (stupidly) Well—er—papa doesn't count.

L. But doesn't Jean count?

Cl. (almost caught again) Why, yes, she *counts* of course—makes up the number—but she doesn't say anything—never talks.

L. Did she walk with you?

Cl. A little way. Then we met the Dodges and she went off coasting with them.

L. (wonderingly) Sunday?

C. (up a stump for a moment,) Well, they don't *every* Sunday. They didn't last Sunday.

[Livy was apparently satisfied. Jean said, some weeks ago, that Clara is the only person who can tell her mother an *improbable* lie and get it believed; and that is because Clara has never before told her any lies.]

L. When did Mark Homburg come?

Cl. Just as John was leaving.

L. I kept waiting to hear the piano. Wasn't it dull for him with no music? Why didn't you take him to the piano?

Cl. I did offer, but he had a headache. [Lie]

[The piano is too close to Jean—it would have disturbed her.]

This is a pretty rude sketch, aunt Sue, and all the *fine* things are left out—I mean the exceedingly close places which Clara is constantly getting into and then slipping out *just* alive by a happy miracle of impromptu subterfuge and fraud. The whole thing would be funny, if it were not so heartbreakingly pathetic and tragic.

I have the strongest desire to call you to us, but the doctor wouldn't let you see Livy; and if he did—but he wouldn't.

Dec. 30. 6 A.M. (which is about dawn) I have been up to Jean's room, and find all quiet there—Jean sleeping. Miss Tobin whispered, "She has had a *splendid* night." The doctor (and Clara) had put in an appearance a couple of times in the night and gone back to bed, finding things going well.

S L C

CHAPTER 70

When one considers that Clara had been practising these ingenuities for two months and a half and that she was to continue to practise them daily for a year and a half longer, one gets something of a realizing sense of the difficulties and perils of the office she was filling. I will furnish here another sample.

Letter to Rev. Joseph H. Twichell.

Riverdale-on-the-Hudson.
The Last Day of a—in some respects—
Tough Year, being A.D. 1902.

DEAR JOE—

It is 10 A.M. and the post has just brought your good greeting of yesterday. Yesterday at mid-afternoon there was a memorable episode: I was in Livy's presence two minutes and odd (the trained nurse holding the watch in her hand) for the first time in three and a half months.

Livy was radiant! (And I didn't spoil it by saying, "Jean is lying low with pneumonia these seven days.")

[A good deal of the rest of the week, Joe, can be found in my Christmas story *(Harper's)* entitled "Was it Heaven? Or Hell?" which is largely a true story and was written in York Harbor in August or September.]

In that story mother and daughter are ill, and the lying is attended to by a pair of aged aunts—assisted by the doctor, of course, though I suppress his share to make the story short. In this Riverdale home the liars are the doctor, Clara and Miss Sherry (Livy's trained nurse). Those are the regulars. I am to see Livy again to-day for two or three minutes and it is possible that she may say, "Who was it you were talking with at breakfast?—I made out a man's voice." (And confuse me.) (The man was the doctor; he spends his nights here with Jean and is not due to visit Livy until noon—he lives two or three miles away.) She sent Miss Sherry down to ask that question, during breakfast. We three consulted and sent back word it was a stranger. It will be like Livy to ask me what stranger it was. Therefore I am to go prepared with a stranger calculated to fill the bill.

Yesterday morning the doctor left here at nine and made his rounds in Yonkers, then came back and paid Livy his usual noon visit; but this morning he had a patient or so within half a mile of here, and to save travel he thought it would be a good idea to go straight up to Livy from the breakfast table; so he sent up to say he had called in passing and couldn't he come up and see

Livy *now?* Of course she said yes, and he went up. He ought to have kept still; but some devil moved him to say—

"Mr. Clemens says you are looking distinctly better than when he last saw you, in York."

Livy was back at him instantly:

"Why—have you seen him? How did you come to see him since yesterday afternoon?"

Luckily the doctor did not exhibit the joggle she had given him, but said composedly—

"I ran across him in the hall a minute ago when I came in."

So then he had to get Miss Sherry outside and arrange with her to tell me that that was how he came to know my opinion of the patient's looks. To make doubly sure, he hunted me up and told me himself; then called Clara and instructed *her;* for although her watch is not in the forenoon, she takes Miss Sherry's place a little while every morning while Miss Sherry goes down and plans Livy's food for the day with the cook.

I am to see Livy a moment every afternoon until she has another bad night; and I stand in dread, for with all my practice I realize that in a sudden emergency I am but a poor clumsy liar, whereas a fine alert and capable emergency-liar is the only sort that is worth anything in a sick-chamber.

Now, Joe, just see what reputation can do. All Clara's life she has told Livy the truth and now the reward comes: Clara lies to her three and a half hours every day, and Livy takes it all at par whereas even when I tell her a truth it isn't worth much without corroboration.

Clara's talents are worked plenty hard enough without this new call upon them—Jean. Of course we do not want Jean to know her own danger and that the doctor is spending his nights thirty feet from her. Yesterday at sunrise Clara carried an order from him to Jean's nurse; and being worn and not at her brightest self, she delivered it in Jean's hearing. At once Jean spoke up:

"What is the doctor doing here—is mamma worse?"

It brought Clara to herself, and she said—

"No. He telephoned this order late last night, and said let it go into effect at six or seven this morning."

This morning Clara forgot herself again. She was in a

long hall that leads past Jean's room, and called out to Katy about something, "Take it to the doctor's room!"

Then she flew to explain to Jean with an explanatory lie and was happy to find that Jean was asleep and hadn't heard.

I wish Clara were not so hard driven—so that she could take a pen and put upon paper all the details of one of her afternoons in her mother's room. Day before yesterday (Monday), for instance. We were all desperately frightened and anxious about Jean (both lungs affected, temperature 104 2/5, with high pulse and blazing fever), the whole household moving aimlessly about with absent and vacant faces—and Clara sitting miserable at heart but outwardly smiling, and telling her happy mother what good times Jean was having, coasting and carrying on out in the snow with the Dodges these splendid winter days! . . .

Joe, Livy is the happiest person you ever saw. And she has had it all to herself for a whole week. What a week! So full of comedy and pathos and tragedy!

Jean had a good night last night and she is doing as well as in the circumstances can be expected.

Joe, don't let those people invite me—I couldn't go. I have canceled all engagements and shan't accept another for a year.

There'll be a full report of that dinner[1]—issued by Col. Harvey as a remembrancer—and of course he will send it to all the guests. If he should overlook you—which he won't—let me know.

Soon my brief visit is due. I've just been up, listening at Livy's door. For the first time in months I heard her break into one of her girlish old-time laughs. With a word I could freeze the blood in her veins!

P. S. 1902

Dec. 31, 5 P.M. A great disappointment. I was sitting outside Livy's door, waiting. Clara came out a minute ago and said Livy is not so well and the nurse can't let me see her to-day. And Clara whispered other things. In the effort to find a new diversion for Jean, she pretended she had sent her down to a matinée in New York this afternoon. Livy was pleased but at once wanted the name of the play. Clara was aground. She was afraid to name

---

[1] My 67th birthday. (M.T.)

one—in fact couldn't for the moment think of any name.
Hesitances won't do; so she said Jean hadn't mentioned
the name of it, but was only full of seeing Fay Davis
again.

That was satisfactory and the incident was closed.
Then—

"Your father is willing to go with you and Jean tomorrow night?" (To Carnegie Hall.)

"Oh, yes. He is reformed since you are sick; never
grumbles about anything he thinks you would like him
to do. He's all alacrity to do the most disagreeable things.
You wouldn't recognize him, now. He's spoiling himself
—getting so vain of himself he—"

And so on and so on—fighting for time—time to think
up material. She had sent back the tickets a week ago,
with a note explaining why we couldn't come; the thing
had passed out of her mind, and to have it sprung up
on her out of the hoary past in this sudden way was a
perilous matter and called for wariness. (It is my little
juvenile piece "The Death-Wafer," which Livy loves and
longs to hear about it from an eyewitness.)

"Who else is going?"

"Mary Foote and—and Elizabeth Dodge—and—I think
that is all."

"Why—has Jean invited Elizabeth and not her *sister?*"

(Clara had forgotten there was a sister, and was
obliged to explain that she didn't really remember, but
believed Jean had mentioned the sister.)

"Well, to make sure, speak to her about it. But is that
all she has invited? It is a great big box, and the management have been very kind. It mustn't have a thin look."

And so Livy began to worry.

"Oh, don't you bother, Mousie. You can depend on
Jean to have it full. She mentioned names, but I had the
cook on my hands and wasn't paying attention."

And at this point, sure enough, I fell heir to *my* share;
for Clara said—

"Day after tomorrow she'll want to know *all* about it.
I can't furnish details, they've gone out of my head. You
must post me thoroughly tomorrow."

She had to get back to Livy's room then—and perhaps
explain what kept her so long.

This is a perplexing place. Livy knows the story and

I don't. I wrote it three years ago or more. I think I will suggest some such procedure as this—to Clara:

"*Generalize*—keep *generalizing*—about the scenery, and the costumes, and how bluff and fine the old Lord Protector was, and how pretty and innocently audacious the child was, and how pathetically bowed and broken the poor parents were, and all that, and how *perfectly* natural and accurate the Tower of London looked—work the Tower hard, and Livy knows the Tower well—work it for all it's worth—keep whirling it in—every time you get stuck, say 'Oh, but the Tower! ah, the Tower!' And keep your ears open—your *mother* will furnish the details, without knowing it. She'll mention the child's climbing up into Cromwell's lap uninvited—and you must break into the middle of her sentence and say 'Oh, you should have *seen* it!' and she'll say, 'When the child put the red wafer into her own father's hand—' you will break in and say, 'Oh, Mousie, it was too pitiful for anything—you could hear the whole house sob'; and she'll say, 'Was the child equal to her part when she flew to Cromwell and dragged him out and stamped her foot and—' you must break in and say, 'It was great! and when he said *"Obey! she spoke by my voice; the prisoner is pardoned—set him free!"* You ought to have been there! it was just grand!' "²

Jan. 1, '03. The doctor did not stay last night. Just as I was beginning to dress for dinner Livy's nurse came for me and I saw the patient four minutes. She was in great spirits—like twenty-five years ago.

She has sent me a New Year greeting this morning and has had a good night.

Jean has had a good night and does not look to me so blasted and blighted as on the previous days. She sleeps all the time. Temperature down to within a shade of normal this morning. Everything looking well here.

MARK.

Jan. 28.

Livy had a slight backset yesterday, so the doctor has just told me he is going to shut off my daily visit for a few days. It will distress her, and may have an ill effect at first; but later, results will show the wisdom of it no doubt.

² June, 1906. Clara follows the instructions and succeeds.

Katy's absence at Old Point Comfort with Jean makes a new difficulty. Livy charges Clara with orders for Katy every day. For months Katy has prepared special dishes for Livy, and now Livy wants her stirred up—she is growing careless in her cooking the past few days and isn't up to standard! By gracious *we* can't counterfeit Katy's cookery!

Yours ever,
Mark.

Jean is enjoying herself very well at Old Point Comfort. Clara has asked Judy to come up, and we are hoping she will say yes.

Toward the end of October[3] we carried Mrs. Clemens aboard ship, her excellent nurse, Miss Sherry, accompanying us. We reached Florence on the 9th of November. We conveyed our patient to that odious Villa di Quarto. Mrs. Clemens was doomed from the beginning but she never suspected it—*we* never suspected it. She had been ill many times in her life but her miraculous recuperative powers always brought her out of these perils safely. We were full of fears and anxieties and solicitudes all the time but I do not think we ever really lost hope. At least, not until the last two or three weeks. It was not like *her* to lose hope. We never expected her to lose it—and so at last when she looked me pathetically in the eyes and said, "You believe I shall get well?" it was a form which she had never used before and it was a betrayal. Her hope was perishing and I recognized it.

During five months I had been trying to find another and satisfactory villa, in the belief that if we could get Mrs. Clemens away from the Villa di Quarto and its fiendish associations, the happier conditions would improve both the health of her spirit and that of her body. I found many villas that had every desired feature save one or two, but the lacking one or two were always essentials—features necessary to the well-being of the invalid. But at last, on Saturday the 4th of June, I heard of a villa which promised to meet all the requirements. Sunday afternoon Jean and I drove to it, examined it and came home satisfied—more than satisfied, delighted. The purchase price was thirty thousand dollars cash and we could have possession at once.

We got back home at five in the afternoon and I waited

<hr>

[3] 1903.

until seven with my news. I was allowed to have fifteen minutes in the sick room two or three times a day—the last of these occasions being seven in the evening—and I was also privileged to step in for a single moment at nine in the evening and say good-night. At seven that evening I was at the bedside. I described the villa, exhibited its plans and said we would buy it tomorrow if she were willing, and move her to it as soon as she could bear the journey. She was pleased. She was satisfied. And her face—snow white, marble white, these latter weeks—was radiant.

◇◇◇◇◇◇◇◇◇◇◇◇◇◇◇◇◇◇

CHAPTER 71

Sunday Evening, June 5, 1904—11:15 o'clock. She has been dead two hours. It is impossible. The words have no meaning. But they are true; I know it, without realizing it. She was my life, and she is gone; she was my riches, and I am a pauper.

How sudden it was, how wholly unexpected! Only this afternoon Clara and Jean and I were talking blithely about her in the corridor, and Clara said "She is better to-day than she has been for three months"—then, half-frightened, she said *"Unberufen!"* and we echoed it hastily, superstitiously.

Only four hours ago I sat by her bedside while Clara and Jean were at dinner, and she was bright and cheerful—a rare thing these last miserable weeks—and she *would* talk, although it was a forbidden privilege, because she was so easily exhausted. She was full of interest in the calls which Jean and I had been making, and asked all about the people, and was like her old self. And smiled! Just her natural smile. It was sunshine breaking through weeks of cloud and gloom and unspoken dread. It lifted me up and made me believe the impossible—that she would walk again, be our comrade again! She startled me by speaking of the house in the country, as if she might yet get strong enough to go to it—a hope which she had given up almost as soon as we secured it a month ago. That gave me another uplift and again I believed there was happiness in store for us. Then a sense of her frailness and weakness came upon her and she said we must not mind it if we could not go, but be content here, she was sure the heat would not be unbearable; and I encouraged her and said it would never be any hotter than to-day, and her room would always be as cool as now. Poor tired child, how she loved her life, how longingly and eagerly she clung to it through all these twenty-two months of captivity and loneliness and bodily suffering, and how pathetically she searched our eyes for hope! And how all these bitter months we lied to her loyally and said she would get well *sure*, when we knew in our hearts it would never be! Only four hours ago—and now there she lies, white and still!

I was deceived by her inspiriting life and animation, and far overstayed my privilege. Only a word and a kiss were permissible, but I stayed a full half hour. Then I blamed myself and said I had done wrong; but she said there was no harm, and lavished caresses upon me in her old natural way, the way which has been hers for thirty-four years, and she said "You will come back?" and I said "Yes, to say good-night"—meaning at half-past nine, as usual these many many months. As usual, I stood a minute in the door, bending inward and throwing kisses, she throwing kisses in response, and her face all bright with that new-found smile—I not dreaming that I was looking upon that dear face for the last time in life. Yet so it was.

For a time I sat in my room, musing, filled with a deep contentment, my heart-burdens strangely gone, my spirit at peace for the first time in so many heavy months. Then that uplift came again, and grew to an exaltation; and under its influence I did a thing which I have hardly done since we lost our incomparable Susy eight years ago, whose death made a wound in her mother's heart which never healed—I went to the piano and sang the old songs, the quaint Negro hymns which no one cared for when I sang them, except Susy and her mother. When I sang them Susy always came and listened; when she died, my interest in them passed away; I could not put force and feeling into them without the inspiration of her approving presence. But now the force and feeling were all back, in full strength, and I was all alive, and it was as if eight years had fallen from me. In the midst of "My Lord He call me! He call me by the thunder!" Jean crept into the room and sat down, to my astonishment and—embarrassment; and I stopped, but when she asked me to go on, only the astonishment remained, and it was a pleasant one and inspiring. With great difficulty I brought up little by little the forgotten words of many songs, and Jean remained until a servant came and called her out. After a little I went to my room, and it was now getting toward time to go downstairs and say good-night; for it was a quarter past nine, and I must not go later than half-past. At that moment Livy was breathing her last!

At the head of the stairs I met Miss Lyon, who had come for me. I thought nothing of that; I merely supposed our old Katy thought Livy was tired and ought to be quieting down for the night. On my way down I framed a remark: "Livy, Jean has paid me a compliment which I have not had since we last—" But no, I must not say that, Susy's name would bring the heartbreak, and she would not sleep. She was already sleeping—and I never suspected!

Livy was sitting up in bed, with her head bent forward— she had not been able to lie down for seven months—and Katy was on one side of the bed and the nurse on the other, supporting her; Clara and Jean were standing near the foot of the bed, looking dazed. I went around and bent over and looked into Livy's face, and I think I spoke to her, I do not know; but she did not speak to me, and that seemed strange, I could not understand it. I kept looking at her and wondering —and never dreaming of what had happened! Then Clara said, "But is it *true*? Katy, *is* it true? it can't be true!" Katy burst into sobbings, and then for the first time I knew.

It was twenty minutes past nine. Only five minutes before, she had been speaking. She had heard me and had said to the nurse, "He is singing a good-night carol for me." They had had no idea that she was near to death. She was happy and was speaking—and in an instant she was gone from this life. How grateful I was that she had been spared the struggle she had so dreaded. And that I, too, had so dreaded for her. Five times in the last four months she spent an hour and more fighting violently for breath, and she lived in the awful fear of death by strangulation. Mercifully she was granted the gentlest and swiftest of deaths—by heart-failure—and she never knew, she never knew!

She was the most beautiful spirit, and the highest and the noblest I have known. And now she is dead.

CHAPTER 72

For good or for evil we continue to educate Europe. We have held the post of instructor for more than a century and a quarter now. We were not elected to it, we merely took it. We are of the Anglo-Saxon race. At the banquet last winter[1] of that organization which calls itself the Ends of the Earth Club, the chairman, a retired regular army officer of high grade, proclaimed in a loud voice, and with fervency, "We are of the Anglo-Saxon race, and when the Anglo-Saxon wants a thing *he just takes it.*"

That utterance was applauded to the echo. There were perhaps seventy-five civilians present and twenty-five military and naval men. It took those people nearly two minutes to work off their stormy admiration of that great sentiment; and meanwhile the inspired prophet who had discharged it—from his liver or his intestines or his esophagus or wherever he had bred it—stood there glowing and beaming and smiling and issuing rays of happiness from every pore, rays that were so intense that they were visible and made him look like the old-time picture in the Almanac of the man who stands discharging signs of the zodiac in every direction, and so absorbed in happiness, so steeped in happiness, that he smiles and smiles and has plainly forgotten that he is painfully and dangerously ruptured and exposed amidships and needs sewing up right away.

The soldier man's great utterance, interpreted by the expression which he put into it, meant in plain English, "The English and the Americans are thieves, highwaymen, pirates, and we are proud to be of the combination."

Out of all the English and Americans present, there was not one with the grace to get up and say he was ashamed of being an Anglo-Saxon, and also ashamed of being a member of the human race, since the race must abide under the presence upon it of the Anglo-Saxon taint. I could not perform this

[1] Written in September, 1906.

office. I could not afford to lose my temper and make a self-righteous exhibition of myself and my superior morals that I might teach this infant class in decency the rudiments of that cult, for they would not be able to grasp it; they would not be able to understand it.

It was an amazing thing to see, that boyishly frank and honest and delighted outburst of enthusiasm over the soldier prophet's mephitic remark. It looked suspiciously like a revelation, a secret feeling of the national heart surprised into expression and exposure by untoward accident, for it was a representative assemblage. All the chief mechanisms that constitute the machine which drives and vitalizes the national civilization were present—lawyers, bankers, merchants, manufacturers, journalists, politicians, soldiers, sailors—they were all there. Apparently it was the United States in banquet assembled, and qualified to speak with authority for the nation and reveal its private morals to the public view.

The initial welcome of that strange sentiment was not an unwary betrayal, to be repented of upon reflection; and this was shown by the fact that whenever during the rest of the evening a speaker found that he was becoming uninteresting and wearisome, he only needed to inject that great Anglo-Saxon moral into the midst of his platitudes to start up that glad storm again. After all, it was only the human race on exhibition. It has always been a peculiarity of the human race that it keeps two sets of morals in stock—the private and real, and the public and artificial.

Our public motto is "In God we trust," and when we see those gracious words on the trade-dollar (worth sixty cents) they always seem to tremble and whimper with pious emotion. That is our public motto. It transpires that our private one is, "When the Anglo-Saxon wants a thing *he just takes it.*" Our public morals are touchingly set forth in that stately and yet gentle and kindly motto which indicates that we are a nation of gracious and affectionate multitudinous brothers compacted into one—"*e pluribus unum.*" Our private morals find the light in the sacred phrase, "Come, *step* lively!"

We imported our imperialism from monarchical Europe, also our curious notions of patriotism—that is, if we have any principle of patriotism which any person can definitely and intelligibly define. It is but fair then, no doubt, that we should instruct Europe in return for these and the other kinds of instruction which we have received from that source.

Something more than a century ago we gave Europe the first notions of liberty it had ever had and thereby largely and happily helped to bring on the French Revolution and claim a share in its beneficent results. We have taught Europe many lessons since. But for us, Europe might never have known the interviewer; but for us certain of the European states might never have experienced the blessing of extravagant imposts; but for us the European Food Trust might never have acquired the art of poisoning the world for cash; but for us her Insurance Trusts might never have found out the best way to work the widow and orphan for profit; but for us the long delayed resumption of Yellow Journalism in Europe might have been postponed for generations to come. Steadily, continuously, persistently, we are Americanizing Europe, and all in good time we shall get the job perfected.

◇◇◇◇◇◇◇◇◇◇◇◇◇◇◇◇◇◇◇◇

CHAPTER 73

A cablegram arrived from England three weeks ago[1] inviting me to come to Oxford and receive an honorary degree on the 26th of next month. Of course I accepted, and without any waste of time. During the past two years I have been saying with great decision that my traveling days were permanently over and that nothing would ever induce me to cross the ocean again, yet I was not surprised at the alacrity with which I put that resolution behind me when this flattering invitation came. I could have declined an invitation to come over and accept of a London town lot and I could have done it without any difficulty, but a university degree is a quite different matter; that is a prize which I would go far to get at any time. I take the same childlike delight in a new degree that an Indian takes in a fresh scalp and I take no more pains to conceal my joy than the Indian does.

I remember the time that I found a battered old-time picayune in the road, when I was a boy, and realized that its value was vastly enhanced to me because I had not earned it. I remember the time, ten years later, in Keokuk, that I found a fifty-dollar bill in the street, and that the value of that bill

---
[1] Written May 23, 1907.

also was vastly enhanced to me by the reflection that I had not earned it. I remember the time in San Francisco, after a further interval of eight years, when I had been out of work and out of money for three months, that I found a ten-cent piece in the crossing at the junction of Commercial and Montgomery Streets, and realized that that dime gave me more joy, because unearned, than a hundred earned dimes could have given me. In my time I have acquired several hundred thousand dollars, but inasmuch as I earned them they have possessed nothing more than their face value to me and so the details and dates of their capture are dim in my memory and in many cases have passed from my memory altogether. On the contrary, how eternally and blazingly vivid in my recollection are those three unearned finds which I have mentioned!

Now then, to me university degrees are unearned finds, and they bring the joy that belongs with property acquired in that way; and the money-finds and the degree-finds are just the same in number up to date—three: two from Yale and one from Missouri University. It pleased me beyond measure when Yale made me a Master of Arts, because I didn't know anything about art; I had another convulsion of pleasure when Yale made me a Doctor of Literature, because I was not competent to doctor anybody's literature but my own, and couldn't even keep my own in a healthy condition without my wife's help. I rejoiced again when Missouri University made me a Doctor of Laws, because it was all clear profit, I not knowing anything about laws except how to evade them and not get caught. And now at Oxford I am to be made a Doctor of Letters—all clear profit, because what I don't know about letters would make me a multi-millionaire if I could turn it into cash.

Oxford is healing a secret old sore of mine which has been causing me sharp anguish once a year for many, many years. Privately I am quite well aware that for a generation I have been as widely celebrated a literary person as America has ever produced, and I am also privately aware that in my own peculiar line I have stood at the head of my guild during all that time, with none to dispute the place with me; and so it has been an annual pain to me to see our universities confer an aggregate of two hundred and fifty honorary degrees upon persons of small and temporary consequence—persons of local and evanescent notoriety, persons who drift into obscurity and are forgotten inside of ten years—and never a degree offered to me! In these past thirty-five or forty years I have seen our universities distribute nine or ten thousand honorary degrees and overlook me every time. Of all those thousands, not fifty were known outside of America, and not a hundred are still famous in it. This neglect would have killed a less robust person than I am, but it has not killed me; it has only shortened my life and weakened my constitution; but I shall get my strength back now. Out of those decorated and forgotten thousands not more than ten have been decorated by Oxford, and I am quite well aware—and so is America, and so is the rest of Christendom—that an Oxford decoration is a loftier distinction than is conferrable by any other university on either side of the ocean, and is worth twenty-five of any other, whether foreign or domestic.

Now then, having purged myself of this thirty-five years' accumulation of bile and injured pride, I will drop the matter and smooth my feathers down and talk about something else.

◇◇◇◇◇◇◇◇◇◇◇◇◇◇◇◇◇◇◇

CHAPTER 74

I met Marie Corelli at a small dinner party in Germany fifteen years ago[1] and took a dislike to her at once, a dislike which expanded and hardened with each successive dinner course until when we parted at last the original mere dislike had grown into a very strong aversion. When I arrived in England I found a letter from her awaiting me at Brown's Hotel. It was warm, affectionate, eloquent, persuasive; under its charm the aversion of fifteen years melted away and disappeared. It seemed to me that that aversion must have been falsely based; I thought I must certainly have been mistaken in the woman and I felt a pang or two of remorse. I answered her letter at once—her love letter I may say—answered it with a love letter. Her home is in Shakespeare's Stratford. She at once wrote again, urging me in the most beguiling language to stop there and lunch with her when I should be on my way to London, on the 29th. It looked like an easy matter; the travel con-

[1] Written in 1907.

nected with it could not amount to much, I supposed, therefore I accepted by return mail.

I had now—not for the first time, nor the thousandth—trampled upon an old and wise and stern maxim of mine, to wit: "Supposing is good, but finding out is better." The supposing was finished, the letter was gone; it was now time to find out. Ashcroft[2] examined the timetables and found that I would leave Oxford at eleven o'clock the 29th, leave Stratford at mid-afternoon and not reach London until about half past six. That is to say, I would be seven and a half hours in the air, so to speak, with no rest for the sole of my foot and a speech at the Lord Mayor's to follow! Necessarily I was aghast; I should probably arrive at the Lord Mayor's banquet in a hearse.

Ashcroft and I then began upon a hopeless task—to persuade a conscienceless fool to mercifully retire from a self-advertising scheme which was dear to her heart. She held her grip; anyone who knew her could have told us she would. She came to Oxford on the 28th to make sure of her prey. I begged her to let me off, I implored, I supplicated; I pleaded my white head and my seventy-two years and the likelihood that the long day in trains that would stop every three hundred yards and rest ten minutes would break me down and send me to the hospital. It had no effect. By God, I might as well have pleaded with Shylock himself! She said she could not release me from my engagement; it would be quite impossible; and added, "Consider my side of the matter a little. I have invited Lady Lucy and two other ladies, and three gentlemen; to cancel the luncheon now would inflict upon them the greatest inconvenience; without doubt they have declined other invitations to accept this one; in my own case I have canceled three social engagements on account of this matter."

I said, "Which is the superior disaster: that your half-dozen guests be inconvenienced, or the Lord Mayor's three hundred? And if you have already canceled three engagements and thereby inconvenienced three sets of guests, canceling seems to come easy to you, and it looks as if you might add just one more to the list, in mercy to a suffering friend."

It hadn't the slightest effect; she was as hard as nails. I think there is no criminal in any jail with a heart so unmalleable, so unmeltable, so unfazeable, so flinty, so uncompro-

[2] Mark Twain's secretary on the trip to England.

misingly hard as Marie Corelli's. I think one could hit it with
a steel and draw a spark from it.

She is about fifty years old but has no gray hairs; she is fat
and shapeless; she has a gross animal face; she dresses for
sixteen, and awkwardly and unsuccessfully and pathetically
imitates the innocent graces and witcheries of that dearest
and sweetest of all ages; and so her exterior matches her interior and harmonizes with it, with the result—as I think—that
she is the most offensive sham, inside and out, that misrepre-
sents and satirizes the human race today. I would willingly say
more about her but it would be futile to try; all the adjectives
seem so poor and feeble and flabby this morning.

So we went to Stratford by rail, with a car change or two,
we not knowing that one could save time and fatigue by
walking. She received us at Stratford station with her carriage
and was going to drive us to Shakespeare's church, but I
canceled that; she insisted, but I said that day's program was
already generous enough in fatigues without adding another.
She said there would be a crowd at the church to welcome
me and they would be greatly disappointed, but I was loaded
to the chin with animosity and childishly eager to be as unpleasant as possible, so I held my ground, particularly as I
was well acquainted with Marie by this time and foresaw that
if I went to church I should find a trap arranged for a speech;
my teeth were already loose from incessant speaking and the
very thought of adding a jabber at this time was a pain to me;
besides, Marie, who never wastes an opportunity to advertise
herself, would work the incident into the newspaper and I,
who could not waste any possible opportunity of disobliging
her, naturally made the best of this one.

She said she had been purchasing the house which the
founder of Harvard College had once lived in and was going
to present it to America—another advertisement. She wanted
to stop at that dwelling and show me over it, and she said
there would be a crowd there. I said I didn't want to see the
damned house. I didn't say it in those words but in that vicious
spirit, and she understood; even her horses understood and
were shocked, for I saw them shudder. She pleaded and said
we need not stop for more than a moment, but I knew the
size of Marie's moments by now, when there was an advertisement to be had, and I declined. As we drove by I saw that the
house and the sidewalk were full of people—which meant that
Marie had arranged for another speech. However, we went

by, bowing in response to the cheers, and presently reached Marie's house, a very attractive and commodious English home.

I said I was exceedingly tired and would like to go immediately to a bedchamber and stretch out and get some rest, if only for fifteen minutes. She was voluble with tender sympathy and said I should have my desire at once; but deftly steered me into the drawing room and introduced me to her company. That being over, I begged leave to retire but she wanted me to see her garden and said it would take only a moment. We examined her garden, I praising it and damning it in the one breath—praising with the mouth and damning with the heart. Then she said there was another garden and dragged me along to look at it. I was ready to drop with fatigue but I praised and damned as before and hoped I was through now and might be suffered to die in peace; but she beguiled me to a grilled iron gate and pulled me through it into a stretch of waste ground where stood fifty pupils of a military school, with their master at their head—arrangement for another advertisement.

She asked me to make a little speech and said the boys were expecting it. I complied briefly, shook hands with the master and talked with him a moment, then—well then we got back to the house. I got a quarter of an hour's rest, then came down to the luncheon. Toward the end of it that implacable woman rose in her place, with a glass of champagne in her hand, and made a speech! With me for a text, of course. Another advertisement, you see—to be worked into the newspapers. When she had finished I said, "I thank you very much"—and sat still. This conduct of mine was compulsory, therefore not avoidable; if I had made a speech, courtesy and custom would have required me to construct it out of thanks and compliments, and there was not a rag of that kind of material lurking anywhere in my system.

We reached London at half past six in the evening in a pouring rain, and half an hour later I was in bed—in bed and tired to the very marrow; but the day was at an end, at any rate, and that was a comfort. This was the most hateful day my seventy-two years have ever known.

I have now exposed myself as being a person capable of entertaining and exhibiting a degraded and brutally ugly spirit, upon occasion, and in making this exposure I have done my duty by myself and by my reader—notwithstanding which I claim and maintain that in any other society than Marie Corelli's my spirit is the sweetest that has ever yet descended upon this planet from my ancestors, the angels.

I spoke at the Lord Mayor's banquet that night and it was a botch.

◇◇◇◇◇◇◇◇◇◇◇◇◇◇◇◇◇

CHAPTER 75

Two or three weeks ago[1] Elinor Glyn called on me one afternoon and we had a long talk, of a distinctly unusual character, in the library. It may be that by the time this chapter reaches print she may be less well known to the world than she is now, therefore I will insert here a word or two of information about her. She is English. She is an author. The newspapers say she is visiting America with the idea of finding just the right kind of a hero for the principal character in a romance which she is purposing to write. She has come to us upon the stormwind of a vast and sudden notoriety.

The source of this notoriety is a novel of hers called *Three Weeks*. In this novel the hero is a fine and gifted and cultivated young English gentleman of good family, who imagines he has fallen in love with the ungifted, uninspired, commonplace daughter of the rector. He goes to the Continent on an outing and there he happens upon a brilliant and beautiful young lady of exceedingly foreign extraction, with a deep mystery hanging over her. It transpires later that she is the childless wife of a king or kinglet, a coarse and unsympathetic animal whom she does not love.

She and the young Englishman fall in love with each other at sight. The hero's feeling for the rector's daughter was pale, not to say colorless, and it is promptly consumed and extinguished in the furnace fires of his passion for the mysterious stranger—passion is the right word, passion is what the pair of strangers feel for each other, what they recognize as real love —the only real love, the only love worthy to be called by that great name—whereas the feeling which the young man had

---

[1] Written January 13, 1908.

for the rector's daughter is perceived to have been only a passing partiality.

The queenlet and the Englishman flit away privately to the mountains and take up sumptuous quarters in a remote and lonely house there—and then business begins. They recognize that they were highly and holily created for each other and that their passion is a sacred thing, that it is their master by divine right and that its commands must be obeyed. They get to obeying them at once and they keep on obeying them and obeying them, to the reader's intense delight and disapproval, and the process of obeying them is described, several times, almost exhaustively, but not quite—some little rag of it being left to the reader's imagination, just at the end of each infraction, the place where his imagination is to take up and do the finish being indicated by stars.

The unstated argument of the book is that the laws of Nature are paramount and properly take precedence of the interfering and impertinent restrictions obtruded upon man's life by man's statutes.

Mme. Glyn called, as I have said, and she was a picture! Slender, young, faultlessly formed and incontestably beautiful —a blonde with blue eyes, the incomparable English complexion and crowned with a glory of red hair of a very peculiar, most rare and quite ravishing tint. She was clad in the choicest stuffs and in the most perfect taste. There she is, just a beautiful girl; yet she has a daughter fourteen years old. She isn't winning; she has no charm but the charm of beauty and youth and grace and intelligence and vivacity; she *acts* charm and does it well, exceedingly well in fact, but it does not convince, it doesn't stir the pulse, it doesn't go to the heart, it leaves the heart serene and unemotional. Her English hero would have prodigiously admired her; he would have loved to sit and look at her and hear her talk, but he would have been able to get away from that lonely house with his purity in good repair, if he wanted to.

I talked with her with daring frankness, frequently calling a spade a spade instead of coldly symbolizing it as a snow shovel; and on her side she was equally frank. It was one of the damnedest conversations I have ever had with a beautiful stranger of her sex, if I do say it myself that shouldn't. She wanted my opinion of her book and I furnished it. I said its literary workmanship was excellent and that I quite agreed with her view that in the matter of the sexual relation man's statutory regulations of it were a distinct interference with a higher law, the law of Nature. I went further and said I couldn't call to mind a written law of any kind that had been promulgated in any age of the world in any statute book or any Bible for the regulation of man's conduct in *any* particular, from assassination all the way up to Sabbath-breaking, that wasn't a violation of the law of Nature, which I regarded as the highest of laws, the most peremptory and absolute of all laws—Nature's laws being in my belief plainly and simply the laws of God, since He instituted them, He and no other, and the said laws, by authority of this divine origin, taking precedence of all the statutes of man. I said that her pair of indelicate lovers were obeying the clearly enunciated law of God, and in His eyes must manifestly be blameless.

Of course what she wanted of me was support and defense —I knew that but I said I couldn't furnish it. I said we were the servants of convention; that we could not subsist, either in a savage or a civilized state, without conventions; that we must accept them and stand by them, even when we disapproved of them; that while the laws of Nature, that is to say the laws of God, plainly made every human being a law unto himself, we must steadfastly refuse to obey those laws, and we must as steadfastly stand by the conventions which ignore them, since the statutes furnish us peace, fairly good government and stability, and therefore are better for us than the laws of God, which would soon plunge us into confusion and disorder and anarchy if we should adopt them. I said her book was an assault upon certain old and well-established and wise conventions and that it would not find many friends, and indeed would not deserve many.

She said I was very brave, the bravest person she had ever met (gross flattery which could have beguiled me when I was very very young), and she implored me to publish these views of mine, but I said, "No, such a thing is unthinkable." I said that if I, or any other wise, intelligent and experienced person, should suddenly throw down the walls that protect and conceal his *real* opinions on almost any subject under the sun, it would at once be perceived that he had lost his intelligence and his wisdom and ought to be sent to the asylum. I said I had been revealing to her my private sentiments, *not* my public ones; that I, like all the other human beings, expose to the world only my trimmed and perfumed and carefully barbered public opinions and conceal carefully, cautiously, wisely, my private ones.

I explained that what I meant by that phrase "public opinions" was *published* opinions, opinions spread broadcast in print. I said I was in the common habit, in private conversation with friends, of revealing every private opinion I possessed relating to religion, politics and men, but that I should never dream of *printing* one of them, because they are individually and collectively at war with almost everybody's public opinion while at the same time they are in happy agreement with almost everybody's private opinion. As an instance, I asked her if she had ever encountered an intelligent person who privately believed in the Immaculate Conception[2]—which of course she hadn't; and I also asked her if she had ever seen an intelligent person who was daring enough to publicly deny his belief in that fable and print the denial. Of course she hadn't encountered any such person.

I said I had a large cargo of most interesting and important private opinions about every great matter under the sun, but that they were not for print. I reminded her that we all break over the rule two or three times in our lives and fire a disagreeable and unpopular private opinion of ours into print, but we never do it when we can help it, we never do it except when the desire to do it is too strong for us and overrides and conquers our cold, calm wise judgment. She mentioned several instances in which I had come out publicly in defense of unpopular causes, and she intimated that what I had been saying about myself was not perhaps in strict accordance with the facts; but I said they were merely illustrations of what I had just been saying, that when I publicly attacked the American missionaries in China and some other iniquitous persons and causes, I did not do it for any reason but just the one: that the inclination to do it was stronger than my diplomatic instincts, and I had to obey and take the consquences. But I said I was not moved to defend her book in public; that it was not a case where inclination was overpowering and unconquerable, and that therefore I could keep diplomatically still and should do it.

The lady was young enough and inexperienced enough to imagine that whenever a person has an unpleasant opinion in stock which could be of educational benefit to Tom, Dick and

[2] "Throughout Mark Twain's writing, he confuses the doctrine of the Immaculate Conception with that of the Virgin Birth of Christ." (DeVoto.)

Harry it is his *duty* to come out in print with it and become its champion. I was not able to get that juvenile idea out of her head. I was not able to convince her that we never do *any* duty for duty's sake but only for the mere personal satisfaction we get out of doing that duty. The fact is, she was brought up just like the rest of the world, with the ingrained and stupid superstition that there is such a thing as *duty for duty's sake*, and so I was obliged to let her abide in her darkness. She believed that when a man held a private unpleasant opinion of an educational sort which would get him hanged if he published it he ought to publish it anyway and was a coward if he didn't. Take it all around, it was a very pleasant conversation and glaringly unprintable, particularly those considerable parts of it which I haven't had the courage to more than vaguely hint at in this account of our talk.

Some days afterward I met her again for a moment and she gave me the startling information that she had written down every word I had said, just as I had said it, without any softening and purifying modifications, and that it was "just splendid, just wonderful." She said she had sent it to her husband in England. Privately I didn't think that that was a very good idea, and yet I believed it would interest him. She begged me to let her publish it and said it would do infinite good in the world, but I said it would damn me before my time and I didn't wish to be useful to the world on such expensive conditions.

◇◇◇◇◇◇◇◇◇◇◇◇◇◇◇◇◇◇◇

CHAPTER 76

Last Monday[1] Albert Bigelow Paine personally conducted me to Boston, and next day to Portsmouth, New Hampshire, to assist at the dedication of the Thomas Bailey Aldrich Memorial Museum.

As text and basis I will here introduce a few simple statistics. The late Thomas Bailey Aldrich was born in his grandfather's house in the little town of Portsmouth, New Hampshire, seventy-two or seventy-three years ago. His widow has lately bought that house and stocked it with odds and ends that once belonged to the child Tom Aldrich and to the

[1] Written July 3, 1908.

schoolboy Tom Aldrich and to the old poet Tom Aldrich, and
turned the place into a memorial museum in honor of Aldrich
and for the preservation of his fame. She has instituted an
Aldrich Memorial Museum Corporation under the laws of the
State of New Hampshire and has turned the museum over to
this corporation, which is acting for the City of Portsmouth,
the ultimate heir of the benefaction, and she has injected the
mayor of Portsmouth and other important people into that
corporation to act as advertisement and directors. A strange
and vanity-devoured, detestable woman! I do not believe I
could ever learn to like her except on a raft at sea with no
other provisions in sight.

The justification for an Aldrich Memorial Museum for pil-
grims to visit and hallow with their homage may exist, but to
me it seems doubtful. Aldrich was never widely known; his
books never attained to a wide circulation; his prose was dif-
fuse, self-conscious and barren of distinction in the matter
of style; his fame as a writer of prose is not considerable; his
fame as a writer of verse is also very limited, but such as it is
it is a matter to be proud of. It is based not upon his output
of poetry as a whole but upon half a dozen small poems
which are not surpassed in our language for exquisite grace and
beauty and finish. These gems are known and admired and
loved by the one person in ten thousand who is capable of
appreciating them at their just value.

It is this sprinkling of people who would reverently visit the
memorial museum if it were situated in a handy place. They
would amount to one visitor per month, no doubt, if the museum were in Boston or New York, but it isn't in those places
—it is in Portsmouth, New Hampshire, an hour and three-
quarters from Boston by the Boston and Maine Railway, which
still uses the cars it employed in its early business fifty years
ago; still passes drinking water around per teapot and tin cup,
and still uses soft coal and vomits the gritty product of it into
those venerable cars at every window and crack and joint. A
memorial museum of George Washington relics could not
excite any considerable interest if it were located in that decayed town and the devotee had to get to it over the Boston
and Maine.

When it came to making fun of a folly, a silliness, a windy
pretense, a wild absurdity, Aldrich the brilliant, Aldrich the
sarcastic, Aldrich the ironical, Aldrich the merciless, was a

master. It was the greatest pity in the world that he could
not be at that memorial function in the Opera House at Portsmouth to make fun of it. Nobody could lash it and blight it
and blister it and scarify it as he could. However, I am overlooking one important detail: he could do all this, and would
do it with enthusiasm, if it were somebody else's foolish memorial, but it would not occur to him to make fun of it if the
function was in his own honor, for he had very nearly as extensive an appreciation of himself and his gifts as had the late
Edmund Clarence Stedman, who believed that the sun merely
rose to admire his poetry and was so reluctant to set at the
end of the day and lose sight of it, that it lingered and lingered
and lost many minutes diurnally and was never able to keep
correct time during his stay in the earth. Stedman was a good
fellow; Aldrich was a good fellow; but vain?—bunched together they were as vain as I am myself, which is saying all
that can be said under that head without being extravagant.

For the protection of the reader I must confess that I am
perhaps prejudiced. It is possible that I would never be able
to see anything creditable in anything Mrs. Aldrich might do.
I conceived an aversion for her the first time I ever saw her,
which was thirty-nine years ago, and that aversion has remained with me ever since. She is one of those people who
are profusely affectionate, and whose demonstrations disorder
your stomach. You never believe in them; you always regard
them as fictions, artificialities, with a selfish motive back of
them. Aldrich was delightful company, but we never saw a
great deal of him because we couldn't have him by himself.

If anything was ever at any time needed to increase and
crystallize and petrify and otherwise perpetuate my aversion
to that lady, that lack was made up three years ago, at a time
when I was to spend six days in Boston and could invent no
plausible excuse for declining to visit the Aldriches at "Ponkapog," a few miles out, a house and estate wheedled out of
poor old Mr. Pierce before the old gentleman died. By the
time he was ready to die, eleven years ago, she had very
comfortably feathered the Aldrich nest in his will. He had
already given them a great dwelling house at 59 Mount Vernon Street, Boston, and had built for them a small cottage
at the seaside; also he had already fed Mrs. Aldrich's appetite
for jimcrack bric-à-brac, at considerable expense to his purse;
also he had long ago grown accustomed to having her buy

pretty much anything she thought she wanted and instruct the tradesmen to send the bill to him; also he had long ago grown accustomed to feeding the Aldrich appetite for travel and had sent them in costly and sumptuous fashion all about the habitable globe at his expense. Once, in Europe, when I was a bankrupt and was finding it difficult to make both ends meet, Mrs. Aldrich entertained Mrs. Clemens and me by exploiting in a large way various vanities of hers in the presence of Aldrich and of poor old Mr. Pierce—they apparently approving. She had projected a trip to Japan for Mr. Pierce, Mr. Aldrich and herself, and had been obliged to postpone it for a while because she was not able to secure anything better than the ordinary first-class accommodations in a steamer. She was full of a fine scorn for that kind of accommodation and told how she made those steamer people to understand that they must do better than that if they wanted her further custom. She waited until they were able to sell her one of the two $750 suites on the promenade deck—a suite with beds for only two in it, but she didn't explain what she did with Mr. Pierce. Shipped him in the steerage, I reckon. Then she got out half a dozen gorgeous gowns, worth several hundred dollars each, and told how she gave Worth, the celebrated Parisian ladies' tailor, a piece of her mind regarding those gowns. She showed him that he was taking up too much of her time in fitting them and fussing at them and she added that she had never asked him the price of a gown, she didn't care what he charged, but she would not have her time wasted by his dalliances with the fitting of the things, and she told him quite plainly that her patience was exhausted and that he would never have any of her custom again.

Think of it! Why damnation! She had been a pauper all her life, and here she was strutting around on these lofty stilts.

Joel Chandler Harris is dead; Uncle Remus, joy of the child and the adult alike, will speak to us no more. It is a heavy loss.

I must try to get back to the incident which enlarged and rounded out and perfected my prejudice against Mrs. Aldrich —a little thing which occurred three years ago at "Ponkapog" and to which I have already made vague reference. I had gone to Boston to spend a week with a friend. I did not want to go to "Ponkapog," but I could think of no good excuse, either truthful or otherwise, so I accepted an urgent invitation and went. I knew what would happen: the talk would be merely about "society"—that is, wealthy society—just as in England when one is with titled people the conversation is nearly exclusively about people with titles, and what they were doing when the talkers met them last or heard of them last; I knew there would be a showy and exultant display of precious vanities acquired through the late Mr. Pierce's benevolence; I knew there would be occasional happy glimpses of the charming and lovable Tom Aldrich of early times, and that the Madam would be both occasionally and always her old-time and ever-and-ever self-centered, self-seeking, self-satisfied, honey-worded, interesting and exasperating sham self.

I knew all this would happen and of course it turned out just so. They had an automobile; an automobile was a new and awesome thing then, and nobody could have it except people who could afford it and people who couldn't. This was a cheap 'mobile but it was showy and had a high complexion; they had a steam yacht but couldn't show it to me, which was a matter of no consequence because they had already shown it to me at Bar Harbor in July; it was a cheap little thing with accommodations for three passengers but it looked as important as it could for the money and it expressed pretense as with a voice that spoke; of course they would have a yacht, it is the sign and advertisement of financial distinction; the son was a polo player, in an indigent way, and I was taken out to the fields to see him and half-a-dozen other men play at that aristocratic game; the "Ponkapog" house would necessarily have to indulge in polo, because it is another symbol and advertisement of financial obesity; the men were up-to-date as regards polo costumery, but as they had only two ponies apiece of course the game was brief—brief and delightfully immature and incompetent; incompetent and dangerous to everybody but the ball; nobody could hit it, and poor Aldrich was full of distressed explanations in amelioration of the pathetic miscarriages which constituted the exhibition.

I have not yet reached the incident which I have been so long trying to overtake, but I think I have arrived at it now. I was shown all over the old farmhouse and I paid my way the best I could with shamelessly insincere compliments when pumped. However there were two details which compelled sincere compliments and I easily furnished them without any pumping. One of these details was the living room, which was satisfyingly cozy and pretty, and tasteful in its colors and appointments, and was in all ways inviting and comfortable; the other detail was the sole and solitary guest room, which was spacious and judiciously furnished and upholstered and had a noble big bed in it. I was given that room and was properly thankful and said so; but a girl of twenty arrived unexpectedly in midafternoon and I was moved out of it and she into it; I was transferred to a remote room which was so narrow and short and comprehensively small that one could hardly turn around in it; it had in it a table, a chair, a small kerosene lamp, a washbowl and pitcher, a cylindrical sheet-iron stove, and no other furniture. It was the meanest cell and the narrowest and the smallest and the shabbiest I had ever been in since I got out of jail. The month was October, the nights were very cool; the little stove's food was white pine fragments fed to it a handful at a time; it would seize upon these with a fierce roar, turn red-hot from base to summit in three minutes and be empty and hungry and cold again in ten; under the fury of its three-minute passion it would make the cell so hot that a person could hardly stay in it, and within half an hour the freeze would come on again. The little kerosene lamp filled the cell with a vague and gentle light while it was going, and with a cordial and energetic stench when it wasn't.

The reason I was transferred to that unwholesome and unsavory closet was soon apparent. Young Aldrich was a bachelor of thirty-seven; that young girl was daughter to an ex-governor of the State and was high up in "society." The matchmaking Madam was setting traps for her and working all the ingenuities of her plotting and planning and scheming machinery to catch her for her son. She was quite frank about the matter and was feeling tranquilly sure she was going to succeed in her designs. But she didn't; the girl escaped.

I have at last disgorged that rankling incident. It makes me angry every time I think of it. That that woman should jump at me and kiss me on both cheeks, unsolicited, when I arrived, and then throw me down cellar, seventy years old as I was, to make sumptuous room for a mere governor's daughter, seemed to me to be carrying insult to the limit.

CHAPTER 77

As to the memorial function, let us take that up again.

I had not inquired into the amount of travel which would be required. It came near being great, for I had supposed we must go to New York and reship thence to Boston, which would have made a hard day of it, considering the character of the weather. And a long day—a very long day—twelve hours between getting out of bed at home and stepping into the hotel in Boston. But by accident we found out that we could change cars at South Norwalk and save four hours, so we reached Boston at two in the afternoon after a dusty and blistering and rather fatiguing journey. We were to go to Portsmouth next day, June 30th. Printed cards had been distributed by mail to the invited guests, containing transportation information. Whereby it appeared that the nine o'clock express for Portsmouth would have a couple of special cars sacred to the guests.

To anybody but me, to any reasonable person, to any unprejudiced person, the providing of special cars by the surviving rich Aldriches would have seemed so natural a thing, so properly courteous a thing—in fact so necessary and unavoidable a politeness—that the information would have excited no comment but would have been unemotionally received as being a wholly matter-of-course thing; but where prejudice exists it always discolors our thoughts and feelings and opinions. I was full of prejudice and so I resented this special train. I said to myself that it was out of character; that it was for other people, ordinary people, the general run of the human race, to provide the simple courtesy of a special train on an occasion like this and pay the cost of it, but it was not for Mrs. Aldrich to do such a thing; it was not for Mrs. Aldrich to squander money on politeness to guests, eleemosynarily rich as she is.

It irritated me, disappointed me, affronted me, to see her rising above herself under the elevating influence of a high family occasion; in my malice I wanted to find some way to account for it that would take the credit out of it, and so I said to myself that she, the great advertiser, the persistent advertiser, the pushing and scrabbling and tireless advertiser, was doing this gaudy thing for the sake of spreading it around in the newspapers and getting her compensation out of it as an advertisement. That seemed a sort of plausible way of accounting for it, but I was so deeply prejudiced that it did not pacify me; I could not reconcile myself to seeing her depart from herself and from her traditions and be hospitable at her own expense—still, she was defeating me, and I had to confess it and take the medicine. However, in my animosity I said to myself that I would not allow her to collect glory from me at an expense to her of two dollars and forty cents, so I made Paine buy tickets to Portsmouth and return. That idea pleased me; indeed there is more real pleasure to be gotten out of a malicious act, where your heart is in it, than out of thirty acts of a nobler sort.

But Paine and I went into one of the two special cars in order to chat with their occupants, who would be male and female authors—friends, some of them, the rest acquaintances. It was lucky that we went in there, the result was joyous. I was sitting where I could carry on a conversational yell with all the males and females at the northern end of the car, when the conductor came along, austere and dignified as is the way of his breed of animals, and began to collect tickets! Several of the guests in my neighborhood I knew to be poor, and I saw—not with any real pleasure—a gasp of surprise catch in their throats and a pathetic look of distress exhibit itself in their faces. They pulled out of their pockets and their reticules the handsomely engraved card of invitation, along with the card specifying the special train, and offered those credentials to the unsympathetic conductor and explained that they were *invited* to the mortuary festival and did not have to pay. The smileless conductor-devil said with his cold and hollow Boston and Maine Railway bark that he hadn't any orders to pass anybody, and he would trouble them for transportation cash.

The incident restored my Mrs. Aldrich to me undamaged and just the same old thing she had always been, unde-odorized and not a whiff of her missing. Here she was, rich, getting all the glory inseparable from the act of indulging in the imposing grandeur of a special train and in the valuable advertising for herself incident to it, and then stepping aside and leaving her sixty hard-worked breadwinners to pay the bill for her. I realized that I had gotten back my lost treasure, the real Mrs. Aldrich, and that she was "all there," as the slang-mongers phrase it.

There was another detail of this sorrowful incident that was undeniably pitiful; persons unused to the luxurious Pullman car and accustomed to travel in the plebian common car have the fashion of sticking their fare tickets in the back of the seat in front of them, where the conductor can see them as he goes along; on a New England railway the conductor goes along every few minutes, glances at the exposed tickets, punches some holes in them and keeps that up all day, until the ticket has at last ceased to be a ticket and consists only of holes; but in the meantime the owner of the ticket has been at peace, he has been saved the trouble of pulling a ticket out of his vest pocket every two or three minutes.

Now then, these special-train guests, naturally thinking that their engraved invitation card was intended to serve as a pay ticket, had stuck it in the back of the seats in front of them so that the conductor could turn it into a colander with his punch and leave the owner unmolested; and now when they pointed out these cards to him with a confident and self-complacent and slightly rebuking air, and he responded by his countenance with a pointedly irreverent though silent scoff, those people were visibly so ashamed, so humiliated, that I think Mrs. Aldrich herself would have been almost sorry for them. I was noble enough to be sorry for them—so sorry that I almost wished I hadn't seen it. There were sixty guests, ten or fifteen of them from New York, the rest from Boston or thereabouts, and the entire transportation bill could have been covered by a hundred and fifty dollars, yet that opulent and stingy woman was graceless enough to let that much-sacrificing company of unwealthy literary people pay the bill out of their own pockets. When I used to see her hanging around poor happy old Mr. Pierce's neck and caressing and fondling him and kissing him on both cheeks and calling him "dearie"—But let that go. I am often subject to seasickness on land, and nearly any little thing can give me the heaves.

At a way station the governor of Massachusetts came on board with his staff—these in modest uniform, with two exceptions; these exceptions were veritable birds of paradise for splendor. One of them was young Aldrich, the remaining child and heir. He is a nice and modest and engaging lad, but his modesty goes for nothing; he is his mother's property, as his father was before him, and will have to be a staff officer, or any other kind of wax figure she may prefer, if so be there is an advertisement in it.

Every now and then in the special train some lamb, undergoing the slaughter, would inquire of some other lamb who this train was in charge of; there was never a lamb that could answer that question; manifestly the special train was not in charge of anybody; there was nobody at the Boston Station to tell any guest where to go or which were the special cars; there was nobody on board the train to see that the tin-pot boy came around, now and then, in the awful swelter of that scorching day; at Portsmouth there was nobody to take charge of any guests save the governor's party and about a dozen others. The Madam's motorcar, which is a sumptuous and costly one, was there to fetch the governor—free of charge, I heard.

At the Opera House about three-fourths of the special-train guests were sent to seats among the general audience, while the governor and staff and several more or less notorious authors were marshaled into the green room to wait until the house should be full and everything ready for the solemnities to begin. The mayor of Portsmouth was there too, a big, hearty, muscular animal, just the ideal municipal mayor of this present squalid century. Presently we marched in onto the stage, receiving the noisy welcome which was our due. Howells and I followed the mayor and the governor and his staff, and the rest of the literary rabble followed us. We sat down in a row stretching across the stage, Howells sitting with me near the center in a short willow sofa.

He glanced down the line and murmured, "What an old-time, pleasant look it has about it! If we were blacked and had sharp-pointed long collars that projected slanting upward past our eyebrows like railway bars, it would be complete; and if Aldrich were here he would want to break out in the old introductory formula of happy memory and say breezily, 'How is you tonight, Brer Bones? How is you feelin', Brer Tamborine? How's yo' symptoms seem to segashuate dis ebenin'?'"

After a time the mayor stepped to the front and thundered

forth a vigorous and confident speech in which he said many fine and deservedly complimentary things about Aldrich, and described the gentle and dreamy and remote Portsmouth of Aldrich's boyhood of sixty years ago and compared it with the booming Portsmouth of today. He didn't use that word; it would have been injudicious; he only implied it. The Portsmouth of today doesn't boom; it is calm, quite calm, and asleep. Also he told about the gathering together of the Aldrich mementoes and the stocking of Aldrich's boyhood home with part of them, and the stocking of a fireproof building in the yard with the rest of them, and the placing of the whole generous deposit in the hands of an Aldrich Museum Corporation, with the privilege of saving it for posterity at the expense of the city.

Governor Guild, talking at ease, made a graceful and animated speech, a speech well suited to the occasion, it having been faultlessly memorized. The delivery was free from halts and stumbles and hesitations. A person who is to make a speech at any time or anywhere, upon any topic whatever, owes it to himself and to his audience to write the speech out and memorize it, if he can find the time for it. In the days when I was still able to memorize a speech I was always faithful to that duty—for my own sake, not the hearers'. A speech that is well memorized can, by trick and art, be made to deceive the hearer completely and make him reverently marvel at the talent that can enable a man to stand up unprepared and pour out perfectly phrased felicities as easily and as comfortably and as confidently as less gifted people talk lusterless commonplaces. I am not talking morals now, I am merely talking sense. It was a good beginning— those well-memorized speeches, the mayor's and the governor's; they were happy, interesting, animated, effective.

Then the funeral began. Mourner after mourner crept to the front and meekly and weakly and sneakingly read the poem which he had written for the occasion; and read it confidentially as a rule, for the voice of the true poet, even the voice of the third-rate poet, is seldom able to carry to the middle benches. Pretty soon I was glad I had come in black clothes; at home they had fitted me out in that way, warning me that the occasion was not of a festive character, but mortuary, and I must dress for sorrow, not for the weather. They were odiously hot and close and suffocating and steamy and sweaty, those black clothes there on that sad platform, but they fitted the poetry to a dot; they fitted the wailing deliveries to a dot; they fitted the weary, hot faces of the audience to another dot; and I was glad my outfit was in harmony with the general suffering.

Poet after poet got up and crawled to the desk and pulled out his manuscript and lamented; and this went on and on and on, till the very solemnness of the thing began to become ludicrous. In my lifetime I have not listened to so much manuscript-reading before upon any occasion. I will not deny that it was good manuscript and I will concede that none of it was bad; but no poet who isn't of the first class knows how to read, and so he is an affliction to everybody but himself when he tries it.

Even Col. Higginson, inconceivably old as he is and inured to platform performances for generations and generations, stood up there, bent by age to the curve of a parenthesis, and piped out his speech from manuscript, doing it with the ghostly and creaky remnant of a voice that long ago had rung like a tocsin when he charged with his regiment and led it to bloody victories. Howell's speech was brief, and naturally and necessarily felicitously worded, for fine thought and perfect wording are a natural gift with Howells, and he had it by heart and delivered it well; but he read his poem from manuscript. He did it gracefully and well, then added it to the pile and came back to his seat by my side, glad it was over and looking like a pardoned convict. Then I abolished my prepared and vaguely and ineffectually memorized solemnities and finished the day's performance with twelve minutes of lawless and unconfined and desecrating nonsense.

The memorial function was over. It was dreary; it was devilish; it was hard to endure; there were two sweltering hours of it, but I would not have missed it for twice the heat and exhaustion and Boston and Maine travel it cost, and the cinders I swallowed.

◆◆◆◆◆◆◆◆◆◆◆◆◆◆◆◆◆◆◆◆◆◆

CHAPTER 78

A few days ago I wrote John Howells some strong and spontaneous praises of his work as architect of this house. I remember John as a little child, and it seems strange and uncanny and impossible that I have lived, and lived, and lived, and gone on continuously and persistently and perpetually living, until at last that child, chasing along in my wake, has built a house for me and put a roof over my head. I can't realize that this is that child. I knew the child well; and I also know that child as it looked at the advanced age of seven, when it and its father[1] came down to Hartford once to stay a day or two with us, it must have been thirty years ago. It was in the earliest years of our lost and lamented friend, the colored butler, George. Howells and John were put into the chamber on the ground floor that was called the mahogany room. John was up early and searching the place over, tip-toeing softly and eagerly around on excursions of discovery. He was unfamiliar with the colored race but, being seven years old, he was of course acquainted with the *Arabian Nights*. At a turn in his voyage he presently caught a glimpse of the dining room; then he fled to his father, woke him up and said in awed half-gasps,

"Get up, papa, the slave is setting the table."

I meant to say my say to the architect in good and strong words and well put together, for in a letter received yesterday evening his father says:

> That was beautiful of you to write John of your pleasure in the house. I believe I would rather have such a letter than the most perfect villa.

I wish to quote still another paragraph from Howells's letter:

> I have been thinking how Aldrich would have enjoyed that thing the other day, and what fun he would have got out of us poor old dodderers. How old is Col. Higginson any way? He made you look young, and me feel so.

Speaking of youth, I am reminded that with some frequency people say to me, "You wouldn't look so young if you had the bald head proper to your time of life; how do you preserve that mop? How do you keep it from falling out?" I have to answer with a theory, for lack of adequately

[1] William Dean Howells.

established knowledge. I tell them I think my hair remains with me because I keep it clean; keep it clean by thoroughly scouring it with soap and water every morning, then rinsing it well; then lathering it heavily, and rubbing off the lather with a coarse towel, a process which leaves a slight coating of oil upon each hair—oil derived from the soap. The cleansing and the oiling combined leave the hair soft and pliant and silky, and very pleasantly and comfortably wearable the whole day through; for although the hair becomes dirty again within ten hours, either in country or city, because there is so much microscopic dust floating in the air, it does not become dirty enough to be really raspy to the touch and delicately uncomfortable under twenty-four hours; yet it does become dirty enough in twenty-four hours to make the water cloudy when I wash it.

Now then we arrive at a curious thing; the answer to my explanation always brings forth the same old unvarying and foolish remark, to wit—"Water ruins the hair because it rots the root of it." The remark is not made in a doubtful tone but in a decided one—a tone which indicates that the speaker has examined the matter and knows all about it. Then I say, "How do you know this?"—and the confident speaker stands exposed; he doesn't quite know what to say. If I ask him if he has ruined his own hair by wetting it it turns out that he doesn't wet it often lest he rot the roots of it, therefore he is not talking from his own experience; if I ask if he has personal knowledge of cases where the roots were rotted by wetting, it turns out that he hasn't a single case of the kind to offer; when I hunt him remorselessly home he has to confess at last that "everybody says" water rots the roots of the hair.

Strange—it is just like religion and politics! In religion and politics people's beliefs and convictions are in almost every case gotten at second-hand, and without examination, from authorities who have not themselves examined the questions at issue but have taken them at second-hand from other non-examiners, whose opinions about them were not worth a brass farthing.

It is an odd and curious and interesting ass, the human race. It is constantly washing its face, its eyes, its ears, its nose, its teeth, its mouth, its hands, its body, its feet, its hind legs, and it is thoroughly convinced that cleanliness is next to godliness, and that water is the noblest and surest of all preservers of health, and wholly undangerous, except in just one case—you mustn't apply it to the hair! You must diligently protect the hair from cleanliness; you must carefully keep it filthy or you will lose it; everybody believes this, yet you can never find any human being who has tried it; you can never find a human being who knows it by personal experience, personal test, personal proof; you can never find a Christian who has acquired this valuable knowledge, this saving knowledge, by any process but the everlasting and all-sufficient "people say." In all my seventy-two years and a half I have never come across such another ass as this human race is.

The more one examines this matter the more curious it becomes. Every man wets and soaps and scours his hands before he goes to dinner; he washes them before supper; he washes them before breakfast; he washes them before luncheon, and he knows, not by guesswork, but by old experience, that in all these cases his hands are dirty and need the washing when he applies it. Does he suppose that his bared and unprotected hair, exposed exactly as his hands are exposed, is not gathering dirt all the time? Does he suppose it is remaining clean while his hands are getting constantly dirty? I am considered eccentric because I wear white clothes both winter and summer. I am eccentric, then, because I prefer to be clean in the matter of raiment—clean in a dirty world; absolutely the only cleanly clothed human being in all Christendom north of the Tropics. And that is what I am. All clothing gets dirty in a single day—as dirty as one's hands would get in that length of time if one washed them only once; a neglect which any lady or gentleman would scorn to be guilty of. All the Christian world wears dark colored clothes; after the first day's wear they are dirty, and they continue to get dirtier and dirtier, day after day, and week after week, to the end of their service. Men look fine in their black dress-clothes at a banquet, but often those dress-suits are rather real estate than personal property; they carry so much soil that you could plant seeds in them and raise a crop.

However, when the human race has once acquired a superstition nothing short of death is ever likely to remove it. Annually, during many years, Mrs. Clemens was promptly cured of desperate attacks of that deadly disease, dysentery,

MARK TWAIN 403

by the pleasant method of substituting a slice of ripe, fresh watermelon for the powerful and poisonous drugs used— frequently ineffectually—by the physician. In no instance, in the long list, did the eating of a slice of watermelon ever fail, in Mrs. Clemens's case, to promptly cure the dysentery and make her immune from it for another year; yet I have never been able to get a physician, or anybody else, to try it. During the Civil War any one caught bringing a watermelon into a military camp down South, where the soldiers were dying in squads from dysentery, was sharply punished. Necessarily the prejudice against the watermelon was founded upon theory, not experience, and it will probably take the medical fraternity several centuries to find out that the theory is theory only, and has no basis of experience to stand upon.

◇◇◇◇◇◇◇◇◇◇◇◇◇◇◇◇◇◇

CHAPTER 79

Stormfield, Christmas Eve, 11 A.M., 1909
Jean is dead![1]

Has any one ever tried to put upon paper all the little happenings connected with a dear one—happenings of the twenty-four hours preceding the sudden and unexpected death of that dear one? Would a book contain them? Would two books contain them? I think not. They pour into the mind in a flood. They are little things that have been always happening every day, and were always so unimportant and easily forgettable before—but now! Now, how different! how precious they are, how dear, how unforgettable, how pathetic, how sacred, how clothed with dignity!

Last night Jean, all flushed with splendid health, and I the same, from the wholesome effects of my Bermuda holiday, strolled hand in hand from the dinner table and sat down in the library and chatted and planned and discussed, cheerily and happily (and how unsuspectingly!) until nine—which is late for us—then went upstairs, Jean's friendly German dog

[1] Jean Clemens died early in the morning of December 24, 1909. Two days later Mark Twain showed the following account to Albert Bigelow Paine and said, "If you think it worthy, some day—at the proper time—it can end my autobiography. It is the final chapter." He died four months later, on April 21, 1910.

following. At my door Jean said, "I can't kiss you good-night, father: I have a cold and you could catch it." I bent and kissed her hand. She was moved—I saw it in her eyes—and she impulsively kissed my hand in return. Then with the usual gay "Sleep well, dear!" from both, we parted.

At half past seven this morning I woke and heard voices outside my door. I said to myself, "Jean is starting on her usual horseback flight to the station for the mail." Then Katy[2] entered, stood quaking and gasping at my bedside a moment, then found her tongue:

"Miss Jean is dead!"

Possibly I know now what the soldier feels when a bullet crashes through his heart.

In her bathroom there she lay, the fair young creature, stretched upon the floor and covered with a sheet. And looking so placid, so natural and as if asleep. We knew what had happened. She was an epileptic: she had been seized with a convulsion and heart failure in her bath. The doctor had to come several miles. His efforts, like our previous ones, failed to bring her back to life.

It is noon, now. How lovable she looks, how sweet and how tranquil! It is a noble face and full of dignity; and that was a good heart that lies there so still.

In England, thirteen years ago, my wife and I were stabbed to the heart with a cablegram which said, "Susy was mercifully released today." I had to send a like shock to Clara, in Berlin, this morning. With the peremptory addition, "You must not come home." Clara and her husband sailed from here on the eleventh of this month. How will Clara bear it? Jean, from her babyhood, was a worshiper of Clara.

Four days ago I came back from a month's holiday in Bermuda in perfected health; but by some accident the reporters failed to perceive this. Day before yesterday, letters and telegrams began to arrive from friends and strangers which indicated that I was supposed to be dangerously ill. Yesterday Jean begged me to explain my case through the Associated Press. I said it was not important enough; but she was distressed and said I must think of Clara. Clara would see the report in the German papers, and as she had been nursing her husband day and night for four months and was worn out and feeble, the shock might be disastrous. There

---

[2] Kate Leary, who had been in the service of the Clemens family for twenty-nine years.

was reason in that; so I sent a humorous paragraph by telephone to the Associated Press denying the "charge" that I was "dying," and saying, "I would not do such a thing at my time of life."

Jean was a little troubled and did not like to see me treat the matter so lightly! but I said it was best to treat it so, for there was nothing serious about it. This morning I sent the sorrowful facts of this day's irremediable disaster to the Associated Press. Will both appear in this evening's papers?—the one so blithe, the other so tragic.

I lost Susy thirteen years ago; I lost her mother—her incomparable mother!—five and a half years ago; Clara has gone away to live in Europe; and now I have lost Jean. How poor I am, who was once so rich! Seven months ago Mr. Rogers died—one of the best friends I ever had, and the nearest perfect, as man and gentleman, I have yet met among my race; within the last six weeks Gilder has passed away, and Laffan—old, old friends of mine. Jean lies yonder, I sit here; we are strangers under our own roof; we kissed hands good-by at this door last night—and it was forever, we never suspecting it. She lies there, and I sit here—writing, busying myself, to keep my heart from breaking. How dazzlingly the sunshine is flooding the hills around! It is like a mockery.

Seventy-four years old, twenty-four hours ago. Seventy-four years old yesterday. Who can estimate my age today?

I have looked upon her again. I wonder I can bear it. She looks just as her mother looked when she lay dead in that Florentine villa so long ago. The sweet placidity of death! It is more beautiful than sleep.

I saw her mother buried. I said I would never endure that horror again; that I would never again look into the grave of any one dear to me. I have kept to that. They will take Jean from this house tomorrow and bear her to Elmira, New York, where lie those of us that have been released, but I shall not follow.

Jean was on the dock when the ship came in only four days ago. She was at the door, beaming a welcome, when I reached this house the next evening. We played cards and she tried to teach me a new game called "Mark Twain." We sat chatting cheerily in the library last night and she wouldn't let me look into the loggia, where she was making Christmas preparations. She said she would finish them in the morning and then her little French friend would arrive from New York—the surprise would follow; the surprise she had been working over for days. While she was out for a moment I disloyally stole a look. The loggia floor was clothed with rugs and furnished with chairs and sofas; and the uncompleted surprise was there: in the form of a Christmas tree that was drenched with silver film in a most wonderful way; and on a table was a prodigal profusion of bright things which she was going to hang upon it today. What desecrating hand will ever banish that eloquent unfinished surprise from that place? Not mine, surely. All these little matters have happened in the last four days. "Little." Yes—*then*. But not now. Nothing she said or thought or did is little now. And all the lavish humor!—what is become of it? It is pathos, now. Pathos, and the thought of it brings tears.

All these little things happened such a few hours ago—and now she lies yonder. Lies yonder, and cares for nothing any more. Strange—marvellous—incredible! I have had this experience before; but it would still be incredible if I had had it a thousand times.

"Miss Jean is dead!"

That is what Katy said. When I heard the door open behind the bed's head without a preliminary knock, I supposed it was Jean coming to kiss me good morning, she being the only person who was used to entering without formalities.

And so—

I have been to Jean's parlor. Such a turmoil of Christmas presents for servants and friends! They are everywhere; tables, chairs, sofas, the floor—everything is occupied and overoccupied. It is many and many a year since I have seen the like. In that ancient day Mrs. Clemens and I used to slip softly into the nursery at midnight on Christmas Eve and look the array of presents over. The children were little then. And now here is Jean's parlor looking just as that nursery used to look. The presents are not labeled—the hands are forever idle that would have labeled them today. Jean's mother always worked herself down with her Christmas preparations. Jean did the same yesterday and the preceding days, and the fatigue has cost her her life. The fatigue caused the convulsion that attacked her this morning. She had had no attack for months.

Jean was so full of life and energy that she was constantly in danger of overtaxing her strength. Every morning she was in the saddle by half past seven and off to the station for her mail. She examined the letters and I distributed them: some to her, some to Mr. Paine, the others to the stenographer and myself. She despatched her share and then mounted her horse again and went around superintending her farm and her poultry the rest of the day. Sometimes she played billiards with me after dinner, but she was usually too tired to play and went early to bed.

Yesterday afternoon I told her about some plans I had been devising while absent in Bermuda, to lighten her burdens. We would get a housekeeper; also we would put her share of the secretary-work into Mr. Paine's hands.

No—she wasn't willing. She had been making plans herself. The matter ended in a compromise. I submitted. I always did. She wouldn't audit the bills and let Paine fill out the checks—she would continue to attend to that herself. Also, she would continue to be housekeeper and let Katy assist. Also, she would continue to answer the letters of personal friends for me. Such was the compromise. Both of us called it by that name, though I was not able to see where any formidable change had been made.

However, Jean was pleased and that was sufficient for me. She was proud of being my secretary, and I was never able to persuade her to give up any part of her share in that unlovely work.

In the talk last night I said I found everything going so smoothly that if she were willing I would go back to Bermuda in February and get blessedly out of the clash and turmoil again for another month. She was urgent that I should do it, and said that if I would put off the trip until March she would take Katy and go with me. We struck hands upon that and said it was settled. I had a mind to write to Bermuda by tomorrow's ship and secure a furnished house and servants. I meant to write the letter this morning. But it will never be written now.

For she lies yonder and before her is another journey than that.

Night is closing down; the rim of the sun barely shows above the sky line of the hills.

I have been looking at that face again that was growing dearer and dearer to me every day. I was getting acquainted with Jean in these last nine months. She had been long an exile from home when she came to us three-quarters of a year ago. She had been shut up in sanitariums, many miles from us. How eloquently glad and grateful she was to cross her father's threshold again!

Would I bring her back to life if I could do it? I would not. If a word would do it, I would beg for strength to withhold the word. And I would have the strength; I am sure of it. In her loss I am almost bankrupt, and my life is a bitterness, but I am content: for she has been enriched with the most precious of all gifts—that gift which makes all other gifts mean and poor—death. I have never wanted any released friend of mine restored to life since I reached manhood. I felt in this way when Susy passed away; and later my wife, and later Mr. Rogers. When Clara met me at the station in New York and told me Mr. Rogers had died suddenly that morning, my thought was, Oh, favorite of fortune—fortunate all his long and lovely life—fortunate to his latest moment! The reporters said there were tears of sorrow in my eyes. True—but they were for *me,* not for him. He had suffered no loss. All the fortunes he had ever made before were poverty compared with this one.

Why did I build this house, two years ago? To shelter this vast emptiness? How foolish I was! But I shall stay in it. The spirits of the dead hallow a house for me. It was not so with other members of my family. Susy died in the house we built in Hartford. Mrs. Clemens would never enter it again. But it made the house dearer to me. I have entered it once since, when it was tenantless and silent and forlorn, but to me it was a holy place and beautiful. It seemed to me that the spirits of the dead were all about me and would speak to me and welcome me if they could: Livy and Susy and George and Henry Robinson and Charles Dudley Warner. How good and kind they were and how lovable their lives! In fancy I could see them all again, I could call the children back and hear them romp again with George—that peerless black ex-slave and children's idol who came one day—a flitting stranger—to wash windows and stayed eighteen years. Until he died. Clara and Jean would never enter again the New York hotel which their mother had frequented in earlier days. They could not bear it. But I shall stay in this house. It is dearer to me tonight than ever it was before. Jean's spirit will make it beautiful for me always. Her lonely and tragic death—but I will not think of that now.

Jean's mother always devoted two or three weeks to Christmas shopping and was always physically exhausted when Christmas Eve came. Jean was her very own child—she wore herself out present-hunting in New York these latter days. Paine has just found on her desk a long list of names—fifty, he thinks—people to whom she sent presents last night. Apparently she forgot no one. And Katy found there a roll of banknotes for the servants.

Her dog has been wandering about the grounds today, comradeless and forlorn. I have seen him from the windows. She got him from Germany. He has tall ears and looks exactly like a wolf. He was educated in Germany and knows no language but the German. Jean gave him no orders save in that tongue. And so, when the burglar alarm made a fierce clamor at midnight a fortnight ago, the butler, who is French and knows no German, tried in vain to interest the dog in the supposed burglar. Jean wrote me, to Bermuda, about the incident. It was the last letter I was ever to receive from her bright head and her competent hand. The dog will not be neglected.

There was never a kinder heart than Jean's. From her childhood up she always spent the most of her allowance on charities of one kind and another. After she became secretary and had her income doubled she spent her money upon these things with a free hand. Mine too, I am glad and grateful to say.

She was a loyal friend to all animals and she loved them all, birds, beasts and everything—even snakes—an inheritance from me. She knew all the birds: she was high up in that lore. She became a member of various humane societies when she was still a little girl—both here and abroad—and she remained an active member to the last. She founded two or three societies for the protection of animals, here and in Europe.

She was an embarrassing secretary, for she fished my correspondence out of the waste basket and answered the letters. She thought all letters deserved the courtesy of an answer. Her mother brought her up in that kindly error.

She could write a good letter and was swift with her pen.

She had but an indifferent ear for music, but her tongue took to languages with an easy facility. She never allowed her Italian, French and German to get rusty through neglect.

The telegrams of sympathy are flowing in from far and wide now, just as they did in Italy five years and a half ago, when this child's mother laid down her blameless life. They cannot heal the hurt, but they take away some of the pain. When Jean and I kissed hands and parted at my door last, how little did we imagine that in twenty-two hours the telegraph would be bringing words like these:

"From the bottom of our hearts we send our sympathy, dearest of friends."

For many and many a day to come, wherever I go in this house, remembrancers of Jean will mutely speak to me of her. Who can count the number of them?

She was in exile two years with the hope of healing her malady—epilepsy. There are no words to express how grateful I am that she did not meet her fate in the hands of strangers, but in the loving shelter of her own home.

"Miss Jean is dead!"

It is true. Jean is dead.

A month ago I was writing bubbling and hilarious articles for magazines yet to appear, and now I am writing—this.

Christmas Day. Noon.—Last night I went to Jean's room at intervals and turned back the sheet and looked at the peaceful face and kissed the cold brow and remembered that heartbreaking night in Florence so long ago, in that cavernous and silent vast villa, when I crept downstairs so many times and turned back a sheet and looked at a face just like this one—Jean's mother's face—and kissed a brow that was just like this one. And last night I saw again what I had seen then —that strange and lovely miracle—the sweet, soft contours of early maidenhood restored by the gracious hand of death! When Jean's mother lay dead, all trace of care and trouble and suffering and the corroding years had vanished out of the face, and I was looking again upon it as I had known and worshipped it in its young bloom and beauty a whole generation before.

About three in the morning, while wandering about the

house in the deep silences, as one does in times like these,
when there is a dumb sense that something has been lost
that will never be found again, yet must be sought, if only
for the employment the useless seeking gives, I came upon
Jean's dog in the hall downstairs, and noted that he did not
spring to greet me, according to his hospitable habit, but
came slow and sorrowfully; also I remembered that he had
not visited Jean's apartment since the tragedy. Poor fellow,
did he know? I think so. Always when Jean was abroad in
the open he was with her; always when she was in the
house he was with her, in the night as well as in the day.
Her parlor was his bedroom. Whenever I happened upon him
on the ground floor he always followed me about, and when I
went upstairs he went too—in a tumultuous gallop. But now
it was different: after patting him a little I went to the library
—he remained behind; when I went up stairs he did not follow me, save with his wistful eyes. He has wonderful eyes—
big and kind and eloquent. He can talk with them. He is a
beautiful creature and is of the breed of the New York police
dogs. I do not like dogs, because they bark when there is no
occasion for it; but I have liked this one from the beginning,
because he belonged to Jean and because he never barks
except when there is occasion—which is not oftener than
twice a week.

In my wanderings I visited Jean's parlor. On a shelf I found
a pile of my books and I knew what it meant. She was waiting
for me to come home from Bermuda and autograph them,
then she would send them away. If I only knew whom she
intended them for! But I shall never know. I will keep them.
Her hand has touched them—it is an accolade—they are noble
now.

And in a closet she had hidden a surprise for me—a
thing I have often wished I owned: a noble big globe. I
couldn't see it for the tears. She will never know the pride
I take in it, and the pleasure. Today the mails are full of loving
remembrances for her: full of those old, old kind words she
loved so well, "Merry Christmas to Jean!" If she could only
have lived one day longer!

At last she ran out of money and would not use mine. So
she sent to one of those New York homes for poor girls all
the clothes she could spare—and more, most likely.

Christmas Night.—This afternoon they took her away from

her room. As soon as I might, I went down to the library and there she lay in her coffin, dressed in exactly the same clothes she wore when she stood at the other end of the same room on the sixth of October last, as Clara's chief bridesmaid. Her face was radiant with happy excitement then; it was the same face now, with the dignity of death and the peace of God upon it.

They told me the first mourner to come was the dog. He came uninvited and stood up on his hind legs and rested his fore paws upon the trestle and took a last long look at the face that was so dear to him, then went his way as silently as he had come. *He knows.*

At midafternoon it began to snow. The pity of it—that Jean could not see it! She so loved the snow.

The snow continued to fall. At six o'clock the hearse drew up to the door to bear away its pathetic burden. As they lifted the casket, Paine began playing on the orchestrelle Schubert's *Impromptu,* which was Jean's favorite. Then he played the *Intermezzo;* that was for Susy! then he played the *Largo;* that was for their mother. He did this at my request.

From my windows I saw the hearse and the carriages wind along the road and gradually grow vague and spectral in the falling snow and presently disappear. Jean was gone out of my life and would not come back any more. Jervis, the cousin she had played with when they were babies together— he and her beloved old Katy—were conducting her to her distant childhood home, where she will lie by her mother's side once more, in the company of Susy and Langdon.

December 26.—The dog came to see me at eight o'clock this morning. He was very affectionate, poor orphan! My room will be his quarters hereafter.

The storm raged all night. It has raged all the morning. The snow drives across the landscape in vast clouds, superb, sublime—and Jean not here to see.

2.30 P.M.—It is the time appointed. The funeral has begun. Four hundred miles away, but I can see it all just as if I were there. The scene is the library in the Langdon homestead. Jean's coffin stands where her mother and I stood, forty years ago, and were married; and where Susy's coffin stood thirteen years ago; where her mother's stood five years and a half ago; and where mine will stand, after a little time.

Five o'clock.—It is all over.

When Clara went away two weeks ago to live in Europe, it was hard but I could bear it, for I had Jean left. I said *we* would be a family. We said we would be close comrades and happy—just we two. That fair dream was in my mind when Jean met me at the steamer last Monday; it was in my mind when she received me at the door last Tuesday evening. We were together; *we were a family!* the dream had come true—oh, preciously true, contentedly true, satisfyingly true! and remained true two whole days.

And now? Now Jean is in her grave!

In the grave—if I can believe it. God rest her sweet spirit!

Index